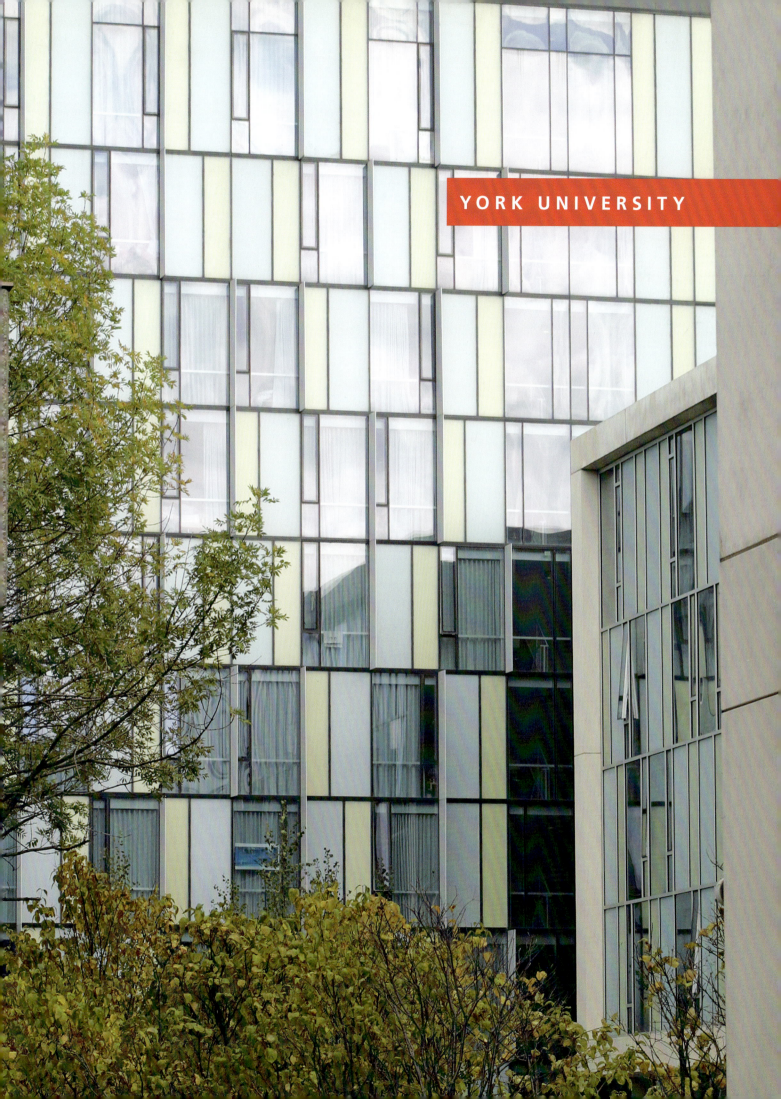
YORK UNIVERSITY

MICHIEL HORN

York University

The Way Must Be Tried

Colour photography by Vincenzo Pietropaolo

Published for York University by McGill-Queen's University Press | Montreal & Kingston · London · Ithaca

© York University 2009
ISBN 978-0-7735-3416-2

Legal deposit first quarter 2009
Bibliothèque nationale du Québec

Printed in Canada on acid-free paper

McGill-Queen's University Press acknowledges the
support of the Canada Council for the Arts for our
publishing program. We also acknowledge the financial
support of the Government of Canada through the Book
Publishing Industry Development Program (BPIDP) for
our publishing activities.

Library and Archives Canada Cataloguing in Publication

Horn, Michiel, 1939–
York University : the way must be tried / Michiel Horn.

Includes bibliographical references and index.
ISBN 978-0-7735-3416-2

1. York University (Toronto, Ont.) – History.   I. Title.

LE3.Y6H67 2009   378.713'541   C2008-903946-7

Set in 11/15 Warnock Pro with Frutiger
Book design & typesetting: Garet Markvoort, zijn digital

Contents

YORK
UNIVERSITÉ
UNIVERSITY

Office of the President

S949 Ross Humanities
and Social Sciences Bldg.
4700 Keele St.
Toronto ON
Canada M3J 1P3
Tel 416 736 5200
Fax 416 736 5641
www.yorku.ca/president

It is my privilege to be president of York University at this exciting time in its history, and my pleasure to introduce this book, published in York's fiftieth anniversary year, 2009. The book navigates the drama and the achievements of this great university, at a time when we are still close enough to that history to touch it and to speak to many of the principals.

Early in the book, in describing York's journey from an idea in the minds of a group of professionals to a leading twenty-first century university, Professor Horn says, "What a difference half a century can make!" He is exactly right: in five short decades, this university has evolved and changed as much as it has helped the world evolve and change.

The history Professor Horn presents in this book is not just a record of York's past; it is also about making history, about the transformative effect York University has had on our society. And as York celebrates its fiftieth year, we do so with a sense of pride in all we have accomplished, but knowing that the best is yet to come.

Mamdouh Shoukri, Ph.D., P.Eng.
President and Vice-Chancellor

When Lorna Marsden asked me to become York's official historian and write this book, I offered two objections. The university was still young, making historical perspective difficult if not impossible. Moreover, I doubted that I was the right person to be York's historian. Having been a member of the faculty since 1968, I would find it hard to adopt a dispassionate point of view.

Perhaps I sounded unsure in my arguments. I had been softened up by Kent Haworth, York's archivist and chair of the search committee for a university historian. (Those of us who had the good fortune to know Kent still regret his untimely death a few years ago. He was a real mensch, committed to York and to the archival profession.) He had listened to my objections, suggested gently they were weaker than I seemed to think, and asked me to consider what President Marsden had to say.

She proved to be persuasive. The conditions she was prepared to recommend to the Board of Governors were financially generous. I would have full access to all university documents, she said, and would enjoy complete independence. I hesitated for a week or two, then accepted the offer.

My appointment took effect in 2002. Having agreed to prepare a book scheduled to appear in 2009, I had ample time to consider what approach I should take. Eventually I decided that the framework would consist of the archival record, but that I would put flesh on the framework by interviewing a large number of people, in an attempt to see the university through their eyes and help bring it to life. My friend Peter L. Smith, who had done something similar in his history of the University of Victoria, agreed to serve on a committee that I established in the hope of gaining useful advice. Alas, in August 2006 he was felled by a massive stroke. Terry Crowley of the University of Guelph, author of a history of the Ontario Agricultural College, kindly took his place. The other members are Paul Axelrod, a historian who has served York as dean of education, Martin Friedland, eminent legal scholar and the official historian of the University of Toronto, and York University Secretary Harriet Lewis.

I am grateful to them for reading all the chapters and responding to them in a helpful fashion. I am also grateful to William Farr, James Gillies, Theodore Olson, John T. Saywell, Clara Thomas, Albert Tucker, and Douglas Verney, each of whom read part of the manuscript and made useful comments. None of these people is in any way responsible for the flaws that remain.

More than 250 people have shared their recollections with me, talked with me about specific issues, or written to me. (Appendix A lists their names). A few declined to be interviewed. I regret this but respect their reasons. I wish to thank all those who spoke with me or wrote to me. Even those I ended up not quoting helped to shape my image of York. I also thank everyone who provided photos or documents. John Court merits special mention: he answered many requests for information about the pre-history and early history of York. I hope his manuscript detailing the earliest origins of the university, "Private Resolve Meets Public Interest," will soon appear in print.

The staff of the Clara Thomas Archives, especially Michael Moir, Suzanne Dubeau, and Julia Holland, were unfailingly helpful. So were Julianna Drexler, director of the Leslie Frost Library and guardian of the archives there, Grace Randell and Berton Woodward in Marketing and Communications, and the staff of Glendon College ITS. I owe thanks to my research assistants Emily Evans, Karen Macfarlane, and Bruce Douville, and above all to my research associate during the last three years of the project, Charles Levi. Sylvia Zingrone and Ijade Maxwell Rodrigues were ever obliging. Vince Pietropaolo, a gifted photographer, was very cooperative. Maya Cruz helped me to copy digital images. Marie Kopf worked on the page proofs. Daniel and Patrick Horn also helped. I wish to thank Philip Cercone, Joan McGilvray, Jonathan Crago, Susanne McAdam, Garet Markvoort, and other staff members at McGill-Queen's University Press, as well as my copy editor, Curtis Fahey. As always, my wife, Cornelia Schuh, read everything and improved it.

A major problem in writing the history of an institution that grew within a dozen years from a tiny college into a large university is that a great deal happened very quickly. There is also an overabundance of information about it. "There are too many origins, too many heroes, too many stories," the historian Peter Seixas has written in another context.[1] I know what he means. In the first three chapters, dealing with York's pre-history and first decade, I was able to aspire to a degree of inclusiveness that proved impossible to maintain in the later chapters. By 1970, there were so many departments, divisions, and administrative units, so many activities, so many concurrent stories by students, faculty members, librarians, administrative officers, support staff, and board members, that it would have swamped my book to mention them all, let alone do them justice. I have selected topics that I consider to be significant or interesting, and, not least important, that interested me. But I had to leave out many things that, given more time and space, I would have wanted to include.

Furthermore, this book very largely ends around 1985. I did feel increasingly inhibited in the role of historian as the story neared the present, but an equally compelling reason was that I ran out of space and time. In the concluding chapter I discuss some recent developments, provide a long glance at the present, and offer a thought or two about the future. My hope is that, when fifty more years have passed, another historian can offer more detail.

My efforts will not, I fear, come close to pleasing everyone. Many readers will look in vain for their names and the record of their accomplishments, and they will very probably be unhappy. I can only ask for their understanding and forgiveness: it was simply not possible to discuss everything and mention everybody. Some readers will fault me for spending too much time on some subjects and too little on others, and they may be right. Some will disagree with my interpretation of events in which they played a part, and they, too, may be right. I have tried to compensate for my own biases and see York's history clearly, but I know that others can and will see it differently. Finally, although I have tried my best to make sure that all names are spelled correctly, a few mistakes will almost certainly remain to mar the book. As someone whose name gets misspelled frequently, I know how irritating this can be. I apologize to anyone I have inadvertantly offended in this way.

Although I am aware that this book falls well short of perfection, working on it has been a pleasure. The people I interviewed have been my teachers, and I have learned a lot from them. Moreover, my appreciation of York has grown. With all its flaws and disagreements, it has stayed true to its original interdisciplinary mission and has expanded it. In common with other Canadian universities, it offers a degree of personal and intellectual freedom that is rarely available in private business or the public service. My forty years at Glendon and York have been, to use a 1960s word, a blast. I am deeply grateful to the university, to all the students I have taught and all the people I have worked with, for making those years possible.

Michiel Horn
Toronto
10 August 2008

YORK UNIVERSITY

Academic processions are sedate but oddly engaging, a curious blend of medieval and modern, of tradition and expectation. One such event took place on the Keele campus of York University on Wednesday, 17 October 2007. Dressed in gowns and hoods of many colours, wearing mortar boards and floppy berets on their heads, a parade of women and men filed into the Tribute Communities Recital Hall of the recently completed Accolade East Building. They had come to attend the installation of York University's seventh president and vice-chancellor, Mamdouh Shoukri. Handel's *Music for the Royal Fireworks* played as everyone waited for the ceremony to get under way.

University Secretary Harriet Lewis having called the assembly to order, the ceremony proceeded at a brisk pace. Four students in the vocal-performance program of the Faculty of Fine Arts led the assembly in the singing of "O Canada." The chair of the university Senate, Brenda Spotton Visano, delivered a few well-chosen words of greeting. Lorna Marsden, the university's sixth president and Shoukri's predecessor, welcomed the participants and guests, noting the presence of the third president, H. Ian Macdonald, and the absence of founding president Murray G. Ross, who had died in 2000 at the age of ninety. The introduction of the platform party, among them representatives from more than thirty sister universities, followed. Representatives of the Association of Universities and Colleges of Canada, the Council of Ontario Universities, the Alumni Association, the faculty, York students, and the non-academic staff expressed greetings to the president-designate.

With the preliminaries completed, four people rose. They were Chancellor Peter Cory, Board of Governors Chair Marshall Cohen, the chair of the Senate, and the president-designate. Off came Shoukri's doctoral hood and gown from McMaster University, to be replaced by the red-and-white robe worn by presidents of York. The distinguished-looking engineering professor, tall, bespectacled, with graying hair, recited the oath of office: "I, Mamdouh Shoukri, do this day affirm my pledge to serve York University, and through it, the cause of learn-

Senate Chair Brenda Spotton Visano, board Chair Marshall Cohen, and Chancellor Peter Cory (right) applaud Mamdouh Shoukri, installed moments earlier as York University's seventh president and vice-chancellor.

ing, and by learning that of humanity. I will do so by every means in my power and with the aid of all those who serve with me. As far as I am able, and with the help of all my colleagues, I shall strive to realize the spirit of the laws and customs of York University."

Then the new president delivered his installation address. It was low key yet effective, expressing gratitude to his parents, greeting his father, "who is watching this ceremony on his computer in Cairo," and expressing pride in his country of birth while praising his adopted country. He acknowledged York's strong record in the humanities and social sciences. "What we need to do now is build on this foundation with further growth in science and the applied sciences, an increased focus on research and graduate studies, and the addition of a medical school right here at the heart of the GTA." He praised the student body, "the best mechanism for the effective dissemination of knowledge ... We are blessed with students who come from every culture, who speak every language. We are connected to the world because we come from every part of it."

The challenges were great, Shoukri said, but he expressed confidence that, with all of its members working together, the university would meet them. "It's time for us to shout about York from the rooftops, to let the world know that York has arrived, and that the best is yet to come!" He concluded by quoting Pierre Trudeau: "The past is to be respected and acknowledged, but not to be worshipped. It is our future in which we will find our greatness."

Enthusiastic applause ensued, and the secretary declared the ceremony at an end. The academic procession filed out, *seniores priores*, to the strains of more baroque music, into a lobby where refreshments were served. A small string ensemble consisting of students in the Department of Music played selections by Bach, Corelli, Handel, Mozart, Massenet, and others. The mood was very much upbeat. The new president, who had left a vice-president's position at McMaster University to assume the new challenge, came highly recommended. He was clearly affable and mixed easily with the guests, who seemed more than ready to share his hopes and dreams for York.

The position he was assuming was anything but a sinecure. In 2006–07 York enrolled almost 52,000 students in eleven faculties on two campuses, making it the third largest university in Canada.[1] More than 3,100 full- and part-time faculty and professional librarians, some 2,300 teaching and research assistants, and roughly 3,500 full-time and casual non-academic staff were on the university payroll. The total budget was well over $600 million. Of the almost one hundred buildings used by the university, the oldest were two (possibly three) nineteenth-century farmhouses on the Keele campus and Glendon Hall, a 1920s villa on the Glendon campus. The newest were the two Accolade buildings recently occupied by the Faculty of Fine Arts. Ten undergraduate residences on the two campuses housed 2,675 students, while the graduate apartments, all on the Keele campus, were home to 1,290 more.[2]

York had become a multiversity, no doubt about that. Yet, if a single term were to be used to describe the York ethos, it was one that linked the institution's present to its past: interdisciplinarity, the commitment of faculty members and students to make an effort to look and reach across disciplinary boundaries in their teaching, learning, and research. The general-education requirement, adopted in York's very early days, was at the heart of this commitment. Over the years, it had inspired or influenced many of the scholars, scientists, writers, and creative artists who had worked at York, as well as many of its alumni, more than 200,000 in number. Individually and collectively, these men and women established and sustained York's reputation across Canada and around the world.

What a difference half a century can make! In 1957 the Keele campus was a farmer's field owned by the Central Mortgage and Housing Corporation (CMHC), and the Glendon campus housed the University of Toronto's Faculty of Law. York University was no more than an idea germinating in the minds of a handful of North Toronto business and professional people. That idea was the beginning of an institutional odyssey that was to mark its fiftieth year in 2009.

They called themselves "the summer's bachelors group," James Keachie remembered.[3] A lawyer employed in the legal department of the S.S. Kresge Company, he was one of a small group of men, ranging in age from their mid-thirties to mid-forties, who began to meet in 1955 to discuss the possibility of expanding the opportunities for adult education in the Toronto area. They had time on their hands, for during the months of July and August their wives and children were in cottages up north, to be joined on weekends by husbands and fathers (the middle-class working world was still very largely male). Significantly, the men had met through the Young Men's Christian Association (YMCA) in north Toronto. The interest of the YMCA in adult education, in both the United States and Canada, was of long standing. Montreal's Sir George Williams College, a YMCA-operated institution, was founded in 1926, mainly to offer evening classes that had earlier been offered through the local YMCA. Ten years later, the college granted its first degrees. Its heavy involvement in adult education offered inspiration to the Toronto group. So did their awareness that Carleton College in Ottawa, which had been founded during the Second World War, owed some of its early impetus to the YMCA.[4]

The area where they lived, the city of Toronto north of St Clair Avenue, had filled up completely very soon after the Second World War, while the population of the suburbs around it – Forest Hill, York, Leaside, and especially North York – was expanding rapidly. That was true also of the townships of Etobicoke and Scarborough. "It was clear to everyone in the early 1950s that Toronto was and would continue to be one of the fastest-growing cities in the western world," James Lemon has written.[5] The elevated birthrate of the post-war years, the so-called baby boom, was combining with high immigration to feed explosive growth. In 1951 the thirteen municipalities in the Toronto area – two years later they were combined into six – had a total population of 1,117,400; in 1956 they were home to 1,358,028. A further 261,000 would be added during the next five years.[6] Symbolic of this growth was the new subway, built along Yonge Street from Union Station north to Eglinton Avenue and completed in 1954. The demand for primary and secondary education was rising. That the demand for university places in Toronto would increase was also clear.

This demand would not be limited to full-time students aged eighteen to twenty-two, of that the north Toronto group was certain. But even conventional high school graduates were likely to have growing difficulty finding university places in the city. University College and the undergraduate colleges of the universities federated with the University of Toronto had some additional capacity – how much, members of the group did not know – but it was more than possible that they would have to turn away qualified students. This, Keachie said, seemed to open the field to a new institution of higher learning.[7]

In 1957 the group expanded to include several people associated with the aircraft and transportation industry. Most prominent among them was Air Marshal Wilfred A. Curtis, vice-chairman of the board of A.V. Roe and Company, which was then involved in its most ambitious project yet, the development of the Avro Arrow, a fighter-interceptor intended for the use of the Royal Canadian Air Force and other air forces. (The project was terminated by the federal government soon afterwards.) Curtis had become concerned about the ability of Canadian universities to meet the needs of the economy and of the wider society, and he was not alone. The post-war years saw greater interest in Canadian higher education than at any time since the first decade of the twentieth century.

The influx of veterans, assisted by federal grants paid directly to them and to the universities that accommodated them, was the initial reason. Even as the last of the veterans were graduating, the 1951 Report of the Royal Commission on National Development in the Arts, Letters and Sciences, better known as the

Chairman of the organizing committee of York University, Air Marshal Wilfred A. Curtis was a member of its provisional board of governors and became the university's first chancellor in 1961.

Massey Commission, recommended that the federal government institute a new program of grants to the universities on the grounds that they served not only personal and provincial but also national goals. Responding to this report and to lobbying by the National Conference of Canadian Universities (NCCU) (later the Association of Universities and Colleges of Canada), Prime Minister Louis St Laurent announced in June 1951 that Ottawa would pay fifty cents per head of provincial population, or a total of approximately $7 million, in aid of higher education, starting in the 1951–52 academic year. Within each province, the money would be divided among universities and colleges on the basis of enrolment and would be paid directly to the institutions, to be spent as they chose.[8]

This intrusion of the federal government into a sphere thought to be the exclusive responsibility of the provinces did not go unchallenged. After one year, the government of Maurice Duplessis indicated that it wanted the Quebec universities to stop accepting the federal funds, offering provincial grants instead. Although all of them were private institutions, they obligingly came to heel. But the governments of the other nine provinces raised no objections, and, in Ontario as elsewhere, universities and colleges gratefully accepted the grants. Whether provincial or private, secular or sectarian, they all could use the money!

Ottawa's action indicated a growing interest in the universities as contributors to national economic growth. At the same time, increasing numbers of Canadians saw post-secondary education as a key to personal success. As the 1950s progressed, a steadily growing number of college-age young people showed up to register. This, and the anticipated impact in the 1960s of the baby boom, led E.F. Sheffield of the Dominion Bureau of Statistics to predict in 1955 that enrolments would double to over 120,000 in ten years. "In fact," he wrote in 1970, "they more than doubled in eight."[9]

"The [Sheffield] report sparked a period of frenetic activity among educators and businessmen," Paul Axelrod has written.[10] The NCCU conference in 1956 highlighted "Canada's Crisis in Higher Education." That year, too, a conference of educators and businessmen took place at St Andrew's, New Brunswick, to discuss what the business community might do to help solve the crisis. Among those attending the St Andrew's conference was Air Marshal Curtis, who mentioned the possibility that another university might be founded in the Toronto area.[11]

These comments may have drawn him to the attention of the group in north Toronto, which now called itself "the organizing committee." By 1957, the group's members were talking about a "Kellock Institute" (giving it the name of the first president of the North Toronto YMCA) that would be committed to adult education. Unsure what direction to take, though, they decided to join forces with the group headed by Curtis, who now became chairman of "the university project" or "Kellock University."

The new organizing committee included three representatives from the North Toronto YMCA, Alan Clarke, A.R. Hackett, and A.R. Jordan. Other members were Stanley H. Deeks, an employee of the Industrial Foundation of Education, which had been established in the aftermath of the St Andrew's conference, and Thomas Loudon, former head of the Department of Aeronautical and Civil Engineering at the University of Toronto. On the industry side were Curtis, E.A.

Alberts, and Arthur D. Margison, a "brilliant and energetic young engineer," as Keachie called him, who soon became chairman of the group's key Facilities Planning Committee. Keachie, who served as its vice-chairman, remembered enjoyable Wednesday evenings in the summer, when the committee met around the swimming pool behind Margison's home to discuss the new university and where it might be located.[12]

In late 1957 the organizing committee's members felt sure enough of themselves to request a meeting with Ontario's minister of education, W.J. Dunlop. Three representatives of the committee, Curtis, Jordan, and Margison, went to Queen's Park to acquaint Dunlop with their plans for "Kellock University." Dunlop reportedly said that "the project was worthwhile,"[13] but he offered no official support. The group's ideas were in any case still relatively unformed. Curtis reported to the larger committee in late November that he had gained the idea that a private university "would be welcomed by the province if properly started." Soon afterwards the committee decided to "proceed towards university status with formal classes."[14] It remained to decide what faculties this new university would include and what it would leave out.

The addition to the group of J. Robbins (Roby) Kidd, director of the Canadian Association of Adult Education, helped the planners to clarify their ideas. A round table to discuss the embryonic institution, in which Kidd participated, took place at the Granite Club (then still on St Clair Avenue West) in February 1958. The committee members present discussed plans to offer courses in business administration, education, and engineering as early as the fall of that year. Other participants suggested that the liberal arts rather than applied courses should be the institution's initial focus.[15] At this meeting, too, Moffatt Woodside, a classicist who was acting president of the University of Toronto, suggested a name for the proposed university. Declaring that universities should be named after their locale rather than after an individual, Woodside proposed "York University,"[16] the reference being to York County, in which Toronto was located. This found approval, and the committee dropped the Kellock name. During the summer it severed its ties with the YMCA's Centre for Adult Education. By this time, the organizing committee consisted of Alberts, Clarke, Curtis, Deeks, Hackett, Kidd, Loudon, and Margison; the secretary was P.R. Woodfield of the Industrial Foundation of Education. Several subcommittees also existed, of which, Margison remembered, the Facilities Planning Committee was easily the most active.[17]

Soon after the round table in February, Margison reported to the Toronto YMCA board that the York University organizing committee hoped to begin with night courses offered in the Yonge-Eglinton area. No doubt the committee felt encouraged by a speech that Claude Bissell, the president of Carleton University, who had recently been named the next president of the University of Toronto, gave to Toronto's Empire Club on 24 April 1958. "I personally welcome the exploratory measures already being taken by a group of citizens that have as their goal the establishment of a second university in this area," Bissell said. "The University of Toronto will gladly offer advice, and will freely offer assistance; but I think it is important that the second university become, as rapidly as possible, a separate and distinctive foundation."[18]

Bissell's positive response found an echo in the Toronto media. In early August 1958 the *Globe and Mail* and the *Telegram* carried editorials welcoming the prospect of a second university, now referred to as York University or York University College, in the Toronto area. "York may expect to grow rapidly," the *Telegram* opined: "All factors favor it. Like an acorn, it can expect to grow impressively."[19] Soon the Toronto *Star* also jumped on the bandwagon, citing the expected demands for admission to university that baby-boom children would be making by 1965. "York University Must Go Ahead," a *Star* editorial stated, arguing that "in this metropolitan area, the fastest growing in Canada, a second university is essential, and perhaps a third, despite University of Toronto plans to expand to more than 20,000 students."[20]

The prospect of a second university in the Toronto area stirred up not only interest but also opposition. The initial attitude of the chairman of the University of Toronto's Board of Governors, Colonel Eric Phillips, verged on hostility. In August 1958 he wrote to the mayor of Toronto, Nathan Phillips (no relation), that "another University in Toronto will not be needed for another ten years." To Premier Leslie Frost, Eric Phillips wrote that the mayor had told him that the organizing group for the new university was asking the city for financial support and that Nathan Phillips did not care for this. Eric Phillips had no wish to denigrate the group, "but if the facts are as Nathan Phillips pointed out, and they are asking for immediate financial support, I would think that their whole planning needs reappraisal."[21] Eric Phillips quite naturally worried about the negative effect that a second university's financial demands might have on the finances of the University of Toronto.

Aware of Colonel Phillips's misgivings, Bissell wrote to him in November to suggest that "we talk to the York University people about the possibility of the new foundation entering our college scheme," offering "modest" financial inducement to that end. Bissell added that he thought Premier Frost "would be receptive to this idea, since it would help to solve the problem of additional facilities for higher education."[22] A few weeks later, Bissell proposed a federation to Curtis. This led the York University committee to visit Bissell and Vice-President Murray G. Ross in early December. Unwilling to abandon the idea of a separate university, yet eager to obtain the University of Toronto's support, the committee agreed to appoint York's first president in consultation with Bissell and his university's Board of Governors.[23]

Several members of the organizing committee met in December 1958 with Frost and the recently created Advisory Committee on University Affairs (ACUA) to plead the case for a second university in Toronto. The response they got was underwhelming. Although not opposed to the proposal, ACUA was disinclined to approve provincial investment in the land needed for a campus. It did express support for the idea of a federation with the University of Toronto in order to get the new institution going. A few days later, having vetted the private bill that proposed the establishment of York – it was drafted by Deeks and Hackett with the help of an interested lawyer, N.T. Berry[24] – ACUA gave the York proposal the green light. "Its sponsors may now proceed to submit it through the regular channels."[25]

As the year 1959 began, the organizing committee was getting mixed signals. The new university seemed to be welcome, but its financial needs were less so, especially those associated with the purchase of land for a campus. This was government policy. "We have to make our money count," Frost wrote to W. Beverley Lewis, the Progressive Conservative MPP for York-Humber and a former reeve of Etobicoke, warning him not to raise the expectations of the organizing group: "200 acres of land in the Toronto area might cost us millions. Frankly, I would prefer to put this money into buildings that would produce students in a short period of time."[26] York University, he added, should look for private money or for less expensive land.

The act chartering the university entered the Ontario legislature in the form of a private member's bill, introduced by H.L. Rowntree, MPP for York West. Approved by the Private Bills Committee in late February, the York University Act, 1959, passed third reading on 16 March and received royal assent ten days later. The "objects and purposes" of the new institution were stated to be: "(a) the advancement of learning and the dissemination of knowledge; and (b) the intellectual, social, moral and physical development of its members and the betterment of society."[27] The new university would have a self-perpetuating lay board as well as an academic senate, which could establish any faculty, school, program, or course and grant "any and all university degrees and honorary degrees and diplomas."

The act stated that seven men, Edgar Alberts, Wilfred Curtis, Stanley Deeks, Arthur Hackett, Roby Kidd, Thomas Loudon, and Arthur Margison, "and any others appointed by them," constituted the "provisional Board of Governors."

Within twenty-four months this board would give way to a permanent board consisting of a chancellor, a president, and twenty-four more members elected or appointed for four-year terms. The university was to be secular: neither religious tests nor religious observances of any kind would be imposed on students or members of the faculty and staff.

Obtaining a charter for the new university was the easy part. Much more difficult tasks awaited: deciding on a home for the institution so that it could open its doors in September 1959, appointing a president and teaching staff of high quality, and finding the funds that would make the other two possible. In late January 1959 the organizing committee decided that at least $100,000 would be needed for the first two years, provided temporary quarters could be found at a reasonable cost. A fund-raising campaign was therefore essential, though no one was quite sure how and where to begin. All the same, the Facilities Planning

In 1958–59 York's organizing committee tried to obtain Chorley Park, former residence of Ontario's lieutenant governors, but failed because of local opposition.

Committee was actively looking for a place where York might start operations as well as for a site that would accommodate the university in the long term.[28]

Offers of land began to trickle in as soon as it became known that a new university was planned for the Toronto area. Most of the sites, located in Etobicoke, North York, Scarborough, Thornhill, and Oshawa, were unattractive, being too small, too expensive, or too remote. In the fall of 1958, committee members had their eyes on an estate east of Woodbine and south of Highway 401 that, when combined with an estate west of Woodbine, would have created a parcel of approximately three hundred acres. This scheme never firmed up, though, and the committee soon became interested in Chorley Park, located in Rosedale, as a temporary site. Among its attractions was a large building, the residence of the lieutenant governor of Ontario until 1937, that would be usable for offices and classrooms. Margison and his associates approached politicians at all three levels in an attempt to secure the property.[29] The city of Toronto wanted the site for a park, however, while the North Rosedale Ratepayers Association adamantly opposed locating a university on the property.

In the course of the summer of 1959, the University of Toronto met York's immediate need for space. Falconer Hall, located on Queen's Park Crescent south of the Royal Ontario Museum, could be lent to York in 1960. Then, should no other site have become available to the university, it could move to the Glendon estate at Bayview and Lawrence in the summer of 1961. The University of Toronto Faculty of Law was still using the Glendon site, but it would soon be housed in a new building on Queen's Park Crescent. The Facilities Planning Committee had earlier considered the Glendon property only to dismiss it as "too small."[30] As a temporary site, though, it was more than acceptable once Chorley Park proved to be unavailable. Meanwhile, the search continued for a larger, more suitable permanent site.

The committee thought it had found one not long after the York University Act was passed. The George Henry farm, a 340-acre property once owned by a premier of the province, was located between Highway 401 and Sheppard Avenue, from Leslie Avenue east to Woodbine. A York University Committee that had been established by the North York Township Council made a formal offer to the Facilities Planning Committee in August 1959. The company owning the property, Hendon Estates, would sell it for $3.4 million. The council was prepared to pay more than a third of this, provided it could obtain legislative approval of the debenture that would be necessary. "Our committee is most anxious that York establish in North York," Councillor James D. Service wrote to Margison, adding that committee members believed this site, close to Highway 401 and the future Don Valley Parkway (its construction had just begun), to be "the most natural and desirable site for York University in the Metro area."[31]

The Facilities Planning Committee agreed. Committee members James Keachie and James Kelley reported to the provisional board of governors the committee's view that "the Henry farm was the ideal site for the University" and secured permission to continue negotiations.[32] By mid-September, a draft agreement was in place. Some weeks later, North York Reeve N.C. Goodhead asked Premier Frost for legislation that would allow the North York council to contribute approximately $1.3 million to York's purchase of the Henry farm without having to obtain the assent of the electors, as the Ontario Municipal Act would have obliged them to do.[33]

Frost's reply was like a cold shower. "While the object is worthy," he wrote in early November, "I am concerned about the ability of North York, with all its other obligations, to enter into any such arrangement."[34] He rejected the request

This dwelling, the home of George Henry, premier of Ontario from 1929 to 1934, was at the centre of a North York estate that the provisional board of York University sought to buy in 1959.

Premier of Ontario from 1949 to 1961, Leslie Frost supported the University of Toronto's proposal to make the Glendon Hall estate available to York University.

for legislation. This in turn wrecked the three-way deal. "It is ... a matter of deep disappointment to us," Margison wrote to Paul Hellyer, president of Hendon Estates, "that we have to inform you of the financial inability of York University to sign the offer to purchase at this time." An arrangement for academic affiliation with the University of Toronto would solve York's short-term needs, he continued, and the Facilities Planning Committee had continued the search for a permanent site. However, "only this week it was found that money will not be available as expected."[35] The members of the Facilities Planning Committee, who had come close to securing a site for York and then had the rug pulled out from under them, submitted their resignations to the provisional board of governors, which disbanded the committee. "We had given it our best shot. There was nothing more for us to do," Margison said forty-four years later.[36]

The collapse of the Henry farm deal was a heavy blow to members of the committee and the provisional board. It is not surprising that Margison eventually came to the view that meddlers from the University of Toronto, eager to gain control of York and determined to deny it what he later described to newspaper columnist Margaret Wente as "the very best site in Toronto,"[37] had prompted Frost's letter to Goodhead. If there *was* such meddling, though, hard evidence of it is missing. A letter that Colonel Phillips wrote to Premier Frost on 10 November comes closest: "Following our talk about Bob Winters and York University, I think we have gained what might be described as control of a potentially very messy situation, and I believe that if you can find it within yourself to encourage Bob in the thought that the birth and weaning, as it were, of this new university is a thoroughly worthwhile task, he will take it. In the opinion of Bissell and myself, no better man could be found." He went on to stress a point that would have been dear to Frost's heart: "The objective I have in mind is that, under no circumstances, will you be approached for any grants for this university for a minimum of five years. The thought is that very little money will be required under our plan, and I propose to furnish it unofficially from the University, including certain services that are of no significance to us but important to the new university in its early stages."[38]

Phillips was probably of the view that, if large sums of money were to be spent on a university, the University of Toronto should be the beneficiary. For his part, Frost was never eager to spend money unless he could see a good reason for it. North York's proposal to help York finance the purchase of the Henry property probably troubled him less than the awareness that York would also need financial help from *his* government to close the deal. Phillips's undertaking to forestall financial appeals from York – a promise he would be unable to make good – must have been music to the premier's ears. But, even if this undertaking had not been forthcoming, it seems very unlikely that Frost would have wanted to help pay for the Henry farm.

"York University Can't Afford Henry Site," a story in the Toronto *Star* stated, noting that negotiations had collapsed even though North York was willing to pay $1,364,000 towards the cost of the site. Margison had declined to say where York had hoped to get the remainder of the money, commenting merely that it was unavailable.[39] A *Globe and Mail* article by a staff writer stated that the problem was the high cost of the site.[40] All was not lost, however. "Opening Date Stands for York University" was the headline over a joint statement by Eric Phillips and Claude Bissell announcing the terms of affiliation between the University of Toronto and York, described as "a private and non-denominational institution of higher learning," and stating that the new university would begin operations in Falconer Hall in 1960 before moving to the Glendon Hall property in 1961.[41]

Seeking to expand beyond the original group of seven, York's organizing committee had added five members in May 1959. They were N.T. Berry, a partner in a downtown Toronto legal firm, D.F. Kent, president of Kendall Company, G.A. Lascelles, commissioner of finance for Metropolitan Toronto, A.D. McKee, president of Perini, and Walter R. McLachlan, president of Orenda Engines. Two months later, this expanded committee formally transformed itself into York's provisional board of governors. It faced a daunting task: to launch a new university in a city that already housed the premier university in English Canada and the three denominational institutions federated with it. How could qualified faculty be brought to join the fledgling institution? How could students be induced to register in it? Small wonder that the organizing committee had already asked Bissell for advice.

Early in 1959 Bissell had appointed a committee chaired by Dean C.A. Wright of the Faculty of Law. Discussions between this committee and an affiliation committee appointed by York's organizers began in February 1959 and lasted well into the summer. An arrangement that was intended to benefit both institutions gradually took shape. The affiliation agreement that was completed by September 1959 gave to York while also taking from it. York would operate under the University of Toronto's wing for a period lasting from four to eight years, initially offering courses approved by the older university. York would offer the University of Toronto three-year ordinary degree to its first class of students, who would begin their courses in September 1960. During the first year, they would use Falconer Hall; then York would move to Glendon Hall. Whether it would become a permanent York site or would in time revert to the University of Toronto's use remained an open question.

The University of Toronto would also offer financial assistance to York. In exchange, York undertook not to look for financial support in the corporate sector until 1964, when the University of Toronto's own financial campaign would have been completed. A major worry for Phillips and members of the Board of Governors, Bissell wrote in a memoir, was that a financial campaign on York's behalf would endanger a similar campaign by the University of Toronto.[42] The affiliation agreement averted that threat. The new university surrendered a large measure of its autonomy in exchange for money and, more important, academic respectability. This was essential if the institution was to attract qualified faculty and staff, including a president.

A suitable candidate for this position seemed close at hand. On 2 July, Curtis reported to the other members of the organizing committee, soon to become the provisional board of governors, that he had approached President Bissell "to determine whether Dr. Murray Ross might be available for the position of Presi-

As president of the University of Toronto (1958–71), Claude Bissell welcomed the founding of York University and promoted its early development.

dent." On Bissell's suggestion, Curtis had then asked Ross directly, and he had said that he would accept the offer "if York University had a strong Board of Governors." After some discussion, a motion carried that Ross would be "a desirable choice as President of York University."[43]

Reporting to Bissell, who was holidaying in Cape Breton, Ross wrote that Phillips seemed to take a dim view of York's future and had discouraged him from taking the presidency. "On the other hand, Air Marshal Curtis is busily engaged trying to get together a Board of the quality you and I have discussed. I came in for a meeting today, attended by two bank presidents and a senior partner of Wood Gundy," all of whom seemed interested in the York project. But key people like Signy Eaton (the wife of department-store owner John David Eaton) and prominent Liberal politician and businessman Robert Winters had not yet been approached. "A good deal will depend on their view of the matter."[44]

Ross's insistence that York should have a strong board was by implication unflattering to the members of the provisional board. The York University Act committed them to resign as soon as a permanent board could be assembled, but its membership was up in the air, and it was by no means a given that members of the provisional board would be excluded from serving on it. When Curtis mentioned the names of possible permanent board members at the 2 July meeting, Margison expressed misgivings, pointing out that all the people named were from business and industry and that the board should represent a cross-section of society. Furthermore, some of the original members of the organizing committee thought that the provisional board ought to overlap with the permanent board in order to provide continuity.[45]

At a September meeting, Curtis proposed the names of five new members: Ray Farquharson, Allan Lambert, John S. Proctor, William P. Scott, and Edwin H. Walker. Proctor was president of the Imperial Bank of Canada and Walker of General Motors of Canada; Lambert was executive vice-president of the Toronto-Dominion Bank and would soon be its president; Scott was vice-president of Wood Gundy Securities. Of the five, only Farquharson, a former dean of medicine at the University of Toronto and the chairman of the Medical Research Council, was not in business.[46]

The provisional board approved these names for future appointment. A debate then followed as to how long the original group should carry on. In the end, Ross's wish, which Curtis conveyed to the board, carried the day: the reconstituted board would consist only of the proposed new members and such other persons as they might choose. The provisional board resigned in October. Especially the members of the organizing committee must have felt rather like Moses, denied entry to the promised land just as it came into view. Still, James Keachie, not a member of the organizing committee but vice-chairman of its Facilities Planning Committee, believed that the resignation of the original members made sense. "Our group didn't have the necessary clout," he said, "the new group did."[47]

Bissell wrote to Curtis to express "great pleasure" over "the progress that has been made in the establishment of the Board of Governors of York University." Both Colonel Phillips and he had been "impressed by the strength of the proposed board," Bissell continued, "and we look forward to our meetings with them." Bissell expressed the hope that Curtis "and two or three other members of [the] pioneering groups" might become members of the new board, but he added that initially "the board should be a small, cohesive group" capable of making "rapid decisions."[48] (Curtis was, in fact, the only one to continue.)

Bissell's letter made no reference to Ross, but his selection as York's first president was a certainty. Tall and handsome, the forty-nine-year-old Cape Bretoner had worked at the University of Toronto since 1951, when he was appointed in the Department of Social Work. He gained the rank of professor in 1955; two years later, President Sidney Smith appointed him vice-president. An undergraduate at Acadia University, he had also studied at the universities of Toronto and Chicago and had earned the ED.D degree from Columbia University in 1949. Before he joined the University of Toronto faculty, he had worked for the Toronto YMCA, the National YMCA Council, the Canadian Youth Mission, and, in the capacity of executive secretary, the Canadian Institute of International Affairs. Jovial and gregarious, he made friends easily and had a wide acquaintance.

Another name Bissell did not mention was that of Robert Winters. On the verge of turning fifty, he was born in Lunenburg, Nova Scotia, and had studied at Mount Allison University and the Massachusetts Institute of Technology before becoming an electrical engineer. During the Second World War he reached the rank of lieutenant-colonel, and in 1945 he entered the House of Commons as a Liberal. Joining Louis St Laurent's cabinet in 1948, he was minister of public works in 1957 when both the party and he personally went down to defeat in a general election. He then entered the business world and by 1959 had become president of Rio Tinto (later Rio Algoma) Mines. He commanded respect, and more than one observer, among them Eric Phillips, saw him as the obvious choice for chairman of York's Board of Governors. So did the provisional board.

LEFT   Murray G. Ross, a professor of social work and vice-president at the University of Toronto, became York's founding president.

RIGHT   Robert Winters, seen here with Ross, was a prominent Liberal politician and businessman who became chairman of York's Board of Governors in late 1959.

Winters accepted the invitation, and on 26 November 1959 Premier Frost announced that the former cabinet minister would be chairman of York's Board of Governors, adding that the event "marked the official birth of Ontario's tenth university."[49] Some newspaper reports implied that Frost had appointed Winters, which caused confusion. As Frost explained to John Bassett of the *Telegram*, he had merely been "asked to announce the Winters appointment and the actual coming of this university into being and operation as a matter of giving the Government's blessing to the undertaking."[50] On 2 December, Winters met with three members of the new board, Lambert, Proctor, and Scott, and announced the resignation of the last remaining members of the provisional board. The board then formally asked Ross to become York's president and vice-chancellor. Next, the board appointed William Small, who until then had been secretary of the University of Toronto's Board of Governors, to the position of secretary of the York board. The transition from the provisional to the permanent board seemed to be complete.

Not quite. Angered by the collapse of the George Henry farm deal, Councillor James Service complained to the *Globe and Mail* about that setback and also claimed that Winters had been appointed improperly.[51] Service's charges led members of the now-defunct provisional board to seek legal advice, and four of them met Winters and his lawyer on 11 December to resolve the matter. Winters assured them that board members would "represent a wide cross-section of the community," that the University of Toronto had placed no restrictions on his selections to the board, that Premier Frost had promised funds that would ensure the growth of York University, and that he would honour the intention of the founding group to keep York independent. In the following discussion it emerged that Murray Ross was a unanimous choice for the presidency. The board then reconstituted itself. Winters would be in the chair; the other members were to be Ross (as president), Curtis, Lambert, Proctor, Scott, and Walker, as well as Senator Thomas D'Arcy Leonard, a prominent Toronto lawyer.[52]

One week later, the board added Farquharson, William C. Harris, president of the investment firm Harris and Partners, and John D. (Jack) Leitch, president of Toronto Elevators and Upper Lakes and St Lawrence Transportation, to their number. "Bob Winters recruited me," Leitch recalled in 2005, adding that he had never regretted his decision to join the board: "We had some really good men, and everybody worked hard to make York a success."[53] The new board re-enacted the decisions made on 2 December, and Ross assumed the presidency. For the time being, though, he and Small continued to be paid by the University of Toronto.

A 19 December press release announced the names of the board members and expressed Winters's pleasure that "men of this caliber" were willing "to devote some of their time to this young and challenging university." Winters also paid tribute "to those dedicated people who, as the prime movers in the project, were responsible for having York incorporated. They contributed much of their time and energies to the initial stages of York University's development to date."[54] He mentioned by name the seven men designated in the act. Thereafter they quickly faded from institutional memory, with the exception of Curtis, who became

York's first chancellor in April 1961. A good twenty years would pass before the university got around to honouring them.

As the year 1959 ended, York was still little more than a concept. But at least it was, nine months hence, going to open its doors to its first class of students; and its new president had already indicated what the new institution might stand for. Even before formally accepting the presidency, Murray Ross announced a three-point plan. York, he stated, would concentrate at first on "a programme of liberal and general education – as opposed to one of specialization." Secondly, it would "place a fresh emphasis on the social sciences and particularly geography," which he held to be neglected in Canada, and thirdly, it would "give special attention to helping students read, write, and speak effectively." Most classes would be seminars, he added, made possible by "a favourable faculty-student ratio."[55]

Oddly enough, this was the first public statement of what York actually proposed to do. Although some members of the organizing committee, notably Roby Kidd, were interested in curricular matters, they had not addressed these publicly,[56] perhaps thinking that it was premature to do so. After all, only one member of the committee, Thomas Loudon, was an academic. As a consequence, the new institution was like a blank slate on which Ross could inscribe his own concept of higher education. Whether his plan was realistic, how it would be paid for, and where it would unfold: these were questions for the future.

Glendon Hall, the country estate of Edward and Agnes Euphemia (Pheme) Wood, came into the possession of the University of Toronto in 1951.

In the early part of the twentieth century, Edward Rogers Wood was one of Canada's leading financiers. Although his name is little known today, it deserves to be remembered at York, with whose early history it is inextricably linked. The first building used by the university, Falconer Hall, as well as its first campus, the Glendon Hall estate, were both once the property of Wood and his wife, Agnes Euphemia (Pheme) Smart. The first of York's residences is named after him.

Falconer Hall, into which York moved in 1960, is a handsome mansion on the west side of Queen's Park Crescent, south of the Royal Ontario Museum. Built around 1900 and named Wymilwood, it came into the hands of Victoria University in 1925, the Woods having moved to their newly built country home on Bayview Avenue, northeast of Toronto. Victoria used the mansion as a residence and social centre until 1949, when it became part of a land swap with the University of Toronto. Since Victoria kept the name and gave it to a new structure east of Queen's Park Crescent, the University of Toronto renamed the mansion in honour of Sir Robert Falconer, president of the university from 1906 to 1932. Serving as a women's social centre and the home of the Margaret Eaton Library, it was supposed to become the nucleus of an athletic complex for women. This plan fell through, and in the late 1950s the demolition of Falconer Hall came under discussion. Instead the university lent the building to York. (Today it is used by the Faculty of Law.)[1]

As he arranged his move from Simcoe Hall to Falconer Hall, Murray Ross faced several daunting tasks. One was assembling a faculty and staff for York. Scarcely less urgent was finding students willing to take a chance on the new institution. Next in line was preparing the Glendon estate for the move that would take place before the fall of 1961. The new university also had to develop its own curriculum, to plan for the opening of its faculty of part-time studies, and to secure land that would serve York as a campus on which it could eventually expand.

According to the affiliation agreement with the University of Toronto, formally signed on 30 June 1960, the affiliation would last for at least four and up

LEFT   Denis Smith, the first registrar, and President Murray Ross in front of Falconer Hall on the University of Toronto campus.

RIGHT   One of York's first employees, Vicky Draper began her career as the registrar's assistant and eventually became senior executive officer, Faculty of Arts.

to eight years.[2] During that time, York courses would be essentially the same as those offered by the older university, and York graduates would receive University of Toronto degrees. York employees and students had access to the University of Toronto's library, laboratory, and athletic facilities. The arrangement gave the fledgling university a stature it would otherwise have lacked, making it easier to attract both faculty members and students.

In January 1960 the provincial Committee on University Affairs recommended that York get a promotional grant of $25,000 and that the University of Toronto budget be increased by $250,000 in 1960–61 to cover York's operating expenses.[3] The grants allowed York to begin hiring staff. The University of Toronto continued to carry Ross and Bill Small on its payroll in 1959–60, as well as Ross's secretary. (The first incumbent of this position was Jackie Atkins, succeeded a few years later by the ever-discreet Yvonne Aziz.) The first employee to be paid by York was Denis Smith, a young political scientist whom Ross put to work as registrar, charging him with student recruitment and the preparation of the first calendar. Smith recalled undertaking these tasks with some trepidation, since he had not been trained for them. In June he got the assistance of a young woman, Victereene (Vicky) Draper, whom he remembered as "extremely competent"[4] and who herself remembered that Smith "wrote beautifully."[5] But in 1961 he was happy to pass his registrarial functions on to a newly appointed lecturer in history, Don Rickerd. Years later Draper, having filled several positions of increasing responsibility, became senior executive officer of the Faculty of Arts.

Smith's name appeared among several whose appointment Ross announced at a meeting of the Board of Governors in late January. They included the librarian and poet Douglas Lochhead and the philosopher George Grant, both recruited from Dalhousie University, and Ross's friend John Seeley. A well-known sociologist, Seeley was the co-author of *Crestwood Heights* (1956), the landmark study of suburban life in the Toronto suburb (as it then was) of Forest Hill. Ross also persuaded the historian Edgar McInnis to come to York. A former professor at the

University of Toronto and national president of the Canadian Institute of International Affairs, he was a real catch. "Many of our colleagues at the University of Toronto had expected York to use senior PHD students from their departments," Ross later wrote, "but when Professor McInnis was appointed it was obvious we were aiming high."[6]

A month later, Ross announced the names of several more recruits, among them York's first female faculty member, the mathematician Alice Turner, a very young psychologist, Norman Endler, and a veteran geographer, George Tatham. Especially Tatham, who had taught at the University of Toronto since 1939, was an inspired choice, a scholar who shared Ross's commitment to general education and, Tatham's biographer John Warkentin writes, may have understood it better than Ross himself.[7] Wiry and fit, keenly interested in the welfare of the students, Tatham was a prominent man about campus. Until his retirement in 1978, he served the university in several positions, among them dean of the faculty, dean of students, and master of McLaughlin College. Douglas Rutherford, a member of the founding class and the first Student Council president, recalled that Tatham was "the best-loved professor, with Alice Turner a close second."[8] Other students of the 1960s and 1970s have also expressed a high regard for him.

Another early appointment was Lionel Rubinoff, still completing his PHD in philosophy at the University of Toronto. His connections in Toronto's artistic and literary circles made him "very useful to Murray," Rubinoff remembered.[9] Endler said that Ross "was a big fan of Rubinoff's" because he knew a lot about cultural matters, of which Ross knew little.[10] In April 1960, Ross told the Board of Governors that Rubinoff would take charge of an informal lecture series called "Tea and Talk" that would bring in visiting speakers and encourage discussion between them and the students. He was also put in charge of arranging exhibitions of art.[11]

York suffered a setback when Grant suddenly resigned in April. He objected to teaching the introductory course under the supervision of Fulton Anderson, chairman of Toronto's Philosophy Department, with whom his relations were strained. Grant also objected to using a textbook of which he disapproved. When he complained about these restraints on his freedom, Ross replied that the tie

LEFT The mathematician Alice Turner was the first woman appointed to the York faculty.

RIGHT The geographer George Tatham (left) is seen here advising Bruce Bryden, who later served as president of the Alumni Association and as chair of the Board of Governors.

to Toronto brought advantages which more than made up for the drawbacks. Disagreeing with Ross, Grant resigned. Efforts to patch things up, with Tatham acting as mediator, failed,[12] and John McFarland, a Toronto-born graduate student working on his doctorate at Oxford University, was hired to join Rubinoff. McFarland said in an interview that the textbook may have been prescribed but that he taught the course pretty much the way he wanted to, and that he believed other faculty members did the same in their courses.[13] A student who registered in 1961, Penny Williams, recalled that, by her third year, the York courses were sufficiently different from the University of Toronto's that York students wrote different exams.[14]

By the time York's first calendar appeared in April 1960, a dozen faculty members had been appointed, with a few others being added between April and July. Richard Coughlin and John Spencer joined Seeley in Sociology, while Irvine Pounder came to join Turner in Mathematics. Hugh Maclean (English), Lester Pronger (French), and the zoologist David Fowle completed the faculty.

The recruitment of students took place alongside that of faculty. A public-relations campaign that drew attention to York in a variety of ways began in February and continued into September. The president's office made articles available to the three Toronto dailies on a regular basis, publicizing various aspects of the new university. In mid-May the university hosted a dinner at the Royal York Hotel for the principals and guidance counsellors of approximately seventy secondary schools in Metropolitan Toronto and the surrounding area.[15]

In July, York secured some unusual publicity. A few months earlier it had announced a contest encouraging Grade 13 students to compete for a $300 entrance scholarship by submitting suggestions for a York University motto. The winner was a student at Richview Collegiate, John Court. He recalled that, partly "to get my Latin teacher and my mother off my case," he came up with a line from Virgil's *Georgics*: "tentanda via," or "the way must be tried." His sugges-

LEFT   The York University coat of arms, designed by Eric Aldwinckle.

RIGHT   Lois Henry (left), Janet Beeby, and Douglas Rutherford registering in Falconer Hall, September 1960.

tion earned him the scholarship and a story with photo in the Toronto *Star*.[16] A few days after the announcement that York had found a motto, the Board of Governors commissioned Eric Aldwinckle, a well-known war artist and graphic designer, to design the university's coat of arms. In it the white rose of the House of York assumed a prominent position.[17]

Advertisements soliciting applications from prospective students began to appear in the Toronto newspapers on a weekly basis in the summer. They stressed the benefits of education in the humanities and social sciences in an intimate setting, with small classes the rule. In response, 76 students – the target had been 100 – registered in mid-September. (Another 75 or so had reportedly been turned down because their grades were too low.)[18]

What brought the first students to York? Rutherford, one of eight University of Toronto Schools (UTS) graduates to register, said that York seemed just a little different, and that attracted him. More to the point, however: "You were on the U of T campus and would get a U of T degree, and you would also have small classes. There really was no downside."[19] Clayton (Clay) Ruby came for a different reason. While still in Grade 13 he had got to know John Seeley and, impressed with the sociologist's insights, decided to register at the university where he was going to be teaching. Seeley became a life-long friend.[20]

Rick Salutin, who also became a friend of Seeley's, had actually registered in University College. He recalled that he "began the year at U of T in Honours English but switched to York, just up the street in Falconer Hall, when some English prof told me to buzz off; he had no time to look at something I'd written."[21] Dale Taylor, a UTS graduate, had planned to go to Trinity College but was intrigued by York's ads and went to talk with Ross, who lived a few blocks away. "He sold me on York University." Ross convinced him that, rather than be a nobody at Trinity in his freshman year, he could make a mark at York from the outset.[22] (Like Rutherford, Taylor got elected to the Student Council.) Heather (McClary) McGoey, one of four students from Etobicoke Collegiate Institute, came because her parents liked the sound of York: "It was a small university in Toronto, which would allow me to live at home, saving the costs of residence." Being sixteen – she had skipped two grades – she thought it natural that her parents should choose her university.[23]

Looking back on the early days of York, George Rust-D'Eye, who registered in 1961, wrote: "Many of the members of the academic community, both in the first year at Falconer Hall and then at Glendon, were there out of a feeling of reaction to what was perceived as the assembly-line anonymity created by the larger established universities." The opportunity to help create something new and important was exciting. "Aside from the traditions and practices common to all universities, here there was no established way of doing things. There were no long-established faculty or student organizations or practices. But there was tremendous potential for the establishment and development of a unique intellectual environment."[24] Fred Gorbet, who registered in 1962 and took a degree in economics (in time he would serve on the Board of Governors), was "very happy with the structures that we had" and remembered with particular pleasure courses taught by George Doxey and an Australian immigrant, James Cutt,

who "was very young and very eager to help students."[25] David Bell, another 1962 entrant (and later dean of graduate studies and then environmental studies), said that York had "the best scholarship program in the province" at the time, and this attracted some excellent students. Moreover, young academics "had time for students," and a "really terrific" student life was one result. He recalled with great pleasure tutorials in which he and Gorbet met two-on-two with Lionel Rubinoff.[26]

Rhapsodizing about the French Revolution, William Wordsworth exclaimed: "Bliss was it in that dawn to be alive, / But to be young was very heaven."[27] It requires little exaggeration to apply this sentiment to York's first class. Like most freshmen, they took to university life with gusto, and because they were all in first year there was none of that kowtowing to upper-year students that is a normal part of the freshman's experience. "We were like prima donnas," McClary recalled, "we felt very special."[28] Clara Thomas, appointed to the English Department in 1961, used similar words in her memoirs. The first class "had been treated as such a special breed and with so much press publicity," she wrote, "that they were notably inclined to prima donna behaviour."[29] One of those students, John Court, later commented in friendly jest: "Damn straight, Clara, and still proud of it."[30]

The half-dozen faculty members surviving from that first year remembered a small, cozy group, housed in a mansion that had just enough space to provide offices, with one large room in which classes and special functions took place. Among the latter was the "Tea and Talk" series, which brought distinguished visitors to the campus and created an opportunity for students to talk with them. The early speakers included the novelist Morley Callaghan (his son

Barry would teach in Atkinson College), the theatre director Mavor Moore (later a member of the Faculty of Fine Arts), and the geophysicist J. Tuzo Wilson (in time a chancellor of the university).[31] Douglas Lochhead, who was busy ordering books for the library, remembered "a very sociable place, with lots of opportunities to meet people."[32] John McFarland said he "loved the old mansion" and liked the intimate atmosphere: "We talked with each other a lot."[33] But Thomas, who had taught at the University of Western Ontario before coming to York, found that the junior faculty members had "little sense of community" and "little idea of what a university was."[34]

The faculty met socially at both informal and formal functions. At some point during that first year, Ross invited all faculty and their spouses to a reception and dinner at the York Club so that they might meet members of the Board of Governors.[35] Black tie being required, Norm Endler had to borrow a dinner jacket from Bill Small. Ross, whom Endler described as "very status-conscious, and evidently proud of his York Club membership," seemed surprised that the young psychologist did not own one.[36]

Lionel Rubinoff recalled that "Murray's vision was very appealing: a small liberal arts college that would focus on interdisciplinary studies."[37] That first year it seemed to be working out, as faculty members taught their classes, met their students, and set out to develop a curriculum in the humanities, social sciences, and natural sciences. There was as yet no talk of a much larger university. The campus that people looked forward to was the one they would be moving to in 1961, the Glendon Hall estate in North York.

Located where Lawrence Avenue East is interrupted by Bayview Avenue, the eighty-four-acre Glendon property came into the hands of the University of Toronto after Pheme Wood's death in 1950. She and her husband shared an interest in botany and landscape architecture, and upon moving to newly finished Glendon Hall in 1925 they devoted a lot of thought to the transformation of a farm into a beautifully wooded estate, stocking the grounds with a large variety of trees and shrubs. After her husband's death in 1941, Wood came to the view that the property should become a botanical garden. She decided to make the University of Toronto's Department of Botany her beneficiary because she believed that her objective would be ill-served by leaving the Glendon property to North York. She was distressed by the fate of the handsome Kilgour estate farther south on Bayview. Donated to North York to be a public park, it had instead been turned over to the federal government for the construction of Sunnybrook Veterans' Hospital.[38]

If the gardens of the Wood estate, which included expansive lawns, two woodlots, and a rose garden (called the Bruce Bryden Rose Garden since 1992), were splendid, so was the villa at their centre, Glendon Hall itself. Designed by the Toronto architectural firm of Molesworth, West and Secord, the structure "drew inspiration from a number of styles, notably the Italian Renaissance Villa school, British baronial revival, and the grand estate homes of Hollywood and Florida."[39] Unfortunately, however, Pheme Wood did not leave an endowment that would have allowed the Botany Department to maintain and develop the villa, the sub-

Glendon Hall housed the president's office and other administrative offices on York's first campus.

sidiary buildings, and the grounds. As a result, the University of Toronto found itself in possession of a magnificent white elephant. Rather than trying to raise money to turn the property into a botanical-research facility, President Sidney Smith pursued other possibilities. In 1952 the design school of the Ontario College of Art (OCA) moved into Glendon Hall, but when the OCA building on McCaul Street opened four years later, the school moved there. The next tenant was the university's new Faculty of Law, which moved into Glendon Hall in 1956, pending the construction of more ample quarters on Queen's Park Crescent.

Incomprehensibly, in 1957 Smith turned down an offer of more than a million dollars that could have been used as an endowment. Made by the landscape architect Howard Dunington-Grubb, who had redesigned the Glendon grounds in the 1930s, the offer would have turned the estate into a botanical-research centre. Smith either misunderstood what Dunington-Grubb intended or was already preoccupied by the prospect of a political career – after the June 1957 general election he became John Diefenbaker's secretary of state for external affairs. In any case, he dropped the ball, and the money ultimately found a haven at Edwards Gardens in North York.[40] The Glendon property remained a financial burden. It probably took no more than a hint from Premier Leslie Frost for the university's board chairman, Eric Phillips, and Smith's successor as president, Claude Bissell, to offer the estate to York. This killed the proverbial two birds with one stone. The University of Toronto would no longer be spending money to maintain Glendon Hall and its expansive grounds. York, on the other hand, acquired an attractive location where the new university could begin to develop.

The prospect of losing Glendon seems to have troubled few at the University of Toronto, except for some members of the Department of Botany and the Faculty of Forestry. They were using the greenhouses at the southwestern corner of the estate to carry out research, and were loath to lose this facility. In early 1960 J.W.B. Sisam of Forestry wrote to Bissell that, even if the Board of Governors would not pay for a botanical garden, surely it was possible to raise private funds to that end. He asked permission to try to raise the money.[41]

It was too late for such an initiative. The two universities had set out on a road that would irrevocably transform the Glendon estate into a campus. The terms of the conveyance of the property, finally completed on 30 June 1962, did make a concession to Sisam and his colleagues. Part of the property remained with the University of Toronto, so that the botanists and foresters could continue using the greenhouses for their research as long as they wished. The last of them died in 1996. Only when they had ceased to use the structures were they converted to York's own use.[42]

In early June 1960 Premier Frost confirmed that the provincial government would pay an initial $1,700,000 for the construction of an academic building on the Glendon site.[43] Two weeks later, the Board of Governors' building committee, consisting of John Proctor, David Mansur, and Edwin Walker, recommended to the full board that the Toronto firm of Marani, Morris and Allan be appointed as architects for the buildings to be constructed at Glendon. The board also selected Thomas Haworth of the University of Toronto's Faculty of Architecture to be architect/planner for the campus.[44] In September the board accepted his plan and approved his choice for the site of the first building.

An ambitious scheme to erect three ten-storey student residences on the valley slope ran into vigorous opposition, led by the Metropolitan Toronto Conservation Authority and the Lawrence Park Property Owners' Association, and had to be abandoned.[45] Indeed, some of York's future neighbours objected to having a university on the site at all, and obtained an injunction that delayed the start of the construction of York Hall for six weeks. At the hearing before the Ontario Municipal Board (OMB), Haworth was asked by the lawyer representing

residents on Valleyanna Drive, just south of Glendon, if he did not think that his clients "would find the behaviour of students disturbing, even shocking." Murray Ross recalled that "Dr. Haworth replied: 'From what I've heard of the behaviour of adults living in Valleyana [sic], I'd fear that students at York might be the ones to be shocked and upset.' That ended that line of questioning."[46]

The OMB ruled in favour of York but forced modifications in the campus plan. A zoning change limited construction to the table lands. Buildings were to be set back at least fifty feet from the property line, and no building was to exceed thirty-five feet in height. Parking had to be available to accommodate half the combined number of faculty and students.[47] The prohibition of construction on the slope and in the valley led Ross to say to the board, with perhaps pardonable exaggeration, that the site was now unsuitable to a residential college of "even 600 students."[48] Unquestionably, the limits imposed on the university at Glendon reinforced the determination to secure a larger site where the university could expand.

Construction of a three-storey structure began in March 1961 and was completed in August, the job being done as quickly and inexpensively as possible. The brick-faced building that arose, housing classrooms, offices, laboratories, a junior and a senior common room, a dining hall, and a servery (with a kitchen below it), was squat, functional, and architecturally undistinguished. Norm Endler remembered with amusement a system whereby the floor covering in an office indicated the rank of its occupant. His office had cheap tiles presumably suitable for a junior faculty member; associate professors had more expensive tiles; department heads had wall-to-wall carpet. Their offices were also bigger and had two windows, while "other faculty members had to be satisfied with one."[49]

At $1.8 million, York Hall was a bargain. This had a downside: Glendon's executive officer in the 1970s, Cy Pilley, sometimes complained about the building's energy inefficiency, epitomized by the single-glazed windows. Before the oil crisis of 1973, of course, the cost of heating oil was low, and an investment in better insulation must have seemed uneconomical.

In the course of August 1961, faculty and staff began moving from Falconer Hall to the new campus. The students, 216 of them in first and second year, followed a month later. In October the dining hall was the scene of the installation of Wilfred Curtis as York's chancellor. After the ceremony, Premier Leslie Frost and Lord James of Rusholme, the vice-chancellor designate of the University of York in England, officially opened York Hall and the latter symbolically planted the white rose of York.[50] More than one student recalled that some of them had gone up to the roof of York Hall and tried to water the rose and the guests from above.

More than forty years later, the early students raved about the Glendon campus, though not about York Hall. Clay Ruby shuddered when he thought of it: "It was awful, really ugly!"[51] The atmosphere was in some ways that of a country club, Dale Taylor said, and some of the students were known as the "country club set."[52] In the winter it took on aspects of a ski resort, Douglas Rutherford recalled, as one of his fellow students, Charles (Chuck) Magwood, led a project to construct a rope tow from the valley floor up to the top, and the York University Ski Club got going. David Bell remembered Magwood's ski lift as a particularly notable feature of the campus, though snow cover was unreliable.[53]

"The grounds were lovely," Rutherford said: "I picture Bruce Bryden in his red Triumph TR3 with the top down. I can see him in the fall, the leaves changing. It was a little piece of heaven back then."[54] (Bryden became the first president of the Alumni Association and also served as chairman of the Board of Governors, the position he held at the time of his untimely death in 1992.) "The problem was paying attention to my studies," Rutherford continued. He was president of the

LEFT York faculty and administrative officers, 1961–62, in front of Glendon Hall. Front row: Douglas Lochhead, Alice Turner, David Fowle, Edith Guild, Murray Ross, Clara Thomas, George Harjan, Edgar McInnis; second row: John Seeley, George Tatham, Norman Endler, Irvine Pounder, John Armour; back: Lloyd Jenkins, Howard Langille, Lester Pronger, Robert Lundell, Arthur Johnson, Douglas Verney, Hugh Maclean, Craufurd Goodwin, Donald Jackson, John McFarland, Denis Smith, Vello Sermat, Donald Rickerd, John Brückmann, Neil Morrison, Lionel Rubinoff.

RIGHT Lord James of Rusholme has just planted the white rose of York on the Glendon campus, 1961.

Student Council for a second year, and more or less in that capacity he led a raid one night on the campus of the Ontario Agricultural College (OAC) (now part of the University of Guelph). The objective was to capture the nineteenth-century cannon that is still a Guelph campus focal point. Finding that the cannon was clamped and bolted firmly to the ground, and then accosted by campus security and warned by a dean to leave town before OAC students showed up to deal ungently with them, Rutherford and his associates returned to Toronto empty-handed "to nurse our wounded pride (and a few beer bottles)."[55]

There was a fair amount of drinking on campus, but in those early years it mostly took place surreptitiously. The drinking age was still twenty-one, so that the Senior Common Room, which occupied three rooms on the third floor of York Hall, had the only licence on campus. Even that licence, Don Rickerd recalled, had not been easy to obtain, the licensing board worrying about student access to alcoholic beverages.[56] Drinking patterns changed somewhat when the E.R. Wood Residence opened in September 1963. George Rust-D'Eye did not live in residence, but when he was editor of the student weekly newspaper, *Pro Tem*, he often found himself sleeping on someone's floor rather than returning home. The consumption of beer in residence rooms, he recalled, though banned by the rules, was substantial.[57] John Lennox, who entered first year in 1963 (he later served as dean of graduate studies), said that students who wanted to drink often found their way over to the Jolly Miller on Yonge Street, in Hogg's Hollow south of York Mills, which remained for years a favourite watering hole.[58]

While York's Senate and board, its faculty members and administrators, sought to give shape to the new university, to formulate its curriculum and teach it, and to found new programs, the students had their own interests and con-

First-year students listen as Denis Smith explains university rules and regulations, 1961.

cerns. Some of them were educational, others were social, political, cultural, and athletic, both formal and informal. Bridge was a major pastime, though some students played hearts and a few others chess. Dale Taylor recalled a professor entering the Junior Common Room in York Hall and finding most of his students – it was a small class – playing bridge. "What's it going to be today?" he asked jocularly, "your game or my seminar?"[59]

During the first five years, student government was under faculty supervision, with successively Denis Smith, the economist Craufurd Goodwin, Alice Turner, and Edward Pattullo, associate dean of arts and science in 1963–64, acting as advisers and attending most meetings. The Student Council got its money from the university in the form of a per-capita grant that was administered by the Board of Governors' Committee on Student Affairs. In turn, the Student Council disbursed money to a variety of clubs and societies. The arrangement was paternalistic, but on the whole the student councils of those early years were tractable and did not object. That changed in 1965, when, Ross wrote in his memoirs, a new Student Council president and his council wanted greater autonomy and got it.[60]

In 1961 the Senate banned fraternities and sororities, widespread at Canada's older universities, chiefly because they were seen as socially exclusive.[61] The Faculty Council, the Student Affairs Committee, and the Board of Governors concurred in the Senate resolution. No opinion seems to have been solicited from the Student Council, but Rust-D'Eye thought that student opinion generally favoured the board's action.[62]

Few of York's early students had time-consuming part-time jobs, so they had the opportunity to found and participate in a variety of clubs, among them the

LEFT Stephanie Hopkins (front left), Bob Witterick, John Court, and Heather McClary in front of York Hall. Court came up with the York motto: "Tentanda via."

RIGHT Seen at the opening of the show "A Decade of Art" in 1962 are Murray Ross, Alan Jarvis, curator of the National Gallery of Canada, and Lionel Rubinoff.

Art Club, Debating Society, Drama Club, Film Society, Cercle Français, Philosophy Club, Poetry Club, United Nations Society, and Inter-Varsity Christian Fellowship, as well as clubs affiliated with the Liberal, Progressive Conservative, and New Democratic parties. In September 1962 *Pro Tem* appeared for the first time, edited by Harold Levy and John Corvese. It joined a literary publication, MC^2, that was first published in 1961. The first student handbook, *Aardvark*, also appeared in the fall of 1962, edited by Corvese, Rust-D'Eye, and P.J. Spencer.[63]

The arts attracted lots of interest in the young university. The Art Club was active from the very outset, with the well-known portrait painter and sculptor Cleeve Horne the first of several artists to work with interested students. Lionel Rubinoff and soon also William (Bill) Kilbourn, a historian who joined York as chairman of the Division of Humanities in 1962, played a key role in bringing exhibitions, of twentieth-century Canadian but also European and U.S. art, to the campus. One such exhibition, "A Decade of Art," was opened by Alan Jarvis, curator of the National Gallery of Canada, in March 1962. Rubinoff was particularly pleased with an exhibition of works by Albert Franck in 1963, the first exhibition that the cityscape painter had in Canada.[64] Another important show took place in February and March 1964. Called "Eight Artists," it exhibited works by Denis Burton, Yves Gaucher, Gerald Gladstone, Robert Hedrick, John Meredith, Guido Molinari, Kazuo Nakamura, and Jack Reppen.

An Art Committee of the Board of Governors, chaired by the only female board member at the time, Signy (Mrs John David) Eaton, supervised these activities. Rubinoff remembered that one half of one per cent of the construction budget was set aside for the purchase of works of art.[65] Most of the works bought were by Canadian artists, among them Gladstone, Jean-Paul Riopelle, and Harold Town. Alas, in time some of the works fell victim to thieves, such as a small work by Town that graced a wall in the Senior Common Room for years before vanishing.

Music flourished in the early days, thanks largely to the efforts of William McCauley, composer, arranger, conductor, performer, and teacher. Endowed with ample energy and great enthusiasm, he came to York on a part-time basis in 1961 to develop a program in music. In short order he organized a choir, a band, and a string quartet. In February 1963 the York Choir, under his direction, won first prize at the Kiwanis Music Festival. It did so again in 1964 and 1965. In 1963 the choir cut an album with the title *From Bach to Rock*, released by Capitol Records.[66]

Founded in 1961, the Drama Club was at first the particular interest of Sandra Bracken, a demonstrator in zoology. As she planned to put on three one-act plays, she found participants among the staff as well as the students. Vivienne James, who joined York as a secretary in 1961 – when she retired thirty-two years later she was administrative officer to the vice-president (academic affairs) – signed up. It seemed the right thing to do. "The university was like a family with a wedding about to take place," she remembered, smiling: "It was organized chaos!"[67] After someone else backed out, James undertook to make the costumes for the plays: "Everybody was participating in things they never thought they would." Performed at Forest Hill Collegiate because York lacked a theatre, the plays were

well received. In 1962 Jack Winter joined the English Department and took over the Drama Club. He arranged for special instruction of its student members in the Workshop Theatre, run by his friend and associate George Luscombe. "This has been stimulating and valuable for the twenty or thirty students involved," George Tatham reported.[68]

The university's cultural life also benefited from the opening of a bookstore, as the SCM Book Room, whose main store was on St Thomas Street just south of Bloor, opened a branch on the campus in 1961. The "Tea and Talk" series brought visiting speakers to the campus, but in 1961–62 student attendance fell, and after two years the series was dropped for lack of interest. A York University Invitation Lecture series began in late 1961. Under the title "The University and the New World," it brought the sociologist David Riesman and the Harvard English scholar Howard Mumford Jones to York. The following year, York received a grant of $4,500 from the Frank Gerstein Charitable Foundation – Bertrand Gerstein, president of Peoples Jewellers, had been a member of the Board of Governors since 1961 – and the Invitation Lecture series became known as the Frank Gerstein Lectures. "They created considerable intellectual excitement," Lionel Rubinoff remembered.[69] With the title "Imagination and the University," the 1963 series featured the historian Henry Steele Commager, the psychologist

Gordon Allport, and the biologist Jacob Bronowski. In 1964 the topic was "Religion and the University," with Rabbi Maurice Eisendrath of Toronto's Holy Blossom Temple and the American historian of religion Jaroslav Jan Pelikan among the participants. The speakers in the 1965 series on "The Fine Arts and the University" included the prominent historian of architecture Vincent J. Scully. No record exists of how many students came to these lectures, which were open to the general public.

Another cultural event began in the fall of 1963, as the Faculty of Arts and Science introduced a public, ticketed lecture series by new faculty members. Alexander Wittenberg of the Mathematics Department kicked the series off with "General Education as a Challenge to Creative Scholarship." From January through April 1964, the lecturers were John Warkentin (Geography), Fred Knelman (Natural Science), John Yolton (Philosophy), and Eli Mandel (English).

Lionel Thomas's 1962 sculpture *The Whole Man*, its angular shapes adorning the outside wall of York Hall's two large lecture theatres, implied that people's bodies as well as their brains should be nurtured. (Today he would almost certainly have called it "The Whole Person.") That message was taken to heart. Heather McClary said that participating in sports was easy: "There were so few of us at the beginning that anyone could make the team." She played touch football, "but often we tackled: it was a fairly rough game, more like rugby."[70] She also played field hockey. By 1961, York had fencing, skiing, and table-tennis clubs, as well as a men's hockey team, but with the exception of an archery range and an outdoor volleyball court, the university lacked athletic facilities. Students used rented accommodation: the gymnasium of Lawrence Park Community United Church for badminton and basketball, and the hockey rink in Leaside Memorial Gardens.[71] Nevertheless, York joined the Ontario Intercollegiate Athletic Asso-

LEFT   International scholarship winners Sani Dauda, Annie Woo, and Michael Findlay on the archery range, 1962.

RIGHT   1964 Olympic Games bronze medal winner Debbi Wilkes, seen here with pairs partner Guy Revell, played for the women's hockey team while studying at York.

ciation (OIAA) in 1962. At that time Howard Langille was the first director of athletics and recreation. (Bryce Taylor joined him as assistant director of athletics in 1964.) The fall of 1962 saw the opening of three tennis courts in the valley, and the following spring the ground was broken for an athletic building. The political scientist Douglas Verney, who arrived in 1961, stressed the importance of the tennis courts: "We got rid of our aggressions by playing tennis with each other."[72] A sports field and softball diamond were laid out between the site of this building and the river, allowing intramural and inter-university competition in soccer, rugby, women's touch football, and field hockey. Vivienne James said that, having played field hockey as a girl in her native Jamaica, she was the only one "who knew the rules," and so she became the first coach.[73]

Although the golf team were the OIAA champions in 1963–64, and Chuck Magwood was victorious in OIAA ski races that winter, athletics remained something of a stepchild until 1964. The opening of the hockey rink in January and, a couple of months later, of the John S. Proctor Field House changed all that. Mal Ransom, who entered York in 1964, recalled that Debbi Wilkes, a student at York from 1965 to 1967, played for the women's hockey team, which he coached, and participated in a show on ice. With her skating partner Guy Revell, Wilkes had won the Canadian pairs championship in 1963 and 1964 and a bronze medal at the 1964 Olympic Games. "She could skate faster backwards than most guys forwards," Ransom marvelled.[74]

The field house got even more use than the hockey rink. Proctor, a board member since late 1959, had been an excellent tennis player in his youth and continued to be keenly interested in physical exercise and well-being. It was appropriate that the new building should carry his name. (In 1981, when he was chair of the Board of Governors and I was standing in for the chair of Senate at a Glendon convocation, we had an opportunity to talk. We quickly found that we had both been members of the YMCA in Victoria, British Columbia, and had made good use of its swimming pool.) The Proctor Field House included a swimming pool,

LEFT The men's hockey team, 1962–63. They are, from left to right, front row: Roger McNealy, Bob Mervold, John Copus, Brian McGee, Tom Wright; back row: John Moore (coach), Douglas Rutherford (captain), Kenneth Campbell, Harvey Sheppard, Douglas Markle (assistant captain), Arthur Boynton (assistant captain), Michael McMullan, Thomas Boehm, Robert Dignan.

RIGHT The John S. Proctor Field House, Glendon campus, opened in 1964.

four North American squash courts – four international courts were added later – a gymnasium, and a weight room. In September 1964 the gymnasium was the site of the meeting at which delegates to the annual conference of the National Federation of Canadian University Students changed the organization's name to the Canadian Union of Students. Part of an effort to retain the allegiance of student organizations in French-speaking Quebec, it failed in that purpose, for they seceded and went their own way.[75]

Because enrolment was rising, and because of the new facilities, sports were a flourishing concern by the time the 1964–65 academic year began. The new field house was the venue for a high school basketball tournament and a three-day Ontario Collegiate Squash Tournament, the women's curling team won the Women's Intercollegiate Curling Championship, the men's hockey team went to Buffalo and defeated the team from the State University of New York in that city, and Wendy Boyd won two races at the OIAA ski championships.[76]

No event looms bigger in the life of university students than the convocation at which they get their first degrees. York's first convocation took place on the morning of Sunday, 29 May, 1963, in Convocation Hall, University of Toronto, where 849 students graduated in the course of the day.[77] Of the 76 students who had registered in York three years earlier, 43 received their BA degree. Almost all of them were there, McClary remembered, but "some of us didn't feel so good" because they had been at "a big party the night before" at which "many of us got fairly drunk." They must have felt better by that afternoon, when the graduates got a second diploma, issued by York, at a ceremony that took place on the Glendon campus. Held in bright sunlight on the lawn, in view of *The Whole Man*, the ceremony was followed by a reception and garden party for the graduates and their parents. "It was the most perfect day!"[78]

Like the students who were on the Glendon campus, faculty and staff members who worked there before moving to Keele tended to be nostalgic about it. Typical were the responses of Clara Thomas – "Glendon was simply lovely"[79] – and Alex Murray, who joined the Department of History in 1962. He said he "loved the Glendon campus" and was "unhappy" to have to leave it.[80] Harold Schiff, who joined York in 1964 and two years later became the first dean of science, remembered with pleasure playing doubles on the tennis courts in the valley, with Murray Ross, Bill Small, and Bob Lundell, also a chemist and his successor as dean, "in the late afternoon whenever the weather permitted," or having a drink in the Senior Common Room with the man who became dean of arts and science in 1964, the "hard-working and hard-living" historian Jack Saywell.[81] Lucille Joseph, who remembered her father, David Fowle, taking science students into the valley to examine its flora and fauna, considered the campus to be her playground. She recalled picnics on the lawns and, in the summers, "family days ... with all of the children of faculty and staff ... Decades later it became a beautiful setting for my wedding."[82]

Access to the campus was initially a source of complaint for those, mostly students, who depended on the public transportation provided by the Toronto Transit Commission (TTC). They had to get off the subway at Davisville station, take the bus to Sunnybrook Hospital, and walk the rest of the way, as George Rust-D'Eye did the first time he went to see the university he would enter in 1961.[83] A bus ran east from Yonge Street along Lawrence Avenue to Mildenhall Road, but that service was infrequent. Fortunately, service soon improved, North York opting to replace the two-lane bridge across the Don River with something wider. Construction of the new Bayview viaduct, the overpass across Bayview, and the on- and off-ramps began in 1961 and was completed within a year. The project forced the relocation of York's main entrance. It had been at the

The Bruce Bryden Rose Garden and Leslie Frost Library, Glendon campus.

Premier John P. Robarts with "The Whole Woman" at a ceremony officially opening the buildings on the Glendon campus, September 1963. Former premier Leslie Frost (left) and University of Toronto President Claude Bissell are enjoying the prank.

southern end of the property but had to be shifted to face Lawrence. The project also brought the TTC to York, since the bus from Davisville to Sunnybrook Hospital now proceeded farther north along Bayview.

During the next few years, campus construction continued under the general supervision of a Campus Planning Department headed by Arthur Johnson. In 1963 and 1964 York Hall gained three additional wings, two consisting of classrooms and the third of offices, as well as a second dining hall (now the Glendon Theatre) and a private dining room with kitchen (in the 1970s it became the Glendon Gallery; today it is a classroom). The new library, after Glendon Hall the most attractive building on campus, opened in September 1963, and the library staff, now led by Director of Libraries Thomas O'Connell, happily vacated their crowded quarters in Glendon Hall. A month later, the new library got its name. Premier John P. Robarts – he would be York's chancellor from 1977 to 1982 – formally opened and dedicated the buildings that had gone up since 1961, naming the library after his predecessor, Leslie Frost, who was present. Robarts praised Frost for his "constant and strong support to the University" and his abiding personal interest in history and in libraries.[84] Students attending the ceremony added a note of levity that was at the same time a comment on the sexism implied by *The Whole Man*. They presented Robarts with "The Whole Woman," a large cardboard figure drawn by cartoonist Barry Base, whose work appeared in *Pro Tem* and in the yearbook, *Janus*.[85]

The opening of the E.R. Wood Residence in the fall of 1963, with Donald Rickerd as the first master of residence, made York University more appealing to students outside Toronto. Men occupied three of its five houses, and women the other two; total capacity was around 180 students. Completed in 1962, the Central Services Building had begun in the midst of controversy. To make room for it, the Woods' coach house had been razed. Because it had served students as office and social space, and because it was torn down on short notice and without consultation, angry students, Douglas Rutherford remembered, burned the director of physical plant, John Armour, in effigy.[86]

Next to be completed was the Proctor Field House. More than two years later, on 30 September 1966, Marion Pearson officially opened the last building constructed on the Glendon site, the Marion Hilliard Residence for women, at the same time that her husband, Prime Minister Lester B. (Mike) Pearson, officially opened Glendon College. By that time, the focus of the university had definitively shifted to the campus on Keele Street, near the northern boundary of Metropolitan Toronto.

In the fall of 2002, Bill Small said over lunch in the Glendon College Senior Common Room how much he regretted that York had been unable to expand on the Glendon site. If the university had been started a few years earlier, he speculated, it might have been able to acquire not only the Wood estate but also the Bruce, McLean, and Vaughan estates to the south. This would have given York the acreage needed to expand along Bayview Avenue, and might have led to the establishment of a faculty of medicine that could have used Sunnybrook Hospital as a teaching facility. Unfortunately, the property that once belonged to Herbert Bruce, the lieutenant governor of Ontario from 1932 to 1937, had been subdivided in the 1950s, creating a barrier to southward expansion. (In time the McLean and Vaughan estates became part of the Sunnybrook Hospital complex, which was acquired by the University of Toronto in 1967.[87]) An attempt in the spring of 1960 to secure land west of Bayview Avenue having failed, "we had no choice but to find some other location."[88]

After the board rejected the Langstaff Jail Farm in Richmond Hill because of the "lack of public services,"[89] Ross and Small zeroed in on a site in the area bounded by Keele Street, Steeles Avenue, Jane Street, and Finch Avenue. It was part of the Central Mortgage and Housing Corporation (CMHC) land bank, earmarked for public housing. This offered the prospect of getting a large parcel of land free of charge, provided support could be secured from all three levels of government. A key figure in the negotiations that enabled York to acquire land in the area was board member David Mansur, who had served as president of the CMHC.[90] The project also received vigorous support from the minister of education (until November 1961, when he became premier), John P. Robarts, from the chairman of Metropolitan Toronto, Frederick Gardiner, and from James D. Service of the North York Committee for York University. Gardiner was particularly effective, arguing that there was enough space for low-cost housing available within the metropolitan area even should the acreage be granted to York.[91] The troubles that beset the federal government led by John Diefenbaker in 1962 delayed negotiations, but Mansur was able to inform fellow board members in October that the deed of transfer of the property at Keele and Steeles had been completed.[92]

Soon after York University opened its doors, Ross had made an official announcement that, in the long run, the institution would consist of a liberal arts college, a large multi-faculty university, and an evening division.[93] Before the spring of 1962, however, neither Ross nor anyone else anticipated that York's growth would be particularly rapid. Ross's book *The New University* (1961), a collection of speeches that was in large part a blueprint for York, stressed the benefits of teaching and learning in the intimate setting provided by a liberal arts college.[94] Ross also expressed reservations about large universities. Growth was inevitable, he wrote, but it must be slow and guided growth if "proper standards and integrity" were to be maintained.[95]

These were not Ross's views alone. His preface acknowledges a particular debt of gratitude to John Seeley "for reading, and commenting on, many of these speeches in their original form."[96] Interviewed in 2003, Seeley recalled that Ross, in inducing him to join the faculty of York, had assured him that it would be limited to 4,000 students at most, to be distributed over two campuses, and that the tutorial system would be continued even as the university grew. In the course of 1962, however, he learned that, by 1970, the new campus at Keele and Steeles would be the home of an institution with a student body almost twice as large as had been planned to that point, with further increases anticipated in the future. He took this as evidence, Seeley said, not only that Ross was breaking his word but also that the university was entering far too hastily upon a new path. Furthermore, there was suddenly uncertainty concerning the future of the Glendon campus and of the tutorial system.[97]

For more than two years, the number 4,000 had something like official status at York. Writing to Premier Robarts in February 1962, Robert Winters noted that the university expected to have a total of 4,000 students in 1970.[98] Nine months later, though, Winters wrote to Robarts that, by 1970, York expected to register 7,000 students on the northern campus alone,[99] while the Glendon campus would register up to a thousand. By this time, too, the board had approved an upper limit of 25,000 students.[100]

Why had the projected number suddenly gone up? The answer lies in a report commissioned by the Committee of Presidents of the Universities of Ontario (CPUO) and submitted to it in May 1962. Chaired by John Deutsch, vice-principal (academic) of Queen's University, the committee warned the presidents that enrolment would grow more rapidly than they had thought or were ready for. Not only would the baby boomers begin to show up in 1964, with their number growing rapidly after that – this was known, of course – but the participation rate, the proportion of university-age young people entering the institutions, was already increasing at a greater pace than the universities had been anticipating, especially because young women were registering in unprecedented numbers, and would continue to increase. About York the report stated: "The committee was of the opinion that the numbers put forward as the highest goal by York University to the Advisory Committee on University Affairs (1,316 students in 1965, 4,014 in 1970) are unrealistically low, in view of the tremendous pressures in the Metropolitan Toronto area."[101]

This was a broad hint. If more were needed, Vincent Bladen, dean of arts and science at the University of Toronto, addressing the York Senate in November 1962, emphasized that "the greatest immediate problem is whether or not York University agrees to expand at the rate suggested in the Report of the Presidents

Students Linda Robinson (left) and Cathy Frost with a model of the new campus, 1964.

of the Universities of Ontario or whether some other institution must be established to do so."[102] The Board of Governors had already chosen the first option,[103] and, after hearing Bladen, the Senate followed suit, approving an expansion to 7,000 students by 1970, 6,200 of whom would be on the new campus.[104] Although founded as a private institution, York depended heavily on public funds. No one could ignore the possibility that those funds might shrink or even disappear if the province were to found another university in the Toronto area.

Under the circumstances, was it realistic to wish to keep the university small? Douglas Verney commented that "it was not a question of being realistic. Early faculty like John Seeley were lured by the promise of smallness."[105] Some of them clung to that promise even when the circumstances changed. York, they thought, should continue to grow at the slower pace originally envisaged. Seeley became their leader in a protest that challenged not only York's revised plan but also, and more significantly, Ross's management of the university.

The issue of expansion arose at a time when several members of the teaching staff were already unhappy on other grounds. Not least among them was the way the president operated. Ross was generally popular with students – "we really liked him," Heather McClary said[106] – but among the faculty he had gained a reputation for telling people what he thought they wanted to hear, for sometimes being cavalier about facts, for making promises, chiefly of administrative positions, that he failed to keep, and for seeking to get his own way by whatever means seemed necessary. John Seeley's personal papers provide evidence of a

The sociologist John Seeley, a founding member of the York faculty, broke with Murray Ross in 1963 over the development of the university and resigned.

growing rift between him and Ross about matters academic and administrative, with Seeley charging that the president was not living up to earlier agreements.[107] Norman Endler praised Ross for having a vision of York's future, but added that he was all too ready to make unrealistic promises in order to attract good faculty to York and keep them there. "I think the only faculty members who weren't promised a deanship that first year were Lionel [Rubinoff], John [McFarland] and me, because we were too young, and Alice [Turner], because she was a woman."[108] Denis Smith objected to what he saw as Ross's habit of "making decisions without consulting the faculty." The early 1960s were a time, he noted, when faculty members at Canadian universities were beginning to seek a greater share in university government.[109] Barbara Moon, a journalist writing for *Maclean's*, found in the spring of 1962 that some professors mistrusted Ross and no longer took him at his word.[110]

Recalling the events and feelings of that distant time, Verney made four important points. "When you start a new university, people come with their own dreams, and they don't realize that their dreams are peculiar to themselves," he said. Secondly, "each year a new group of professors arrived at York, and the president had to lure them with a story that might change over the years." Seeley was recruited with the promise of a small campus; Verney was lured with the prospect of a large one. Thirdly, "Ross gave the impression to each new cohort that they were to be the stars," the implication being that the people who were already there were "less important." Finally, "Ross tended to be devious, but it wasn't always clear whether he was being devious or simply forgetful."[111] By 1963, some of his faculty were all too ready to assume the worst.

The "revolt" against Ross's leadership simmered for more than a year. In the formation of the York University Faculty Association (YUFA) in the fall of 1962 it is possible to discern the opinion of some faculty members that they needed an alternate way of making their views heard. In February 1963 a few professors brought out a "faculty edition" of the student newspaper, *Pro Tem*, that was critical of Ross's leadership. Some months later, several faculty members resigned, mainly in protest against the way Ross was running things.

When this story broke in the Toronto newspapers, Seeley, who was about to take a year's leave at Brandeis University, became the spokesman for the dissidents. Charging that Ross was antagonizing members of the faculty, and that there was acrimonious disagreement on the campus, Seeley referred to a number of staff complaints involving appointments, scholarships, unfulfilled promises to faculty members, and public attacks on some of them. One man who was leaving, Richard J. Coughlin, a founding member of the Sociology Department, said that "York is an administrative muddle, and that additional trouble can be expected."[112]

Since Ross and Winters were absent overseas, two administrators answered the charges. Rollo Earl, the dean of arts and science, controverted every point that Seeley and Coughlin had made, while Ross's assistant, D. McCormack (Del) Smyth, "claimed that a few members of the staff disagreed with the policy of expansion," and said that this, rather than disagreement with Ross's administration, had prompted their resignations.[113] Two days later, Smyth stated that most of those who had resigned had done so for reasons other than unhappiness with Ross, although he was vague on what those reasons were.[114] In an interview Smyth said that he greatly admired Ross but that he had never understood his decision to appoint Seeley, whom he regarded as "unrealistic" and "unreasonable."[115]

Four letters of protest against Ross's administration – three were letters of resignation – reached the board, from Coughlin, Walter Simon of the Division of Social Science, Neil Morrison, the dean of Atkinson College, and Seeley, who was going on leave but resigned soon afterwards.[116] Another man who resigned, Denis Smith, stated to the press that "the impropriety and muddle of the university" was responsible for his move to Trent University, adding that "if [the projected size of the university] had been the only major disagreement, he would have remained at York."[117] Two others, chairman of English Hugh Maclean and the psychologist Vello Sermat, offered no public explanation for their departure, although Maclean expressed harsh criticism of Ross and of York in a private letter to Endler.[118]

One of those who resigned, Douglas Lochhead, later spoke of Ross in warm terms – "I hit if off well with him; he was very kind to my wife, who like Murray was from Cape Breton, and to me" – and said that Ross's administrative style had nothing to do with his decision to resign. He had left Dalhousie University to go to York because he wanted to work in the intimate setting of a liberal arts college, which Ross had given him to understand York would be. When he learned in 1962 that a much larger library would soon be built and that he was expected to supervise its growth, he felt "a bit betrayed" and started looking for another job. He found his niche at Massey College in the University of Toronto, taking his "highly competent secretary" at York, Patricia Kennedy, with him.[119]

Some students were unhappy. The president of the Student Council, Gary Caldwell, said that he had resigned his position because York's administration had "made a favorable academic environment impossible." Two other members of the graduating class, Anne Dalziel and Clay Ruby, wrote a letter to the *Globe and Mail* stating that Seeley had accurately described "a disgraceful situation," that he was the only "prominent faculty member" whom students felt they could trust, and that good students were leaving the university because they were unhappy with it. A former secretary of the Student Council, Shari Braithwaite, "asserted that the real issue was whether York was going to be a first-rate liberal arts university." She charged that "the better people were leaving because the administration were more interested in quantity and show than in quality."[120]

More than forty years later, Ruby still spoke of the incident with passion. He remembered helping to paint a broad yellow stripe down the back of the small statue in front of Glendon Hall one night, implying that Ross was a coward for not facing students who were unhappy about the proposed change in the enrolment target. "Murray was very upset about the protest and tried to find who was behind it." Ruby said he thought all students felt "a commitment to what they thought was the original vision, but many decided not to make an issue of it."[121] Fellow students Heather McClary, George Rust-D'Eye, Douglas Rutherford, and Penny Williams confirmed this. All four knew that trouble was brewing but did not think it was their quarrel. "We were graduating," Rutherford said of his year, adding that he knew the struggle was a big issue for some of the faculty and a handful of students, but that he saw it as an unavoidable part of "York's growing pains. Dr Ross couldn't please everybody."[122] When the news came that most of York would soon move to the new campus, McClary recalled thinking: "Who would want to go up there?" But it did not affect her and her friends: "We just felt lucky to have been at Glendon."[123]

Robert Winters returned to Canada on 30 June and took charge, calling a board meeting for 3 July. Ross, who returned from Europe later that summer, stated in his memoirs that Rollo Earl's statement, supplemented by a confidential report from board member Ray F. Farquharson supporting him and criticizing Seeley, seem together to have settled the issue in his favour.[124] He added that Winters had engaged a private investigator to get an independent assessment of the charges. But the report this investigator made, favourable to Ross, was not available to the board when it rejected the complaints by Seeley and his associates, "deplored the actions of the dissatisfied professors in making public controversy out of their grievances to the detriment of York," expressed "full confidence in Dr. Murray Ross ... and in his ability to handle whatever genuine grievances there might be," and declared the matter closed.[125]

A different outcome had always been unlikely, unless Ross's offences had been truly egregious and a much larger proportion of the faculty had resigned in pro-

Glendon campus's Marion Hilliard Residence.

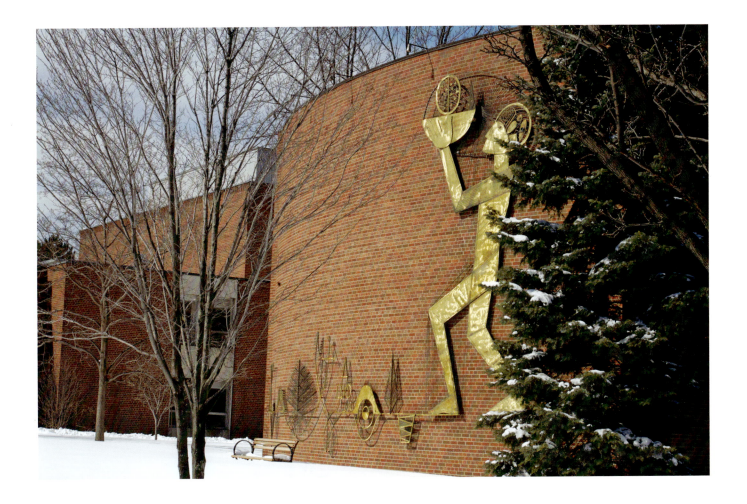

The Whole Man on Glendon campus.

test against his leadership. The Board of Governors had no compelling reason to second-guess its president. For many of its members, he was their only direct link to the university. Then, too, institutional solidarity and personal loyalty were matters of importance to the board. The last surviving member of the board at that time, Jack Leitch, said that he thought it was "presumptuous" of Seeley to try to "take over" the university: "If you don't like what the university is going to be, you go to another university."[126]

The incident highlighted a tension that always exists in a modern university. On the one hand, it is a corporate enterprise in the services sector of the economy, with a governing board, a chief executive officer, a hierarchy of administrators, and several different categories of employees. On the other hand, it is a collaborative enterprise of scholars, scientists, and teachers, often more committed to their students, their research, and their disciplines than to the institution in which they work, of which they ask chiefly that it be organized to facilitate what they see as their calling. Over the years, York University has usually managed to maintain a balance between the two. But the balance has sometimes been more or less uneasy, and occasionally, as in 1963, York came close to losing it.

Important for the future of the institution was that most faculty members stuck with Ross or, if not with Ross personally, with the university. Douglas Verney, for example, described himself as "non-partisan," which was in effect a

The Escott Reid Walk, Glendon campus.

vote for the status quo.[127] Clara Thomas remembered that other senior people, such as Edgar McInnis, Irvine Pounder, and H.S. Harris, the famously absent-minded chairman of the Philosophy Department, "studiously avoided taking sides." Most of the more junior faculty, she added, "feeling confident that York was here to stay, and that was what mattered," kept their heads well down. She also said that Mortimer Appley, the highly respected head of Psychology, repeatedly expressed faith in York's future. This had a steadying influence, she recalled: "Mort absolutely saved Murray."[128] Possibly as a result of Appley's intervention, a YUFA meeting on 5 July passed an anodyne motion that took no sides and looked with confidence to the future.[129]

Some of those who stayed had misgivings, and a few of them might have resigned had they had somewhere to go. John Brückmann, a medievalist who had joined York in 1961, wrote to Endler: "At the moment things look very discouraging ... Oh, to hell with it all!"[130] In a conversation during the 1970s, Brückmann said that, had he been able to find another job, he would have left. He added that he was glad he had not done so, having found a niche at Glendon College that suited him very nicely. Others were glad he stayed. "John was such a lovely man," Johanna Stuckey, who joined the Division of Humanities in 1964, recalled.[131] Walter Beringer, a classicist who arrived in 1965 and was perhaps closer to Brückmann than anyone else at York, called him "a fine colleague and a true friend."[132] "We all loved him," Penny Williams said, not just for his "inspired teaching" but for "his urbane and cheerful subversiveness."[133] John McNee, a student from 1969 to 1973, remembered him as a "great teacher" who "really identified with the period he taught."[134] Sad to say, he died prematurely in 1982.

The incident faded quickly. In the summer of 1963, eighteen new faculty members joined York. One of them was William Whitla, recruited by Bill Kilbourn for the Division of Humanities.[135] With a background in classics, English, and theology – he was ordained in the Anglican Church – Whitla had an interest in the interdisciplinary work that was central to the division and relished "the opportunity to work with people in other fields."[136] People still talked about the recent revolt, he said, but it meant little to him. Two new associate deans of arts and science, Edward (Pat) Pattullo and John T. (Jack) Saywell, also joined the university in 1963. Saywell, who would become the central figure in the expansion of the Faculty of Arts in the 1960s, was in his early thirties, a rising star of the University of Toronto's History Department. His friend Bill Kilbourn urged him "to lend my energies to the young institution," he recalled. He responded because the prospect of building a new university suited his temperament. Claude Bissell told him that an administrative career was open to him at Toronto as well, but Saywell did not relish such a career in an institution that was firmly set in its ways.[137]

In September a fresh group of students arrived to join those who were continuing their studies. The incident passed into memory, but accounts of it, often

Looking towards the dining hall on Glendon campus.

distorted by emotion and the passage of time, have become part of York University folklore and mythology.

Another issue that disturbed the waters in the early years was the curriculum. From the outset, Murray Ross had stressed the need for a curriculum that differed from the widely accepted model in Canada, in which specialization at the undergraduate level, epitomized by the University of Toronto honours BA, enjoyed high status. "The decision to emphasize general and liberal education at York arose out of what appeared to be a significant gap in higher education in Canada," he wrote in 1961. "No one will question this century's need for specialists in a wide variety of fields. But when specialization requires or implies that knowledge be limited to one narrow area of life, and that an individual's view of mankind be lacking in perspective and that he be insensitive to the problems of the modern world, then certainly there is need to question the adequacy of an educational system that produces such specialists."[138]

Seeking to avoid the dangers of specialization in the undergraduate curriculum that he had identified, in May 1960 Ross presented the Board of Governors with a scheme that he hoped York would adopt. After a required two-year program in which students would take courses in humanities, social science, and natural science, they would proceed to a further two years in liberal arts and science, in a specialized program focusing on a chosen discipline, or in a professional program. Here Ross mentioned communications, fine arts, business, education, journalism, and medicine.[139]

September 1960 saw the appointment of a small committee charged with developing the curriculum. George Tatham (chair), John Seeley, Hugh Maclean, and Lionel Rubinoff (secretary) found their task challenging and time-consuming. "In various degrees, all four members were enthusiastic about the idea of liberal education," Tatham later wrote. This prompted "a sense of unity" and implied a high level of agreement, "but it was illusory."[140] Each man had more or less strongly held views about what general education should entail and what it could exclude. In the fall of 1960 a spirited discussion took place as to what requirements York should make of students, and whether these requirements should be athletic, aesthetic, and social, as well as intellectual.

Seeley was particularly concerned that York should not merely tinker with the structure of higher learning and the organization of its branches but rather strike out in a new direction. "What is ... overdue," he wrote to the other committee members in December 1960, "is, I feel certain, the kind of re-examination of virtually everything we believe about what we are doing that will, if acted upon, make everything that follows radically different from what has gone before." What, he asked, "is the place, the power, the function of the University in *this* world?"[141] What could York do to encourage the desirable development of its students?

In response, Maclean expressed the fear that "in our determination to be 'new' we may choose the merely novel and ignore or chuck overboard the traditional without sufficient thought for the continuing value of much that is traditional."[142] The ensuing debate led committee members to the view that "it could best settle such questions only after an attempt has been made to establish a curriculum." The first stab at this had first-year students taking six courses, one each in humanities, social science, English and rhetoric, natural science, a language (to be continued in second year if the student had not previously studied it), and mathematics and logic. In their second year, students would take five courses, one each in humanities, social science, and natural science, a language course (if a new language had been started in first year), and one or two specialized courses in a discipline.

"The third year is primarily intended to relate the student to the division in which he is specializing," the report continued, "while the fourth year attempts to relate him to his specialized subject." To this end, third-year students would take "three courses in the subject of specialization" and "two courses in a relevant subject chosen from outside the department." Fourth-year students would take "a seminar course [and] two reading courses in the subject of specialization" and would complete a thesis in that subject. They would also take "the synthesizing course," which would pull everything together. Like much else, this course remained "to be discussed."[143]

The discussion, within the committee and within Faculty Council, went on and on. Council meetings in the spring of 1961 offered evidence of support for the committee's work but also of misgivings, especially the fear that the proposed curriculum was trying to do too much. Nevertheless, Ross indicated that "he would ... be discussing financing of the curriculum with the board of governors and that he wished to open discussions with a foundation." He was of the view that the Senate should adopt a curriculum in the autumn.[144]

During the summer the committee was enlarged to include Lester Pronger, representing Languages, David Fowle, representing the Natural Science subcommittee, and Douglas Verney, representing the Social Science subcommittee. Later in 1961, Alice Turner joined the committee to represent Mathematics. Committee members visited a number of colleges and universities in the United States, among them Harvard, Yale, Brandeis, and Columbia universities, the Massachusetts Institute of Technology, and Reed College, and, in England, Keele and Leeds universities. Rubinoff recalled that he and the others learned a lot about liberal-arts undergraduate programs but that the shape of the new curriculum remained elusive.[145] Towards the end of 1961, the committee decided to recommend that adoption of the new curriculum be postponed to the fall of 1963, even though this ran the risk of multiplying the problems involved in its introduction. Not least of these was that new faculty members might object to what had already been agreed on, especially since many of them would be expected to teach part of the interdisciplinary courses that were being proposed.[146]

Two confidential memoranda, drafted in March 1962, outlined continuing difficulties with the curriculum, particularly in drafting the courses in social science. With eight members (two political scientists, two psychologists, two sociologists, one economist, one geographer), the Social Science subcommittee was twice the size of the next largest, Humanities. The image of too many cooks spoiling the broth comes to mind. Some were unhappy that Ross had approached the Ford Foundation with a curriculum proposal, drafted by Seeley, that differed in some ways from the committee document, about which there was in any case much disagreement.[147] Small wonder that the chairmen of the three subcommittees, Fowle, Maclean, and Verney, reported on 9 March 1962: "The question of the new curriculum is becoming acute."[148]

In her *Maclean's* article of April 1962, Barbara Moon wrote that York's students were "making out all right," but that "a goodly number of the current staff were less than happy." Many of their anxieties centred around the curriculum, still "little more than the original pious outline." She quoted Rubinoff: "Some time before next year, we've got to establish whether we're going to have scholarship here, or just a Unique Rich Experience." The first economist appointed by York, Craufurd Goodwin, "so distrusts the shape the curriculum is taking that he has accepted a post elsewhere at the end of this session."[149]

At much the same time that Moon's article appeared, the York Senate committed the university to introducing its new curriculum in September 1963. At that time York would offer two four-year programs of study to incoming students, general honours and specialized honours, "each leading to the Honours Bachelor of Arts degree." The first two years would be devoted to "liberal and general education," with all students taking introductory English and mathematics, a "foreign language" – since most students would be taking French, this suggests that the committee did not yet fully grasp the bilingual nature of Canada – "and a series of comprehensive courses in the Natural Sciences, the Social Sciences and the Humanities." Students in general honours would take some subject courses, but much of their third year would be spent "studying an alien culture such as that of the Soviet Union, China or Islam." Their fourth year would focus on "selected contemporary problems such as that of world population, the growth of metropolitan centres, and international organization." Students in specialized honours would, in their third and fourth years, take mainly "specialized courses in their chosen field of study. This work will correspond to the Honours program at other Canadian universities." However, in their final year, "students in both programs will come together again in a course designed to integrate and assess their whole educational experience."[150]

A recasting of Ross's original suggestions for the curriculum, the proposal was nothing if not ambitious. Was it realistic? Speaking at a dinner that York held for high school principals in April 1962, Hugh Maclean contended that it was. However, his account of the past two years rang truer than his optimistic speculations about the curricular future. Among York's characteristics that he singled out were "the *esprit de corps* of the student body, and the remarkable way in which staff-student relations have developed."[151] The relative youth of much of the faculty and their willingness to engage with students and each other created an enriched educational environment that, to this day, students of that time talk about with affection and a certain awe. As examples of the "cross-disciplinary encounters" that York was fostering, Maclean cited a seminar in which a biologist, a sociologist, a political scientist, a psychologist, and a philosopher discussed evolution with each other and with a large audience. Instructors in French and English collaborated in seminars and play readings that illustrated eighteenth-century life and literature. A philosopher and a historian "conducted a joint seminar on what [John] Brückmann pleasantly called 'The Mystique of Monarchy.'"[152] Such seminars were exciting but time-consuming, Rubinoff remembered, and for that reason "difficult to sustain."[153]

York's curriculum *was* in place by the fall of 1963, but it turned out to be a lot more conventional than the one described eighteen months earlier. This development owed much to the first person to hold the position of dean of arts and science, Rollo Earl, remembered by Clara Thomas as "a straight arrow ... a man who, like Mort Appley, knew which end was up."[154] A biologist who was dean of arts and science at Queen's University in the 1950s but had recently retired, Earl arrived at York in 1962 and soon made his influence felt. That influence was towards curricular conservatism.

Under Earl's supervision as chairman of the committee on undergraduate studies, the York curriculum came to resemble other arts and science programs in Ontario more closely than before. By the end of 1962, the committee was recommending that York offer a three-year ordinary BA program, a four-year general honours BA program, and a four-year specialized honours program leading to either a BA or a BSc. The Senate approved this in January 1963, for introduc-

Dean of Arts and Science Rollo Earl came out of retirement to help develop York's curriculum.

tion in the fall. The required number of interdisciplinary courses (humanities, social science, and natural science) that students had to take had fallen to four, one of them to be taken in the second year. The other required courses included one in English and one in "a language other than English" – two courses if a student had not taken such a language in Grade 13. Finally, students had to take a course in calculus or, substituting for mathematics, a course in modes of reasoning, to be taught by members of the mathematics and philosophy departments. This course, John McFarland recalled, was the "brainchild" of the members of the Philosophy Department, McFarland himself, Rubinoff, and H.S. Harris, an expert on Hegel who came to York in 1962. It would, they thought, guarantee that the Philosophy Department would have an ample number of students.[155] In the upper years, students would be taking courses in their major department.[156]

If the York curriculum was more conventional than the original plan, the distinctive commitment to general education remained. The curriculum diverged sufficiently from earlier proposals, however, that some faculty members and students perceived it as a dilution of York's founding vision.[157] Thereby it contributed to the "faculty revolt" of 1963. Nevertheless, in September of that year, incoming students were the first to register in York's own courses rather than those of the University of Toronto. It was a huge step on the road to independence.

One assumption implicit in the discussions of the curriculum was that students in the Faculty of Arts and Science would pursue their studies on a full-time basis. From the outset, though, York undertook an innovative policy with respect to part-time students, who at the time were almost invariably adults already in the working world. At other universities they received their instruction through a department of university extension or something similar, staffed by faculty members or sometimes graduate students in the university proper. Ross's long-range vision for York included an evening college with its own program of study tailored to the needs of working people. He also proposed that part-time students should have their own faculty with their own building and full-time professors, and should have to meet the same academic standards as full-time students.[158] These were central parts of an appeal for financial support made in November 1960 to the Atkinson Charitable Foundation.

The appeal was timely. A report issued early in 1961 by the Toronto Board of Education stressed the need for improved access to higher education by adult students. Prepared by J. Roby Kidd, a member of York's 1959 provisional board, the report stated that "many *excellent* students of age 25 or over who want a university education cannot secure it on any basis that suits their present income or present family or job responsibilities," asserted that Canada was "falling behind other countries in the education and training of our able people," and urged that this matter receive early attention. One suggestion was that York offer some of its courses in the evening.[159]

Evidently the new university was proposing to meet a real need, and the Atkinson Charitable Foundation, named after the crusading publisher and social reformer who led the Toronto *Star* from 1899 to 1948, was willing to assist York in meeting it. In February 1961 the university received a grant of $782,000, the

exact amount asked for, towards the establishment of the Joseph E. Atkinson College.[160] Of this money, $700,000 was a capital grant and the other $82,000 a grant to help defray operating costs during the early years.

That summer, Douglas Verney became acting dean of the college, while Neil Morrison, who had considerable experience with adult education, was appointed assistant dean. He became dean in 1962, the year that Atkinson College admitted its first students. There were 287 of them, and they took one or more of three courses, taught in the evening, that had been designed with the needs of adult learners in mind. Harry Girling, added to the faculty in 1962, taught introductory English, Alice Turner taught introductory mathematics, and Bill Kilbourn taught a course in humanities. All three courses were compulsory in a curriculum that, initially at least, closely resembled the one that was being developed for the Faculty of Arts and Science, with the same commitment to general and liberal education.[161]

By September 1963, Morrison had resigned in protest against Murray Ross's leadership. Del Smyth succeeded him, becoming acting dean in 1963 and dean in 1964. He held the position for five years. Many years later, recalling his decision to accept the deanship, Smyth called it "a leap in the dark."[162] Atkinson was an untried entity, and "York was undergoing a good deal of stress at the time." However, the challenges were "interesting, even exhilarating."[163]

Atkinson College expanded rapidly. Early in 1964 the Board of Governors approved a recommendation that the college establish the Division of Continuing Education to provide non-degree courses. Also in 1964, Atkinson College offered summer courses, held in the late afternoon and early evening, for the first time. A year later, Atkinson appointed the first members of its own full-time faculty, Walter Carter (Philosophy), Michael Creal (Humanities), W.E. (Ted) Mann (Sociology), Donald Theall (English), and David Wood (Geography). Smyth wrote in 1965 that the college also wanted to "appoint a substantial number of highly competent and academically-trained members of the community on a part-time basis so that the skills and knowledge of such people may be added to the academic skills of the full-time staff."[164] The first two were Leslie Mezei in Mathematics and Computer Science and Ralph Blackmore in Economics.[165]

The Board of Governors, acting on the advice of the Atkinson College committee chaired by Jack Leitch, decided to locate the Atkinson College building on the new campus. Initially there was talk of acquiring the Fingold property, just north of the Glendon campus, for this purpose. But this idea yielded to the recognition that there were major long-term advantages to being near Keele and Steeles "since the population of Metropolitan Toronto is growing in a north-westerly direction."[166] For many years, Atkinson College continued to offer courses at the Glendon campus, but over time a growing proportion of students came from north and west of the Keele campus and preferred to take their courses there.

For understandable reasons, student government and extracurricular activities developed somewhat more slowly in Atkinson than in Arts and Science. Even when an autonomous student life did develop, many Atkinson students were unable to take part in it. The demands made on their time by full-time jobs and, in a good many cases, by families, made many students reluctant to participate in clubs and societies. In 1963–64, however, a student government did take form. That year, too, some students launched a newspaper called *COASSIP* (College of Atkinson Students Speak in Print), forerunner of the *Atkinsonian*, edited by Carl Garry,[167] for him the start of a long association with York.

The terms of affiliation with the University of Toronto obliged York not to begin a fund-raising campaign until Toronto's own campaign was finished in 1964.[168] Nevertheless, by 1965, the university had attracted well over a million dollars for scholarships, bursaries, prizes, buildings, departments, the "new curriculum project," and other purposes.[169] Many of the donations were for

relatively small amounts. Exceptions were the gift by the Atkinson Charitable Foundation, the largest made to York in its early years, and a grant from the Fund for the Advancement of Education, a subsidiary of the Ford Foundation. It provided $125,000 (US) in 1963 to help pay for the expenses involved in planning and designing York's curriculum. Although welcome, the money was all too quickly spent.

The decision in 1962 that York would expand more rapidly than had originally been planned prompted talk of additional faculties. In the fall, Claude Bissell suggested to Murray Ross that representatives of the two universities should meet to discuss what York might do in order to take some of the growing load off the University of Toronto. The meeting, which took place on 31 October 1962, led to further discussion. As one result, early in 1963 the York Senate established a committee of graduate studies, headed by the psychologist Mortimer Appley. The committee reported within months, and in September 1963 the Senate and Board of Governors approved the creation of the Faculty of Graduate Studies, with the recommendation that graduate instruction begin in 1967. Edgar McInnis became the first dean and kept the position for two years, Appley succeeding him in 1965.[170]

In fact, York's first graduate students arrived well before 1967. In the fall of 1964, eleven students registered, all of them in Psychology, where Wesley Coons, newly come from Dalhousie University, became director of the graduate program.[171] The psychologists were not alone for long. In January 1965 the council of the Faculty of Graduate Studies recommended the establishment of an interdisciplinary Centre for Research in Experimental and Space Science (CRESS), which would offer graduate degrees in chemistry and physics. In the first few years, these two fields had not been areas of strength. Although the first chemist, Robert Lundell, was appointed in 1961, the initial bias was towards the life sciences, with Peter Moens joining David Fowle in 1962 and James Tait arriving in 1964. The appointment of Harold Schiff in 1964 and Ralph Nicholls in 1965 signalled change. Schiff, who came from McGill University to be chairman of the Chemistry Department, became director of natural science in 1965 and dean of science the following year. (The Faculty of Science was not fully separated from the Faculty of Arts until 1968.[172]) Nicholls, who arrived at York from the University of Western Ontario, became chairman of Physics and director of CRESS.[173] Nicholls recalled that his move to York was facilitated because Jack Saywell, the dean of arts and science, was able to offer Nicholls's wife, Doris, a position in biology, where the graduate department registered *its* first students in 1965. What really attracted Nicholls, though, was that at York "the slate was clean" and that the interdisciplinary approach allowed people to do things in a different way.[174] Schiff and Nicholls were established researchers; both brought graduate students and research grants to York. Soon joined by others, such as John Goodings, Robert Haynes, and Huw Pritchard, described by Ralph Nicholls as "the best scientist we ever had at York,"[175] they gave the sciences a prominence at York that they had not initially had.[176]

The first meeting of the Faculty of Graduate Studies council took place in September 1965, with Appley in the chair. Five graduate programs were available to students: psychology (MA, PHD), chemistry (MSc, PHD), physics (MSc, PHD), biology (MSc), and CRESS (MSc, PHD). Thirty-seven students registered in the faculty that session.[177]

York reached two milestones in the early summer of 1965. The first was the passage of a new York University Act. The second was the severing of the tie with the University of Toronto.

In the spring of 1964 the Board of Governors struck a committee to consider revisions of the 1959 act. It was ambiguous in places, Murray Ross wrote in his memoirs, and the lines of authority stated in it were not fully clear. "Bob Winters was anxious to review and change it, for he thought the board required more authority and that this should be clearly stated in the act."[178] Winters believed the board should have the authority to appoint the chancellor and to select the recipients of honorary degrees. Some faculty members, on the other hand, in line with the attitudes expressed in *A Place of Liberty*,[179] a book of essays issued by the Canadian Association of University Teachers in 1964, thought that the Senate should retain these powers, should, in fact, gain power at the expense of the board.

The suggestions sent by the board committee to the Executive Committee of the Senate ran into heavy weather there. A joint Board of Governors-Senate committee was created to try to resolve the differences, and its deliberations continued through the 1964–65 academic year. In time a compromise document took shape that received unanimous support from the Board of Governors, the Senate, and YUFA. The changes made were not dramatic. They did increase somewhat the board's powers to make appointments, but they also provided for consultation concerning the appointment of the chancellor and the president and the awarding of honorary degrees. A joint Board of Governors-Senate committee was established to facilitate this process. The new act also removed the clause banning faculty members from the board and increased the maximum number of governors from twenty-four to thirty.[180]

The revised York University Act gained royal assent on 13 June 1965.[181] The new consultative procedures proved to be generally satisfactory. In his memoirs, Ross offered as an example the choice of a successor to Wilfred Curtis. When the joint committee met to discuss who should succeed him as chancellor, a Senate member proposed the name of Floyd S. Chalmers, newspaper executive and generous and innovative patron of the arts. "There was immediate and unanimous approval," Ross wrote. Chalmers was installed during the fall convocation, held in October 1968, at which Curtis received an honorary doctorate of laws. "Floyd served with great distinction," Ross wrote. "His period of service ... was marked by creative and intelligent leadership seldom found in this largely ceremonial office."[182]

Severing the tie with the University of Toronto took much less time than revising the act. The connection with the older university brought significant advantages to York, but as soon as the new institution introduced its own curriculum, the days of that connection were numbered. Moreover, the University of Toronto's attitude to York was changing. Ross said in his memoirs that Eric Phillips told some members of the York board in 1965 that their university was moving "too fast," that York's plans were "unrealistic" and "too ambitious," and that it would be a good thing to bring Ross under control, to "slow him down" and "have him talk less in public."[183] The historian Willard Piepenburg, who came to York from Toronto in 1964, following the path trod by his colleague Jack Saywell the year before, recalled that in the first few years the University of Toronto's attitude was "patronizing" but that by the mid-1960s it was becoming "slightly hostile," certainly in the Department of History.[184]

By 1965, there was no strong reason to continue the affiliation, so it was allowed to come to an end. On 24 June, York University hosted a dinner in recognition of what the University of Toronto had done for York. Winters and Ross presented ornamental keys to Claude Bissell and Henry Borden, Phillips's successor as the University of Toronto's board chairman, as well as an illustrated scroll. In their turn, Borden and Bissell presented Winters and Ross with a guest book bound in red morocco leather, decorated with the white rose of York, and the deed to the Glendon property. The invited guests listened, one assumes approvingly, to several suitable speeches. "Done with goodwill and relief on both sides," Ross wrote, "this dinner terminated the legal association of the two universities."[185] A week later, on 1 July 1965, York University, about to open its second campus, became independent.

More than forty years after the tie was severed, few people at York remember that their institution was once affiliated with the University of Toronto. Some graduates *do* remember. One consequence of the affiliation has been that members of the first three graduating classes, those of 1963, 1964, and 1965, tend to feel uncertain about their status. Although they were educated at York, they received University of Toronto degrees. A few have called themselves members of "the lost years."[186] As this chronicle ought to make clear, nothing and nobody in that time should be thought of as in any way "lost." They were immensely important in York University's growth and development.

During 1965 and 1966, York's focus shifted from its first to its second campus. The move to the new location on Keele Street, south of Steeles Avenue, began in August 1965. But planning for the move had begun three years earlier, when the university acquired the land it wanted for expansion in the long run, expansion that was hastened by the appearance of the 1962 Deutsch Report.

The acreage that York obtained in North York had been farmed from the early decades of the nineteenth century into the middle of the twentieth. Four of the five settlers on the land that is now the Keele campus were of Pennsylvania Dutch origin, Mennonites attracted by the promise of free land in Upper Canada. The Fisher, Stong, Kaiser, and Hoover families settled on several lots between what are now Steeles and Finch avenues; the English-born John Boynton settled south of them.[1] The still-extant Stong House on Steeles, built by Jacob Stong on land bought from his father, Daniel, dates from 1859–60. The farm stayed in the hands of the Stong family until 1952, when a speculator bought the land and then sold it to the Central Mortgage and Housing Corporation. It in turn made the property available to York, along with land once owned by two branches of the Kaiser family.

In the 1950s a speculator bought land that had been opened up by Abraham Hoover and John Boynton, selling it to York in 1964. Hoover House, which dates from 1843, is located southwest of Stong Pond and has been occupied by York people almost continuously since John Conway, the first master of Founders College, moved into it in 1965. Stong House became an artists' studio. The painter Ronald Bloore was using it by 1966; other artists soon joined him. A third dwelling, Hart House, located southwest of Osgoode Hall Law School, is of uncertain date and origin. David Fowle moved into it with his young family upon becoming master of Vanier College in 1966. Subsequently, William Farr, who succeeded James Flynn as secretary of the university in 1969 and became vice-president four years later, lived in Hart House for years before making way for English professor Elizabeth Hopkins, the provost and a vice-president of the university at

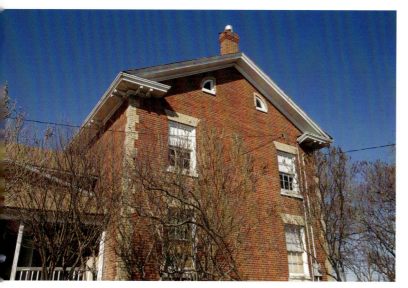 

LEFT Built in 1859–60, Jacob Stong House became studio space for several artists, among them Tim Whiten and Ronald Bloore.

RIGHT Abraham Hoover House, the oldest structure on the Keele campus.

the time, and her family. Later, another vice-president, Gary Smith, lived there. More recently it has been used for meetings and receptions;[2] it is now in the care of Osgoode Hall Law School.

Although the Board of Governors expected that much of the money for construction at the new campus would come from the provincial government, it was eager to launch a fund-raising campaign as soon as possible after the University of Toronto's was finished. "Like all new universities," Paul Axelrod has written, "York was seriously handicapped by an absence of endowment funds which older institutions had gathered over previous decades."[3] A further handicap was that York had few alumni as yet, and those it did have were just starting their careers, so that little financial help could be expected from them. Much depended, therefore, on a campaign for public support.

It was bold to launch the York University Founders Fund Campaign, with a target of $15 million, right after the University of Toronto finished its own attempt to raise $51 million. Murray Ross wrote that G.A. Brakeley, a fund-raising firm retained in 1964, initially suggested a target of $9 million, which the board then raised to $15 million.[4] Brakeley advised that one key to success was a generous response by board members personally, followed by large contributions from the companies they were associated with. Such donations would present an image of a self-confident institution "well on the way to success," not a struggling university desperate for support.[5]

Allan Lambert, president of the Toronto-Dominion Bank and chairman of the board's Finance Committee, played a central role, but he had the essential support of other board members, almost all of them at or very near the top of major companies. Among them were Senator T. D'Arcy Leonard, Edgar Burton of the Robert Simpson Company, William Harris of Harris and Partners, John S. Proctor of the Bank of Nova Scotia, William P. Scott of Wood Gundy, Edwin Walker of General Motors of Canada, John D. Leitch of Toronto Elevators, Bertrand Gerstein of Peoples Credit Jewellers, W.F. McLean of Canada Packers, Leonard

Lumbers of Canada Wire and Cable, William Horsey of Maubank Associates, and John H. Taylor of Liquifuels. Robert Winters, too, was a key figure before he resigned at the end of 1965 in order to return to politics and enter Lester B. Pearson's cabinet. Scott succeeded him as board chairman on 1 January 1966.

The Board of Governors launched the Founders Fund Campaign at a media dinner on 19 December 1964. Its guest list included the names of every important figure in the Toronto-based television and radio industry, as well as leading representatives of the daily newspapers and periodicals such as *Saturday Night*. "The menu was planned meticulously: a seafood cocktail, filet mignon or roast beef, and ample liquor before, during, and after dinner."[6] Brakeley was at least as meticulous in tracking the media coverage of the campaign, which ran for several months. Soon the fund-raisers were able to point to the large donations made by members of the board themselves and by the enterprises they led. By the end of January 1965, board members had collectively donated $1,167,500, with a further $1,325,000 coming from their companies.[7] If nothing else, this underlined the wisdom of Ross's insistence, back in 1959, that the board must consist of men of influence and financial means.

The Founders Fund Campaign was, in Axelrod's view, "a qualified success."[8] Somewhat disappointingly, by the middle of 1966, the campaign had covered little more than two-thirds of the distance towards the goal of $15 million, although it had passed the original target suggested by Brakeley. The campaign was closed by then, but "contributions continued to trickle in until 1970, when the $15 million dollar figure (less expenses and including interest from investments) was finally obtained."[9] Although it fell somewhat short of expectations, the campaign did allow York to build and grow more rapidly than government grants alone would have permitted, and, in enabling this growth, the Board of Governors played a crucial role. The board was important, too, because the financial stature of its members helped the university to borrow when funds were needed quickly. In looking back on York's first decade, Ross wrote: "There would be no York University without its Board of Governors."[10] No informed person is likely to argue with this.

In the fall of 1962, with the campus now in York's possession, the board asked University Planners, Architects and Consulting Engineers (UPACE), a joint venture by three Toronto firms, Gordon S. Adamson and Associates, John B. Parkin Associates, and Shore and Moffatt and Partners, to develop a master plan and design the first four buildings. Thomas Haworth, the architect-planner of the Glendon campus, continued to serve as architectural consultant and adviser to the board, and Hideo Sasaki, head of the Department of Landscape Architecture at Harvard University, became a special consultant to UPACE.[11] (This should put to rest the persistent myth, which I started hearing soon after I came to York in 1968, that the campus was designed by California-based planners ignorant of the Ontario climate.) The board, of course, took a lively and continuing interest in the process.

After more than a year of work, the Campus Planning Committee released a twenty-year master plan for York University that had clearly been influenced by the recommendations of the Deutsch Report. The university was expected to

William Pearson Scott, board chairman from 1966 to 1971.

"Where is my university?" Murray Ross at his desk on the new campus.

have some 20,000 students by 1980 as well as 1,700 faculty and 3,200 other staff members. The Glendon campus would be home to a liberal arts college modelled on U.S. institutions such as Amherst, Swarthmore, and Reed. Atkinson College was to continue on its chosen course. The "York campus" was to become home to a multi-faculty university with undergraduate and graduate programs in the sciences, social sciences, humanities, medicine, dentistry, pharmacy, engineering, and so on. There would be one main library and several subsidiaries. Six buildings were projected to be ready by the fall of 1965, among them the first of the residential colleges, a science building, a library, and a large auditorium. The estimated total cost of all the buildings planned for completion by 1980 was $150 million, money that was expected to come from the provincial government and the York Founders Fund Campaign.[12]

The plan projected the eventual construction of twelve colleges, each with approximately 1,000 undergraduates, with classrooms, faculty offices, a dining hall, senior and junior common rooms, and a student residence. The colleges were intended to serve as centres for athletic and other extracurricular activities and provide students with "a home on the campus." The hope was that this would allow students to develop "a sense of identity" and forge "intimate contacts with fellow students and teachers," even as the university grew.[13] Of the twelve colleges originally planned, only seven actually took full form, with Stong (1970–71), Bethune (1972), and Calumet, its building finally completed in 1990, joining the four built in the 1960s.

Time would show that the colleges worked reasonably well for the faculty members who became fellows and the students who lived in them, but generally, though with exceptions, they were less successful in meeting the needs and wishes of students who lived off campus. Don Rickerd, who in 1967 became the first master of Winters College, said that Ross revered Oxford and Cambridge without knowing much about them and had not conceptualized how the colleges would fit into the larger university. Rickerd, who *had* been at Oxford, noted that there the masters usually lived in the colleges, and at York they did not – he lived in Maple – and said that he soon came to the view that "the colleges had no future."[14] Steve Dranitsaris, on the other hand, did not see it that way. A student in geography from 1969 to 1973, he became "extremely active" in Stong College, the fifth of the colleges to open, and in the university, "sometimes to the detriment of my studies."[15] He lived off campus and later in residence, and found the college to be an exciting place both ways. At a time when the great majority of students were undergraduates in arts and science, he recalled, York's life was college-based. Only more recently did "ethnic and group identification become more important."[16] The colleges survived, and they continued to do interesting things. Nancy Accinelli, who assisted Michael Creal when he was master of Vanier College in the 1980s, very much enjoyed working there: "I loved being able to know kids from first year to last; they belonged to a community."[17] But according to John Becker, secretary of the Council of College Masters from 1969 to 1984, "the colleges never worked as they were meant to."[18]

Early in 1964 York received a grant of $336,000 from the Advisory Committee on University Affairs, enabling the university to purchase two parcels of land south and west of the site obtained from the CMHC and thereby increase the size of the campus from 475 to 600 acres.[19] At this time the Board of Governors' committee on names outlined a policy that would govern the naming of buildings. If a building was used by a single faculty or discipline, its members would be allowed to propose the name. Otherwise, buildings would be named after large donors or after well-known Canadians, according to guidelines to be set out by the board.[20]

Three months later, on 23 April 1964, a sod-turning ceremony took place for the university's first building on the Keele campus, the Natural Sciences Building. Upon the death in 1965 of Ray F. Farquharson, a member of the board since

LEFT   Founders College, one of the first buildings to open on the Keele campus.

RIGHT   Burton Auditorium was built to function as both lecture hall and theatre.

1959, it was named the Farquharson Life Sciences Building. Work soon began on other buildings as well: a library, an auditorium that could do double duty as a theatre, and the first of the projected twelve colleges, as well as a central services building. In early 1965 the board, on a recommendation from the committee on names, gave the first of the colleges the name of Founders College.

The first building to open was the library, with most of the staff at Glendon's Leslie Frost Library moving to occupy their new quarters in August 1965. It was named the Steacie Science Library, after the eminent chemist E.W.R. Steacie, president of the National Research Council at the time of his death in 1962. The Burton Auditorium, which opened a few days later, carried the name of the late Charles L. Burton, a Canadian businessman and philanthropist who had actively supported Canadian education.

Founders College opened in September, though it was not quite finished when students and faculty began to move in. On a crisp fall day a few weeks later, the governor general, Georges P. Vanier, officially opened the campus. Approximately 2,500 people attended the event, at which Nathan Pusey, the president of Harvard University, spoke briefly. Robert Winters announced that the second residential college, to be opened in 1966, would be named after the governor general.[21]

The Faculty of Arts and Science was now physically divided, and it would not be fully reunited until 1968. This contributed to the confusion, sometimes verging on chaos, that was part of life at York in that first decade. For up to three years, some faculty members taught and had offices on both campuses. Most faculty and staff members, led by the natural scientists, the members of Atkinson College, and almost all librarians, knew in 1965 that they would soon be working on the new campus full time. Still, the physical comparison with Glendon remained unflattering to the Keele campus, and few fell in love with it.

The location on the northern fringe of the metropolitan area did not help. "The first time I went up to the wilds of North York," said Brian Dixon, who joined the Faculty of Administrative Studies (FAS) in 1967, "I began to have second thoughts about my decision to come to York." He soon found that many of the faculty were commuters who taught their classes and then left the campus. Something like the McGill Faculty Club, where he had met the likes of Frank Scott, Donald Hebb, and the painter Arthur Lismer, who encouraged his interest in sculpture, was missing at York. A few people gathered in the Winters College Common Room in the late afternoon, but a sense of collegiality proved "very difficult to establish."[22] Frances Henry, who joined the Anthropology Department in 1970 after teaching at McGill for a decade, found when she arrived at York that a commuter mentality dominated among her colleagues, many of whom were managing to get their classes scheduled on just two days a week. "They did most of their scholarly work at home," she recalled. At McGill, she added, people had been happy to teach several days a week and worked in their offices when they were not teaching.[23] John Warkentin, who joined the Geography Department in 1963, remembered that on the Glendon campus people were in their offices a lot but that on the Keele campus this happened much less often.[24]

From the outset, Murray Ross had said that York would consist of three components: a residential liberal arts college, a multi-faculty university, and an evening division. In this plan, the Glendon site was the logical home for the liberal arts college. However, if the new campus was going to be the main focus of York's development, did it make sense to continue to devote resources to a college that lay outside that focus? Ross recalled in his memoirs that some faculty members were ready to cut not only Glendon but also Atkinson College loose. "Better by far, they said, to let them grow on their own."[25] Others felt that, even if the Glendon site were kept and Atkinson College continued to function, all faculty members teaching the liberal arts should be in the Faculty of Arts and Science. Ross thought that neither of these options was appropriate.[26]

The Board of Governors never seriously considered abandoning the Glendon campus, which had to be used for educational purposes or be returned to the University of Toronto for the dollar York had paid for it. Too much money had been invested at Glendon for this to make any sense. Besides, by 1964, board members were meeting in the handsome, if somewhat gloomy, Board-Senate Chamber built as part of the York Hall extension, and they were disinclined to relocate to the Keele campus. (Sometime in the 1980s I asked Vice-President Bill Farr half-facetiously whether the board had retained the Glendon site mainly because its members wished to continue meeting there. For a few seconds he chewed pensively on one of the plastic stirrers that had replaced the cigarettes he used to smoke, then a slow smile passed over his face: "There *is* some truth to that.")

If most faculty members assumed that Glendon would become a conventional liberal arts college, one of them had a different idea. Late in 1962 the head of the French Department, Lester J. Pronger, drafted "A Proposal for the Small Campus of York University." As presented to the Senate a year later, the document asserted that the original plan of "a small, elite, experimental college with a unique and distinctive curriculum [can] be achieved in a way which will also solve the major Canadian social problem: the misunderstanding, ignorance and intolerance which separate Canadians of the two founding races."[27] Pronger's "National College of York University" would be bilingual and bicultural; English

The anthropologist and race-relations expert Frances Henry came to York from McGill in 1970.

and French Canadians would live side by side. Half the faculty and staff would be French Canadian or bilingual, and students would take courses in both languages. Since the function of the college would be to educate Canada's future leaders, a small number of departments in the humanities and social sciences would suffice. Science would not be taught, thereby reducing costs.[28]

At a December 1963 Senate meeting, "Professor Pronger expressed the hope that the statement would be accepted and that the Planning Committee for Glendon College might consider the possibility of creating a bicultural college on the Glendon Campus."[29] What the committee did with the document is unclear, and no further discussion of it took place in the Senate during that academic year. Several faculty members have said that they did not take Pronger's scheme very seriously.[30] One who did, though, was a young Québécois recruit to the French Department, Jacques Cotnam, who learned about Pronger's proposal soon after arriving in 1964 and welcomed its commitment to bilingualism and biculturalism.[31]

Early in 1965 Ross announced that a former Canadian diplomat then employed by the World Bank, Escott Reid, would be the founding principal of Glendon College. Acting on Jack Saywell's suggestion,[32] Ross had written to Reid the previous July, suggesting that "our own college at Glendon Hall" should become "a first-rate residential college such as Swarthmore, Amherst, Reed etc. ... We thought also that our college might have as its distinctive ethos, both in its curriculum and outside, a compelling interest in public affairs – perhaps a college from which would come people interested in politics and the civil service."[33] The influence of Pronger's ideas is evident here.

Asked about the offer, Reid's son Timothy, who was Ross's assistant at the time, told his father that "the Principalship of Glendon College is one of [the plums], if not 'the' plum in Canadian universities."[34] Recalling the occasion forty years later, Tim Reid said that "for obvious reasons" he had "stayed completely out of the matter."[35] Besides, his father did not need prompting. He was interested in Ross's offer from the outset and before long was sending letters that outlined ambitious proposals, among them the notion that Glendon's "one thousand students" should all live in residence (Reid foresaw five residences in all!) and that "all students should acquire the ability to read and speak French." Reid went on to say: "Glendon College should play a great role in helping to train a new generation of Canadians who would make a better job of relations between English- and French-speaking Canadians than their parents and grandparents. This task will remain whether or not Canada breaks up. Indeed it would be even more important if the secession of Quebec were to take place with great bitterness on both sides."[36] Post-1960 events and intellectual currents in Quebec, and their implications for Canada as a whole, shaped Reid's proposals as they did Pronger's, as, indeed, they shaped the policies of the government of Canada at the time. In the spring of 1963 the Liberal government led by Lester Pearson took office. Soon afterwards, it established the Royal Commission on Bilingualism and Biculturalism, whose *Preliminary Report* appeared in early 1965.[37]

When Jacques Cotnam read a copy of a memorandum Reid had sent to Ross in the spring of 1965, outlining his ideas for Glendon College,[38] he addressed

an enthusiastic letter to Reid, welcoming his commitment to bilingualism and expressing the wish to discuss his own ideas with him.[39] He also sent Reid a copy of Pronger's memorandum.[40] It was more grist for Reid's mill. For months he had been asking friends for advice, among them the political scientist John Holmes, who later taught at Glendon, the international-law scholar Norman MacKenzie, and the historian Frank Underhill. MacKenzie, until recently the president of the University of British Columbia, said that Ross was a good man, but warned Reid that "he may not be able to deliver all he would like or has promised."[41] Underhill, who had taught at the universities of Saskatchewan and Toronto, took issue with Reid's exclusion of the natural sciences and of sociology, and also thought students should be "exposed to music and the fine arts."[42] Reid responded that he had already decided to add sociology and drop philosophy from the honours courses to be offered.[43] This proposal ran into heavy weather when Reid addressed the York faculty in late February, testing his ideas against theirs. John

McFarland recalled that the historian W.R. (Bob) Augustine made a persuasive case for including philosophy.[44] Augustine, who had come to York in 1964 and ended up staying at Glendon College, said he was impressed with the way Reid listened to the faculty when he met them, and with his willingness to accommodate his thinking to theirs.[45]

Some months later, Reid informed the York Senate that the college's emphasis on public affairs required "first-rate departments in at least economics, history, political science and sociology" as well as English, French, and philosophy. "It would seem best to begin with these seven departments," he stated, "with mathematics, geography, psychology and modern languages" to be added later. The natural sciences were left out because they cost too much.[46] A newspaper article that appeared in the *Globe and Mail* not long afterwards stated in comment that the college would be a "hotbed of politics" and a "bilingual incubator for tomorrow's elite."[47]

A good many faculty members would divide their teaching time between the two campuses for two or even three years, but some of the early arrivals stayed at Glendon permanently. Among them was the eminent Hegel scholar H.S. Harris. His colleague Lionel Rubinoff said that Harris, who had taught in a large U.S. university, wanted to be part of a liberal arts college.[48] In addition, Reid, an outsider in the university world, asked Harris to be his academic dean.

The newly created Glendon College, which was officially opened by Prime Minister Pearson in October 1966, registered its first students in September of that year. It offered instruction in humanities, social science, natural science, modes of reasoning, and the seven academic departments that Reid had earlier identified. The limited offerings undermined Glendon's appeal. So did the require-

LEFT   The official opening of Glendon College, 1966. Left to right: Lester B. Pearson, Murray Ross, George Tatham, Wilfred Curtis, Richard Schultz, unidentified student, Marion Pearson.

ment that all students take English and French through the second year. David Clipsham, who joined the Glendon English Department in 1967, recalled that he and his colleagues opposed the principle of compulsion, prompting the Faculty Council to drop the English requirement over Reid's protests in 1968–69.[49] The French requirement remained in force, though, in part because the chairman of the Glendon English Department, Michael Gregory, did not oppose *it*. "I would have been hung, drawn, and quartered," Gregory said with a smile, adding that he did believe in a bilingual college.[50]

At the time, universities across Canada were dropping language requirements in response to student pressure, so that Glendon College was rowing against the current. Not only did first-year registration fall short of expectations, but not a few students transferred to the Faculty of Arts or another university after the first year, often citing the French requirement as a reason.[51] Disappointing enrolment figures prompted the establishment in 1968 of a board/Senate committee, chaired by board member George Gardiner, to investigate the prospects of the college. It reaffirmed the university's commitment to Glendon's objectives but raised the target enrolment from 800 to 1,250, to be reached by the year 1971–72.[52]

The faculty who came to Glendon often were or became strongly committed to its ethos as enunciated by Reid. One was the historian Albert Tucker, who had been educated at the University of Toronto and Harvard University. Jack Saywell recruited him from the University of Western Ontario in 1966, but Reid and McInnis persuaded him to stay at Glendon rather than join most of the historians in moving to the new campus. Although he knew that he would have "trouble with French," Tucker remembered, he was "fascinated by the idea of a liberal arts college."[53] He became chairman of History and in 1969 succeeded Reid as principal.

In a different category was Alain Baudot, one of five *coopérants culturels*[54] recruited in France by Reid, whom Baudot described as "perhaps the most decent human being I have ever known."[55] Completely ignorant about Toronto when he got here in 1966, he came to love the city, the college, and the close contacts he forged there with colleagues and students.[56] He stayed at Glendon, becoming one

LEFT Lester B. Pearson, Murray Ross, William Davis (minister of colleges and universities), and Principal Escott Reid chat after the opening ceremony at Glendon.

RIGHT Leslie Frost, Marion Pearson, and Escott Reid at the official opening of the Marion Hilliard Residence on the Glendon campus, 1966.

of its strongest champions as well the founder in 1984 of the Groupe de recherche en études francophones (GREF), which he turned three years later into a small publisher of books from and about all parts of *la francophonie*.

Of the students who came to Glendon, some were drawn by its smallness and beauty, others by the opportunity to improve or maintain their French. Lesley Lewis was one of three students who arrived at Glendon from Neuchâtel Junior College in Switzerland in 1966. Having become fluent in French, Lewis was attracted by Glendon's commitment to bilingualism and by Reid's vision of public service, although she said: "How I heard about it in Neuchâtel I can't remember."[57] She lived in residence and soon made friends among the Quebec students who were registering in small but growing numbers by 1968, such as Alain Picard and Renault Marier. In the summer of 1969 she and Picard went on a two-week recruiting tour for Glendon in Quebec. Among her professors she remembered with particular affection Jean Burnet, Louise Rockman, and Stuart Schoenfeld: "They encouraged me to go on to graduate school."[58]

One of her new friends was David Cole, who came to Glendon quite serendipitously. Having graduated from a school in England, he was finding it hard to get his transcript evaluated by Canadian universities. His parents, who had heard of the new college at York, encouraged him to see its dean of students. George Tatham took one look at his transcript and said: "The admissions committee will have to confirm this, but I can tell you that you're in."[59] Like Lewis, Cole took to Glendon like the proverbial duck to water. Decades later he remembered his time there as "the happiest four years of my life." Within a year he was the chief organizer of a conference on the changing scene in Quebec. The first of Glendon's public forums, "Quebec: Year Eight," took place in November 1967. It brought, among others, Ramsay Cook, Eric Kierans, Jean-Luc Pepin, Claude Ryan, Frank Scott, and a chain-smoking René Lévesque to the campus. A genuine charmer, Lévesque was a popular favourite with students, and Cole stayed in touch with him.[60]

Almost eighteen months later, Lévesque was in Toronto again as part of a countrywide speaking tour, with the journalist Graham Fraser in tow.[61] He spoke at Glendon again, introducing a fresh crop of students to the separatist message. "He was sensational!" Rives (Dalley) Hewitt recalled.[62] Some of the students who had been involved in the conference decided to throw a dinner party, with Lévesque and Fraser as the guests of honour. It was held in the mid-town apartment of Lewis's parents, who were in Germany at the time, and she invited her friend Ruth Mesbur, who had come to Glendon from Regina on a scholarship in 1966, to help with the cooking, something Lewis had little experience with. Mesbur set out to prepare a turkey, noodle kugel, and sweet carrot tsimmes; Lewis worked on a trifle. Lévesque and Fraser were late for dinner, however, and frantic telephone calls to Regina and Frankfurt ensued, soliciting maternal advice as to how to slow things down.

Eventually the guests did arrive, and eight people sat down to dinner. Although she did understand the language, Mesbur was the only one who did not speak French fluently. When Lévesque noticed that she was not taking part in the conversation, he switched to English: "After all, we're in English Canada

here."[63] After dinner, it seemed a matter of course that the women should do the clean-up. (The women's liberation movement was still in its infancy. "I don't recall the role of women being an issue when I was a student," Cole said.[64]) The kitchen did not have an automatic dishwasher, so this was a major chore. Lewis and Mesbur were not far into it when someone knocked on the kitchen door. It was Lévesque, who asked if he could help. This was the signal for the other men to volunteer as well, Lewis remembered, but the politician warded them off. "He was such a charming man!"[65] Ron Kanter, one of the dinner guests, said with a grin: "He obviously preferred spending time with the women."[66]

Jan Armstrong, who came from Ottawa's Glebe Collegiate in 1967, was influenced by her older brother Hugh. "I had been accepted at Trent, Queen's and Glendon, but decided to go to Glendon because it was small, near a large urban centre, was bilingual, and, perhaps more importantly, had a politically active student population. This last bit of information I got from Hugh, who was president of the Canadian Union of Students in 1966–67 and knew and liked a number of the student activists on the Glendon Campus."[67] Armstrong lived in Hilliard Residence and loved it: "We residence students ran student life at the college."[68] Another student who entered in 1967, Julie Drexler, confirmed this. A graduate of Forest Hill Collegiate, she lived at home and felt herself to be an outsider as a result, "definitely not part of the 'in-crowd,'" who included the "theatre crowd" and the "actively sociable students" in the residences. However, she found Glendon's commitment to bilingualism to be a key attraction. Having come from France as a child, and having attended the École sécondaire de Charbonnel through Grade 11, she found Glendon to be "a wonderful continuation" of her French education.[69] She took an honours degree in French and English; three years after graduating, she joined the staff of the Frost Library, of which she is now the director.

Rives Dalley registered in 1968. She lived in Ancaster and had intended to go to the University of Western Ontario, but then she heard about Glendon and thought it would be a more stimulating environment. She loved her three years there and went to Sainte-Foy, Quebec, for a summer to improve her French. Among her professors she singled out the historian Irving Abella – "he was really interested in us as students and what we thought" – and Michael Gregory, whom she described as "charismatic." Several fellow students also stood out, especially Ron Triffon, who died of cancer in 1971. "He was such a nice fellow, so thoroughly decent," she said with regret.[70]

John McNee, intent on maintaining French-language skills acquired at Neuchâtel Junior College, chose Glendon in 1969 because Tatham's successor as dean of students, the economist Brian Bixley, took the time to show him around the campus. He never regretted his choice. Having honoured in history and English, he spoke appreciatively of his professors, among them Albert Tucker, John Brückmann, the historian Don Pilgrim, and a teacher of English medieval literature, Penelope Reed Doob: "She was so smart and had such a wide range of interests!"[71] In contrast, French played no part in bringing Adrienne Hood to Glendon in 1969. She had applied to the University of Toronto but was turned down at the St George campus and offered a place at Erindale or Scarborough College instead. She fancied neither, and chose Glendon because "it looked better than the other two." Drifting into the unilingual stream that opened up in 1971, she took an ordinary degree in English; almost a decade later, she returned to complete an honours degree in English and history. She particularly appreciated courses with Pilgrim and the poet and novelist Michael Ondaatje – "he was really great!" She also liked the small classes at Glendon: "We really did get to discuss things, and that forced us to think."[72]

Like McNee and Hood, Helen Sinclair, currently an honorary member of the Board of Governors, registered in 1969. Reid had addressed her graduating class at Havergal College, Toronto, and impressed her with his account of Glendon and its prospects. Many of her fellow Glendon students were of "high quality," she remembered. One of them, Charles Stedman, persuaded her to study economics after she had a difficult time in philosophy. She loved the "beautiful rose garden," enjoyed living in residence, where she found Sally Bowen a particularly

Glendon student Helen Sinclair later joined York's Board of Governors.

congenial don, and appreciated the opportunity to meet students from Quebec such as Lucy Bigué, Denis Massicotte, and Hubert Saint-Onge. But she was "most impressed by the teaching," singling out Abella in history and Roger Gannon in linguistics, as well as the economists David McQueen and James Savary.[73]

Paul Cantor was a don in Wood Residence from 1966 to 1970 while he studied law at the University of Toronto, articled, and took his bar-admission course. A native of Edmonton and a graduate of the University of Alberta, he came to Toronto and worked for World University Service (WUS) for three years. That was how he got to know Don Rickerd, who encouraged him to apply for a don-ship at Glendon. His years in Wood were, he said with humorous exaggeration, "the last days of booze and the first days of pot." He enjoyed meeting students as well as the other dons and the deans of students, Tatham and Bixley, and spoke feelingly of the beauty of the campus and the facilities of Proctor Field House (he introduced me to the game of squash on its courts). His agreeable memories of and attachment to the Glendon campus made it easy for him to agree to join the Board of Governors in 1998 when Lorna Marsden invited him.[74]

During the early years, a number of students registered in arts and science augmented Glendon's enrolment. Among them was Bob Drummond, a later dean of arts who entered York in 1963 and graduated in 1967 with an honours degree in political science. Although the Political Science Department moved to the new campus in 1966, and he had to take one course there, he had no trouble completing his degree at Glendon, and he said there was no pressure on him to move from one campus to the other.[75] Marion Boyd, who registered in 1964 and completed her honours BA in English and history four years later, had a somewhat different experience. Having been attracted by York's modest size and the beauty of the Glendon campus, she wished to stay, but she said that Ross wanted her year to move north in 1966. She and others resisted. "It was quite a fight," she recalled, but in the end there was a deal: students who had started at Glendon could finish their degrees there if they wished and if the courses they needed were available.[76] Since she had taken French for the first two years, she did not feel out of place in the college that was beginning to take form.

That was true also of Rick Schultz, who came to York from South Porcupine, Ontario, in 1964 and took an honours degree in political science. Later he completed a doctorate at York under the supervision of Fred Fletcher: "He was superb!" Schultz quickly became active in student government, and in 1965–66 he wrote a brief that argued for greater student participation in university government. When Reid arrived to become principal, Schultz quickly learned to love him because of his honesty and his ability to differ in argument without taking disagreement personally. (Michael Gregory also stressed this very appealing side of Reid's character.[77]) Besides, they used to meet and chat while walking in the Don Valley below the college. "I've had two heroes in my life, my father and Escott Reid," Schultz said, adding: "I loved the Glendon campus, I loved my time there, and I loved my professors." He spoke highly of Bill Kilbourn, the political scientist Harold Kaplan, and Douglas Verney but saved his highest praise for Bob Augustine, the historian Sydney Eisen, and the political scientist Magnus Gunther: "They were really great!"[78]

David Collenette, who registered in 1965 and would take an honours degree in political science, also said that he had very happy memories of Glendon. Like Schultz, whom he remembered as "very bright," Collenette enjoyed long walks in the valley. He took French, which he saw as essential to a career in public affairs, and joined the campus Liberals, the first steps in a political journey that would take him to federal office. He enjoyed meeting the students from Quebec who registered after Glendon College got started, and he remembered the "Quebec: Year Eight" conference as an "incredible experience." Although he remained on the Glendon campus until his graduation in 1969, he took several courses on the new campus, where he enjoyed lectures by Gunther, Verney, and "a very young Harvey Simmons." However, Collenette did not enjoy the shuttle-bus trips there and back, or the "utterly bleak" appearance of the Keele campus.[79]

Other students did go north, usually because their departments did. Geography moved to the new campus in 1966, although enough geographers continued to teach at Glendon that Mal Ransom was able to complete his third year there in 1967. To get his fourth year, he had to go in pursuit of professors like John Warkentin. "I didn't like it much," he recalled, because most of his friends, among them Schultz, were able to complete their degrees at Glendon. Besides, "York Main was a pretty desolate place."[80] But he got used to it. In 1969 he joined the university secretariat, and four years later he succeeded Bill Farr as secretary to the Senate and the Board of Governors, serving in that capacity until 1998.

Harriet Lewis, an honours English student who entered York in 1965, moved north when the early members of the English Department went to the Keele campus almost en masse. One reason was, as Clara Thomas said, that graduate teaching would be concentrated there.[81] Another was that the new chairman of English at Glendon, Michael Gregory, favoured a linguistics-oriented approach and preferred to build his own department.[82] As a result, Lewis migrated to Keele and Steeles in 1967. Ten buildings had been completed by then, and more were under construction, but the campus still looked "pretty raw." Asked for her reaction to it, Lewis, who succeeded Ransom as York's secretary, laughed: "I was from Medicine Hat, you know, so it was a bit like going home."[83]

After 1965, a growing number of faculty members and students inhabited the new campus at Keele and Steeles. At first they were associated with the Faculty of Arts and Science (not fully separated until 1968), Atkinson College, and the Faculty of Graduate Studies, but within a very few years several other faculties opened their doors.

Among the early arrivals were members of the Psychology Department. Kurt Danziger, who joined the department in 1965, came directly from South Africa. Accustomed to Cape Town's mild climate, he found the Keele campus, especially in mid-winter, a severe shock to the system: "It was Siberia!"[84] Neil Agnew, who left a clinical-research position in Saskatoon to become a professor of psychology and take charge of Psychological (today Counselling) Services on the Keele campus, was understandably less shocked.[85] The psychologist Sandra Pyke, who

A herd of cows ignores the construction taking place on the Keele campus.

arrived from Saskatoon in 1966, said: "When we moved down here I thought we had moved to the banana belt." But, while the campus looked "raw," she was not as dismayed as some: "I think I'm fairly insensitive to my environment."[86] Johanna Stuckey went to the new campus in the winter of 1965–66 to see what it looked like and get a sense of where her new office would be. "It was a hideous wasteland," she recalled, with the detritus of construction scattered everywhere. "The wind seemed to be blowing at 100 miles per hour. 'Oh God, how am I going to stand it,' I asked myself."[87] But she moved to the new campus permanently in the fall of 1966 and got used to it.

The early students often saw themselves as pioneers, not only because the campus was brand new, but also because they were the first in their families to attend university. In that category were Jackie Robinson and Sandra Noble Goss, graduates of Downsview High School who later called themselves "suburban Toronto working-class kids" and said that they knew of no classmates whose parents had gone to university.[88] (This pattern has continued, especially at the Keele campus, as Esther Greenglass, a member of the Psychology Department since 1968, noted.[89]) What struck Robinson and Goss about the campus was "the vastness of it, and the cold in the winter." There was construction everywhere. "I constantly had muddy shoes," Robinson recalled.[90] It was easy for them to take the Keele bus north, but, because it did not enter the campus, they faced a long walk along St Lawrence (now York) Boulevard to the few buildings that had opened. Well into the 1970s the Toronto Transit Commission resisted pressure to increase the frequency of service and reroute the Keele bus through the campus, so that hitchhikers standing along St Lawrence Boulevard remained a feature of life at York for years. The hike from the Steacie Library, where Robinson had a part-time job, or from Founders College, to the Burton Auditorium, venue of the lectures in first-year humanities and social science, was also long. So was the trek up to Steeles Avenue, to Stong House, which Robinson helped to fix up that first winter so that it could be used as studio space. Ronald Bloore, who joined the Humanities Division in 1966 as director of art and later moved to the Faculty of Fine Arts, remembered that "the house was exposed and not easy to keep warm." One day the overworked furnace began to spout flames, and he had to call the fire department to get things under control.[91]

Asked about her professors, Robinson mentioned Michael Collie in English – "he wore tweed jackets and was our image of what a professor should be" – and John Conway – "his humanities lectures were very dramatic and interesting." Ruth Straka in French also made a lasting impression on her: "She was the reason I became a French teacher." However, it was Donald Summerhayes who provided the occasion for her most memorable moment. "In September 1965 he put a brick through a window because it was very hot in the classroom, the air conditioning wasn't working, and there was no other way of letting air in."[92] Goss appreciated Bloore, who taught the visual art part of her humanities course, but her political-science courses really opened her eyes: "I hadn't known that political science existed!" Ed Broadbent made the subject "very exciting," but he left York in 1968 to enter federal politics. Magnus Gunther and Douglas Verney were also good. Together they were a large part of the reason that she went to work at

Queen's Park for Tim Reid, who taught economics on the Keele campus by this time but had also become a Liberal MPP.[93]

Cathie Stone lived in Founders College Residence, still unfinished when she moved in. Some steps were missing and students had to use a plank to enter the building. Furthermore, there were no carpets in the halls as yet, the showers were not working, and, since the residence lacked air conditioning, her room was very hot: "My father was ready to turn around and take me back to Barrie." She, too, remembered the inadequate bus service as "a real pain." On the other hand, York's isolation fostered strong bonds between residence students: "I'm still close to many of my floormates."[94] Rex Lingwood also lived in Founders College and found it to be congenial if at times noisy, though he added that his floor was less given to partying than some others.[95] Sandra Goss, who believed that residence students had a richer university experience, had this confirmed when she finally moved into Founders College in her fourth year. "That last year was great, just being here all the time."[96]

John Nagel arrived in 1967 to study economics. He was from upstate New York but, because his godparents lived in Toronto, he already knew the city. Although

he had been accepted by Trinity College, University of Toronto, he decided to attend York "because it was new and exciting and still relatively small." He lived with his godparents and was in a carpool, so that the commute, while irksome, was less of a problem than for students dependent on the TTC. The master of Vanier College, David Fowle, was a "key influence," and the Vanier common room – "we played a lot of euchre and bridge, and we debated many topics" – became the focus of his university life. He even met his wife-to-be there. Among his professors he remembered the historian Arthur Haberman, the psychologist Esther Greenglass, and the economists Ronald House, John Beare, and Alan Shapiro. The latter, he said, "was great. He kept us sharp and focused."[97]

Harriet Lewis, who lived in Winters College, the third of the colleges to open (Vanier College was the second), from 1967 to 1969, and Marie Rickard, who lived in Winters in 1970–71, confirmed that residence life was all the more cozy because of the remoteness from places of entertainment and the problems involved in getting there if you did not own a car and could not hitch a ride with someone.[98] Wendy Mitchinson, who came to York because its first-year general education program gave her time to make up her mind what to study and because York gave her a bigger scholarship than the University of Toronto, lived at home in Thornhill for two years, then entered McLaughlin College Residence when it opened in 1968. Until people agreed on some basic rules, residence life was rather chaotic, she recalled, but she liked being on campus. She never regretted going to York, where several of her history professors were "truly memorable." She singled out Jack Granatstein, whom she described as "a wonderful lecturer who led me to go into history," Paul Stevens, and Peter Oliver, and, at the graduate level, Ramsay Cook. "Besides, I fell in love at York. That colours my attitude." She married fine-arts student Rex Lingwood, who actually "liked that York was a construction site." "There was a real energy there as a result," Mitchinson added.[99]

She was not the only history major to find Granatstein to be a fine teacher. Paul Axelrod entered York in 1968 because he could not afford to leave the city to attend university and did not want to go to the University of Toronto because of its image: "traditional, huge, conservative." He liked professors such as the poet Eli Mandel, who taught a third-year humanities course on Canadian culture and was "incredibly engaging," and Don Coles. But Axelrod remembered most vividly the second day of a fourth-year course with Granatstein: "He gave the class an article he had written, and told people to come back the next week and criticize it." This really impressed Axelrod: "I argued with him all year."[100]

A key event in student social life took place when the 1969 session began. On 11 September, the Green Bush Inn, the first student-run pub on campus, served its first drink. (Glendon students had to wait until 1970, when the Café de la Terrasse in the basement of Glendon Hall got a licence.) The Green Bush Inn had a temporary location in Central Square, the hope being that the York Student Federation (YSF) would succeed in preserving the original Green Bush Inn building from demolition and transferring it to the York campus from its location on the northwest corner of Steeles Avenue and Yonge Street. This project did not succeed, but the presence of a pub, made possible by the decision of the provincial government to lower the drinking age to eighteen, significantly

The poet Eli Mandel was a member of the Department of English and the Division of Humanities, Faculty of Arts.

enhanced campus social life. There were also six coffee houses spread around the campus by September 1969, but for many students coffee, especially at night, did not match the attractions of beer.

Lots of students drank on campus before the fall of 1969, of course, but the practice was largely confined to residence rooms. So was another indulgence, the smoking of marijuana. How widespread it was is impossible to ascertain, but the scent of burning marijuana was a regular feature of residence life. Not everyone recognized it. "I was so innocent," Mitchinson remembered, "that I thought the pot I smelled in McLaughlin Residence was incense."[101] Paul Axelrod recalled that marijuana "was smoked quite regularly in the Winters Junior Common Room and elsewhere in the basement of Winters College, where there were alcoves allowing greater discretion."[102] (From my own experience as a don in Wood Residence in the late 1960s and early 1970s, I would say that marijuana use was fairly common but not a significant problem. Heavy drinking and "dropping acid," the use of LSD, were. Several times I was pressed into service in the middle of the night to drive a student experiencing a "bad trip" to the emergency department of Sunnybrook Hospital.) Early in 1969, *Excalibur*, the Keele campus student newspaper, argued in an editorial for the legalization of marijuana, on the grounds that it was hypocritical not to do so since it was no more dangerous than alcohol, tobacco, or sex.[103] Although the drug was illegal, there was no clear-cut policy on its use at York, so that academic administrators dealt with cases on an ad hoc basis.[104] This led to inconsistencies and did nothing to improve the attitude of students towards "the administration," in any case too easily seen as slightly malevolent. Finally, it must be noted that, when the federal government appointed a Commission of Inquiry into the Non-Medical Use of Drugs in 1969, Gerald LeDain, dean of York's Osgoode Hall Law School, became its chairman.

The Keele campus pioneers included not just the students who began their studies at York in 1965 and the faculty members who taught them. A large number of staff members migrated north in the late summer of 1965. One was Rasma Rugelis, who had joined the library's Technical Services Department in 1963. She liked working in the Frost Library and remembered that "no one wanted to go to the new campus – it was bleak and far away, and lacked proper public transportation." But technical services, including acquisitions and cataloguing, were going to the Steacie Library, "so there was no choice."[105] She did not own a car but fortunately managed to get a ride from another librarian.

Another pioneer was Raymond Hudson, York's first computer programmer. Freshly arrived from Australia, he met Cy Pilley, York's assistant registrar, at a computer-programming course early in 1965 and soon afterwards went to work for York, spending three months at Glendon before moving to an office in the Steacie Library. Decades later, he raved about the beauties of the Glendon campus and about the Proctor Field House, where he played squash and swam. The Keele campus was a let-down – "acres of nothing" – but he "enjoyed the job and the brilliant work atmosphere." Nostalgically he recalled the IBM1401, with its 4K of memory – the data were stored on punchcards – and the IBM360 (with 32K of memory) that succeeded it.

Aside from the director, Wallace Fraser, who had come to York from teaching mathematics and computer science at the University of Toronto, Hudson and Richard (Dick) Riley were the only two people in the department well into 1966.[106] The first jobs were student-records management and payroll calculation. Hudson affectionately remembered "lovely people" such as Vicky Draper, Milton Bider, who became the director of admissions, Bill Farr, still working on his master's degree, and, in financial management, Hugh Wareham, Flo Steen, and Kenneth Clements. He lunched in the Founders College dining room and was "amazed" that senior staff people were willing to talk with him. Almost forty years later, during a visit to Toronto, he still marvelled at the "wonderful collegiality" he had found at the university in those early days.[107]

Like Hudson, Vicky Draper moved into an office in the Steacie Library in the fall of 1965. There she reported to Edward Pattullo, who had become a vice-president. She had a very high opinion of him, describing his return to the United States a year later as "a great loss to York." (In his memoirs, Ross stated that a misunderstanding and subsequent quarrel between John Conway and Pattullo, in which Ross took Conway's side, led Pattullo to resign.[108]) After his departure, she once again reported to Don Rickerd, who was acting secretary to the Board of Governors. She herself became director of the Office of Student Programs. She was realistic about the new campus: "It was new and growing rapidly, so a bit of a mess was to be expected. And I worked with good people."[109]

Bruce Dugelby, who joined York in 1965 as accounts-payable clerk and would serve the university in the accounting and financial areas for four decades, remembered the mud that came with the constant construction. The term "muddy York" took on new meaning, he said – but he focused on the "camaraderie" and "spirit" of the campus: "You knew everybody; people were helpful to newcomers." York was "isolated physically but not emotionally or intellectu-

ally," he said, referring also to the "enthusiasm" of young people working things out "when there was no handbook to guide them." He also recalled that, being young, lots of people took part in the "keep fit" courses held at the Tait McKenzie Physical Education Centre, completed in 1966.[110]

For three years Dugelby hitched a ride from Mississauga with Owen Winchcombe, a former military man who worked in Physical Plant. The drive did not take very long, because, other than the oil tanks east of Keele, there was little development north of Highway 401 as yet and few traffic lights. In 1968 he moved to the campus, becoming a don in Winters and then in McLaughlin College, where George Tatham was the first master. Dugelby enjoyed living on campus, especially after he moved into Stong House as joint custodian in 1969 and got to know "the artists who had studios there, Ron Bloore, Doug Morton, and Tim Whiten." Enjoyable, too, were the "memorable parties" he and his housemates threw.[111]

York's first year of transition effectively ended on 1 June 1966. That day saw the first convocation of York as an independent university. Gathering in Burton Auditorium, proud parents and other relatives watched as 119 students graduated in the ordinary program, all of them having taken York's own curriculum throughout their three years. Among the graduands were the first two from Atkinson College, George Plue and Jean Sophia Taylor. The first honorary degrees granted by York went to Baron Noël Annan, vice-chancellor of the University of London, the artist Harold Town, John J. Deutsch, principal of Queen's University, George E. Gathercole, chairman of Ontario Hydro, Ruth Atkinson Hindmarsh of the Joseph Atkinson Foundation, and Robert S. McLaughlin, pioneer of the Canadian automobile industry and philanthropist. Lord Annan gave the convocation address. That evening a banquet for the new graduates and their parents took place on the Glendon campus.[112] It was thoroughly appropriate that the celebrations were spread over the two campuses.

The 1962 meeting of representatives from York and the University of Toronto had suggested that York should soon establish professional faculties that might reduce the pressure on the senior institution. In 1964 Ross appointed a small committee on professional faculties, chaired by Henry Best, a young historian who had joined his staff as research associate (he later taught in Atkinson College and served as its associate dean). The committee reported later in the year. It recommended that York establish a faculty of administrative studies, rather than simply one of business administration, on the grounds that a body of knowledge about administration had developed that applied to more than just a business setting: "Anyone who understood the fundamental principles of planning, staffing, organizing , directing, and controlling, could apply them in any institutional setting."[113] The first governing board had shown an interest in business administration, and Ross was also interested in it. He believed it to be a field well worth studying. Furthermore, it was one to which the University of Toronto did not, in his view, pay sufficient attention.[114]

Early in 1965, the Board of Governors gave approval to a faculty of administrative studies and a division of business within the faculty. Instruction was supposed to begin in September 1966. Looking for someone who could assemble the personnel of the new faculty, Ross turned to James Gillies, an Ontario-born acquaintance who taught at the business school of the University of California in Los Angeles (UCLA). Gillies had no wish to leave UCLA, he recalled, but he did agree to visit Toronto in March 1965 to discuss the York project. Ross's enthusiasm, and the commitment shown by the Board of Governors, especially Robert Winters, impressed him. The new campus, to which Henry Best drove him, did not. Gillies smiled as he remembered the experience: "It was a godforsaken place. 'When's the next plane back to L.A.?' I thought."[115] Nevertheless, intrigued by the challenge of building a faculty from scratch, he agreed to take a year's leave from UCLA in order to get the new faculty started.

Arriving in Toronto in early July, he got an office in the Leslie Frost Library and began to work. As he later wrote: "If the faculty was to open on schedule, [I] had to do a variety of things within the university, within the general academic community, and within the business community."[116] None of these tasks proved to be unusually difficult. In December 1965 the Senate approved his proposals for master's degrees in business administration and public administration. Although Gillies believed that the faculty should offer graduate instruction only, he had to agree to submit a proposal that "the new faculty should offer a small, experimental, undergraduate program" leading to the BBA degree.[117] The Senate and board then approved the proposal and its financial implications.

After the Senate approved the MBA program as presented by the Graduate Council, in February 1966, with Gillies still on leave from UCLA, the board formally appointed him a vice-president of York University as well as dean of administrative studies.[118] In the former capacity he replaced Edward Pattullo, who had been one of three vice-presidents appointed in January 1965 (the other two were

 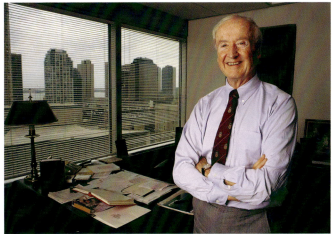

Bruce Parkes, finance, and Bill Small, administration). Soon afterwards, Gillies decided to stay at York to guide the early development of the expanding faculty and to continue to serve as vice-president.[119] In that role Gillies assisted in finding deans for the other new faculties, interviewed senior faculty recruited from other universities, and served as "a listening post for Murray." But "my position was unsustainable," he recalled. He could not simultaneously allocate resources to other units while seeking to secure them for his own faculty. Forced to choose between the vice-presidency and his deanship, he did not hesitate: "The business school was my passion."[120] In July 1968 he made way for Dennis Healy, who came to York from being dean of arts at the University of British Columbia.

Instruction in the Faculty of Administrative Studies began in the fall of 1966. William Dimma, who entered the business program as a part-time student that year (in the 1970s he would be dean of the faculty; two decades later he would be chair of the Board of Governors), remembered as its "big strength" the fact that the University of Toronto business school was "pretty bad" at that time. The weakness of the immediate competition meant that FAS attracted very good students from the outset. "It also soon had some brilliant professors," Dimma recalled, among them Associate Dean Tom Beechy, Charles Mayer (marketing), Mel Moyer (voluntary sector and arts management), Rein Peterson (small business), Al Rosen (accounting), and the "very colourful" Seymour Friedland (finance).[121]

At the 1967 spring convocation, held in the Tait McKenzie Physical Education Centre, twenty-two MBA students received their degrees. That summer Brian Dixon (later an acting dean of the faculty) came to York. Having been asked by a friend at the Stratford Festival to investigate what university might house a program in theatre management, Dixon had interviewed Gillies among others, and had got the sense that "York was the only university new enough that you could still move the walls."[122] Gillies ended up recruiting Dixon, and soon Dixon was, with his colleague Paul Schafer and Joe Green of the Faculty of Fine Arts, on a committee formed to look into training arts administrators. In 1970 he became the founding director of the arts administration program.

LEFT   James Gillies (right), the first dean of administrative studies, talks with Robert Winters.

RIGHT   A part-time student in the Faculty of Administrative Studies in the 1960s, William Dimma later served as its dean and was board chair from 1992 to 1997.

Among the earliest faculty members in FAS were Victor Murray, Gordon Shaw, and Elmer Phillips. But the appointment Gillies recalled with most affection was that of Lyndon Urwick, one of the founders of modern organization theory. Already well into his seventies, he lectured in the faculty for one semester, declining a salary and asking only for "a car and a driver and a drawing account for warm winter clothes."[123]

In the fall of 1967 the Senate approved the master of public administration program, with the first students scheduled to register in September 1968. That year Malcolm Taylor, "one of the jewels of the university," Gillies called him,[124] came from the presidency of the University of Victoria to take charge of public administration. Also important to the success of the faculty, Gillies remembered, was its advisory council, with a member of the Board of Governors, George Gardiner, in the chair. Gardiner was well connected in the business world, Gillies said, and was able to attract the support of CEOs of many of the top Canadian corporations.[125]

Henry Best's committee recommended not only the establishment of a faculty of administrative studies but also faculties of fine arts and environmental design. These had a harder time than administrative studies in getting Senate approval, because there were doubts about their financial viability.[126] All the same, theatre, music, and the visual arts had enjoyed a significant place in the university from the outset. The York theatre program was officially opened late in 1965, with performances in Burton Auditorium. In November 1966 the York Colleges Drama Festival of One-Act Plays took place, with participation from Atkinson, Glendon, Founders, and Vanier colleges. The York University Players, founded in 1965 by John M. Smith, were active until 1970, with Nick Ayre, Brian Meeson, and *Globe and Mail* theatre critic Herbert Whittaker among the directors. In Atkinson

The painter Ronald Bloore (left) became an early member of the Faculty of Fine Arts.

College, the New World Players, led by English professor Matthew Ahern, staged works well into the 1970s.[127]

Theatre loomed at least as large on the Glendon as on the Keele campus. Michael Gregory, who had been a professional actor, believed that dramatic literature should be not merely read but, whenever possible, seen on stage. He set out to make drama a major component of the English Department he was shaping. "The dramatic side of literature was well received by students," he recalled.[128] Some very good actors took part in the program. One of them was Trish Nelligan, a student in the Glendon English Department from 1967 to 1969, who went on to a career on the stage, in film, and in television, using the name Kate Nelligan. Few who saw it will have forgotten her bravura performance as Gertrude in a 1969 production of *Hamlet*, directed by Gregory and staged in Burton Auditorium.

By 1966, William McCauley, who later became director of music in the Faculty of Fine Arts, had announced the founding of the York University Band and the York University String Orchestra.[129] In 1966, too, the painter Ronald Bloore was recruited by Bill Kilbourn and Jack Saywell to teach in the Humanities Division.[130] Bloore and McCauley were among the participants in the "Centennial Performing Arts Festival," held in February 1967, an event that saw participation from other faculty members, among them Michael Collie and Robert Fothergill, who had been appointed in 1966 to the English Department of Atkinson College (three decades later he would transfer to the Department of Theatre in Fine Arts). Guests from outside the university included the poet Leonard Cohen and the artist Greg Curnoe.[131] By the spring of 1967, the Senate and board had given approval to the establishment of the Faculty of Fine Arts.[132]

As so often, Saywell took the lead in finding faculty members. Early in 1968 he recruited Joe Green, a graduate of the University of Indiana who was teaching at Hunter College in New York, to take charge of the Theatre Department. Green did not know much about Toronto and even less about York University, he

LEFT Joe Green was founding chair of Theatre and later served as dean of the Faculty of Fine Arts.

RIGHT Fine Arts Dean Jules Heller and his wife, Gloria, with Janet and Murray Ross.

recalled, but in 1968 Canada looked attractive to a growing number of Americans who opposed the war in Vietnam.[133] He soon recruited Don Rubin, a young American-born theatre critic for the Toronto *Star* and the CBC. "I think Joe just needed someone to boss around," Rubin said in jest. "I thought I'd be here for a few years," he added, "and now it's almost forty!"[134] The first dean of the new faculty, the printmaker and art historian Jules Heller, joined the York faculty a few weeks later. Another early appointment was Marc Rosen in Film. Like the others, he taught in the Humanities Division that first year. He had taken his first degree in comparative literature, which, he remembered, persuaded Saywell that he should be able to lead tutorial groups in the introductory course.[135] Other appointments included Bloore in Visual Arts and McCauley in Music, though Green recalled arguing against the creation of a music department since strong programs already existed at Queen's, Western Ontario, and the University of Toronto. However, Heller wanted to include all five major areas, and his opinion won the day.[136]

Officially opened in 1968, with departments of Theatre, Music, Film, Visual Arts, and Dance, the Faculty of Fine Arts sought to recruit people with unconventional backgrounds. On Heller's insistence, art history was included with the visual arts, in order to allow the linking of history and theory with studio practice. The combination was not free of conflict, and it did not please everybody. Green said that the art historian Zdenka Volavka tried to move art history into the Faculty of Arts. Others thought that the linking of the two fields was desirable. Joyce Zemans, who came from teaching the history of art at the Ontario College of Art and at York was to be appointed chair of visual arts in 1975 (later she served as dean), said that she "believed very strongly in the philosophy of integration."[137]

Fine Arts registered its first students in September 1969. One of them was Rex Lingwood, a Keele-campus pioneer who studied psychology but was interested in art and soon began to visit Stong House. After dropping out for a year, he registered in the Faculty of Fine Arts, starting in visual arts, with a minor in theatre design. He fondly remembered Frank Salerno, an Italian-born cabinetmaker who made props for faculty productions and also a spectacular round walnut desk for Germain Bazin, a French art historian who was a former curator of paintings at the Louvre. (When Bazin left York in 1973, Green appropriated the desk, which has been used by every fine arts dean since.[138]) Lingwood took a memorable course in art history from Ted Heinrich and studied sculpture with Tim Whiten and Ted Bieler – "they were both great!"[139]

The first production of the Theatre Department took place in November 1969. Directed by Green, the two one-act plays by Tennessee Williams, *27 Wagons Full of Cotton* and *This Property Is Condemned*, featured Michael Burgess (later an actor and singer in musicals), Alain Goldfarb, Donna Farron Slivinski, and Charlotte Weisberg.[140] Performance in the Music Department was slower to get under way. In an interview carried out in 2000, the first chairman of Music, Sterling Beckwith, remembered that he spent much of the first year buying "a few new pianos, a Canadian-built baroque pipe organ (my pride and joy!), a small harpsichord, various other musical instruments, and some good playback equipment for classroom use."[141] He needed to buy records and sheet music, and ordered

many books, many of which, along with the general music books already in the library, became part of the Sound and Moving Image Library. He also scouted the York campus, looking for rooms that might be adapted as interim space for the program's use. The university's architects, he found, had not taken the needs of music teaching, rehearsal, recording, and public performance into account.

The attraction of the faculty for people in the arts was the same as the one that drew scholars and scientists to York in the 1960s: the opportunity to do new things. York was starting from scratch, and this appealed to people with a taste for innovation. Among those who came were the painter Douglas Morton, well known as one of the "Regina Five," the theatre director Mavor Moore, the choreographer Grant Strate, the musicologist Austin Clarkson, and the art historian and arts administrator David Silcox, who became an associate dean of the faculty. Heller worked with Jim Gillies to develop an MBA program in arts management, an innovation that created a link between two apparently very different academic units. Expansion was rapid, in Fine Arts as in the larger university, with people eager to try new approaches. Green, who became dean in 1973, thirty years later said wistfully: "There was a vision and energy at York in those days that has largely been lost."[142] Marc Rosen, who left York's Film Department to enter the private sector in 1978, recalled that "there was a tremendous energy in the early years," later sapped by increasing financial stringency. Still, three decades after leaving, he regarded his work at York as "one of the most exciting things I did in my life."[143]

The Best committee having also recommended the founding of a faculty of environmental design, the Senate gave first reading in February 1967 to a motion to establish "a Faculty of Environmental Design with a School of Architecture as its first component," provided the provincial government would offer financial support.[144] Two months later, the Senate's Committee on Professional Faculties urged a reconsideration of the issue, since the University of Waterloo and Carleton University were both in the process of setting up such a faculty.[145] As a result, the focus of the proposed faculty shifted away from design, while the idea of a school of architecture was dropped altogether.[146] Early in 1968, the Senate approved the establishment of the Faculty of Environmental Studies (FES), something Harold Schiff remembered as "Jack Saywell's idea."[147] Saywell did not remember it that way, but wrote: "We needed something broader based on the land and human side. I didn't realize then how offbeat it would become!"[148] Alex Murray, a member of the History Department since 1962, welcomed a broad-based program. He had begun to study the history of landscape architecture and park design and tried to interest Escott Reid in establishing a program in urban studies within Glendon College, "but Escott didn't want one." Murray surmised that Reid saw the study of cities as "unworthy and unimportant." Murray then moved to the Keele campus, though "with considerable reluctance."[149] He took an early interest in the proposed faculty of environmental design, and in 1968, encouraged by Saywell, he joined James Gillies in drafting an outline of the objectives and curriculum of the Faculty of Environmental Studies. Daniel Cappon, a psychiatrist then teaching at the University of Toronto (he would join the faculty in 1970), took a hand in preparing the draft and in convincing Ross of the value of the proposal. Gerald Carrothers, an architect who had earlier taught at the universities of Manitoba, Toronto, and Pennsylvania, came from the Central Mortgage and Housing Corporation in 1968 to became the first dean of the faculty.

The Faculty of Environmental Studies embodied, in Ross's words, "an entirely new conception of environmental study and planning."[150] "Fundamental to FES was that things were not in boxes," Carrothers said. "There would be no departments and no schools" to act as boxes; "the only box is the student's head."[151] This was something he believed to be in line with the interdisciplinary spirit of York. The faculty allowed students to apply with an undergraduate degree in any discipline and granted only graduate degrees, initially just at the master's level (a doctoral program came into existence in the 1990s). This meant that the Ontario Council of Graduate Studies had to approve the program if the students were to be funded. Alex Murray, the only faculty member already at York to join FES, recalled that the council's assessor, a biologist from Queen's, asked some very

The architect Gerald Carrothers was the first dean of environmental studies.

sceptical questions. Ross's advice, Murray said, was "to tell him what he wants to hear."[152]

Sylvia Zingrone, who joined York as secretary to Henry Best in 1967 but became Carrothers's assistant in the fall of 1969, said that he "was extremely hands-on in an intellectual way."[153] He was the principal author of *FESKIT: Essays into Environmental Studies, Being Interpretations and Amplifications of the FES Curriculum Model*, prepared with Stephen Kline and John Livingston, and several others. Students received a copy when they registered; it was supposed to serve them as a guide throughout their years of study. First drafted in 1968, *FESKIT* was regularly updated. "The FES approach is based on connected concepts of 'environment' and 'study,'" *FESKIT* stated: "Environmental not only defines that which is to be studied but also indicates the way in which study may be pursued."[154] "Self-directed learning is fundamental in the process," *FESKIT* continued: students enjoyed the freedom to create their own courses of studies. They would do so by way of the plan of study, defined as "a 'learning contract' between the student and the Faculty" that could be changed "as often as needed to guide the student through to the end of the program." Individual plans would be devised by students and their faculty advisers to meet individual needs and would be examined at general examinations "to confirm relevance and validity." Students could take courses anywhere, provided the professors accepted them. They were assessed on a pass/fail basis, but faculty members had to do written evaluations of each of their students. "This constituted a fairly complete system of monitoring," Carrothers stated: "We did not want a quick and dirty way of rating our students."[155] Monitoring was more time-consuming than grading, but it was also more rigorous, he recalled, though from the outside it may not have looked that way.

Carrothers conceded that FES had a "flaky reputation" from the start, and that some York faculty regarded it with misgiving, even hostility. It continued to be embattled for at least a decade. When interviewed, Harold Schiff was critical of the decision to exclude the sciences from the faculty. He had been dismayed by the lack of clarity in Carrothers's conception of the environment, he said, and he regretted that "Gerry was not interested in working together."[156] The program did not steer clear of the Faculty of Science, Carrothers said in response: "We supported the Centre for Research on Environmental Quality." However, FES wanted to avoid the sort of compartmentalization that traditional science faculties represented, because that would have been a box, too.[157] One FES student of the 1970s, Adèle Hurley, noted with mild regret the near-absence of a scientific side to the faculty at that time, although she was able to compensate for it.[158] There is no doubt, however, that many of the faculty members and students appreciated the flexibility of the curriculum and the freedom they enjoyed in shaping their own programs.

York acquired one more faculty in 1968. The adhesion of Osgoode Hall Law School to the university was almost three years in the making. Days after the formal opening of the Keele campus, Ross and John D. Arnup, treasurer of the Law Society of Upper Canada, jointly announced that, subject to approval by the Board of Governors and the benchers of the Law Society, Osgoode Hall Law

School, which had been operated by the society for decades, would become a faculty of York, effective 1 July 1968.

In 1967 Harry Arthurs – he would be president of York from 1985 to 1992 – wrote an article describing and analysing the process whereby Osgoode joined York. He saw the affiliation as more or less the logical outcome of a process that began with the resignation of Dean Cecil A. Wright and several of his colleagues from Osgoode Hall in 1949 in protest against the Law Society's rejection of a full-time law school.[159] Several developments in the decade before 1965 pointed towards a change in direction, among them Osgoode Hall's loss of its monopoly of legal education in Ontario in 1957, changes in the faculty and their research interests as well as in the Osgoode curriculum, a growing demand for legal education in the Toronto area, and Osgoode's inability to expand on its downtown site. "Thus the stage was set for formal affiliation with a university, and York was the obvious choice. It was Toronto's second university, and it had plans for its own professional faculties."[160]

Affiliation did not occur without conflict and division. The younger faculty were eager for the link with York, Arthurs remembered years later, but most of the older faculty were opposed.[161] One proposal, that Osgoode should join the University of Toronto law school in creating a single large faculty, seemed briefly attractive, but it ultimately went nowhere.

By 1966, the plans for affiliation, the development of a curriculum that linked the law to society in new ways, and the establishment of targets for faculty and student numbers were all well under way. When Dean H. Allan Leal announced that he did not intend to join York upon affiliation, an acting dean, A.W. Mewett, took over. A search committee chaired by Justice Bora Laskin of the Ontario Court of Appeal, who joined the Board of Governors in 1967, came up with the name of Gerald E. LeDain, a professor of law at McGill University. "He was an inspired choice for Osgoode at a critical moment," Laskin's biographer writes: "LeDain's experience in a prominent corporate counsel setting afforded him instant legitimacy with the bar, his teaching and scholarship in public law fields endeared him to the faculty, and his service as counsel to Quebec Attorney-General Claude Wagner on several constitutional files had given him a high public profile."[162] In 1968 he became the first dean of York's newly acquired Faculty of Law. Osgoode remained downtown for one more year, however, since its new building on the Keele campus was not completed until 1969.

The name of the faculty remained controversial for a few years, as the Law Society of Upper Canada sought to deny the use of the name "Osgoode Hall" for York's new Faculty of Law. In late 1972 LeDain's successor as dean, Harry Arthurs, appeared before a meeting of the Board of Governors to present a brief on the subject. In summary, he asserted "the belief of members of the faculty that the work of the Law School brought credit … to bear upon the historic name, and asked for the support of members of the Board both individually and collectively in resisting the action by the Law Society."[163] The board unanimously declared its support for the school's position, and asked two of its members, William R. Allen, a former chairman of Metropolitan Toronto, and James L. Lewtas, senior partner of a major downtown law firm (and later briefly board chairman),

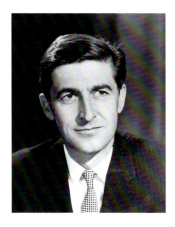

Gerald LeDain was dean of the Osgoode Hall Law School when it joined York in 1968.

to coordinate the board's activities in dealing with the Law Society. Evidently the board's efforts met with success, and the Law Society abandoned its quest.

Osgoode quickly developed a reputation for engaging the law with other disciplines in innovative ways. This attracted faculty and students. Fred Zemans, who joined the faculty in 1971 with a joint appointment to Parkdale Community Legal Services, referred to an atmosphere of "intellectual excitement" that encouraged him to leave a downtown legal firm.[164] John McCamus, who would be the dean from 1982 to 1987, joined Osgoode in 1971. Although the Keele campus was "unimpressive" and the drive up to it "anything but attractive," he said, the school "was the biggest and best in Toronto," and "the library was a joy to work in."[165] Marion Lane, who registered as a student in 1971, said she did not want to attend the University of Toronto law school. She described its curriculum at the time as "narrow and rigid," whereas Osgoode's was "imaginative ... Osgoode was light years ahead."[166] The remote location did not trouble her the way it did some others. It *was* a drawback, though, and it did discourage some potential students. Ruth Mesbur, who graduated from Glendon in 1969, chose the University of Toronto Faculty of Law in part because she did not want to go to the Keele campus.[167] Marilyn Pilkington, who in 1993 became dean of Osgoode and thereby the first woman dean of a law faculty in Ontario, entered the University of Toronto Faculty of Law in 1972 even though Osgoode was known to be "a much more interesting place." Why had she nevertheless gone to the University of Toronto? She smiled and answered: "Location, location, location."[168]

The Faculty of Graduate Studies was expanding rapidly at the same time. By 1967, English, geography, mathematics, political science, and sociology had joined psychology and several flourishing programs in the natural sciences, and other programs were under consideration. With graduate students now numbering well over a hundred, they founded the Graduate Students' Association. Soon afterwards the Board of Governors gave its approval to an agreement

LEFT   The Osgoode Hall Law School building was completed in 1969.

RIGHT   Passy Gardens and graduate residences, seen from Stong Pond.

between York and the Ontario Housing Corporation for the construction of the Graduate Student Residence Number One, the first of several built south of The Pond Road.[169]

Not only did York establish several new faculties from 1965 through 1969, but it was branching out in other ways as well. Founded in March 1965, the Institute for Behavioural Research (IBR) joined the two-month-old CRESS as a research centre.[170] Initially under the direction of Mortimer Appley, the new institute undertook to coordinate research activities in the departments of economics, political science, psychology, and sociology, to facilitate post-doctoral training and research, especially of an interdisciplinary nature, and to sponsor large-scale research projects. By 1967, an office with three staff members had come into being, with the political scientist Fred Schindeler as director. The IBR initiated research programs in ethnic, family, political, and psychological research. In 1967, too, its first conference, on "The Theory of Organization," took place, the institute's publication series got under way, and the data bank began acquiring early Canadian Gallup Poll survey data. In 1968 the IBR's Survey Research Centre was started, as a young sociologist, Michael Lanphier, came from a position at Pennsylvania State University to take charge of it. He found York to be "extremely accommodating," he later recalled, and, although a serious budgetary problem occurred in 1972, the centre generally accomplished what he hoped it would.[171] He established a field staff and a "sampling frame" for Ontario, the initial project being a survey of political attitudes of Ontario voters. By 1970, the IBR was offering a course in survey-research methods in conjunction with the Faculty of Graduate Studies. The IBR changed its name to the Institute for Social Research (ISR) in 1984 because this better described the broadly interdisciplinary work that its members were carrying out. In time it gave birth to several other organized research units (ORUs) at York, including the Centre for Refugee Studies (1981), the York Centre for Health Studies (1990), and the Centre for Feminist Research (1991).

Two other research centres got their start in the late 1960s. One was the Centre for Research on Environmental Quality (CREQ). Harold McFarland of the Department of Natural Science became the first director; others involved with the centre were the biologists David Fowle and Michael Boyer, after whom the Boyer wood lot was later named, and the chemist Morris Katz. The other was the Transport Centre, under the direction of Ivan Feltham of Osgoode Hall Law School, which developed into the University of Toronto-York University Joint Program in Transportation in 1970. Funded by the Canadian Transport Commission with an initial grant of $140,000, it undertook to coordinate research into transportation at both universities.[172]

A centre of a different kind received autonomy in 1969. Initially the Centre for Continuing Education (CCE) was located within Atkinson College. A president's committee chaired by board member Bertrand Gerstein, with Arthur Johnson as secretary, recommended in 1967 that the centre be separated from Atkinson, and that the functions of the dean of Atkinson College and the director of CCE also be separated. The centre was to be financially self-supporting, with the profits (if any) from its operations going to the university rather than to Atkinson. "The

Centre should call upon and make use of not only the faculty and physical facilities of the University, but also the appropriate teaching and physical resources available within the general community of the Toronto metropolitan area whenever the demand for programs is sufficient to support the expense involved."[173] The Senate accepted this recommendation but also released a policy statement establishing Atkinson College as an equal academic partner with the other faculties in the overall undertakings of York, including, as recommended by the Gerstein report, involvement in graduate teaching. At the same time, the Senate approved the creation of a "Diploma for Science Teachers," to be administered by the CCE.[174] Under the direction of Lloyd Duncan, the centre thrived, offering non-degree courses on both campuses.

Another important initiative of the later 1960s was the Kenya Project. In October 1969 the Board of Governors approved an agreement between York University and the Canadian International Development Agency (CIDA) whereby the university would provide economic-assessment services, research, and training to the government of Kenya, a former British colony in eastern Africa. By the end of November, York and CIDA had concluded their negotiations, which led to the establishment of a project planning and evaluation unit in the Kenyan Ministry of Economic Planning for a five-year period. Tillo Kuhn of the Economics Department became the first head of the field unit in Kenya, while Andreas Papandreou assumed responsibility for supervising the Kenyan fellows who would come to York.[175] In exile from Greece after that country suffered a military coup in 1967, Papandreou was a charismatic figure who some years later became his country's prime minister. He was cross-appointed in Economics and the Faculty of Administrative Studies; Jim Gillies remembered him as "a wonderful teacher and a wonderful man."[176] The Kenya project was York's first major venture in the international realm. There would be many more.

The university grew quickly in the later 1960s, too quickly, some have said. Brian Dixon commented that, like other Canadian universities, York was forced by rapid expansion to reach out for faculty that, in his view, "we would not have hired if growth had been slower."[177] In order to accommodate the exploding student body on the Keele campus, which approached 12,000 (full and part time) in September 1969, buildings went up at breakneck speed, and scores of new faculty and staff members had to be recruited each year. The hiring process was casual by current standards. Although a measure of central control remained, deans and non-academic administrators had a fairly free hand. Everyone sought to strike deals quickly. The sellers' market in which York was operating, with several new universities having recently opened in Ontario alone, rewarded swift and decisive action. Until 1971, when the academic labour market began to change, prospective university teachers hardly needed to look for jobs. The jobs came looking for them! Furthermore, it was unnecessary to have a doctoral degree in hand. Many of those hired were still working on their PHDs (some never completed them). This is not to say that the appointment procedure was altogether perfunctory. Deans needed to provide the vice-president in charge of academic matters – Gillies until 1968, Dennis Healy after that – with a curriculum vitae and three letters of reference, so that these were available to the president and the Board of Governors, formally responsible for making prospective appointments. This was true even of people with established reputations, such as the historian Ramsay Cook.[178] All the same, the atmosphere of the later 1960s was one that graduate students who took their doctorates after the early 1970s could only dream about with justified envy.

Scholars and scientists who were already teaching but wanted a new challenge or a promotion found that it was easy to move. The sociologist Fred Elkin was teaching at the Université de Montréal when Jack Saywell, who had obtained his name from Everett Wilson at the University of North Carolina, wrote in the fall of 1963 to ask whether he might be interested in coming to York. Saywell, "young and very dynamic," came to Montreal to have lunch with him and then invited him to a meeting in Toronto with the other associate dean, Edward Pattullo, and Dan Rossides of the Sociology and Anthropology Department. The upshot was that Elkin accepted an offer to become chairman of Sociology and Anthropology. "It was new, and I would be coming as chairman, and there was the challenge of building a department because there was hardly anybody here."[179] Elkin in turn recruited Thelma McCormack, whom he had met at McGill when he taught there before 1962.

Another sociologist, John O'Neill, who was teaching at Stanford, arrived in 1964 on Saywell's urging. York "intrigued" him, he recalled: "Jack collected an original faculty in arts, with a very creative tension between interdisciplinarity and the disciplines."[180] Gordon Darroch was completing his doctorate in sociology at Duke University when Ted Mann, who chaired the Atkinson College Sociology Department, approached him in 1967. Darroch was from Toronto and liked what he heard about York, but he did not care to teach in the evenings. So he got in touch with Elkin and was interviewed by him and by Saywell, who asked him sceptically why anybody would want to do quantitative sociology. Darroch

Thelma McCormack began teaching in the Sociology Department in 1964.

remembered that when he started at York he was the only native Canadian in the department: "The rest were all Americans or Brits." This was not surprising, he added. There were few graduate programs in sociology in Canada at the time, and every university was hiring. "Jobs were chasing people, especially Canadians with U.S. degrees," he recalled: he got unsolicited job offers from several Canadian universities.[181]

Virginia Rock was teaching at Michigan State University (MSU) when she attended the 1964 convention of the Modern Languages Association. An acquaintance, the Faulkner scholar James Meriwether, told her that "Michael Millgate was looking for people in English for a new campus of York University." Feeling blocked at MSU, she approached Millgate, who interviewed her informally. All positions were filled, he said, but he would stay in touch. Two months later she got a telegram asking her to come to Toronto for an interview. She met Millgate and Harry Girling, the chairman of English; she also talked with Saywell and Clara Thomas. A job offer soon followed. She liked Millgate, a noted Thomas Hardy and Faulkner scholar who later went to the University of Toronto, and she liked the idea of helping to build a new university.[182] In 1969 she became the master of College E, which soon became Stong College.

By 1964, Kurt Danziger, head of the Department of Psychology at the University of Cape Town, was feeling political pressure because of his opposition to apartheid and started looking for opportunities elsewhere. A friend who had moved to Toronto encouraged him to apply to York. "Mort Appley and Jack Saywell hired me, sight unseen,"[183] he remembered. He arrived in 1965; a year later he became chairman of the York department. Much of his time was taken up by recruiting: "The atmosphere was hectic." Saywell participated in the hiring of senior faculty members, with City Limits, a Yonge Street restaurant at the top of the hill south of Hogg's Hollow, serving as a popular place for interview dinners during which the dean, chairman, graduate director, and a couple of senior members of the department sized up potential recruits. Saywell had veto power over the appointment of associate and full professors; the hiring of more junior faculty members was the concern of the department's executive committee, which consisted of the chairman and full professors such as Neil Agnew, Wesley Coons, and John Gaito.

Arthur Haberman was teaching at Temple University when Sydney Eisen of the Faculty of Arts History Department invited him up in January 1967. Saywell and his associate dean, Willard Piepenburg, took him out to dinner, Haberman remembered, and talked with him about York and about his own interests. When a letter offering him a position arrived two weeks later, Haberman scarcely hesitated. With the war in Vietnam expanding, American campuses were increasingly troubled places. "Canada seemed lovely, York seemed an interesting place," he said, adding: "One of the attractions of York was to be in on the creation."[184] This also influenced another historian, Ramsay Cook. By 1968, having taught at the University of Toronto for nine years, he "needed a change and thought we could do some new things in a graduate program that was to be created" at York.[185] When Saywell, Piepenburg, and Lewis Hertzman, chairman of the History Department, came to his house in January, they found in him an interested

A founding member of the Glendon College English Department, Elizabeth Hopkins was later provost and vice-president (campus relations and student affairs).

listener. He did not meet Ross, he said, but Gillies interviewed him before he got a formal offer.[186]

Ken Carpenter, working on his doctorate in economics at Berkeley, was visiting his parents in Toronto in the summer of 1964 when his mother urged him to apply for a job at York. Although he was not really interested, he secured an interview with George Doxey and James Cutt. "I said some pretty outrageous things about economics," he recalled. Then he decided for family reasons to interrupt his studies and got a second interview. The upshot was that Doxey persuaded Saywell to hire Carpenter even though he had not yet written his comprehensive exams, on the understanding that "I would complete my degree when I could."[187] When he did get a doctorate, it was in art history from the University of London, and the year was 2000. By this time he had been teaching visual arts in the fine arts faculty for many years. York had a "marvellous flexibility" in those early days, he said with a hearty laugh.

The political scientist Harvey Simmons came to York in 1965 *without* an interview. A fellow graduate student from Cornell, Selwyn Ryan, was already at York, having been recruited by Douglas Verney. After Verney became ill, the acting chairman, Harold Kaplan, phoned Simmons. "'Do you want a job?' he asked." Simmons had a job offer from the University of Wisconsin, but he checked with Ryan, who "said that York was a good place."[188] A year later, Simmons suggested to Verney and Kaplan that they approach another Cornell graduate student, Bernard Frolic, who then also joined York.

Elizabeth Hopkins, enrolled as a graduate student in English at Queen's University in 1965–66, decided to look for employment, expecting her theatre experience to be an asset. She wrote to Michael Collie, who had become chair of English at York; he forwarded her letter to Escott Reid at Glendon College. With the assistance of H.S. Harris, Reid was doing the early hiring for Glendon, and she soon got a letter from him, offering her a job as instructor in English. She remembered that she, Joan McKibbin, also in English, and Monique Nemni in the French Department were the first women taken on to the Glendon College faculty.[189]

Robert Fothergill was a graduate student in English at the University of Toronto when he applied for a job at Atkinson College in 1966. The person who hired him was Donald Theall, who was briefly chairman of English at Atkinson before he quarrelled with the dean, Del Smyth, and went on to teach at McGill (later he was president of Trent University).[190] Fothergill had taken an M.Phil. at Toronto, a degree that was intended to get students through graduate school and into teaching jobs more expeditiously than the PHD. Later, however, he did take a doctorate.

Christopher Innes, who spent 1968–69 at the Free University in Berlin, recalled that little was known about York in Europe, but that it was supposed to be "an exciting place with a reputation for encouraging interdisciplinary studies." His job interview took place in Cambridge, England, in the spring of 1969. Because of trouble with his car he arrived late for the meeting, and the interviewers, Michael Collie and Desmond Maxwell, Don Rickerd's successor as master of Winters

College, took him to a pub, where they had lunch. A beer-irrigated conversation followed, and "by the end of the afternoon I knew I had a job."[191]

Bernard Wolf responded to a notice that Brian Bixley, chairman of the Glendon Economics Department, had asked to have posted in the Graduate Department at Yale in the fall of 1967. Bixley invited him to visit Toronto, and Wolf fell in love with the Glendon campus. He also liked the idea of being in a small college that was attached to a larger university (later he transferred to Administrative Studies). And he noted that there was a sweetener: academic immigrants did not have to pay income tax for the first eighteen months.[192] This was a temporary expedient the federal and provincial governments had adopted to facilitate academic recruiting abroad. Although Canadian graduate programs were expanding in the 1960s, in most fields they were quite unable to meet the demand for teachers and researchers.

Not only was York hiring at high speed, money was available for other objectives, too. With Jules Heller recovering from a heart attack, Joe Green was acting dean of fine arts in the late winter and spring of 1969. In mid-April he got a phone call from Murray Ross: "Can you spend $250,000 in two weeks?" Green was equal to the challenge. "I went out and bought forty or fifty Super 8 cameras as well as a couple of huge refrigerators that I stocked with film."[193]

The heavy recruitment abroad, where scholars in most disciplines were more readily available than in Canada, produced a backlash in the later 1960s. In 1969 two English professors at Carleton University, Robin Mathews and James Steele, published a book, *The Struggle for Canadian Universities: A Dossier,* in which they asserted that academic immigrants had come to dominate the humanities and social-science departments in many Canadian universities, and that this posed problems both for curriculum content and for future hiring.[194] Part of a wider concern in the late 1960s about the influence of the United States on Canada, the controversy that began at Carleton found an echo at York, which had recruited south of the border at least as heavily as any other English-Canadian university.

Joe Green remembered an "awkward moment" during the reception at which Heller was introduced to the Toronto arts community. Someone asked why York could not have hired a Canadian as dean. "Signy Eaton said: 'We couldn't find one who had a PHD.'"[195] This was more an excuse than anything else, Green said, and it seemed to convince nobody. The incident passed, but the issue did not go away.

In early 1969 *Excalibur* carried an article on the "Americanization of York," complete with a photo that showed the raising of the American flag over the campus in a fashion reminiscent of the iconic photo of the raising of the flag over Iwo Jima during the Second World War.[196] A year later, an *Excalibur* article claimed that "Canada is a whore for Captain America," called for the resignation of Saywell, held responsible for the hiring of "too many" Americans, and demanded the adoption of more Canadian content in courses as well as more courses focused on Canada.[197] During the year that followed, the issue became a topic of interest to the Council of York Students Federation (CYSF). Its president in 1970–71 was Paul Axelrod, who recalled decades later that anti-Americanism

President of the York Student Federation in 1970–71, Paul Axelrod took a PHD in history and in time became dean of education.

was a significant feature of the student movement at York and elsewhere in Canada at the time.[198] A key concern was to publicize what proportion of York's new appointments was non-Canadian: 57 per cent in 1970 and 55 per cent in 1971 according to *Excalibur*, using data supplied to the York Senate.[199] Presumably this was a problem of some kind, but what precisely its nature was and how it should be solved were occasions for debate and sometimes noisy disagreement.

A landmark in that debate was a book edited by Ian Lumsden, an Atkinson College political scientist, which examined and criticized "the Americanization of Canada" in a number of areas of the economy and society. One of the essays was by Mathews and Steele: "The Universities: Takeover of the Mind."[200] The scholars contributing to the volume included several from York: Irving Abella, the political scientists Neal Wood and Ellen Meiksins Wood (both Americans but on the political left), and Lumsden himself. Two other contributors joined the Atkinson College faculty soon afterwards, the political scientists Daniel Drache and James Laxer.

Interviewed more than thirty years later, several faculty members mentioned that they had been troubled or annoyed by what Thelma McCormack saw as

"a deliberate rejection of foreign influences."[201] Arthur Haberman said that by 1970 anti-Americanism had become disagreeably noticeable. He was stunned when a colleague described him as "part of the American colonial invasion." After careful thought he decided to ignore the comment, and he recalled that by the mid-1970s anti-American sentiment seemed to have passed.[202] Joe Green remembered with wry amusement that his election to the Fine Arts deanship in 1973 led a rival to berate the Faculty Council for having chosen an American.[203] It also prompted a couple of letters of complaint to the president of the university and to the Faculty Association.[204]

Some of the newcomers saw merit in the criticism that they knew too little of Canadian life. There were significant issues of where one published, and where one's network of scholarly colleagues was, Michael Lanphier said.[205] He did not feel threatened by anti-Americanism, though, and he did not engage in the debate, which he thought would go nowhere. Bernie Wolf, teaching the introductory course in economics in his first year, was dismayed to find how little he knew about Canada, so that he had no Canadian examples to offer. In order "to teach the course properly," he quickly set out to learn as much as possible about the Canadian economy.[206] This aspect of the matter influenced a number of the critics, who feared that Canadian topics in fields like history, literature, and the social sciences were getting short shrift from scholars whose background was in the United States or the United Kingdom or who had received most of their education there. This, Axelrod wrote, was a more important issue than that of national origin.[207]

For a few years the issue agitated the academic world, but interest in it was declining by 1973. The Canadian Association of University Teachers (CAUT) tried to frame a policy on the "Canadianization" of the universities, including preferential hiring of Canadians and landed immigrants, but faculty associations as well as universities were divided on the issue. Many professors and academic administrators, Canadians as well as immigrants, thought that adopting any policy at all would be a mistake. (When I briefly served as chair of the CAUT's ad hoc committee on Canadianization and the university in 1974, I became fully aware how divided the professoriate was. The 1974 CAUT national council meeting rejected our report, which counselled preferential hiring. Not until 1977 did a diluted version pass.[208]) Eventually the Canadian government introduced a regulation governing recruitment in most fields. Canadians and landed immigrants had to be given priority, and a second-tier search among other candidates was permitted only if no qualified first-tier candidates were judged to have applied.

Organized student activities began slowly on the Keele campus, but by 1966 students had a widening range of clubs and societies open to them. Many sports got a shot in the arm when the Tait McKenzie Physical Education Centre opened in December 1966. Its swimming pool, squash courts, and gymnasia soon had many users.

In 1967 Bryce Taylor succeeded Howard Langille as athletic director as well as first chair of the Department of Physical Education. By this time, York sports teams as well as individuals were already distinguishing themselves.[209] Murray

LEFT Ontario-Quebec championship-winning women's badminton team, 1968. Left to right: Sue Ward, Bev Pugh, Mary Lyons (coach), Nancy Green, Kathy Troyer.

RIGHT Men's basketball team, 1965. Left to right, front row: Warren Major, Nick Christian, Peter Clute, Ed Friedman, Jim Forsyth; back row: Ron Lieberman, Brian Lennox, John Lennox, Alan Young, Tom Hooper, Chuck Gordon, Arthur Johnson (coach).

Young, an honours student in political science from 1965 to 1969, "was the king-pin of the University's swim team during those four years." The team captured three consecutive Ontario Inter-Athletic Association (OIAA) championships, starting in 1967. At the 1966–67 Canadian Interuniversity Athletic Union (CIAU) swimming finals, Young "finished first in the men's 500 metre freestyle event and was selected to the CIAU All-Canadian team."[210] Joan Featherstonehaugh, who graduated with an honours history degree in 1968, won three gold medals at the 1967–68 Ontario-Quebec Women's Interuniversity Athletic Association (OQWIAA) synchronized swim championships and also won a silver medal in the Canadian University Games held in Edmonton in 1967. In 1967–68 the men's and women's badminton teams, and the men's volleyball team, were victorious at the provincial level, and the volleyball team repeated in 1968–69 and 1969–70.

Other teams to win conference titles in 1968–69 and 1969–70 included women's gymnastics, synchronized swimming, and tennis, as well as men's swimming and tennis; in addition, fencing, squash, and skiing championships were secured in the latter year. Nancy Green anchored the women's tennis team and won the singles championship. David M. Smith, a student first in mathematics and then in business administration, "led York's cross-country team to gold in the OIAA championships in 1967 through 1970, finishing first individually each year."[211] Smith also won the individual title at the CIAU cross-country meet in 1968 and again in 1970, when he had returned to York to pursue an MBA degree. Along with Bryce Taylor, Featherstonehaugh, Smith, and Young were the first athletes to be inducted into the York University Sports Hall of Fame in 1980.

Bill Purcell, a Toronto firefighter and a former professional hockey player, began coaching the men's hockey team in his spare time in 1963.[212] The team moved from the outdoor rink at Glendon to the Keele campus in 1968, the new indoor rink having opened in September. Known for a time as the Jolly Millers in honour of the pub in Hogg's Hollow, in 1969 the team got a new name, the Yeomen. Women's teams were now known as the Yeowomen.

In 1967–68 the men's hockey team finished in second place in the OIAA league. A year later, York, now reinforced by players from Osgoode Hall Law School, scored its first victory over the University of Toronto Varsity Blues. Greater success followed in 1969–70. Both Purcell and one of his star players, Murray Stroud, remembered it as a magical year. Stroud, a centre who had been MVP with the Varsity Blues the year before, volunteered for the York team, along with several other Osgoode students. The only position at which the team was weak was goalie. "I had to wait and see what would turn up," Purcell said. What turned up was a student who had been goalie on a ball hockey team, Bill Holden. He did not even have goalie skates, Purcell recalled, but "he could stand up, and he had great hand-eye coordination." A couple of people, former goalie Mert Prophet among them, worked with Holden, "and he did just fine." Stroud commented that "Purcell was an excellent coach; he brought us together as a team."[213]

The Yeomen won ten straight league games and went to the national championships. "In the first game, against the Saint Mary's Huskies, we ran into a hot goalie, while Bill had his worst game of the season," Stroud said: "We lost 4–1. We wouldn't have lost to Saint Mary's a second time." The team did not lose another game and won the consolation final. Stroud played one more year, in 1970–71, when the Yeomen were again very strong. Remembering with pleasure fellow players like Roger Gallipeau, Dave Kosay, John Robb, and Bruce Penny, Stroud said: "I enjoyed my time at York."[214] Purcell remembered the friendships he made, working with "a great bunch of guys."[215] In 1972 he gave way, with some regret, to a full-time coach, Dave Chambers, who in 1985 led the team to a national title.

Football was slower to take off than hockey, and success proved much harder to achieve. By 1968, a team, the Windigos, had been formed. Its first game was a "friendly" against a team from Laurentian University. The Windigos lost. In 1969 the renamed Yeomen joined the OIAA – in 1971 it became the Ontario Universities Athletic Association (OUAA) – but several years would pass before they gained their first victory on the field.

Intramural sports had many more participants than interuniversity sports. Starting in 1966, the colleges played for the York Torch in a range of sports. For five years Glendon College won the trophy handily, but in 1971, to the delight of self-described sports fanatic and Stong College partisan Steve Dranitsaris, Stong beat out Glendon. He laughed as he recalled that, early on, the Stong hockey

LEFT The York Yeomen football team, established in 1969, struggled for years to become competitive.

RIGHT Glendon faculty men's soccer team, 1969. Left to right, front row: Roger LeBras, Gilbert Dussuyer, Lewis Rosen, Roger Gannon, Orest Kruhlak; back row: Rick Schultz, Dick Tursman, Brian Bixley, Nollaig MacKenzie, Terry Fowler, Pierre Fortier, Michiel Horn, Irving Abella, Alain Baudot, Bob Brough.

team had recruited Gordon Albright of the Atkinson College Mathematics Department, jocularly known as "Leaky," to be the goalie.[216] In 1980 Dranitsaris helped Frank Cosentino, a former Canadian Football League star who had joined the Department of Physical Education, and Carol Wilson to organize the York University Sports Hall of Fame.[217] Nor was Dranitsaris just a sports fan. The classicist Michael Herren remembered him as "such a gung-ho Yorkie that he didn't want to leave."[218] Upon graduation, he became student liaison officer in Stong College; currently he is senior executive officer in the Office of the Vice-President (Finance and Administration).

Especially Glendon was a hotbed of intramural sports in the late 1960s. For example, each of the five houses in Wood Residence fielded a flag-football team. So did the faculty, with the political scientist Orest Kruhlak starring as the quarterback in 1969 and Irving "Golden Hands" Abella as his favourite receiver. When the faculty, many still in their twenties or early thirties and very largely male, fielded a soccer team in the fall of 1969, the historian became "Golden Boots" Abella. These nicknames he owed to a remarkable *Pro Tem* sports journalist, Nick Martin, a history major who peppered his accounts of athletic events with characters of his own invention, among them Viet Squirrel, Captain Bourgeois, the Masked Beaver, and the Serpent of the Don. Asked decades later how he had come to write this way, Martin said that at the time someone at the *Varsity*, the University of Toronto newspaper, was taking an irreverent approach to sports writing, and that he "had adopted the approach after doing it straight for a year [because] it was more fun to write." When readers responded favourably, he felt encouraged to continue.[219]

Student journalism absorbed the excess intellectual energy of many students. The first student newspaper, *Pro Tem*, served both campuses during the transitional year 1965–66, until the founding of *Excalibur* in October 1966 brought an end to this arrangement. Henceforth *Pro Tem* would be the Glendon weekly only. Similarly, the 1966 yearbook, *Janus*, covered both campuses, but it was the last to do so. As it happened, yearbooks ceased to appear altogether within a very few years. At York and everywhere else in the country, students found other uses for their time.

A notable feature of the later 1960s was the increased interest by students in social and political issues and the rise of the student movement. The reasons for these developments were complex.[220] An early manifestation of the increasingly fractious attitude of North American students was the "Free Speech" movement at Berkeley in the fall of 1964. In Canada the opening shot seems to have been a short-lived fees strike at the University of Victoria in the 1965–66 academic year.[221] But it was especially the war in Vietnam that galvanized many students, in Canada as in the United States.

As a member of the International Control Commission (ICC), formed as part of the Geneva Accords that ended French rule in Indo-China and temporarily partitioned Vietnam, Canada was not a belligerent. Some Canadians felt concern, however, about the possibility that Canadian companies were exporting war-related commodities to the United States, or about the role that Canada was playing in the ICC. By 1966, anti-war sentiment was growing in the United

States, especially on the campuses, and this was bound to have an effect in Canadian universities, especially since some of the U.S. professors being hired were critical of the American presence in Vietnam. Rick Schultz, who studied political science, remembered that war protesters, as well as students demanding universal access to higher education, greeted Prime Minister Pearson when he officially opened Glendon College in October 1966. Murray Ross had hoped to prevent a demonstration by bringing police on campus, Schultz said, but the Student Council had strenuously opposed this, and Escott Reid had sided with the students.[222] In December 1966 a panel discussion on how to end the war in Vietnam took place in Founders College. The founding of the York Committee to End the War in Vietnam followed in February 1967. Three days of debates on the Vietnam War took place on the first weekend in April, bringing twenty debating teams from Canada and the United States to the campus, as well as a team from the University of Moscow.[223]

In late 1967 some students demanded that Hawker Siddeley, a military contractor, be banned from recruiting on campus; others signed a petition opposing such a ban.[224] The recruiters nevertheless came to the campus, and, although they were met by a picket line consisting of war protesters, there was no direct interference. The issue dragged on for a year. In the late fall of 1968 Henry Best, director of student services, asked Hawker Siddeley to postpone its visit until student opinion could be ascertained through a referendum.[225] This took place on 10 December 1968 and the result surprised some observers: the vote was 1,226 to 294 in favour of campus recruitment by military contractors.[226]

Opposition to the war found a different form at Glendon. In February 1969 the Student Council decided to test the attitude of Canadian border guards to deserters from the U.S. armed forces. By this time "draft dodgers," young men escaping military service, often because they had no wish to serve in Vietnam, were increasingly numerous in Canada. Their passage into the country was relatively uncomplicated, but that was not true for deserters. Bob Waller remembered that he, Graham Muir, John Thompson, Jim Weston, and Chris Wilson went into the United States and, carrying the papers of a U.S. Air Force deserter, approached five different border crossings at much the same time. Masterminded by Larry Goldstein, a Keele-campus student in history and philosophy, the scheme was intended to show that the Canadian immigration authorities were "conniving" with the Americans, and in this they believed they were successful. All five were refused entry into Canada.[227] The incident gained some newspaper attention and prompted a Toronto *Star* editorial pointing out that young Americans seeking to escape the draft faced discriminatory policies in Canada.[228]

An unknown number of draft dodgers entered York as students. Earle Nestmann was one. A physician's son from West Virginia and a graduate of Marietta College in Ohio, he was set to begin graduate studies in biology at the University of Michigan in September 1968 when he received a notice to report for military service. He and his wife scarcely hesitated. August found them in Toronto, and Nestmann started looking for a place to continue his studies. At the University of Toronto, people were "courteous but not particularly helpful," he recalled. It was otherwise at York, where David Fowle, Michael Boyer, Robert Haynes, and

Robert Winters, a contestant for the leadership of the federal Liberal Party in 1968, talks with a student protester at the official opening of Winters College.

Barry Loughton in the Department of Biology were "interested in me and welcoming," allowing him to enter the graduate program, although he had to make up some courses in science, and, in Fowle's case, giving him some part-time work to do. He remembered that he enjoyed talking with the professors, mentioning by name Haynes, Brian Colman, David Logan, Peter Moens, Sal Saleuddin, and James Tait.[229]

Initially Haynes was Nestmann's supervisor. Haynes was very impressive – "he was one of the brightest people I ever met" – but after Ruth Hill arrived from Columbia and immediately got her laboratory set up, Nestmann started working on DNA repair under her supervision. Having completed his MSC in 1971, he began his PHD, still under Hill's supervision, in the field of mutagenesis. In November 1973 Hill had a stroke, dying a few days later. Nestmann was in shock: "She was a wonderful supervisor; her passing was a great loss." He took over a course she had been teaching, and this slowed him down, but he completed his dissertation under Haynes's supervision in 1974. York had its downside, he remembered. It was "isolated, desolate, and sterile; walking to the Farquharson Building from one of the outer parking lots in the winter was not a happy experience." Moreover, "the architecture was not exactly charming." On the other hand, the human environment was great: "York was new and growing, and there was a sense of excitement and opportunity."[230] He stayed in Canada and eventually became active in the Alumni Association.

The war in Vietnam was only one source of unrest. Students in more than one country were forging a critique of society that cast the universities as servants of the corporations and more particularly of a "military-industrial complex." The year 1968 witnessed serious disturbances especially among students in France and Germany, and also on some American and a few Canadian campuses. However, students at the Keele campus were generally calm, though there was a successful protest during the fall against a single compulsory Modes of Reasoning course. "That was John Yolton's idea," John McFarland remembered, referring to the chair of the Philosophy Department who thought that teaching a course analogous to the introductory courses taught in humanities and social science made good sense. Students disagreed. McFarland, who was in charge of the course, lectured in the largest room in Stedman Hall, with the overflow accommodated in smaller rooms equipped with closed-circuit television. This proved unsatisfactory. "The thing was pretty close to being a disaster," he said.[231] Students protested, and early in 1969 Jack Saywell agreed to the abandonment of an introductory course in Modes and the establishment of college tutorials, which could be taken as a course for credit. Other than this, the main evidence of student unrest was a protest against "faculty only" parking signs, held to be a form of social injustice.[232] When Christopher Innes started teaching in September, he found York's students "very docile" compared with those at the Free University of Berlin, where he had spent the 1968–69 academic year.[233]

If the Keele campus largely escaped student agitation in 1968, this was not true of Glendon. In late August the Student Council launched an ambitious campaign called Liber-Action 68, intended "to generate an intellectual confrontation between what presently exists at the College and what we feel the College should

Liber-Action, September 1968. Left to right: H.S. Harris, Glendon College academic dean, Stephen Langdon, University of Toronto student leader, Jim Park, Glendon College Student Union president, and the poet Dennis Lee, representing Rochdale College, an experiment in student-run alternative education and cooperative living on Bloor Street (now the Senator David A. Croll Apartments).

become."[234] "A University Is for People" was the title of the manifesto issued in September. Critical of the college and of higher education in general, the document proposed a thoroughgoing reorganization of college governance, major changes in the organization of the curriculum and of courses, the elimination of grading, the "removal of all symbols of social stratification in the college," and the augmentation of bilingualism.[235] This sounded stirring to socially committed students at Glendon and on the Keele campus as well. "There was nothing like Liber-Action at York main," Paul Axelrod said somewhat wistfully.[236]

The manifesto's rhetoric may have been confrontational, but Liber-Action was on the whole good-natured. Student leaders like Glen Williams and Student Council president Jim Park were generally reasonable and not discourteous. The three students on Faculty Council, David Copp, Kathy Hamilton, and Graham Muir, sounded at least as sensible as members of the faculty. As for the proposals for change, most of them went nowhere. This was partly because most students were not committed to change in the way members of the Student Council and their supporters were. "Liber-Action meant nothing to me," Julie Drexler said: "it was a resident-student thing."[237] Although he lived in residence, David Cole declined to get involved.[238] Another resident student, Lesley Lewis, hardly remembered Liber-Action, though she did recall working on a campaign to get a fellow Glendon student, Ron Kanter, into the York Senate.[239] Rives Dalley, who entered the college that September, was intrigued but also confused by the appeals from Liber-Action's organizers not to sign up for courses but to hold back and audit various courses instead, registering only when students thought they had found the right ones. "I did audit a couple," she recalled, "but I was petrified that I wouldn't get the courses I wanted, so I registered anyway."[240]

At least as important as the disengagement of many students was that Glendon formed part of the larger university. Student activists no doubt got tired of hearing the academic dean, H.S. Harris, intone: "I do not think Senate will care for that." But he was right.

Then, too, Reid and Harris reacted calmly and quickly removed the most obvious "symbols of social stratification," ending the separation of washrooms for faculty/staff and students and eliminating high table, where servers waited on faculty. The latter would save the college hundreds of dollars annually, Glendon's executive officer, Victor Berg, said with a pleased smirk. (Students wonder to this day why there are two women's washrooms side by side on the second floor of York Hall's main wing. Incredulity has invariably greeted my explanation.) It helped, too, that the faculty were mostly young and showed some sympathy for student concerns. Finally, that winter the college was united in self-defence by rumours, quickly denied by Ross and the Board of Governors, that the board was seeking to turn the Glendon campus to another use.[241]

Possibly the last hurrah of Liber-Action took place at convocation in late May 1969, held outside in the quadrangle. Ruth Mesbur, who graduated that year, remembered it as a blisteringly hot day. At some point during the ceremony, several students, led by Bob McGaw, walked in with large pieces of watermelon, which they presented to the graduating students. The references were lost on few of the participants: Jerry Farber's 1967 essay "The Student as Nigger" (it was later expanded into a book), and the 1968 book by Pierre Vallières, *Nègres blancs d'Amérique: autobiographie précoce d'un 'terroriste' québécois*, which was well known among Glendon's bilingual radicals.[242] Mesbur had not been part of Liber-Action, and she thought the incident was amusing more than anything else. "And I enjoyed the cool watermelon."[243]

Liber-Action had some significant long-range results. It facilitated the expansion of student representation on the Faculty Council and its committees, and it gave added impetus to the hiring of bilingual faculty. Albert Tucker, for example, who became chairman of History in 1968, was moved to insist that new appointments to the department, starting with Ian Gentles in 1969, be bilingual.[244] His predecessor, Edgar McInnis, had been dubious about Escott Reid's project and failed to mention bilingualism when he offered Irving Abella a position.[245] (Nor did he mention bilingualism when he hired me.) Tucker took a different tack, both as chairman and as principal.

By 1969, some students on the Keele campus were becoming feistier. In September a group calling itself the York Student Movement (YSM) disrupted a teach-in on "The Faces of Toronto" in Winters College. Among the speakers were Jack Saywell and Phil Givens, a Liberal MP and an ex-mayor of Toronto. A YSM member, Andy Stanley, interrupted Givens and effectively forced him to abandon his talk. Saywell walked out in disgust, leaving members of the YSM to conduct the meeting. A YSM spokesperson reportedly expressed the hope that "in the weeks to come students would become less concerned with marks and listening to professors and more concerned with organizing themselves to deal with people's real problems."[246] Two months later, the YSM joined the Committee to End the War in Vietnam and the Young Socialists in holding a teach-in on the Vietnam War in the Winters College dining hall. *Excalibur* reported that the dining hall was packed and that classes were poorly attended on that day.[247]

Unhappiness with two introductory natural-science courses on the Keele campus led to student unrest in the Faculty of Arts in 1970 and 1971. Late in 1971, students founded a Natural Science Course Union whose objective was to do away with compulsory introductory courses. In retrospect, Harold Schiff conceded that the unhappy students had a point. The attempts at interdisciplinary teaching "did not work," he said. The faculty members teaching the courses came from "traditional backgrounds," and, although they "might pay lip service to interdisciplinarity, they hankered after their own departments."[248] The outcome of the protest was greater choice for students in their natural-science courses.

Protest also greeted the appearance of the report of the Presidential Committee on Rights and Responsibilities in the fall of 1969. Appointed in February 1968 in response to the student protest against on-campus recruiting by military contractors, but also as a reaction to growing student unrest that had begun with the "Free Speech" movement at the University of California in 1964, the committee included representatives from the Board of Governors, the faculty, and the students. Its chairman was Justice Bora Laskin, who was also the principal author of its report.[249] It made eighty-two recommendations, of which the first was probably the most momentous: "The *in loco parentis* relationship of the University to the student should be abandoned."[250] The university had become a community of faculty and students, in which internal courts should deal with misconduct. The report rejected a detailed code of conduct, but it did enunciate some general standards "such as the duty to refrain from destruction of property, from invasion of premises, from violence and from incitement of violence, from assault or threat of assault, from unjustified interference with the conduct of classes or of meetings, from obstruction of passage of others, and from obstruction of ingress to or egress from campus buildings."[251] No specific penalties were stated. Offences might be dealt with by an internal tribunal or by the courts of the land, or both, depending on the circumstances.

Reactions to the report were mixed. The Faculty Association expressed misgivings,[252] and when Paul Axelrod read it, he decided to make opposition to it the launching pad for his campaign to become president of the York Student Federation.[253] Upon his election, he wrote what he later sarcastically referred to as "my modest 75 page response ... to the Laskin Report," adding: "I cringe a bit when I think of it."[254] His report proposed a thoroughgoing reform of university government before York tackled the question of disciplining students for alleged disruptions of the university's activities. Among other things, he called for openness in decision making, equality in the classroom, and a unicameral governing body in which faculty, students, and community representatives would each constitute a third. He was particularly critical of the Board of Governors for its narrow socio-economic base, its self-selection and self-perpetuation, and its continued insistence on meeting privately.[255]

By this time, student participation in university governance was a fact, although it did not extend nearly far enough for student leaders like Axelrod, "a pain-in-the-ass radical" as he called himself much later (in time he would become the dean of education at York).[256] One recommendation of the 1966 report by Sir James Duff and Robert O. Berdahl on university government, which had been commissioned by the CAUT and the Association of Universities and Colleges in Canada, was that students should have representation on the academic decision-making body.[257] A Senate committee established to study the recommendations of the report recommended early in 1969 that the number of students on Senate and faculty councils be increased. As a consequence, the number of student senators was increased to ten for the 1969–70 session. Another sign of the times was a change in the search committee for a new president that the board and Senate executive committees put together after Murray Ross announced his retirement. In April 1969 the Board of Governors recommended the addition of three students to the committee. Originally there had been none.[258]

The influence of students on the governance of York and its faculties was still small, but it was growing. The influence of the faculty was growing, too. Another one of the Duff-Berdahl recommendations was that faculty members should have representation on governing boards, something not a few Canadian academics had been calling for since the late 1950s.[259] The Board of Governors did not embrace this proposed innovation hastily, but in April 1969 two faculty members joined the board – Eli Mandel and Ivan Feltham.[260]

In 1969 Douglas Verney contributed an article to the *Review of Politics* whose subject was York. He analysed its early growth and development in the context of the rapid growth of Canadian higher education in the 1960s, and compared its experience with that of Simon Fraser University in Burnaby, British Columbia, founded a few years after York. Even though Canada had no Vietnam and no black ghettoes, Canadian university problems, Verney demonstrated, were very similar to those experienced in the United States, particularly with respect to the issue of student power. "We are heirs of the great universities of Europe and the United States. And increasingly we find ourselves heirs of Cromwell, Jefferson, Robespierre, Lenin, Mao, Castro, and above all of Mario Savio and his friends at Berkeley in 1964."[261]

Verney concluded his article on a note of cautious optimism. The challenges students were making to received ideas would continue, he wrote. But he thought it possible that "calmer counsels will ultimately prevail." Though he looked to the future "with some trepidation," he admitted that the experience of dealing with student reformers had been "as exhilarating as it has been humiliating." Facing "the prospect of being considered obsolescent by the young" was disconcerting. "But it has been exhilarating in that never have I met such lively students, eager for me to read and enjoy the books that have stimulated them, interested in knowing my gut reaction to arguments and events, and willing patiently to explain to me how we can learn together."[262] As it happened, the radical student movement was already in decline by the time Verney's article appeared.[263] But at York as in other universities it had long-lasting effects, notably in the feminist and environmentalist movements and in the increased part that students, and faculty, played in university governance.

York's cultural life continued to flourish, on both campuses. Continuity was evident in the Frank Gerstein lectures. In 1966 they focused on government-university relations, with a key contribution made by William G. Davis, Ontario's minister of education (and a future premier of the province). The five questions he posed implied that Ontario universities were not always using their resources wisely. First, "have our universities given full recognition to the need for economy and taken steps to practise it?" Second, "should boards of governors launch new programs and projects without assurance of the necessary government funds to support them?" Third, "can universities curtail the non-constructive aspects of competitiveness that now prevail among them?" Fourth, "is there a willingness on the part of individual institutions to subordinate their individual ambitions if society, as a whole, would be better served by such action?" Fifth and last, "can we expect the universities of this province to work in close co-operation with other institutions at the post-secondary level?"[264]

Davis did not challenge the economic benefits of the money Ontario was spending on higher education. Only a year earlier, the Economic Council of Canada had argued in its *Second Annual Review* that both the public and private returns on investment in higher education were substantial. Costs were clearly becoming a cause for concern, though. Davis's address was an indication that the provincial government wanted to get "more bang for the post-secondary buck" and that it was hoping for cooperation between the universities and the recently established Colleges of Applied Arts and Technology (CAATs). The speech was a harbinger of the Commission on Post-Secondary Education in Ontario, established in 1969, and of the gradually shorter rations for the universities that came into effect after 1968.

The 1967 Gerstein lectures, held in March and April, examined the relationship between science and the university. The lectures dealt with "The University and the New Intellectual Environment" in 1968 and with "The City and the University" in 1969. That same year, the so-called Learned Societies met at York in early June. For a week, more than five thousand humanists and social scien-

Art exhibit, Keele campus, 1969.

tists from all over Canada and from several other countries wandered around a campus that the great majority of them had never seen before, trying, not always successfully, to find their way through the college complex, filing into seminar rooms and lecture halls, and listening to academic papers of varying degrees of interest. If their taste ran to the visual arts, they were able to admire an exhibition of "American Art in the Sixties," assembled by York's curator, Michael Greenwood, and featuring mostly graphic works by artists like Josef Albers, Roy Lichtenstein, Louise Nevelson, Kenneth Noland, Jules Olitski, Frank Stella, and Andy Warhol.[265] Ken Carpenter, who lent a small Olitski painting to the exhibition, remembered it as "an excellent show."[266]

The Gerstein lectures drew good audiences. So did the student-run conferences of the later 1960s. In addition to the already mentioned debate on the Vietnam War, the "Quebec: Year Eight" forum held at Glendon College in November 1967 received national media coverage and led to the publication of the conference proceedings by the CBC.[267] Its success led to another well-attended Glendon forum in the fall of 1968. Again organized by students, with Bob McGaw as the committee coordinator, it was called "The Canadians" and focused on the experiences and condition of Canada's aboriginal peoples. A first stage began in mid-September and prepared students for the conference by means of films and lectures, while the conference itself ran for three days in late October and attracted participants from the Department of Indian Affairs and the Indian-Eskimo Association, as well as leading members of various aboriginal groups, among them Tony Antoine, Harold Cardinal, Andrew Delisle, Carol Lavallee, and Harold Staats. It, too, gained media attention as well as a *Globe and Mail* editorial praising the forum.[268] Rives Dalley remembered that, although she was a freshman, she "really became involved in the organization of that conference" and found the experience "fascinating." She was particularly impressed by Cardinal.[269]

The third and final student-organized forum, "The Year of the Barricade," an examination and celebration of the student movement, took place at Glendon in October 1969. This was the most controversial of the three, and it received more media coverage than the other two combined. Asked in late 1968 to approve the use of university property for the forum, some members of the Board of Governors expressed "doubts about the benefit to be obtained from the holding of [the] proposed forum."[270] Perhaps they were worried about the negative publicity it might generate. If so, they may have felt justified when they read that "leaders of the fast-growing women's movement" had asserted that "the traditional family structure must be destroyed if women are to be truly free,"[271] yet perhaps a bit relieved when a noted neo-Marxist academic came in for the loudest heckling. A panel on radicalism and the university included C.B. Macpherson, a University of Toronto political theorist whose left-wing credentials seemed beyond reproach. Nevertheless, his assertion that modern universities could be "centres of independent criticism and analysis" met with jeers and catcalls.[272] One student accused him of being, at bottom, no more than an apologist for capitalist and reactionary social forces in Canada! (Sitting beside me on the floor of the Old Dining Hall, Escott Reid whispered: "Michiel, please pinch me. I want to make sure that I'm not dreaming.")

At the end of the conference, about two hundred of the participants picketed the offices of the *Globe and Mail* to protest the newspaper's "campaign of hysteria against the Quebec people." The story that appeared in the newspaper made much of the fact that several of the student leaders were from abroad.[273]

Conferences on the Keele campus at this time were less controversial. In the spring of 1970 College E, soon to be named Stong College in honour of the pioneer who opened up the land along Steeles Avenue west of Keele, sponsored the first James Joyce seminar in Canada as part of the York 10 celebrations.[274] Also part of those celebrations, which used the registration of the first students in 1960 rather than the first York University Act as York's starting date, were the 1970 Gerstein lectures, organized by Lionel Rubinoff. The first four took place in March, with "Tradition and Revolution" the subject. Among the speakers were the Austrian-born educational reformer Ivan Illich, then domiciled in Mexico, and McMaster University's George Grant, author of the influential book *Lament for a Nation: The Defeat of Canadian Nationalism* (1965).

Two weeks later, as its contribution to the York 10 celebrations, Vanier College held a two-day conference on French Canada with the title "Canadians-Canadiens: Two Cultures or Two Nations?" Claude Ryan, Jean-Paul Desbiens, Claude-Armand Sheppard, John Porter, Mavor Moore, and Keith Spicer presented papers offering a French- or English-Canadian perspective on topics such as "The State Versus the Individual" and "Culture and the Constitution."[275] The main celebration, held during the last week of May 1970, was a university-wide festival. Steve Dranitsaris, who had just completed first year, got a job helping to organize York 10. He remembered it as "one big party."[276] An "open house" brought many curious people to the Keele campus. Those with an interest in sculpture had an opportunity to admire the maquette of the Alexander Calder stabile created for Expo '67 in Montreal, donated to York by the International Nickel Company of Canada

The Murray G. Ross Humanities and Social Sciences Building under construction.

and placed near the entrance to the Burton auditorium. An international squash tournament took place in the Tait McKenzie Physical Education Centre, three exhibitions were open to the public, a collection of rare bibles was on display in Central Square, which had opened in 1969, and the Department of Instructional Aid Resources (DIAR) showed a film its staff had produced.[277]

An extension of the 1970 Gerstein lectures took place from 26 to 28 May. Harold Taylor, the ex-president of Sarah Lawrence College, spoke about "The Student Revolution," and Jacob Bronowski of the Salk Institute for Biological Studies in San Diego lectured on "Protest and Prospect." On the final day a panel discussion took place, with Lord James of Rusholme also participating and Rubinoff in the chair.[278] As was the custom, the lectures later appeared in printed form.[279]

A different kind of conference took place in August 1970, when the Canadian Federation of University Women met on the Keele campus. Organized by the University Women's Club of North York (UWCNY), the conference brought 450 women to the campus as well as a hundred native people. Barbara McNutt, long the archivist of the UWCNY, recalled that it attracted a good deal of publicity for York.[280] The women's club had taken an interest in the university from the outset, funding scholarships and bursaries and donating books to the library.

The convocation ceremonies were part of the Year 10 celebrations. Receiving degrees *honoris causa* at the Keele campus convocation on 29 May – the Glendon convocation was a day later, the Osgoode convocation a week later – were Lord James of Rusholme, Ralph Bunche, under-secretary general of the United Nations and a Nobel Peace Prize laureate, and the actress Kate Reid. After the convocation, the Ross Humanities and Social Sciences Building and the adjacent Amphitheatre were officially opened.[281] (Built in the architectural style known as brutalism, the Ross Building soon gained the nicknames "Ministry of Love" and "Ministry of Truth," used whimsically by students acquainted with George Orwell's *Nineteen eighty-four*.) It must have seemed appropriate that Ralph Lamoureux had won the university's first Rhodes Scholarship in 1969, the tenth anniversary of the first York University Act. In spite of difficulties in the recent past, the general mood was upbeat. York had passed through what might be called its institutional adolescence and seemed to be coming of age.

The spirit of York 10 was one of celebration, at times even exuberance. It masked for a while the ill feeling created by a struggle over the succession to the presidency which disturbed the university from the fall of 1969 into the spring of 1970. Some of the ill feeling lingered, however, and it would complicate York's affairs two years later, when the institution entered a major budgetary crisis. This in turn led to an event at that time unique in Canadian university history. At the end of 1972, York's deans, in full revolt against President David Slater, effectively forced the Board of Governors to secure his resignation.

To this day, the crisis of 1972–73 remains the most dramatic and disruptive episode in York's history, one that threatened to push the university into chaos. It undermined the confidence fostered by the growth of the 1960s and prompted searching questions about York's future. It was the most serious of the shocks that the institution sustained in the 1970s and 1980s, but there were others. And yet it was also a period in which the institution successfully met significant challenges and in which it accomplished much.

Early in 1969 Murray Ross announced his retirement, effective 30 June 1970. Consultation between the board and Senate executive committees led to the nomination of a six-person search committee charged with finding a successor, three each from the board and Senate.[1] This prompted student criticism, and in April the board proposed a reconstituted search committee, consisting of three representatives each from the board, Senate, and student body, and one from the York University Faculty Association. The committee met for the first time on 1 May 1969, with Justice Bora Laskin in the chair and Bill Farr as secretary. Joining Laskin as board representatives were Bertrand Gerstein and A.J. (Pete) Little. Michael Creal, Harold Schiff, and Albert Tucker represented the Senate; the student members were David Coombs, Paul Koster, and Michael Woolnough. Wesley Coons represented Y U F A.[2]

"The almost surreal misadventures of this tortured search process," Laskin's biographer has written, "provide a perfect microcosm of academic life in the later 1960s."[3] While the 1959 York University Act gave the Board of Governors power to appoint the president, the 1965 act added the phrase "after consultation with the Senate." What this would mean in practice went unstated, and no clear consensus developed in the course of the search as to the full implications of this consultation, although the board and Senate executive committees did reach a measure of agreement in early December. Partly as a result of the lack of clarity, the search turned into a power struggle between the board and Senate.

The Senate was the chief academic decision-making body, dominated numerically by faculty members. Its membership, totalling 150, consisted of senior professors and administrators serving ex officio, a number of academics elected by faculty councils, a handful of student senators elected by the student body, two members of the Board of Governors, and several representatives of outside agencies. Although the Senate was hardly dominated by social or political radicals, some of its members did hope to expand its power at the expense of that of the board, particularly when the matter at issue was the selection of a new president. This was part of a growing tendency among Canadian academics in the 1960s to challenge the role of lay people, especially businessmen, in governing the universities.[4]

Suspicion of the businessmen who dominated boards of governors found clearest expression in "The Law of the University Constitution" by Frank Scott, dean of law at McGill University. (In 1976 he received an honorary doctorate of laws from York.) The essay appeared in a 1964 book about university government to which Laskin also contributed. Attitudes and preferences that might be appropriate in the world of business could be "fatal" to a university, Scott wrote. "The special nature of a university cannot be understood except by those who devote their lives to teaching and scholarship, in the same way that the nature of medical practice cannot be comprehended by non-doctors, or the nature of corporate business enterprise by those who have never served in a corporation. Better have scholars running banks than bankers governing scholars."[5]

Few if any academics showed an interest in running banks, but more than a few wanted a bigger role in governing their own universities. Some faculty members at York believed that, as part of an attempt to have the Senate assume an expanded role in running the institution, it should effectively choose the successful candidate by voting for the candidates on the short list proposed by the search committee, with the nod going to the person who enjoyed most Senate support. Board members, on the other hand, wanted to receive a short list, preferably unranked, so that they could choose among the candidates acceptable to the search committee.[6] Student leaders, led by YSF president Paul Koster and student senator John Bosley, argued that the student body should also be asked to express a preference,[7] but this proposal went nowhere.

Many people, including most of the members of the search committee, knew from the outset whom they wanted to succeed Ross. Schiff, the dean of science, said that he realized before the search got under way that "Ross and the board wanted Jim Gillies," the dean of administrative studies, while many faculty

members, including a majority of those in the Senate (and Schiff himself), preferred Jack Saywell, the dean of arts.[8] Tucker, who became principal of Glendon College while the search was going on, believed that "Gillies was recruited from California to succeed Ross" and that "the board wanted Gillies very badly."[9] He contrasted this with "the judgment of many of the senior faculty in Arts that Gillies had never given any indication [that] he would make a president who understood the real academic roots of the university."[10] Creal, who taught humanities in the Faculty of Arts, backed Saywell.[11] Coons, a member of the Arts Psychology Department who was YUFA chairman in 1969–70, said that he liked Gillies personally but believed Saywell to be more suitable.[12]

Of the three student members, Coombs, a history major, favoured Saywell, and Woolnough, a student in administrative studies, leaned to Gillies.[13] Koster was harder to classify. Saywell recalled that, during the interview he had with the committee, Koster seemed to see him as hostile to the interests of students: "He gave me a hard time."[14] Yet in the end he gave the nod to Saywell, perhaps as the lesser of evils. Among the board members, Little wanted Gillies and so, at least initially, did Gerstein. Laskin maintained neutrality until the short list was drawn up.[15]

Robert MacIntosh, who joined the board while the search committee was getting under way, confirmed that there was strong support for Gillies among his colleagues, while Saywell was seen as "able" but "a bit irreverent." Especially George Gardiner was "militantly pro-Gillies."[16] Jack Leitch remembered that many board members, he among them, were impressed with Gillies when they first met him in 1965. He had been born and raised in Ontario, was successful in business and academe in California, and seemed eminently suited to the task of getting a business school under way. "Already at that point some of us started thinking of him as a future president." By way of contrast, although Leitch had met Saywell several times, "I knew little about him and never considered him to be presidential timber."[17]

Ross, who favoured Gillies, confirmed in his memoirs that many board members hoped to appoint him. Ross also opined that there were a number of people at York who would have done a good job, among them Dennis Healy, Jules Heller, and Gerald LeDain, as well as Gillies and Saywell.[18] He did not include the dean of Atkinson College, the historian Harry Crowe. He was a marked man: in 1958 he had been at the centre of a highly public dispute about academic freedom, tenure, and faculty rights at United College (now the University of Winnipeg) that Laskin had helped to investigate.[19] He joined the faculty of Atkinson College in 1966 after seven years as research director for a labour union and newspaper columnist. Del Smyth, who recruited him, recalled that he asked Crowe to promise he would concentrate on teaching and research, and "not become actively involved in politics at York." Crowe agreed to this, but "soon afterwards it became clear that his agenda included the presidency of a Canadian university."[20] In 1969 Crowe succeeded Smyth as dean of Atkinson College, where he presided over what the mathematician Pinayur Rajagopal has called "the golden years of Atkinson."[21] This gave him a base of support, but it was not enough to gain him serious consideration. Crowe was "not really acceptable," Schiff stated, without specifying why.[22] Coons said that Crowe's health – he had heart trouble – concerned him.[23] Tucker recalled that, although he liked Crowe, he thought him "insufficiently immersed" in the world of scholarship.[24] Crowe did get nominated, as did Gillies, LeDain, Saywell, and the historian John Conway.[25] But only Gillies and Saywell had significant faculty support.

Gillies denied that he had been promised the presidency when he decided to leave UCLA for York, or that he badly wanted to be president.[26] Saywell, too, denied that he ever genuinely wanted the job. Nor did it seem likely that he would get it, he added. Not only did he believe that "Gillies was the board's man," but he knew that he himself was not. His relations with the chairman were particularly strained: "Pete Scott and I deeply disliked each other."[27] Saywell's raffish private life and sardonic attitude apparently offended Scott. Saywell resented the implied moral judgment, disliked Scott's "pomposity," and considered him to be a man "who, unlike Winters and others on the Board, had no idea of what we did, who we were, and how a university functioned."[28]

Although neither Gillies nor Saywell may have been keen to be president, each would surely have accepted the job provided he knew that he enjoyed broad support. On each side, though, some were determined that *their* man should be chief and, failing that, that the other should not. Creal believed that "the board found Saywell impossible" and would never appoint him.[29] At the same time, many faculty members found Gillies unacceptable, probably less for who he was than what he represented. As dean of the business school, he was under a cloud at a time when corporate influence on the universities was suspect and faculty across the country were challenging the legitimacy of lay boards. Brian Dixon – he became associate dean of administrative studies in 1972 – remembered that he advised Gillies in 1968 to retain the post of vice-president and resign the deanship: "I knew the prejudice that existed against business education would keep him from becoming president."[30] Gillies seemed too chummy by half with businessmen, moreover, making him look to many arts professors like "one of them" rather than "one of us." He was not without faculty support, however: he had strong partisans in his own faculty as well as in Osgoode Hall Law School.

The physicist Ralph Nicholls also backed him: "Jim would have made an excellent second president for York. I was ... a little saddened that people voted slavishly by faculty, rather than for persons."[31]

Saywell's attraction to many faculty members, especially in the Faculty of Arts and Glendon College, was that he was so clearly "one of us." Dean since 1964, he had built Arts into a large unit that was home to numerous scholars with national and international reputations. He epitomized an institution in which the humanities and social sciences were dominant.

The search process was bedevilled by the leaks that quickly sprang up and the rumours they fed. Although the committee's deliberations were supposed to be confidential, they soon were anything but. "The first hint of trouble," Ross wrote in his memoirs, "came as regular reports of the search committee discussions and activities spread over the campus ... Somebody on the search committee was leaking the news."[32] In fact, there was more than one leak. Bob Waller, editor-in-chief of *Excalibur* in 1969–70, recalled that he had "a couple of very good sources." (Since they were both still alive, he declined to reveal their names.) Moreover, he believed that a board member was also betraying confidentiality.[33] John Adams, a stringer for the *Globe and Mail*, told *Excalibur* in December 1969 that "he received his information from a member of the board of governors."[34]

Waller, who was editor-in-chief of *Pro Tem* before moving to *Excalibur*, said that staff members of both student newspapers saw themselves as an "extra-parliamentary opposition" seeking to keep the university's governing bodies as well as student government accountable. He and his associates were keen to "get the scoop" on who would be president because they "were interested in the road the university would follow." The issues of Americanization and university governance loomed large at the time, Waller recalled, and *Excalibur* staff wanted to know where the candidates stood on these issues.[35] Given this perspective, it is easy to understand why they did not respect the confidentiality of the proceedings. But then, neither did the *Globe and Mail*.

In spite of considerable differences within the committee, by late November agreement had been reached on the short list. In an interview conducted not

LEFT Bob Waller was the well-informed editor of *Pro Tem* in 1968–69 and *Excalibur* in 1969–70.

RIGHT *Excalibur* staffers, 1978–79.

long after the search process ended, Schiff recalled that both Laskin and he had put Gillies at the bottom of the list of four candidates from which the short list was chosen. "Laskin gave ... the same general reason that I did, namely that the President should not be somebody from a professional faculty, particularly not a graduate professional faculty." Initially the other board members still wanted Gillies, Schiff said, but after a full discussion, Bertrand Gerstein had said he could see why Gillies should not be in first place.[36]

On 9 December 1969 both *Excalibur* and the *Globe and Mail* published the leaked names of the three men whom the committee was recommending to the Senate and board: Albert Allen, dean of arts and science at the University of Toronto, Michael Oliver, vice-principal of McGill University, and Saywell.[37] Speculation began at once about the absence of Gillies's name, and Schiff remembered that "there seemed to be a strong degree of indignation among some faculty members ... a feeling that Gillies's name should be on the list."[38] A rumour was soon circulating that W.P. Scott was trying to claim for the board the right to add names. This rumour quickly became irrelevant, however, because Oliver withdrew his name. Since the understanding was that the list should contain a minimum of three names, this put the search in limbo.

Who leaked the list? In his memoirs, Ross claimed to know the person responsible and said that he confronted him. While implying that it was a Senate representative on the committee, however, he did not identify him by name.[39] Five committee members, Coombs, Coons, Creal, Schiff, and Tucker, have denied responsibility. Coombs speculated that it might have been someone who favoured Gillies and hoped that leaking the list would lead one of the short-listed candidates to withdraw his name, thereby forcing a new search that might have the effect of getting Gillies on the short list after all.[40] But this is an educated guess, no more.

In early January, Saywell also withdrew his name, soon followed by Allen.[41] Both men criticized the procedures used. Saywell's letter singled out "the haggle over procedure, which seems to have left suspicion and mistrust on all sides, and the flood of rumour, fabrications and slander that has circulated on the campus over the past few months." He deplored the secrecy of the process and stated his belief that Senate should have the "preponderant voice" in selecting the president.[42]

According to Laskin's biographer, "the board was furious, Laskin disgusted, and York appeared ridiculous in the public eye."[43] That last assessment seems overstated. Ross Munro's comment in the *Globe and Mail* was more to the point. Seeing Saywell's letter as evidence of coming changes in the university, Munro wrote that it had "forced York to come to terms with the province-wide trend toward downgrading boards of governors in favor of new governing structures which go a long way toward making universities self-governing communities of students, faculty members and administrators."[44]

After some hemming and hawing, the Senate endorsed a continued search, having been "reassured that no one would become president without its broad support."[45] The committee went back to work, but the task proved no easier the second time around. In late March senators and board members received a con-

fidential long list that almost immediately appeared in *Excalibur* under a cheeky byline: "With a Little Help from Our Friends." The eight candidates included Allen, Gillies, Saywell, Crowe, Andrew Booth, dean of engineering at the University of Saskatchewan, John Crispo, director of the Centre for Industrial Relations at the University of Toronto, Ivan Feltham, an Osgoode Hall Law School professor, and David Slater, dean of graduate studies at Queen's University.[46] The Senate ballot, analysed for the committee by Michael Lanphier, director of the IBR's survey research centre, revealed that only Slater, Saywell, Allen, and Gillies, in that order, enjoyed "substantial" support. The board voted overwhelmingly for Gillies, followed by Slater, Allen, and Saywell.[47]

This confronted a divided search committee with a difficult problem. As Laskin wrote in the report he submitted: "The Committee's own ranking ... was preceded by a lengthy and frank discussion which revealed great disquiet by the faculty members and by a majority of the student members (a disquiet shared to a degree by the Board members) that the Board might appoint someone agreeable only to it rather than one who, in the opinion of the faculty and student members, would better be able to provide academic leadership, imagination, and effective administration at this stage in the history of York."[48] More than three decades later, Schiff said: "We figured the board would choose Jim if his name appeared on the short list."[49] Yet leaving his name off was out of the question, since he enjoyed Senate as well as board support.

According to a tally kept by David Coombs, six committee members put Saywell and four put Slater first. Allen was the second choice of nine committee members, with the tenth (Pete Little) choosing Gillies. Slater got six third-place votes, with Gillies and Saywell splitting the other four. Gillies placed last on seven ballots, Saywell on two (Bertrand Gerstein and Michael Woolnough), and Allen on one (Little).[50] The most common ranking, adopted by all four faculty members and two of the students, was: Saywell, Allen, Slater, and Gillies. According to Tucker, it was Schiff, desirous that the board should know the misgivings the committee majority entertained concerning Gillies, who insisted that these be stated in the report. "Michael and I then agreed, and so did Wes."[51] Upon hearing this account, Wesley Coons nodded: "That's the way it was."[52]

The resulting confidential report ranked the candidates as follows: Saywell, Allen, Slater, Gillies. "This ranking is that of the Committee alone and does not take into account the results of either the vote of the Senate or the vote of the Board," Laskin wrote. "Saywell had the largest number of first choice votes, ranking considerably ahead of all other candidates." Allen and Slater were almost in a dead heat. "Gillies ranked far below the other three candidates in the committee's overall assessment."[53]

Whether the misgivings that Gillies inspired were justified or not, they were real, and Laskin gave them unmistakable expression. Nevertheless, MacIntosh recalled, board members believed they were free to choose whomever *they* judged to be the best candidate, given that each of those on the short list enjoyed substantial support in the Senate.[54] They had already appointed a special four-person board committee, headed by Scott, to interview the four men, consult widely, and then report back to the full board. The feedback that this committee received clearly favoured Gillies over the other three.[55]

The activities of the special board committee did not go unnoticed. They aroused concern among members of the search committee as well as the Senate Executive Committee that the board would exercise its authority in defiance of the report of the search committee. In a mid-April letter to Scott, the Executive Committee stated its concern.[56] To the Senate, the Executive Committee reported "that one candidate was the subject of negative comments, and that if the Board ignores these comments it would be showing bad judgment, but not bad faith, and would be exercising its legal power to appoint within the limits of the Board/Senate agreement."[57] This would have put the cat among the pigeons had it not been there already. Rumours were swirling around the university that the board was about to appoint Gillies. On 23 April the *Globe and Mail* reported that the board was on the verge of naming him and stated that this could lead to a crisis in the university.[58]

From the point of view of those who favoured Gillies, this article was most untimely, for it galvanized the pro-Saywell forces. The article appeared on the morning of the day the Senate met. The mood was testy. Senators spent close to three hours discussing the presumed contents of the search committee report. In his memoirs, Ross, who chaired the meeting, showed annoyance with Creal and Schiff, saying that they muddied the waters by shifting the debate from one about the selection of any one of the four candidates to one about the powers of the Senate.[59] (Schiff also seems to have aroused Scott's ire by insisting at a meeting of the joint board and Senate executive committees that the search committee had attached qualifications to Gillies's name strong enough to keep him from being ranked with the other three.[60]) Eventually the Senate voted, 72 to 22, for a motion asserting that "the Board of Governors would display bad judgment unless it appoints a candidate from among those receiving unqualified support by the Search Committee."[61] As the meeting adjourned, Osgoode associate dean and labour mediator Harry Arthurs remembered, "Murray Ross signalled to me from the front of the room, obviously seeking my valuable advice or assistance on an urgent basis. 'Tell me,' he said when I reached him, 'where did you get your sports jacket?'"[62]

The YUFA executive met on 30 April. The mood of the meeting was strongly pro-Saywell (I was there as the Glendon representative). Upon hearing Coons's report and discussing it, a resolution passed unanimously to send a letter to Ross and the board, asking them to heed the Senate resolution and informing them that an emergency YUFA meeting would be called should the board not do so. At this meeting the executive would recommend "further appropriate actions."[63] What might these be? A Toronto *Star* article stated that YUFA was raising the possibility of a boycott of convocation ceremonies.[64]

Would the Board of Governors, which was due to meet on 1 May, stick to its guns and appoint Gillies? Absolutely! The question soon became moot, however. Gillies confirmed in an interview that Scott offered him the presidency, reportedly with the approval of the full board, but he decided to decline it. Although he knew he had some faculty support, the awareness that many in Arts, easily the largest faculty, opposed him made the prospect of being president unappealing. "Under the circumstances the job just wasn't worth it."[65] He appeared at the board meeting to withdraw his name. In a press release issued the same day, the board regretted his withdrawal, rejected the reservations expressed by members of the search committee concerning him, said that the special committee had found "wide appreciation" of his "abilities and strong support for his candidacy," stated that he had been "very much in the Board's mind as a candidate for appointment to the Presidency," and expressed its belief that he had been "done a disservice and that the University community owes him an apology."[66]

Gillies having sidelined himself, the board was left with three names. Appointing Saywell was not an option, for this must have seemed like a capitulation to those who had opposed the board's preference. Scott said that a quick decision was needed to get the story out of the newspapers, MacIntosh recalled, and recommended that Slater be appointed. The board concurred.[67]

On the face of it, this was a sound decision. Slater was a tall, personable forty-eight-year-old with an excellent curriculum vitae. A native of Winnipeg, he had served in the Canadian Army during the Second World War and had studied at the University of Manitoba, Queen's University, and the University of Chicago, where he earned a doctorate in economics. He had been a member of the Royal Commission on Canada's Economic Prospects (1956) and had served as editor of the *Canadian Banker* for eleven years. A former treasurer of the Canadian Association of University Teachers and former president of the Queen's Faculty Association, in 1970 he was dean of graduate studies at Queen's as well as a member of Ontario's Advisory Committee on University Affairs. He was short on administrative experience, but he was otherwise well qualified and seemed altogether suitable. Scott reported in early June that Slater had accepted the position for a seven-year term, renewable for three to five years by mutual agreement between him and the board.[68] The dominant feeling, both Leitch and MacIntosh remembered, was one of relief. The board had not got the president it wanted, but it had found one it could live with and who was also acceptable to the Senate. However, one board member, George Gardiner, was so furious about the failure to appoint Gillies that he resigned. "He was a real loss to York," MacIntosh commented.[69]

In 1970 the economist David W. Slater became York's second president and vice-chancellor.

The board's relief was all the greater because the search had been so contentious and disruptive. Gillies is surely right in his continuing belief that the struggle damaged York in the long as well as the short term.[70] It gave the institution an image of being given to rancorous infighting, an image that would all too soon be reinforced. Were the issues at stake in the dispute worth the negative publicity it generated? Back in 1970 many academics would have replied in the affirmative. Almost forty years later, an answer seems much less obvious. Howard Adelman, a member of the Atkinson Philosophy Department who at the time supported Crowe's candidacy, said that, on reflection, he believed either Saywell or Gillies would have done a good job as president. "But a president has to work well with a board,"[71] he added, and that pointed implicitly to Gillies. Preferring somebody as president whom they saw as one of their own and in whom they had confidence, many faculty members were unwilling to grant the point.

When Murray Ross left the presidency, the university he led for a decade had expanded enormously since the first seventy-six students registered in Falconer Hall. By September 1970, there would be roughly 9,000 full-time and 6,300 part-time undergraduate students on two campuses, while graduate enrolment comprised 785 full-time and 774 part-time students, for a total of 16,860.[72] This exceeded by a wide margin the 8,000 students on two campuses to which the Board of Governors had committed York late in 1962.[73] The fifteen faculty members of 1960 had grown to approximately 700, full and part time, in 1970; the administrative and support staff had gone from seven to 1,700. By 1970, almost forty buildings were in use at the Glendon and Keele campuses, and the university's budget had grown to more than $29 million.[74]

Bigger is not necessarily better, and the rapid growth of the later 1960s was in sharp contrast with the more sedate expansion that Ross had counselled in his 1961 book *The New University*.[75] To this day there are people like Henry Jackman, a member of the Board of Governors in the 1970s, who believe that "York grew too fast,"[76] creating problems of staffing and organization that might have been avoided. They have a point. Rapid growth was what the government wanted, however, and what the demographic realities of the period required. Having accepted these realities, Ross was forced to make the best of them. If he felt a warm sense of accomplishment as he passed his responsibilities on to David Slater, who can blame him?

Both Ross and Slater must have been pleased with a very positive cover story on York that appeared in the October 1970 issue of *Toronto Life*. The subhead read: "Its realistic views on education, mingling of the sexes and student protests have made it the happiest campus in Canada."[77] As partial evidence of the university's "realism," the authors revealed that Slater, like Ross before him, regularly had a beer in the Green Bush Inn, mixing with students and soliciting their opinions. "York will go on being fresh, innovative, and somehow always right for its time," the article concluded, referring to "York's knack of making a university work" and suggesting that "if more campuses played it as cool as does this one, they too would find human beings under those student bodies."[78]

Howard Adelman was a member of Atkinson College's Department of Philosophy.

York continued to expand. By the late 1960s, there was talk of three additional faculties, in education, engineering, and medicine. Plans for two of the three had to be shelved, however. Planning for a faculty of engineering was still at a very early stage in the fall of 1969 when the Committee of Presidents of the Universities of Ontario (CPUO) and the Committee of Ontario Deans of Engineering (CODE) jointly appointed a director, Philip A. Lapp, and a three-person study group consisting of the director and two other members. Their assignment was to study engineering in Ontario, and they submitted their report, *Ring of Iron*, to the CPUO in December 1970. From York's point of view, its key recommendations were that "no further engineering schools be established prior to 1980" and that "York devote its ambitions, energies and resources not to engineering but to applied science."[79] The committee understood applied science to be "fundamentally different" from engineering: "Engineering curricula are relatively more structured to satisfy the basic requirements of the profession, while the applied scientist requires a relatively unstructured curriculum so that he may pursue his scientific interests without severe constraints."[80] York had the staff and facilities to build up a "high reputation" in applied science, but should stay out of engineering. "Bob Lundell never forgave me," Lapp, who joined the Board of Governors in 1979, recalled with a wry smile.[81]

Plans for a medical school were more advanced when they, too, had to be abandoned. During a meeting of the Board of Governors in early 1968, W.P. Scott noted that preliminary planning had begun on "the teaching of health sciences" and that the province seemed to be considering York's claims in this area.[82] In 1970 the Senate formed a Committee on the Study of Health Sciences, among whose members were Howard Adelman, the psychologist Kurt Danziger, and the biochemist Doris Nicholls. She remembered that the committee met "almost weekly for dinner on the Glendon campus for two terms at least, often entertaining distinguished and knowledgeable guests." She wrote that the committee was concerned "to propose a radically new and different kind of medical school with concentrated training at the 'practical' bedside level, and in particular the training of nurse practitioners, a new idea at the time. Howard Adelman ... was a vigorous proponent of this proposal."[83]

The committee issued its first report in July 1971. Its chief recommendation was the creation of a four-year Bachelor of Health (BH) program, which would both be a terminal degree and serve future physicians as a superior preparation for their medical studies. In the longer run, the committee stated, the program would serve as the platform for the establishment of a full-fledged medical school in the 1980s. This would require major provincial support as, indeed, would the BH program.[84] Nicholls remembered that the proposal led to a good deal of opposition among the deans and in the Senate, where fears existed that a medical school would divert funds from other academic programs and faculties.[85] These worries turned out to be groundless in more than one way, because in the summer of 1971 the provincial government received a report from a committee, chaired by J. Fraser Mustard, which recommended that no new health science complexes be built in Ontario. Undeterred, the York committee recommended in January 1972 that York University "consider the possibility of introducing a B.H. programme ... with modified clinical content."[86] At much the same time, the Board of Governors, noting that the Mustard report seemed to be a public document and that it had recommended against the opening of a new medical school in Ontario, evidently decided to drop the matter.[87] (While I was attending a meeting of the provincial council of the Ontario Confederation of University Faculty Associations [OCUFA] in May 1972, a member of the McMaster Economics Department congratulated me on York's failure to secure a medical faculty. McMaster's new school, he claimed, had become a financial drain on the rest of the university.)

In 1972 York *did* get a Faculty of Education. Interest in this had built over several years, as the Senate and its Academic Policy and Planning Committee (APPC) discussed a report on teacher education in 1965 and approved its transmission to the Minister's Committee on the Training of Elementary School Teachers. At the time, primary school teachers received their education and training in teachers' colleges (earlier known as normal schools), while secondary teachers took degrees in arts and science, followed by a year in one of three Ontario colleges of education, located at Queen's, Toronto, and Western Ontario. York's faculty of education was to be different. The York report recommended that "the functions of a Faculty of Education be absorbed within the programmes of the Faculty of Arts and Science," and that "a new experiment in teacher education be launched," integrating education into the second and third years of undergraduate studies in arts.[88] The following year, the Minister's Committee recommended to the minister "that programmes in teacher education be provided by the Universities and that the first steps towards the setting up of these programmes be taken without delay."[89] However, not until February 1969 did a "memorandum of understanding" between the minister of education and representatives of the CPUO appear, setting down general principles and guidelines for agreements to be negotiated between the ministry and individual universities concerning the integration of the teachers' colleges.

A discussion between President Slater and Deputy Minister of Education J.R. McCarthy followed, leading to negotiations between York and the Ministry of Education about financing, programming, and the like. While these negotiations were taking place, the Council on University Affairs (CUA) and CPUO issued a report in December 1970 dealing with the financing of undergraduate teacher-training programs. The terms proposed seemed satisfactory, and in March 1971 Slater established an Interim Committee on the Planning and Implementation of a Faculty of Education at York. By June, both board and Senate felt confident enough to establish the faculty and to move to take over the operation of Lakeshore Teachers' College in Etobicoke on 1 July 1971.[90]

On the faculty of Lakeshore at the time was Peter Ross, who had joined the college in 1970 knowing that it was going to become part of York. "I was the last person hired by the Ministry of Education to work in a Teachers' College," he recalled.[91] He was well aware that York University, and especially Jack Saywell, wanted to take the education of teachers out of the hands of professional educators and put it into the hands of academics in the faculties of arts and science. However, since he had obtained his doctorate in the history of education at the

Robert Overing came from the University of British Columbia to be the founding dean of the Faculty of Education.

Ontario Institute for Studies in Education (OISE), this did not bother him. It *did* bother most of the staff of Lakeshore, he said. Their qualifications being solely in education, they knew that York did not want to give them a long-term home. The deal made with the Department of Education was that York would guarantee them jobs for up to four years only. As a result, most of the Lakeshore teachers were "dispirited" and "hostile towards York *and* the Ministry" and took no part in the York community. Ross remembered that he was the only member of the Lakeshore faculty to attend a reception organized for them in the fall of 1971.

Principal William McClure was in charge until a new dean took over in July 1972. The challenge of a new kind of teacher education, unique in Canada, drew Robert Overing from the University of British Columbia.[92] McClure continued as principal of Lakeshore in 1972–73, after which the teachers' college closed forever and he became the new faculty's administrative officer. That fall, York's new "concurrent" program began, with students pursuing a BA or BSc degree as well as a BEd degree and spending one day a week in the classroom, elementary or secondary depending on the level at which they eventually wanted to teach. Ross, who had served on the search committee to find a dean, became Overing's all-purpose assistant for a year. He recalled the "sense of excitement" he felt about being at York, "working in an education program that looked as if it could be very different from anything else being done in the country."[93]

The historian Arthur Haberman, who joined Education on cross-appointment from the Faculty of Arts in 1972 and served as associate dean from 1975 to 1978, noted that there were no other concurrent programs in the country at the time. The environment was "wonderful," he found: "We were shaping something out of nothing."[94] However, supervising the students in the program required a lot of time from the faculty, many of whom had their appointments elsewhere in York. Among them were Gwenda Echard, Don Coles, Elaine Newton, Donald Solitar, and Martin Muldoon in Arts, Mary Lyons and Stuart Robbins in Physical Education, Neil Freeman in Fine Arts, and Brian Cragg in Science, as well as Glendon professors David Cooke, Jos Lennards, Tim Moore, and Page Westcott. The faculty also had a large number of adjunct professors, full-time teachers in the public and separate school boards of Toronto and York who took charge of the students on their days in the classroom. Haberman remembered that a study done in the 1970s by Harvey Kolodny of the University of Toronto's Faculty of Management Studies predicted that the model would not survive in the long run because the commitment in time that it required was too heavy.

Overing left the deanship in 1981 and the university a year later. The new dean, Andrew Effrat, had no strong commitment to cross-appointments, which in any case, Overing said, had proved increasingly difficult to arrange because they were so time-consuming for the faculty holding them. In the 1980s they came to an end, and the faculty was increasingly staffed with professional educators. In staffing, "the original vision did not persist," Haberman said a bit wistfully.[95] Overing and Ross expressed a similar opinion.[96]

A student enrolled in the program from 1977 to 1982, Liz Lundell, might have chosen York because her father was dean of science there, but she remembered that this played only a minor role in her decision. She wanted the concurrent program, in her case in primary education, and York was alone in offering it. She also wanted to take an honours degree in history and English, and "the Canadian historians I knew from reading books in high school were all at York – Ramsay Cook, Jack Granatstein, Jack Saywell." She remembered taking rewarding courses in history with Peter Oliver and H.V. (Viv) Nelles, and in English with Derek Cohen, but the professors she remembered with greatest enthusiasm were Don Coles in Humanities – "I thought he was a great lecturer, and he was really approachable!" – and Marsha Forest, who taught special education. As for the concurrent program, it lived up to her expectations: "I liked it. It was far more realistic than two-week stints in the classroom."[97] Forest also looms large among Donna Paterson's recollections of the Faculty of Education. Forest's commitment to the idea that students with special needs should not be segregated but should be integrated into regular classrooms inspired her as it did Lundell. Paterson had begun her education studies at McGill but transferred to York in 1980 partly for personal reasons and partly because of the concurrent program. She resented the time that it took her to commute from her place near Yonge and St Clair. "But I have no regrets," she said: "The concurrent program was great!"[98]

Another notable curricular innovation was the Parkdale legal clinic operated by Osgoode Hall Law School. Made possible by the Legal Aid Act of 1966, which created the Ontario Legal Aid Plan (OLAP), a publicly funded "judicare" program, Parkdale Community Legal Services came into existence in 1971. During the preceding academic year, Osgoode's clinical-program training committee had recommended that a clinical training centre be established in a community law office, to be run by the law school, that was to serve as the site of a full-semester academic program. Osgoode's Faculty Council approved the centre for two years provided the necessary funding could be secured. Fred Zemans, the clinic's first director, who got a joint appointment to the faculty and the clinic in 1971, said that Osgoode managed to obtain seed funding from the federal government and from the Council on Legal Education for Professional Responsibility, a Ford Foundation project that was principally active in the United States. He later wrote: "From the outset, there were two central elements in Osgoode's development of a poverty law program: exploring the possibilities of clinical legal education and developing an alternative model of legal aid services."[99] Although the original plan had been to locate the clinic in Rexdale, Zemans said, it was established in Parkdale instead because that part of the city already had a tenants' association and a single parents' association, and seemed to have more use for a community-based legal-services clinic.[100]

The legal profession had less use for it. The Law Society of Upper Canada opposed the project, Zemans remembered: "Basically they were unhappy that it was not under their control." The first student to article at the clinic was Mary Jane Mossman, who showed up in September 1971, fresh from writing her exams for the LLM degree at the London School of Economics. She found upon her arrival that Zemans was subject to disciplinary proceedings (eventually withdrawn) at the Law Society because the sign advertising the clinic's services, intended to make it visible to potential clients, exceeded the maximum size the society permitted![101]

From the outset, the Parkdale clinic, one of four pilot projects in Canada, was a success. Twenty law students per semester could be found there, and they made a difference to the lives of the people among whom they worked. As described by Zemans in a book published in 1974, *Community Legal Services in Perspective*, this attracted the attention of the attorney general and later chancellor of York, Roy McMurtry, who decided to fund the project after the initial grants had run out. By 2005, Zemans said, Ontario had seventy-five clinics more or less modelled on Parkdale. The pilot project was still a going concern and was considered to be "a jewel in the crown of the legal clinic system."[102]

Among the students who worked and studied at Parkdale in the first couple of years was Marion Lane. Having registered in Osgoode in 1971, she spent the 1973 winter semester at Parkdale and later remembered it as an "exciting" place. She and her fellow students – she mentioned Harriet Sachs and Esther Lenkinski – not only did clinical work but sought to "reflect on its practice," which they believed had wider relevance. In a report to the Long Range Academic Planning Committee, Lane recommended that practical experience in law school need not occur only in the context of poverty law. One of her recommendations was that

clinical programs be established in areas such as criminal law. In light of her research on clinical education, she wrote an evaluation of the Parkdale program, which found that it should be dealt with in a more academic manner. There were those who feared that such criticism might lead to the cancellation of the program. This did not happen, though, and "the academic side *was* beefed up."[103]

Lane noted that the Parkdale clinic gave rise to other initiatives. In 1974 she, Sachs, and a few others, using money obtained from the federal Opportunities for Youth program, started the Toronto Community Law School, which is now Community Legal Education Ontario. Other initiatives were Flemingdon Community Legal Services and Justice for Children, now the Canadian Foundation for Children, Youth, and the Law. As a consequence, Osgoode co-sponsored a pioneer interdisciplinary training program for lawyers on children and the law. "Ann Montgomery, the administrative assistant to the dean, worked very hard on this project."[104]

In 1969 the presidential committee headed by George Gardiner had recommended raising the enrolment target of Glendon College from 800 to 1,250,[105] a recommendation that the board and Senate had accepted. This number was nothing if not ambitious. The college came reasonably close to reaching its enrolment target in 1969–70 because first-year Arts students who could not be accommodated at the Keele campus were redirected to Glendon. But in 1970 this source dried up, leaving classrooms emptier and classes smaller than planned. The budgetary officers of the university did not see this as sustainable, and Glendon's Policy and Planning Committee recommended the introduction of a unilingual stream of students who would not be required to take French.[106] After a long debate, Faculty Council narrowly approved the recommendation.

Some observers, among them Edgar McInnis, were not surprised. When he had first read Escott Reid's proposal for a bilingual college, McInnis had been sceptical, and he continued to be so after he retired. (Indicative of his attitude was a comment during a reception hosted by George Tatham after the 1970 fall convocation. "How goes it with bilingualism?" McInnis asked in his pipe-tobacco voice. After I had told him about the proposed unilingual stream, he shook his head and said: "I *told* Escott that if you want young English Canadians to learn French, you send them to Quebec or to France. You don't ask them to come to Toronto. But Escott wouldn't listen.") Students who came to Glendon were often keenly interested in bilingualism, but there were not enough of them to justify the number of faculty teaching at Glendon or to fill the space available on the campus.

The unilingual stream weakened the bilingual ethos. On the other hand, that ethos received a boost from the introduction of a certificate of bilingual competence, obtainable only after a rigorous exam in both official languages. Bilingualism also benefited from the changing conditions of academic employment. What had been a sellers' market became in 1972 a buyers' market. To that point, it was simply impossible to secure faculty able to teach in both languages, and some department chairs did not even try. Alan Sangster, for example, a botanist who joined Natural Science in 1968, said that neither Bob Snow, who was effectively

the head of the department, nor H.S. Harris, who as academic dean interviewed Sangster, mentioned either French *or* bilingualism.[107] This changed quickly. When William Irvine joined the History Department in 1971, taking "the only substantial job in Canada" in his field that year, his ability to speak French and lecture in it was crucial to his appointment.[108] The requirement was still unofficial, however. The psychologist James Alcock, who arrived in 1973, recalled that the departmental chairman, Ronald Cohen, "who spoke no French," assumed he was bilingual simply because he had received his undergraduate degree from McGill! "Cohen's assumption was quite wrong," Alcock said, laughing: "I had a lot to learn. I sometimes wonder how the students in that first year understood me."[109] A few years later, his appointment would have been unlikely. In 1975 the demonstrated ability to teach in both official languages became a condition of appointment in the tenure stream in every department except English. At the same time, bilingual competence became a requirement for non-academic staff.[110]

Students in the unilingual stream had to take a course focused on French Canada. After an unsuccessful experiment with a single team-taught course, students were allowed to satisfy the unilingual requirement by taking any course that dealt at least in part with French Canada. Diluted in this way, the unilingual stream was an affront to those who believed in Escott Reid's bilingual vision. Among them was Philippe Garigue, a political scientist who came from the Université de Montréal in 1980 to become Glendon's fourth principal. Aware that the existence of the unilingual stream complicated dealings with the provincial government and with groups interested in promoting bilingualism, he eventually initiated the process that led to its phasing out.

Although student numbers had been rising, some people feared that they would fall again, prompting yet another reassessment of Glendon's future. Many remembered that in 1974 acting president John Yolton, on the occasion of receiving an honorary degree, had proposed that Glendon College be moved to the Keele campus, making room for Osgoode Hall Law School and the Faculty of Administrative Studies on the Glendon site. (More than thirty years later, Brian

Dixon still thought that this would have been a positive move from the point of view of the professional schools, locating them closer to the centre of Toronto's business and legal worlds.[111]) The proposal had appalled Glendon's faculty and administration. If enrolment were to fall, who could say such a proposal would not re-emerge?

The debate that took place in the Faculty Council in November 1985 was vigorous, but the historian Ian Gentles, the associate principal (academic) at the time, recalled that "the motion to end the unilingual stream passed with few opposing voices."[112] Starting in the fall of 1987, all students registering in the first year of a degree program at Glendon would be required to complete by graduation a course in their second language at the second-year level.[113] Reporting on the phase-out, the sociologist Don Willmott informed the Faculty Council in early 1988 that "enrolment had not declined sharply. Projections were not alarming though they fell short of the University's suggested enrolment target."[114] That target was 1,900 by now, having been raised twice since the Gardiner report had set it at 1,250. If nothing else, this was a graphic illustration of the effects that the underfunding of universities was having on Glendon.

All the same, faculty members continued to find Glendon a satisfying place. Irving Abella remembered it as "a glorious place to teach" and reeled off the names of more than a dozen students who had done well in his history courses and after leaving Glendon.[115] Alain Baudot, who taught French and humanities, raved about the quality of students in the 1970s.[116] Elizabeth Hopkins described as "a real delight" the courses in creative writing and dramatic arts that she taught and the students she met in them, among them M.T. (Terry) Kelly and Trish Nelligan.[117] Stanley Tweyman said that the Philosophy Department was "small, but it worked," and added that H.S. Harris was "a wonderful human being and a wonderful mentor."[118] Gail Cuthbert Brandt, who joined the History Department in 1975 to teach courses on French Canada and women's history, remembered Glendon as "a close-knit community, with a faculty that was young and really engaged." She, too, was "impressed by the students of those early days."[119]

Among the students of that time was Adèle Hurley. She loved the small campus, residence life, and her courses in English: "Barry Olshen, Ann Mandel, and Michael Ondaatje were great profs!" But nothing influenced her more than a third-year course in natural science taught by Alan Sangster. "I was prepared to be bored, but for the first time I found myself reading books not required in the course." With Sangster's support, she gained admission to the Faculty of Environmental Studies in 1975.[120] In 1981 she and another York alumnus, Michael Perley, founded the Canadian Coalition on Acid Rain; later she served on York's Board of Governors.

David Trick, who came from Winnipeg in 1973, was drawn by Glendon's bilingual ethos. He enjoyed the small classes and the opportunity to meet faculty informally: "Some of the things that people have discovered are good for students, Glendon has had all along." He lived in B House, Hilliard, where the actor Charles Northcote was the don, and remembered seeing a Northcote-directed play, Larry Kardish's *Brussels Sprouts*, in the Pipe Room, a small space in the bowels of Glendon Hall. John Frankie and Gordon McIvor performed in the buff;

Doreen Hess, with a nod to modesty, wore briefs. It was *the* ticket of the year: "We all went to see it." Above all, though, Trick remembered H.S. Harris. "I took three courses from him. When I left Glendon I wanted to become a professor of political theory, and that was because of Harris."[121]

Catherine Limbertie also remembered *Brussels Sprouts* vividly: "It was a big hit!" She studied political science and French, and fondly remembered courses by Edward Appathurai, Norman Penner, and John Holmes. "Living in residence was great for learning French if you made the effort," she said. Chantal Hébert, later a Toronto *Star* columnist, read her French papers for mistakes. "I returned the favour, but her English was better than my French." Aside from residence food, "life at Glendon was absolutely wonderful."[122]

Julie Pärna, who arrived in 1975, loved the campus, residence life, and most of her teachers. "But my favourite professor in the world, ever, was Jeannie Bartha," who taught Spanish. Pärna, who held jobs of increasing seniority at Glendon from 1979 to 1994 and more recently has worked in the Schulich School of Business and the Registrar's Office, said: "The bilingualism at Glendon is what drew me, and what kept me working there for years."[123] Another student who later worked for York, Gwyneth Buck, showed up with a pass degree from the University of Toronto, intending to work towards an honours degree in history as a part-time student. After completing the degree in 1979, she went on to take an MA at York. Compared to the University of Toronto, she said, Glendon was "small and very friendly ... You could talk to your professors and other students; people knew your name and you knew theirs ... Glendon was a very positive experience."[124]

If some York old-timers look back to 1971–72 as the last good year, they have grounds for their nostalgia. The university was booming. Full-time undergraduate enrolment on the two campuses was almost 20 per cent higher in the fall of 1971 than the year before. Full-time graduate enrolment was up approximately

LEFT Convocation, 1980, Glendon campus. From left to right: John Proctor, Murray Ross, Norman Endler, William Small, John Armour, Vicky Draper, five graduating students, honorary graduates Sir Hugh Springer and Steven Staryk, Ian Macdonald.

RIGHT Official opening of the William Pearson Scott Library, 1971.

10 per cent, and part-time enrolment, both graduate and undergraduate, rose by roughly the same proportion.[125] "The construction site," as some students called the Keele campus, remained true to its name. In 1970 the Curtis Lecture Hall opened, as did two graduate student residences, joining the one completed in 1969. Stong College, begun in 1970, was completed in 1971. So was the central library. On 13 October 1971 a special convocation marked the official opening of the William Pearson Scott Library, as it was henceforth called.

Held in the atrium of the library, the ceremony granted honorary degrees to Richard Blackwell, the British bookseller, Archibald MacLeish, American poet and former Librarian of Congress, and Samuel Rothstein, director of the University of British Columbia Library, as well as to Scott himself. Among those who spoke was special guest Gérard Pelletier, the secretary of state. Ellen Hoffmann, who had recently left the Yale University library to take a position at York (she became director of libraries in 1983), attended the ceremony. She remembered the opening chiefly because of what MacLeish said. "His speech on the meaning of libraries has, I am sure, provided quotes for a number of library administrators over the years. My favourite has always been that the library is not a scholarly filling station where students can get a tankful of titles."[126]

Phase Two of Atkinson College and the Stong College Residence opened in 1971; the Administrative Studies Building as well as Bethune College and its residence followed in 1972. By this time, Fine Arts Phase Two, designed by Raymond Moriyama, was under construction, as were a fourth residence for graduate students and the Atkinson College residence. Although none of the others matched the visual appeal of Moriyama's building, several of them were pleasing and together with those constructed earlier they gave the Keele campus a more settled look. Except in the four wood lots on the edge of the campus, trees were still scarce, but the grounds crew were taking steps to ensure that this lack would be corrected in the future.

On the surface the institution seemed to be flourishing. Not everyone was satisfied, however. There were repeated complaints from the YUFA leadership about the alleged inadequacy of the increases in salaries and improvements in

benefits that the board proposed in more-or-less informal negotiations. More than once in the later 1960s, YUFA threatened some kind of "job action," with the withholding of grades the preferred option, in an attempt to secure a better settlement, and during a YUFA meeting in March 1970 attended by 120 members, those present voted almost unanimously to censure the board.[127] How many of the faculty would have gone along with any kind of job action is difficult to determine, because on each occasion the contending parties reached agreement. In the early summer of 1972 a strike of the International Union of Operating Engineers took place, but it was soon settled "with a result generally satisfactory to the University."[128]

From the board's point of view, YUFA's demands, usually based on comparisons with settlements at other Ontario universities, were apt to seem excessive given the money available and the many demands on it in a rapidly growing institution. Since 1968 the provincial government's grants to the universities had been falling increasingly short of institutional expectations. By 1971, if anyone was in doubt about the direction of government policy, that doubt should have been dispelled when John White, the new minister of colleges and universities, announced that henceforth the government would be expecting to get "more scholar for the dollar."[129] This did not bode well for the future of the Ontario universities.

The crisis that dominated the fall of 1972 took shape during the preceding academic year. Anticipating another increase in enrolment, many departments and units recruited additional faculty. Employment offers had been made to more than a hundred new faculty members by the time it became known that applications were well below what had been anticipated and that an unexpectedly high number of students were leaving York after their first year. Not only income from tuition fees would be lower than anticipated, but also the size of the provincial government grant, which was determined by the enrolment count on 1 December.

Projecting enrolment was not easy. "From 1968 to 1970," Paul Axelrod has written, "enrolment estimates fell significantly short of the numbers actually registering in Ontario universities."[130] The Department of University Affairs believed the universities were using faulty data; the Committee of Presidents believed the government was too conservative in predicting enrolment. "But as university officials grappled with the problem of meeting possible enrolment over-runs in the years ahead, the system suddenly faced the opposite problem in the fall of 1971 ... Expected to rise by over 9 per cent, undergraduate registration rose by only 5 per cent."[131] York's full-time undergraduate enrolment was not affected, however, rising by almost 20 per cent in 1971. Indeed, York's success in bucking the trend may have encouraged academic planners to make optimistic forecasts for 1972, thus helping to bring about the crisis of that year.

In the summer of 1972 York made a valiant effort to boost enrolment. The university launched "Operation Breakthrough," designed, as *Excalibur*'s Marilyn Smith put it, "to sell the university to wavering students and project the image of a with-it place responsive to the needs of its members."[132] How much success the campaign had is unclear, but it was unable to make up the shortfall. When the numbers were finally in, they showed that full-time undergraduate enrolment was down over 300 students, from 10,735 to 10,427. The enrolment of part-time undergraduates and graduate students, both full and part time, rose by several percentage points, and the total number of students was up from 19,349 to 19,778. But this modest 2 per cent rise left York well short of where the academic planners and budget makers had expected it to be.

The raw numbers did not tell the whole story. That autumn, faculty members started hearing about FTE students and BIUs, concepts of which many had so far been blissfully ignorant. An FTE (full-time-equivalent) student was one who took five full-session courses; five part-time students, each taking one course, equalled one FTE student. The BIU (Basic Income Unit) was the amount of the provincial grant ($1,785 in 1972–73) for one FTE student in the ordinary program in humanities and social sciences, with students in the honours program, in science, and in the professional and graduate faculties worth multiples ranging from 1.5 to 6 BIUs. In October 1972 the Registrar's Office estimated that York's BIU count would fall 10 per cent short of what had been anticipated when the board approved the 1972–73 operating budget. That 10 per cent translated into roughly four million dollars![133]

When the prospect of a deficit opened up, it affected budget planning at once. Units and departments were asked to scale back projected expenses. "In the spring of 1972," Ellen Hoffmann remembered, "the library had unspent funds and sent six librarians to British Columbia ... to visit libraries and get ideas. I learned a lot (and loved staying at the Hotel Vancouver and Empress). On the day we left, the Associate Director who went with us, Natsuko Furuya, got a call to say that there was a big budget cut, and she spent the whole flight home working on what to do."[134]

The deficit prompted the trimming of a good many sails. It also affected the work of the Senate Committee on Academic Dismissal (SCAD). Established by a Senate resolution late in 1971, its mandate was to deal with gaps in the policy

Floyd S. Chalmers, chancellor of York University, 1968–73.

statement on tenure and promotions that the Senate and board had approved in the fall of 1968 and amended in 1970.[135] However, soon after the committee members met for the first time and elected the biologist John Heddle as their chairman, they found themselves charged with an additional task. In mid-July the committee discussed with President Slater his request that "the matter of dismissal of tenured as well as untenured faculty for budgetary reasons be considered by the committee," and agreed to consider whether it should make recommendations on this to the Senate.[136] Heddle recalled that, as a recent arrival at York – he had joined Atkinson College and the Faculty of Science in 1971 – he did not at once grasp the full implications of the request: "I was an innocent scientist."[137] Another committee member, Wesley Coons, *was* aware of what the request meant: "I knew that the prospect of dismissals was due to an anticipated budget crunch. In the Psychology Department we had a fair amount of informal discussion of the matter and I suspect we were not alone in that."[138]

Hearing that SCAD had been asked to develop guidelines for dismissals on financial grounds, the Faculty Association executive drew the committee's attention to a document adopted recently by the national council of the CAUT, which stated that cuts in academic positions should be considered "only after reasonable cuts have been made in all other budgetary areas such as administration, publicity, and budgetary reserves," and insisted that faculty members must be fully involved in budget making, including the process of apportioning cuts.[139] The YUFA executive, Michiel Horn wrote, adopted the position that "we cannot, at this time, endorse the principle of dismissal of faculty members merely on budgetary grounds ... The central functions of a university are teaching, learning, and research, and we believe that these will suffer severely if faculty members ... have to live in constant fear of being found 'redundant' for purely financial reasons."[140] Soon afterwards YUFA set up an ad hoc Prevention of Dismissals Committee, chaired by a member of the Faculty of Arts English Department, Annabel Patterson.

YUFA's primary interest was the welfare and security of its members. Husbanding York's financial resources and keeping the budget in balance were the responsibility of David Slater and his main administrative officers, Walter Tarnopolsky, a law professor who had become vice-president (academic) in July 1972, and the two vice-presidents in charge of administration and finance, Bill Small and Bruce Parkes. Ultimately, of course, responsibility rested with the Board of Governors. Also involved, though not responsible for the budget, was the Senate's Academic Policy and Planning Committee, which was examining information it received from the president with a view to making recommendations to the Senate.

With rumours swirling around the two campuses, the level of anxiety among academic and non-academic staff was rising. But most students, it is safe to say, were unconcerned, even though *Excalibur*, edited that year by Marilyn Smith, provided a well-informed picture of what was happening. Smith remembered the fall as "unsettling" but "exciting." Used to Glendon College, where she registered in 1967 and was a reporter with *Pro Tem*, she thought the Keele campus was "like that gangly kid who is growing too quickly and trying to find him-

self." But getting information was easy. "Plenty of people were willing to talk ... I could phone the president and knew that he would return my call. David was very friendly."[141]

The Board of Governors knew about the general nature of the problem by the early summer, but not until its regular meeting of 10 October did it get some reasonably exact numbers. Slater reported that shortfalls in enrolment in Arts, Science, Glendon, and Atkinson had already prompted budget cuts totalling $1.2 million, and that the target for further cuts was $2 million, leaving a projected deficit of close to a million. He alerted board members that "it might be necessary to reduce the number of faculty," adding that "a decision to separate faculty members from the University for budgetary reasons must be correct" or the consequences for morale could be "devastating."[142]

The Senate got its first official whiff of calamity at a special meeting on 19 October. The report presented by Theodore (Ted) Olson, chairman of the APPC, was a shocker. It stated that "a sufficient case has been made by the University's responsible administrative officers indicating that a multi-year problem of some magnitude exists" and that "there must be a substantial cut in numbers of faculty for 1973–74." Normal attrition should yield twenty positions; the release of roughly half of the full-time faculty employed on annual contracts might yield some fifty more. Beyond this, *"it is our preliminary judgement that perhaps another 60–70 terminations may have to be made* in order to achieve balance as an institution."[143] In other words, up to 140 people would need to be shed.

After Olson sat down, Slater spoke. The enrolment shortfall, he said, meant that income would be 10 per cent lower than anticipated. In order to achieve balance and "maintain room for manoeuvre, development, and innovation," budgets needed to be adjusted along the lines proposed by the APPC, "with a severe cut of faculty" in the immediate future "rather than a protracted grinding down to recovery over several years."[144]

The way the report was presented implied unanimity on the part of the APPC. But this unanimity was absent. One committee member, Pinayur Rajagopal, remembered feeling resentment that his name had been attached to the document, since he had expressed reservations about the financial data supplied by Vice-President Parkes – the effort to determine precisely what they were would take several weeks – and had questioned the report's major recommendation. "Financial exigency had not been proven yet," he said, "and so it was too early for the university to decide to let people go."[145] At the Senate meeting he criticized the report, as did several other members of the committee, among them two of the deans. They had not expressed this criticism during the APPC meeting, Olson recalled: "There was no feeling that there should be a majority and minority report." In the APPC meeting the deans "had seemed a bit stunned" by what they were discussing. The Senate's mood was sufficiently ugly, however, that they may have felt a need to distance themselves from the report. "It was a horrible day," Olson said: "I was merely the chair of the committee, but everybody dumped on me."[146]

Eventually Slater "suggested that the possibility of terminations was distinct enough that Senate should move to consideration of procedures to govern such terminations."[147] With these words in their ears, senators moved on to discuss the SCAD report. That report consisted of two schedules, the first dealing with recommendations emerging from the committee's original mandate, and the second consisting of "rules for reductions in teaching staff for reasons of budget necessity."[148] Not surprisingly, most of the debate focused on Schedule II. The recommendation that tenured faculty be subject to dismissal on budgetary grounds proved particularly contentious.[149] Albert Tucker remembered that he was appalled: "It would have wrecked York. Nobody who was any good would have come to us after that."[150] The meeting, which had begun at 4:30, dragged on until after eight. By this time, only an amended version of Schedule I had been adopted, and it was clear that if the number of probationary and tenured faculty were to be reduced in time for the 1973–74 academic year, the Board of Governors would need to impose reductions that administrators would have to carry out without guidelines or significant consultation.

It briefly seemed that this might happen. The board's executive and finance committees met on 20 October, approved Slater's revised budget for 1972–73, and authorized the borrowing of $750,000 to cover the remaining deficit. The year 1973–74 posed a greater problem. At a further meeting of the board's Executive Committee on 23 October, Slater stated as a "basic fact" that "the 1972–73 actual enrolment for the University will fall somewhere between 8% and 10% below the projections which were used for staffing and budgeting." This meant that York was overstaffed by the same percentage. The board would have to discuss "the programs which may cushion whatever reductions of staff may turn out to be required."[151]

The Executive Committee understood this to mean that reductions *would* be required, and that they would have to be set in train quickly. "In view of the impending November 1st deadline for notice of terminations to take effect June 30, 1973, it was agreed to propose to the Board a request to the President to take the steps necessary to effect a 10% reduction in the academic salary load."[152] The full board met in special session on 24 October. Robert MacIntosh, who had succeeded Scott as board chair in 1971, remembered it as "a difficult meeting."[153] Slater, who had evidently had second thoughts, stated that the resolution passed the day before was too blunt an instrument. The board must involve the faculty, for the administration needed faculty support to be able to make the necessary reductions without plunging the university into turmoil. "On the other hand, the faculty are not their own employer, and Senate cannot be the body to determine the University's position in such matters." A serious problem was that notice had to be given to probationary faculty by 1 November. Walter Tarnopolsky suggested that this might not be the relevant date if the dismissals were for financial rather than academic reasons, and that "a reasonable date, such as December 1st or 15th, might be acceptable to the courts." Slater agreed, then added that the magnitude of the problem facing York was still unclear.

Slater's argumentation was confusing. The board was the employer and had the right to dismiss, but it should not be hasty in exercising this right, not even when time was of the essence. Every possible alternative needed to be examined and explored. Adrienne Clarkson, who had joined the board in the summer of 1972, thought that Slater was "floundering."[154] "David gave us one scenario, and another, and yet another," MacIntosh recalled. "Finally someone said: 'David, just tell us what you think we should do.'"[155]

The difficulty was that Slater could not decide what should be done. As a thoroughly decent human being, he could not have taken any pleasure in the prospect of dismissals. He understood, as Clarkson pointed out, that "the Draft Resolution ... would require that some 110 faculty be given notice within the next seven days, resulting doubtless in an almost incredible amount of attention, calumny, and litigation being focused on York." He knew that if tenured faculty were included all hell would break loose. He must have been appalled by a motion proposing to protect the university's legal position by giving notice to all those whose contracts required notice by 1 November, although the president was to assure these people that their contracts would probably be renewed when the university's finances had been clarified. Several board members, among them Clarkson and Bertrand Gerstein, opposed the motion "on the grounds that such widespread giving of notice would throw York into internal chaos," and it was defeated. In the end the board suspended all construction projects not yet started and passed a motion asking the president "to take all necessary steps to achieve a reduction in the academic budget of 10%, or $2,700,000, in fiscal 1973–74."[156] No opposing votes or abstentions are recorded.

When Slater appeared before the Senate on 25 October, he seemed troubled and looked uncomfortable. The thought of making a major cut in the budget must have been far from his mind when he accepted the presidency, and he was apparently unsure how to proceed. Howard Adelman, who was York's academic colleague at the CPUO in 1970–71 and had an opportunity to observe Slater at that level, said that "he was a decent man but unable to make a decision."[157] Harry Arthurs remembered Slater as "a very nice man and an appalling president," indecisive and unable to manage a complex situation.[158] Arthurs himself was highly

Dean of Osgoode Hall Law School from 1972 to 1977, Harry Arthurs was later president and vice-chancellor of York.

organized and "could make fast decisions," Ann Montgomery, his administrative assistant at the time of the crisis, recalled: "He realized that things needed to keep moving."[159] It evidently bothered Arthurs to be working with someone who could not make up his mind.

Not only was Slater indecisive, but he was also largely isolated. He had gained few allies since he began his presidency. In the eyes of many, he continued to be an outsider, president only because the supporters of Gillies and Saywell had fought each other to a draw. Moreover, he had made little effort to become an insider. David McQueen, a Glendon economist who knew Slater before he came to York, liked him and valued his personal integrity and scholarly qualities,[160] but few others knew him well. Marion Boyd, who became his personal assistant in 1971, said that Slater was likable and kind but not easy to get to know. People were used to the gregarious Ross, who always had "an air of being in charge." Slater was much more reserved and scholarly, wanting "space and time for academic work." Ross had chaired the Senate during his entire presidency. After a year, Slater yielded the position of Senate chair to an elected successor, John Yolton. Senators by and large welcomed this. (Albert Tucker later wrote: "It ... seemed odd to me that the president of the university should also chair the Senate," and he was not alone.[161]) Still, as a participant in the debate, Slater was less in control than Ross had been as chair. Moreover, Boyd said, Slater "didn't like campus politics. He never got the hang of it." Having largely failed to put together the team he hoped would assist him in running the university, in 1972 "he had no real support."[162]

The lack of support was not just personal, it was institutional. Administrative structures and processes that had served well enough during the years of growth proved quite inadequate when growth suddenly ended. The difficulties Parkes had in coming up with numbers that stood up to analysis by critics like Rajagopal were symptomatic of a larger problem. York had become too large and too complex to function with administrative structures that, like the university itself, had grown almost helter-skelter. These structures made it possible for forceful deans to make budgetary claims on the basis of enrolment projections that in 1972 turned out to be unrealistic. As a senior administrator who wishes to remain anonymous has said: "Large amounts of real expense were committed on the strength only of hypothetical income. Whatever the general university system funding constraints, York was the author of its own particular misfortune."[163]

That realization took a long time to sink in. In 1972 people were looking for someone to blame, and Slater provided the obvious target. This was evident at the meeting of 25 October, where Tarnopolsky, Olson, and law librarian Balfour Halevy were conspicuous in failing to join the chorus of criticism and attack. The meeting had been called to continue discussion of the SCAD report and to consider a motion by Harry Crowe and Pinayur Rajagopal that no notice of nonrenewal or termination of appointment on grounds of budget necessity should be given to a faculty member until appropriate regulations had been adopted by the Senate. Fully a hundred senators, two-thirds of the membership, and a large number of observers listened as the secretary read the communications

Bertrand Gerstein served on the Board of Governors for almost two decades and was its chairman from 1975 to 1979.

the Senate had received, among them the resolution the board had passed the day before. Asked what advice the board had received, whether the president had been present at the approval of the resolution, and whether he had supported it or not, a visibly nervous Slater offered a rambling reply: "He had been present at the approval of the Board's resolution which had arisen out of a draft resolution to which he had objected." The board's executive and finance committees had drafted the resolution on the basis of "highly tentative" data he had supplied. "He interpreted the figures in the Board's resolution as 'stylized facts,' and the effect of the resolution as an instruction to find solutions to York's problems, not an instruction to terminate faculty. The resolution should not be taken literally, but as an expression of the Board's concern for the fiscal integrity of the institution." Several senators thought that this defied belief: $2.7 million was a very specific amount. Where had it come from? Slater denied he was the source. "Others must take the responsibility for it, although the figure is not outlandish, since it is, by a combination of pessimistic approaches, [possible] to approximate a figure of $2.7 million as a potential deficit for 1973–74."[164]

We cannot know how the discussion would have gone if neither of the board members who were also members of the Senate, Doris Anderson and Bertrand Gerstein, had been at the meeting. (No senators were attending board meetings at this time because the Senate had not yet replaced those who had left in the spring.) Both *were* present, however, and Gerstein now challenged Slater's version of events. The board had received estimates for 1973–74, he said, "presumably developed by the President and Vice-President in consultation with the Deans," suggesting that a reduction of $2.7 million would be needed if the university was to return to budgetary health in 1973–74. The board's "first concern" was to foster academic excellence while preserving the institution's fiscal integrity, he continued, and it had tried by its resolution "to leave internal decisions to internal decision-making bodies, while requiring that reduction in the University's commitments which financial responsibility would seem to require."[165]

Disagreeing with Gerstein, Slater insisted that he had not given the board a budget for 1973–74. Gerstein asked where the figure of $2.7 million had come from. Slater answered that others than himself – he did not say who – had "generated the figures on the basis of a series of pessimistic hypotheses as to 1973–74 enrolment. His own presentation had been clearly not a budget recommendation, but a highly speculative preliminary exploration." Gerstein remembered it differently. (I recall him saying: "The board was under the impression it was dealing with a recommendation from the president.") The exchange with Gerstein, which left the impression that Slater either had tried to deceive the Senate or simply could not decide what to do, significantly weakened his authority.

Eventually a motion passed (39 in favour, 17 opposed, 11 abstentions) "that Senate has received with reluctance the communication from the Board, and it is the consensus of Senate that we reject the communication, feeling that much more time is necessary to establish the exact nature of the facts underlying the University's financial problem." Slater, who had spoken against the motion because "it invited confrontation with the Board," said he would inform the board of his intention to interpret its resolution "in general terms only, implying the presentation of further recommendations to the Board on the size and nature of the real and immediate problem of austerity and retrenchment and solutions to the problem."[166]

The Crowe/Rajagopal motion, amended to state that faculty on one-year contracts *could* be let go on budgetary grounds, passed unanimously. The debate on Schedule II of the SCAD report then resumed. Not far into it, Jack Saywell made an intervention that proved to be crucial. Indeed, it is no exaggeration to say that it changed the course of York's history. Not only did it all but end any attempt to balance the budget by dismissing probationary and tenured faculty, it also, although quite unintentionally, set the stage for the eventual deans' revolt against the president. "The debate on Schedule II should be suspended," Saywell said, "in order that a better factual base be provided for Senate's discussions." He moved that an ad hoc committee be created and charged with providing that base. Consisting of the president and vice-presidents, the deans, and the chairmen of the Senate, the APPC, and YUFA, its mandate would be to study the academic budget and the projections of enrolment, "to examine and place before Senate all alternatives to cutting faculty as a means of introducing budget constraints or reductions," to explore with the board the possibility of deficit financing, "and if there seems to be no alternative to terminations of faculty for budgetary purposes, to place before Senate a clear and concise statement of the likely number of terminations of faculty."[167] An objection from student senator Peter McGoey led Saywell to amend his motion in order to add a student to the committee, to be chosen by the student senators. They selected a man well into his twenties, Cal Graham.

The creation of this ad hoc committee, soon known as the Joint Committee on Alternatives (JCOA), turned out to be momentous. Because neither the president nor the board challenged its mandate, JCOA effectively seized control of staffing and, by extension, of the budget. Provisionally passed during the special meeting, the motion to create JCOA was confirmed at the regular meeting of the Senate, held the following day. At this time Rajagopal joined the committee as the YUFA representative. (A check with other members of the YUFA executive had persuaded me that I should not be a member, since this might prove to be a problem if JCOA were to recommend that faculty members be dismissed. However, I attended almost every meeting as an observer.) Also added were Don Hathaway, representing the York University Staff Association (YUSA), Ian Sowton as the chairman of the Council of College Masters, and a member of SCAD, Ann Wilbur MacKenzie of the Glendon Philosophy Department. She was the only woman on the committee and very probably its only untenured faculty member. Bill Farr and his assistant, Mal Ransom, served as co-secretaries.

The committee's initial meeting took place on Saturday, 28 October. Since it proved impossible on short notice to find a time that suited everybody's schedule, the second meeting took place at 11 p.m. on Wednesday, 1 November, in the principal's apartment in Glendon Hall, with Albert Tucker serving drinks. Barry Richman, who had become dean of administrative studies in July 1972, showed up in pyjamas and dressing gown as a humorous protest against the late hour! Before adjourning well after midnight, JCOA spun off several subcommittees

A York graduate, William D. Farr was secretary of the university from 1969 and, in 1973, became a vice-president.

York graduate Malcolm Ransom was secretary of York from 1973 to 1998.

Robert Lundell, professor of chemistry and dean of the Faculty of Science, 1972–82.

The historian Harry S. Crowe was twice dean of Atkinson College.

that would gather information about enrolment, the budget, and related subjects, and undertook to meet regularly to discuss what had been learned and examine proposed initiatives to raise enrolment or curtail budgets.

At a special Senate meeting on 8 November, a motion passed authorizing a continuation of the committee and its work. By this time the committee had already begun to resemble a decanal coup d'état. "The deans and senate, in defying the board and the president, have created a major tremor in York's power structure," an *Excalibur* staff writer commented shrewdly.[168] As president, Slater was the university's chief executive officer. As a member of JCOA, he was one of a group dominated numerically by the deans, who increasingly acted like medieval barons seeking to limit the power of the king. Not that they necessarily made common cause, or that they were equally influential. Jack Saywell, calm and in command, had a lot more clout than, say, Bob Overing, who remembered: "As a newcomer to York, I was still finding my feet."[169] Harry Arthurs was clearly a man of influence, and he and Bob Lundell, the acting dean of science (he was confirmed in the deanship early in 1973), made their views heard more readily than Gerald Carrothers, Jules Heller, or Albert Tucker. However, when one of Heller's associate deans, Joe Green or David Silcox, turned up in his stead, they were vocal participants. William McClure of Lakeshore Teachers' College and Michael Collie, the dean of graduate studies, rarely spoke. Richman spoke often, but he was a recent arrival and young, and lacked the gravitas of the older men. "He had no weight among the other deans," Tucker recalled.[170]

The dean who threw his weight around most was Harry Crowe. Marion Boyd said he made Slater's life miserable. "Harry constantly surprised him ... I felt that Harry was stabbing him in the back."[171] Saywell recalled that "Harry was out to get David from the moment he arrived."[172] Crowe had hoped to be president himself and had not abandoned this ambition. Moreover, he had doubts about Slater's suitability for the job. To everyone who cared to listen he would say: "At Queen's he was just a paper dean."[173] Crowe was also determined to protect the members of the Atkinson faculty, many of them junior and vulnerable. One was Wallace Northover, who taught social psychology. He remembered getting a telephone call from Walter Tarnopolsky that fall, advising him to look for another position. Others received the same advice, he said. "When Harry heard about it, he hit the ceiling. He went to bat for us." This is why, he said, "the younger faculty would have walked on hot coals for Harry."[174] And Crowe was a formidable opponent. He did not shrink from a fight, possessed political skills in abundance, and could be very ruthless. Aware that Slater lacked political savvy as well as toughness, Howard Adelman said, "Harry simply pounced on David."[175]

Although Crowe's political skills were impressive, he would have had little influence had he been the only dissident dean. However, in the course of November, several other deans gradually lost confidence in Slater's ability to lead York through the crisis. His capacity for seeing more than one side of an issue was a strength, but that strength became a weakness when he kept on talking about the options, seemingly unable to decide which to choose. Henry Jackman, who joined the Board of Governors in November 1972, recalled that another board member warned him not to ask Slater a question unless it was essential, because "the answer could add forty minutes to the meeting."[176] Saywell's assessment was blunter: "David couldn't stop talking."[177] Some of the deans got tired of listening to Slater, MacIntosh remembered, and phoned him to complain. One dean who must go nameless informed MacIntosh even *before* the crisis that he intended to boycott all further meetings chaired by the president.[178]

Nevertheless, it seems surprising that dissatisfaction with Slater grew during November, because, so far as many faculty members were concerned, the crisis was receding, at least in its most menacing aspect. Reintroducing Schedule 11 of the SCAD report on 8 November, committee member Deborah (Hobson) Samuel explained that "the committee wished to give sufficient time for submissions respecting Schedule 11 ... given the fact that the urgent application of the procedures proposed ... seems less and less likely."[179] Slater stated that, "based on legal opinions received from the University's solicitors," York could not terminate probationary or tenured faculty for budgetary reasons for effect in 1973 and he would so advise the board.[180] Should contract faculty and non-academic staff receive the same assurance? Slater advised against this, noting that "extreme pressure had already been placed on many budgets, and all options should not be closed off."[181]

Meeting with the board's executive and finance committees on 10 November, Slater said that JCOA should be able "to devise a strategy for the next 2½ years." A balanced budget was impossible in 1973–74, but it should be an attainable goal for 1974–75. "If this kind of budgetary situation cannot be confidently foreseen, then faculty terminations for effect in 1974–75 will have to be planned for."[182] This seemed to satisfy her colleagues, Clarkson recalled, but she and Anderson had come to the view that Slater "wasn't up to the job." She thought that "the men were kind of protective of David. After all, they had appointed him."[183]

At a special Senate meeting on 22 November, Slater acknowledged that "earlier attempts to force an almost immediate return to a balanced budget by terminating faculty for 1973–74 were rather short-sighted" and reported a general conviction that "faculty terminations should be only a last resort, if other alternatives fail to improve the University's position sufficiently."[184] The Senate then approved a further extension of the Joint Committee until 13 December, when it would make a final report. Thus validated, JCOA continued its assessment of the university's services, prospects, and proposals for change.

The most fascinating and sobering report received by the committee came from the subcommittee on enrolment. Based on careful research and, as Ted Olson recalled, shaped by the decision not to indulge in wishful thinking,[185] it stated: "The rate of growth in Metro Grade 13 population has been slowing for several years. This year the Grade 13 population went into absolute decline and now stands 1500 below projections made only two or three years ago." Together, Metropolitan Toronto and York County were down 5.8 per cent from previous years. "It is clear that over the next few years, there will be no population pressure to drive up an intake of students automatically."[186] The report identified another variable that was undermining York's enrolment, one that has affected the university more than once over the years. In order to maintain its intake, the University of Toronto had lowered its entrance requirements and was expected

Robert MacIntosh was chairman of the Board of Governors, 1971–75.

Petrie Science Building.

to continue to do so whenever necessary. "Its basic attractiveness, unlikely to decline in the near future, guarantees, under these circumstances, that U of T takes a larger and larger proportion of a shrinking number. This leaves York in the position of competing with other universities for the smaller remainder."[187] Most arts faculties in the province had fallen short of their projections in 1972, the report continued, but York's enrolment had suffered more than most because of the impact of the University of Toronto's intake, especially noticeable in York's Faculty of Science.

The subcommittee speculated about the reasons, other than demographic change, for the decrease in the pool of students, identifying two: the negative impact of student activism on public opinion, and growing unemployment among university graduates. The prognosis for the future was uncertain. "At the very least, we cannot as a University community go on making projections as if the bulge in the birth rate had continued."[188]

The report was disturbing. Evidently York could not expect to grow out of its predicament. The report also prompted questions damaging to Slater's leadership. Why had this research not been done when it might have done some good, might, indeed, have prevented the recruitment of professors in the undergraduate arts and science faculties? Moreover, should the enrolment shortfalls experienced by other institutions in 1971 not have prompted caution on York's part?

The report did identify opportunities to be exploited. For example, one area where Grade 13 numbers were still growing was southern Etobicoke. Unhappily, the transportation links to this part of the city were particularly awkward. A subcommittee proposal, later approved, was to lease buses and run them into this area. Also, the Yonge Street subway line would soon extend north to York Mills, and the subcommittee proposed that the university operate an express line from the York Mills station to the Keele campus, supplementing the service that already connected the Keele and Glendon campuses.[189]

(Only after Finch station opened in 1974 did public transportation to the campus improve significantly. The opening of the University-Spadina line to Wilson station in 1978 and to Downsview eighteen years later, with express buses running to the Keele campus, was an even more positive development. But, as more than one user of those buses has recalled, there could be as many as two or three hundred people waiting to get on the bus in the morning, and the ride to and from the campus was often maddeningly slow. The fervently hoped-for extension of the subway line to York would remain a mirage into the early years of the twenty-first century, when the growth of population north of the campus finally forced the TTC and governments to acknowledge the obvious and commit themselves to construct the line that should have been built three decades earlier.)

JCOA was not alone in coming up with innovations. The Faculty of Arts developed a "Drop-In-Year Proposal" that gained approval at the regular Senate meeting on 23 November. It permitted students to begin their courses in January and complete the academic session by mid-August.[190] This required the adjustment of some teaching schedules and the hiring of part-time faculty, but it promised significant financial rewards.

By December, the deans were in control of the Joint Committee. This is not to say that they always saw eye to eye on things. Olson recalled that each dean tended to be defensive when *his* faculty came under discussion.[191] But, on the subject of decanal power in general, the deans seemed to be united. The faculty members were independent, but Rajagopal and Sowton, both professors in Atkinson College, were understandably close to Crowe.[192] So was MacKenzie: "I was talking a lot with Harry at the time and was strongly influenced by his view of things."[193] All three tended to support the deans, as did the YUSA representative, Don Hathaway, and the student senator, Cal Graham. Howard Robertson, who chaired the committee as well as the Senate, sought to maintain neutrality and generally succeeded, while Olson was regarded as a Slater loyalist. Tarnopolsky also stood loyally by the president, in spite of the fact that, in Arthurs's phrase, "he got hung out to dry" after declaring himself to be in favour of dismissals during the Senate meeting of 25 October.[194] The other two vice-presidents, Bill Small and Bruce Parkes, said little, though Arthurs remembered that of all the committee members Small seemed closest to Slater. When interviewed, however, Small chose to remain silent about the episode.[195]

In early December, Tarnopolsky suddenly resigned, effective at the end of the month, when he would become a professor in Osgoode Hall Law School. *Excalibur* reported him as saying that it was not the budget crisis that had driven him out: "That was hard work, but not reason enough to quit. It was my feeling that I was ineffective in my post." He added that "there's no need for an academic vice-president and ... he will recommend the position be dissolved." The official reasons given for his departure were vague, "but unofficially it's said that Tarnopolsky clashed head-on with York's deans."[196] However, in January 1973 *Excalibur*'s Jim Daw wrote: "It was later learned that Slater had failed to define the role of the academic vice-president or to delegate effective authority."[197] Whatever the grounds for Tarnopolsky's resignation, Slater lost an ally.

Perhaps it was this resignation that drove Slater to act. Perhaps it was the deans' dominance of the Joint Committee. He was aware that some of them were disaffected. After meeting with a couple of the deans in Crowe's office, David McQueen and Howard Robertson had told Slater on 8 December that most of the deans had lost confidence in him,[198] and he must have known that Crowe was openly critical of him. Perhaps Slater acted on his belief, gleaned from talking to several professors, that he had more support among the faculty than among the deans. Perhaps, as Arthurs has suggested, the stress of the past few months had begun to affect Slater's judgment, prompting "some bizarre behaviour."[199] Certainly the step he took on 10 December was little short of bizarre.

The Joint Committee met in the Principal's Dining Room on the Glendon campus all day Saturday and Sunday, 9 and 10 December. The Sunday meeting began with a morning session held in camera at Slater's request. (I was not permitted to attend it but heard what had happened immediately afterwards.) He said he wished to resume the full exercise of his presidential powers and believed he could count on the support of the Senate and most of the deans. One, however, had made his job particularly hard. He turned to Crowe and faced him with an ultimatum: either commit yourself to support me or resign as dean. There was a moment of stunned silence, then Crowe got up and, without saying a word, left the room. MacKenzie remembered she was so astonished by what Slater had just done that she got up and sternly said to him: "David, you *can't* ask what you're asking for."[200] Robertson promptly called a ten-minute recess. Crowe returned, but not before he had phoned his associate dean, Henry Best, who set a pre-arranged "telephone tree" into motion. An hour later a large group of Atkinson College faculty were gathering in the Junior Common Room to show their support for Crowe and discuss what they could do to fight off the threat to him.

They had less cause for concern than they thought. When the committee reconvened in open session, disapproval of Slater's action was almost universal. Indeed, the ultimatum to Crowe convinced at least three of the deans, Carrothers, Overing, and Tucker, that the president's judgment was temporarily impaired, so that it would be ill-advised to have him resume the full exercise of his powers at this point.[201] The members of a JCOA delegation said nothing about the incident when they met the board on the afternoon of Monday, 11 December, but the story quickly spread and some board members had already heard it.[202] It was in any case clear that something was wrong. Slater did not attend the board meeting, and Tarnopolsky's resignation was a disagreeable surprise.[203]

Slater also skipped the last meeting of the Joint Committee, held Monday evening in the Board-Senate Chamber at Glendon. After JCOA approved the final version of the report to be presented to the Senate, the discussion turned to the presidency. Eventually a motion passed to recommend to the Senate that, for the remainder of the academic year, executive power be exercised by a five-person Coordinating Committee, chaired by Saywell and consisting also of Parkes and Richman, a student member – Cal Graham was the obvious choice – and a faculty member to be chosen by the Senate. Its function would be to oversee the implementation and continuation of the work started by the Joint Committee.[204] Whether Slater would accept this remained to be seen.

He would not. He objected strenuously, in fact, and urged Robertson to call yet one more meeting of the Joint Committee. Addressing the other members of JCOA in the Founders College Master's Dining Room on Tuesday evening, Slater said he interpreted the motion to continue the work of JCOA after 13 December as a clear indication of non-confidence in himself. If the Senate were to accept it, "he would take it as a further expression of non-confidence."[205] He urged committee members to reconsider their motion and presented three proposals of his own. As an alternative, he offered amendments to Monday's motion that would enable him to live with it. He then left the meeting.

The restive mood that evening can be inferred from Farr's minutes. Those who had agreed to serve on the Coordinating Committee withdrew their names, and, in the course of a discussion that went late into the evening, efforts to find a formula for the composition and mandate of the committee that would be acceptable to Slater alternated with "attempts by some members to have the committee discuss or vote upon the matter of its confidence or non-confidence in the President." In the end, with several members opposed and others abstaining, a compromise motion passed proposing the creation of a Coordinating Committee whose membership would include three members chosen by the Senate and two by Slater, and that would serve until 30 June 1973. "The meeting, and the Committee, then adjourned for good."[206] Reading the words, one can almost hear Farr's sigh of relief.

The Senate met on 13 December to receive the final report of the Joint Committee. Most of the recommendations dealt with initiatives designed to increase enrolment or to reduce the operating deficit in 1973–74. Slater said he supported the recommendations, recognized "the need for continuity from the work of the Joint Committee," undertook to cooperate fully with the new committee, and thanked JCOA and the staff who worked with them. "I readily acknowledge that the University has found itself in troubles in the last year and that I share in the responsibility for those difficulties," he concluded, "but I am optimistic that we have found the course that will solve the difficulties and serve the University more effectively in the future."[207]

Alas, neither York nor Slater was out of the woods. The 14 December issue of *Excalibur* carried the story of Slater's ultimatum to Crowe.[208] A day later it appeared in the Toronto *Star*.[209] On the afternoon of the fourteenth, MacIntosh, believing the situation to be deteriorating, "called an emergency meeting of the Executive Committee to meet as many deans as could be found on short notice … together with the Vice-Presidents, the Chairman of Senate, and three other senior senators including the Senate members on the Board." Those attending were "nearly unanimous" in indicating "lack of confidence" in the president.

Confronted with this information on 15 December, however, Slater responded that he "retained the confidence of a significant majority in Senate and held the view that he should continue in office."[210]

A difficult situation was made even more difficult by Barry Richman. Around this time, MacIntosh recalled, Richman approached him and threatened to resign unless the board dismissed Slater. MacIntosh rejected the threat, but a few days later he received a telegram from Richman, who had gone to Hawaii with his family for the holidays, signalling his intention to resign. Worse: he instructed Len Birchall, executive officer of administrative studies, to convey his letter of resignation to the faculty, and asked Howard Robertson to have it read to the Senate. Alert to the implications, Colonel Birchall – Brian Dixon remembered him as "the consummate executive officer"[211] – warned MacIntosh. Almost forty years later, MacIntosh still got angry thinking about Richman's lack of good sense. The letter was critical of Slater and, if published, would prove embarrassing to him *and* the university, but "Richman refused to withdraw it or block its publication."[212] As a result, the story spread to the media. "York Dean Quits, Criticizes President," read a headline in the Toronto *Star*; the article contained the text of Richman's letter.[213] "Leadership Crisis Pits York Deans against President," a *Globe and Mail* headline shouted.[214] MacIntosh, who feared that public controversy would worsen York's enrolment and financial problems while damaging university morale, said he was deeply dismayed.[215]

The *Globe and Mail* article appeared on 22 December. By this time, Slater had agreed in principle to resign, effective 30 June 1973, with discussion of the details postponed until after the Christmas break. After the university reopened on 8 January, intense and difficult negotiations took place for two weeks, with Ian Douglas of McCarthy and McCarthy acting for the board and board member (and lawyer) James Lewtas playing a key role.[216] On 22 January, Slater resigned, effective immediately. "In my view," he wrote, "acceptance of this request is in the best interests of the university."[217] It was a sad end to a presidency that under more favourable circumstances could have been a successful one. York's structures were unequal to the challenges posed by the 1972 budgetary shortfall, unfortunately, and Slater became its most prominent victim. A more determined and self-assured president might have weathered the crisis successfully; so might one who enjoyed greater support. Slater, however, was largely isolated. Moreover, he was unprepared by his background and ill-suited by his temperament to deal with a major financial crisis, and he was distracted by the activities of a disaffected dean. Severe stress impaired his judgment and led him to make the grave error of presenting Harry Crowe with an ultimatum. This misstep lost him much of whatever support he still had among the other deans. Few if any people questioned Slater's essential decency and fair-mindedness. It was doubts about his ability to lead York through the most difficult period in its history that brought him down.

On 22 January, MacIntosh asked Richard Storr, who had come to York in 1968, was the first graduate director of history, and in 1972–73 was co-chair of the Board-Senate Governance Committee, to be acting president. Storr accepted the position for a period of up to eighteen months.[218] MacIntosh recalled that

In 1973 the historian Richard Storr was briefly acting president.

Storr, who was fifty-seven, said he was fit but would get a physical check-up. That seemed a formality. "He looked healthy enough to me," MacIntosh said, "but I should have waited before making the announcement." Two days later, Storr phoned and said the recurrence of an old illness forced him to withdraw. "It was like a blow to the solar plexus," MacIntosh remembered. The announcement had been made the day before; how would York look when it lost its second president within three days?[219]

The nature of the illness was not revealed to the board or to the public. A *Globe and Mail* article mentioned "a heart condition."[220] That was a guess. In fact, Storr said in an interview, the illness was war-related. It recurred when he found himself in the president's office. "I felt immobilized, and instead of fooling around with it, I just resigned."[221]

The board met again, this time to accept Storr's resignation and appoint John Yolton, a member of the Philosophy Department since 1963 and a Senate representative on the Board of Governors, in his place.[222] His name had been suggested by Sydney Eisen, dean elect of the Faculty of Arts, with other members of the Senate Executive Committee concurring. Yolton was reluctant to take the job, but his acceptance was made easier by Bill Farr's promotion to a vice-presidency.[223] (Mal Ransom succeeded him as university secretary.) With Farr to assist him, Yolton must have felt equal to the task he faced.

Should Farr have been made acting president? Marion Boyd said that for many practical purposes he acted in that capacity while Yolton had the title; she thought Farr should have had the title himself.[224] Dixon, appointed acting dean of administrative studies in January 1973 to replace Richman, agreed.[225] But MacIntosh, while conceding that Farr was the most competent senior administrator, said that making him acting president never occurred to him: "He was so young, and he was not an academic."[226] Henry Jackman noticed from the moment he joined the board that his colleagues had "more confidence in Farr than anyone else and constantly sought his advice," but he, too, cited his youth and lack of academic stature as reasons for not considering him for the top job, even in an interim capacity.[227] Was this realism or a failure of imagination? Whatever the answer, the arrangement reached in January 1973 helped to settle the university down.

Some bad moments were still to come. On 25 January a Toronto *Star* editorial asked: "Is Canadian higher education so weak in administrative talent that York University can find only American citizens to qualify for its presidency?"[228] (Both Storr and Yolton were Americans.) A front-page article in the 1 February issue of the *Globe and Mail* asserted that "David Slater resigned as president of York University only after the board of governors said he would be fired if he did not," and offered an account of the "extraordinary meeting of top university officials" that was held at the Bank of Nova Scotia, where MacIntosh was the executive vice-president, on 14 December, complete with a list of those attending.[229] Evidently leaks to the media continued to be part of York's culture. But after this the storm subsided. "I worked well with John," MacIntosh said: "Things went smoothly."[230]

And yet one aspect of the arrangement may, in the long run, have damaged York. Sheldon Levy, who was doing an MA in mathematics in 1972–73 and had

John Yolton of the Department of Philosophy was acting president from 1973 to 1974.

York graduate Sheldon Levy would rise to the rank of vice-president.

a part-time job helping to prepare the Faculty of Arts budget (later he was a vice-president), speculated that the interregnum between two presidents hurt York where funding was concerned. During that time, the Ontario Council of University Affairs (OCUA) adopted a new funding formula that discounted both decreases and increases in student enrolment. "This protected mature institutions like the University of Toronto, which wanted a stable income," Levy said, "but it turned out to be very unfair to York" once growth resumed in the 1980s. He suggested that Yolton's lack of interest in the issue put York at a disadvantage, the more so because Farr, in any case not fond of public confrontation, felt that he lacked the authority to challenge OCUA or the presidents of the other universities. He might have been able to defend York's interests more vigorously had *he* been acting president.[231]

What did the events of 1972 mean to faculty, staff, and students? Well-established members of the faculty and administrative staff probably felt fairly sure of their positions. Most students neither knew nor cared what was happening, and this in spite of *Excalibur*'s coverage of the crisis. The response of Rosemarie Schade, who was in second year at Glendon, may have been typical: "It meant nothing to me. Students have no idea what goes on at the top."[232] "I have no recollection [of a crisis]," Marion Lane, a second-year student at Osgoode, said.[233] Sandie Rinaldo, a fourth-year student in Fine Arts, said: "What crisis? I don't remember anything."[234] On the other hand, Jamie Laws, a fourth-year student in Arts, had no difficulty recalling the crisis. He was a student member of the Senate at the time and would soon be the first student member of the Board of Governors. He was therefore well informed. But he surmised that most students had other things to think about. "I don't think every student read the campus paper, especially the political parts. Many students simply didn't realize there was a financial problem."[235]

Not surprisingly, some junior faculty members felt seriously threatened. Barbara Godard, who held a one-year renewable contract in the Arts English Department at the time, felt "very vulnerable and fragile. I wondered if I would survive."[236] Cyndi Zimmerman of the Glendon English Department was in the tenure stream, but because she had not yet completed her PHD she, too, felt vulnerable: "I was very worried; that's why I went on POD [YUFA's Prevention of Dismissals Committee]. What drove me was the fear of losing my job."[237] Daniel Drache, who joined the Atkinson Political Science Department in 1971, believed that Slater hoped to use the crisis to fire radicals like him "for discrediting the university."[238] On the other hand, Gerald Jordan, appointed in the Arts History Department in 1970, said: "I don't remember worrying about my job. I was too busy teaching and raising children. Besides, I realized that there was nothing I could do about the situation, and I had a lot of faith in Syd Eisen."[239] Bill Irvine, who arrived with his Princeton doctorate in hand, said he thought there were enough faculty members without PHD degrees around that he was probably safe.[240] Marc Rosen, who had taught film in Fine Arts since 1968 but did not yet have tenure, said he hardly noticed the crisis and did not worry about it: "It didn't really affect Fine Arts. We had lots of students."[241]

It *is* true that the enrolment shortfall barely touched the professional and graduate faculties. Brian Dixon recalled reacting with outrage when the Coordinating Committee established by the Senate in December 1972 asked Administrative Studies to make a 15 per cent budget cut for 1973–74. "Who were these guys?" he asked, answering his own question: "They were mainly from Arts or Science!" (For its representatives on this committee, the Senate elected Michael Creal and the economist John Buttrick, both from Arts, and David McQueen from Glendon College; Slater appointed the chemist John Goodings and Warren Grover of Osgoode Hall Law School. Of the five, none had significant experience with budgets.) Dixon complained to Yolton and Farr, pointing out that Administrative Studies had made its enrolment target in 1972–73 and fully expected to see enrolment increase again in 1973–74. "In the end I got permission to make six appointments and my budget increased by 20 per cent!"[242]

One urgent task in 1973 was finding a new president. The events of 1969–70 and the troubles York had just passed through strongly influenced the new search committee. Guidelines for the search, developed by the Senate Executive Committee and approved by the board, were clearer than those the previous committee had worked with. The search committee, consisting of three members each from the board, the Senate, and the student body, worked expeditiously and in a spirit of cooperation. Chair of the committee was Mavor Moore of the Theatre Department in Fine Arts. A board representative on the committee, Henry Jackman, recalled him as "an exceptionally good chairman," equipped with superb political antennae. "He insisted: 'We have to consult everyone; we have to get the sense of the community first.'" There was interest in only one internal candidate, Saywell, "and he took himself out." (Gillies had done so by obtaining political leave in 1972 to run for the House of Commons. He represented Don Valley for the Progressive Conservatives until 1979, when he returned to York.) All the deans were interviewed, Jackman said, "but that was only for courtesy." The dominant attitude was that "the president had to come from outside." Asked to present a list of candidates to the Senate, "we gave them twenty-odd names."[243] Most promptly withdrew, leaving a list of eight.[244] Only two got more than 50 per cent of the Senate vote, and only their names were forwarded to the board: H. Ian Macdonald, the deputy treasurer and deputy minister of economics and intergovernmental affairs of Ontario, and Brian Wilson, vice-president (academic) at Simon Fraser University.[245] "The board all knew Macdonald," Jackman said, "the fellow from British Columbia nobody knew."[246] On 13 November a press release announced that Macdonald would become York's third president and vice-chancellor as well as a professor in the Faculty of Administrative Studies, assuming office on 1 July 1974.[247]

Tall and athletic, born and raised in Toronto, Hugh Ian Macdonald was in his forty-fifth year. He had taken a B.Comm. degree at the University of Toronto in 1952 and gone on to Balliol College, Oxford, as a Rhodes Scholar. He still played recreational hockey and would continue to do so for years to come. More important from the point of view of the search committee was that he had a background in academe augmented by recent administrative experience. Upon returning to Canada after three years at Oxford, having gained the B.Phil. degree in economics, he taught at the University of Toronto for a decade before becoming chief economist of the province of Ontario in 1965. Two years later he became deputy provincial treasurer and deputy minister of economics; the appointment to intergovernmental affairs followed in 1972. His financial background and connections to the provincial government were strong points in his favour.

Newspaper responses to the appointment were highly positive. The *Globe and Mail* stated that the Board of Governors had made "an eminently wise decision in its appointment of Ian Macdonald as its next president."[248] A few days later, Norman Webster wrote: "It is not really stretching things to say that H. Ian Macdonald has been one of the most influential Canadians of the past decade."[249] The *Star's* Hartley Steward referred to York's new president as "Ontario's quiet doer,"

Keele campus, aerial view, taken between 1975 and 1985.

and lauded his ability and achievements in words supplied by former Premier John Robarts, current Premier William Davis, provincial NDP leader Stephen Lewis, and a former federal Liberal cabinet minister, Walter Gordon.[250] (Both Gordon and Robarts were later chancellor of York.) This was music to the ears of many at York.

Davis advised him against accepting the offer, Macdonald remembered. York was known to be in trouble, and the premier questioned whether the presidency would be a good thing for him, although Davis recognized the contribution Macdonald could make to York. Moreover, Davis was not eager to lose Macdonald's services and would have preferred him to stay with the Ontario government, Macdonald said. However, he had never thought he would spend the rest of his working life in the public service. When he had left the University of Toronto in 1965, it was an opportunity for a change, "but I still thought of myself as a university man, and I was happy to return to a university." And York appealed to him as a project: "How do you build a first-rate institution close to an old, established one?" He knew some of the people at York, among them Ramsay Cook, Bob Haynes, Bill Kilbourn, and David McQueen, and thought that they and others like them "were the basis of a strong university." The biggest challenge was the "bad press" York had at the time. The image of a distant suburban university, wracked by conflict, was unappealing. He added that "businessmen saw York as a place full of 'pinkos.'"[251] His new job, he realized, would not be easy.

Since Macdonald had been out of academe for almost a decade, he thought that he should teach a course, at least initially. Among other things the use of language had changed a bit, he found. He smiled as he remembered meeting one of his students in a corridor of the Ross Building: "We greeted each other, and I asked him how he was. 'I'm good, sir,' he replied. 'You mean you're well,' I said. 'Oh, I'm not *that* good.'"[252]

The crisis of 1972 cast a long shadow. Among its consequences were a debt of $2 million, whose servicing and retirement burdened York for several years to come; an unbalanced faculty complement that permitted more favourable faculty-student ratios in some areas of the university than in others, with inter-unit tensions and envy as a result; salary increases that lagged behind those awarded in other Ontario universities; and troubled labour relations. Compounding York's problems was that, in Paul Axelrod's words, "the process of financial retrenchment ushered in at the beginning of the 1970s continued largely unabated throughout the rest of the decade." Kept on a very tight budgetary leash by the provincial government, some Ontario institutions endured a "steady state," while others, York among them, "suffered through a depressing period of permanent underfunding."[253] How long this period would last was unclear in 1974, but it was a major part of the challenge facing Macdonald as well as the university whose presidency he had assumed.

The decade that began in 1973 is sometimes called "the big freeze." The Scott Religious Centre, financed by a large gift from W.P. Scott, was completed in 1974. In the decade that followed, construction was limited to the first tennis centre, located near Keele and Steeles, and the track-and-field complex farther west on Steeles. Neither was a York project. The university leased land to Tennis Canada and the municipality of Metropolitan Toronto so that they could build facilities for their own use, which York got to use as well. These projects did not alter the appearance of the built-up campus, which ceased to resemble a construction site. It did retain a certain unfinished suburban look.

When Ian Macdonald assumed his duties on 1 July 1974, enrolment was growing once again, but the increase was largely confined to Atkinson College and the graduate faculties. In the fall of 1974, full-time undergraduate enrolment was 10,720, just below the high of 10,735 attained in 1971. The modest rise in the number of undergraduates and in total enrolment that took place in 1975 and 1976 went into reverse in 1977, and over the next two years enrolments in most categories continued a slight downward trend. In 1979 full-time undergraduate enrolment reached a post-1970 low of 10,714.[1]

If York's steady-state enrolment in the mid- to late 1970s prescribed caution, so did the financial context the university operated in. In the second half of the 1970s, "higher education absorbed a diminishing proportion of public funds; corporate support of Canadian universities was further eroded; and an entire generation of highly trained doctoral graduates faced the dismal prospect of permanent underemployment."[2] This affected every Ontario university. Martin Friedland has shown that the University of Toronto suffered significantly from cutbacks in both provincial funding and research funding from the federal granting agencies.[3] Continued uncertainty about the intentions of the provincial government, reinforced by the awareness that there were other urgent claims on its resources, notably the rising costs of health care, prompted a defensive attitude.

One of the more startling developments of the 1970s was the decision of the teaching staff to seek certification as a labour union. A few years earlier this had seemed improbable. In 1968 Albert Robinson, an economist in Arts, asked whether "the loss of professional status and of the informal atmosphere of the university community," resulting from the creation of a union, would be compensated for "by significant gains in salaries and other material benefits." He thought not, and, in any event, the demand for faculty was likely to remain strong and the outlook for salaries good.[4] Soon provincial governments were cutting back on financial support, however, and recruitment dropped off. At the same time, public outrage prompted by the more confrontational aspects of the student movement exposed the universities *and* their faculty to attack. A 1971 report prepared for the Council of Presidents of the Universities of Ontario cited newspaper articles indicating that "the attitude of the public at large to the universities of Ontario is entirely hostile." Moreover, "expressions of editorial outrage" that for a time had been directed against students were now also aimed at professors.[5]

At York, the crisis of 1972, and the evidence it offered of administrative disarray, reinforced the anxieties prompted by provincial cutbacks and public criticism and led some faculty members to look for protection in a union. Another reason for exploring certification was dissatisfaction with the results of informal negotiations about salaries and benefits. Faculty members' belief that negotiators for the administration and board tended to adopt a "take it or leave it" attitude was reinforced in the spring of 1973. With inflation running in excess of 7 per cent, the board's final offer, shaped by York's financial problems, was a 4¼ per cent cost-of-living increase. Upon being told by George Eaton, an Atkinson College economist who chaired the Faculty Association negotiating committee, that the membership might turn this down, board member Henry Jackman said: "Let them! We can use the money to reduce the deficit."[6]

In 1974, a year when close to ten faculty associations across the country had already unionized or were unionizing, the York University Faculty Association took the first tentative step along the road to certification. In the spring two members of the executive met with two labour lawyers to gather information and solicit advice. However, it took another unsatisfactory experience with negotiations to push the process along. The political scientist Harvey Simmons, who led the association in 1974–75, recalled that YUFA was at a disadvantage in dealing with the board: "It had all the power. YUFA couldn't do much." He remembered saying that "things couldn't go on this way. The faculty would have to unionize to be taken seriously."[7] At a meeting on 17 April 1975, members voted 120 to 10 to instruct the executive to seek certification.[8]

A key figure was the historian Jack L. Granatstein. When he succeeded Simmons as chairman of YUFA in the spring of 1975, he was determined to help turn YUFA into a certified bargaining agent. His immediate reason, he said, was unhappiness with the way Paul Stevens, who chaired the Faculty of Arts History Department, had dealt with the money allocated for merit in the 1974–75 salary agreement. Stevens had awarded the money in equal amounts to the lowest-paid members of the department. Granatstein disagreed – "merit should go to the meritorious, to those who have published"[9] – and launched an informal griev-

The historian Jack L. Granatstein headed the York University Faculty Association from 1975 into early 1977.

ance followed by a formal one. Both failed. This convinced him that there should be rules and regulations "to prevent departmental chairs from making arbitrary decisions." Unionization seemed the best way of achieving them.

Granatstein's stature as a scholar helped the campaign for certification along. Still in his mid-thirties, he was already the author and editor of more than a dozen books, among them the magisterial *Canada's War: The Politics of the Mackenzie King Government 1939–1945*, which appeared in 1975. He was able to interest some other "big names" in signing a pamphlet entitled "Who Supports the Union," he recalled, and he was pleased that members of all three history departments gave solid support to the campaign. His new persona as a labour leader surprised some. He recalled going to a meeting of the Board of Governors and being quizzed by several of its members. "'Why do you want to do this thing?' Hal Jackman asked. Then Walter Gordon [the chancellor at the time] said: 'You have the votes, don't you, Jack?' I didn't know whether we had the votes or not, but I said: 'Yes, sir.'"[10]

There *was* strong opposition, in fact, especially in Administrative Studies, Science, and Osgoode Hall Law School. The Osgoode teaching staff managed to stay out of the bargaining unit, organizing themselves into the Osgoode Hall Faculty Association. This disappointed Granatstein, who remembered that the Osgoode professors were divided on the issue.[11] Furthermore, after the Ontario Labour Relations Board certified YUFA in 1976, a group of six faculty members, among them William Jordan of Administrative Studies and Del Smyth of Atkinson College, formed the Independent Faculty Movement (IFM) and took legal action to stay YUFA's certification.[12]

By the time this challenge was resolved in YUFA's favour, Granatstein was no longer YUFA chair. He was not on the team seeking to negotiate a first contract, but he was closely involved. It was a trying experience, he said. The historian Sidney Kanya-Forstner headed YUFA's negotiating committee, "and he was the only one on it who kept me sane." He, like Granatstein, wanted compensation for merit to be an important component of the salary settlement. Several other members of the negotiating committee or executive, such as David Clipsham, Virginia Hunter, and J. Ian McDonald, attached little or no importance to it. Hunter, one of Granatstein's colleagues in the Arts History Department, said that she opposed merit because of the distorting effects that merit payments had on salaries over time.[13]

Fortunately, from Granatstein's point of view, the administration team, which included Vice-President Bill Farr and the dean of science, Bob Lundell, insisted that merit pay must be part of the settlement. The document Farr drew up to guide the administration's negotiating team asserted: "Quality differences exist, can be identified, and ought to be rewarded differentially."[14] "I agreed with that," Granatstein said: "Merit was a sine qua non for me, but I had to fight like hell to keep it in. By the time I left the chair I was under no illusion as to what would happen to it if YUFA had anything to do with it." He began his term with the idea that "the university *was* the faculty," but he discovered that, from his perspective, the administrators were "less antipathetic to the interests of the university than many of the faculty." He found the struggle with his colleagues frustrating: "My blood pressure went through the roof." Early in 1977 he resigned, making way for the joint presidency of Hunter and Clipsham, who served out his term. "I have enjoyed my 20 months as Chairperson," Granatstein wrote to YUFA's secretary, "and I am genuinely sorry to leave before my time and with the task still incomplete."[15] Three decades later he expressed himself differently: "They were the most unpleasant two years of my life."[16] It was a difficult year for the executive, Hunter recalled. Fortunately, the chairman who followed her and Clipsham, the Glendon historian William Echard, had "a calming influence."[17]

The contract that was signed in 1976 for a two-year period assigned 1 per cent to merit, to be distributed according to some rather complicated rules. More significant, given York's history in the early 1970s, was an article dealing with financial exigency. In principle, the article established guidelines for the dismissal of faculty members on budgetary grounds. However, the burden of proof needed to demonstrate the existence of a financial crisis, and the procedures to be followed before anyone could be dismissed, were sufficiently cumbersome that they virtually guaranteed the article would not be used. In 1977–78, when major reductions had to be made in the budget, the axe spared the full-time faculty – there *was* a freeze on hiring – and fell on the part-time faculty instead.[18]

The York University Staff Association, which had been formed in 1970, had preceded YUFA down the road to unionization. Responding to the insecurity felt by many of *its* members in 1972 as well as to York's straitened circumstances, YUSA achieved certification in 1975. Ian Macdonald regarded this as one of his early disappointments as president. Seeing the secretarial staff as "the unsung heroes of York," he had authorized a salary increase for YUSA that other groups did not get. "My intention was to do something the staff needed and wanted. Nevertheless, they unionized."[19] When YUFA followed a year later, "this put additional strain on the budget" and contributed to the 1977–78 budget crunch.

The Staff Association launched the first seriously disruptive strike in York's history in September 1978. Just after the start of classes, with the administration and union far apart, YUSA's members "voted in favour of strike action to back their demands for improved wages and job security by a margin of 551 (71.9 per cent) to 222 (27.9 per cent)."[20] Myriam Obadia-Hazan, administrative assistant in the Glendon College French Department, said the strike had a lot of support on the Keele campus but less at Glendon, where most of the support staff were satisfied with their jobs and were not eager to strike for more money. "Some people couldn't really afford to go on strike; the strike pay was so low." Still, she and most other YUSA members joined the picket line: "Those who needed the strike pay were there every day."[21]

The strike, which lasted eighteen days, opened wide fissures in the university. Some professors refused to cross the picket lines, cancelling classes or holding them off campus; a few professors and students even joined the picket lines. Most tried to carry on as usual. Obadia-Hazan remembered that "the spirit on the picket line was good. Faculty members came and gave us food and coffee."[22] Even though many faculty members continued to meet their classes, some students complained they were not getting the education they had paid for. Their professors might be teaching, but the libraries and bookstores were closed.

Margaret Knittl, a historian who was dean of Atkinson College from 1974 to 1979, recalled the strike as a "particularly difficult period." Many Atkinson professors supported the strike and approximately half signalled their intention not to begin teaching until it had been settled. "Ian [Macdonald] wanted me to get the faculty back on the job," Knittl said, "but he knew and I knew that was impossible."[23] Some thirty Osgoode professors also indicated that they would cancel classes or teach them off campus. "A university spokesman said about 20 per cent of classes have been cancelled," a Toronto *Star* staff writer reported on 22 September, adding that student support for the strike seemed to be limited.[24] Students living in residence were particularly inconvenienced by the strike, and there was relief on all sides when renewed bargaining produced agreement on a one-year contract in early October, with YUSA president Laura Avens claiming victory. Macdonald reportedly said that he was "happy with the settlement" and hoped there would be "no animosity on either side."[25] Knittl remembered that "we got back on an even keel very quickly."[26]

A strike by the Graduate Assistants Association was averted later in 1978, but in 1981 its successor, Local 3 of the Canadian Union of Educational Workers (CUEW), which consisted of part-time faculty and graduate assistants, walked off the job. One part-time teacher, Ildikó Kovács, recalled that she was paid $1,000 when she taught her first language course in the Faculty of Arts French Department in 1974 (the starting salary of an assistant professor, teaching three full courses, would have been around $13,000). "There was no union to look out for us," she said. This changed in 1979, when the part-time faculty, who had been left out of YUFA and were eager for allies, joined forces with the Graduate Students Association in a new bargaining unit. The new union seemed to pay off quickly. "We got our first good contract in 1979," Kovács recalled, complete with a seniority clause.[27] Two years later, when the CUEW embarked on its first strike, money was not the main issue, according to union president Janet Patterson. Matters such as job posting, seniority, and class size were of greater importance.[28] But the union was divided, as teaching assistants in the Faculty of Science crossed the picket line to go to work and a number of part-time faculty members did as well. Richard Dubinsky, president of the Graduate Students Association, noted that classes in science could not be expanded as easily as those in arts, leaving graduate teaching assistants in science feeling less aggrieved. Moreover, teaching and lab assistants in science were closer to their professors, many of whom were anti-union, than were teaching assistants in the arts faculties.[29] The strike lasted a week, with a settlement that included a wage increase averaging 14 per cent but no limitation on class sizes. Aside from the interruption of classes, the strike had proved an inconvenience to students living in residence because postal workers, beer-store truck drivers, and TTC drivers had honoured the picket lines.[30]

For a few years there was labour peace, but 1984–85 witnessed three strikes. They were the result chiefly of the growing stress caused by rapid growth and a system of funding that did not fully reward it. Whereas most of the 1970s had been a period of stagnating enrolment, the early 1980s presented a very different picture. Vigorous growth resumed, and by 1984, the year Ian Macdonald left the presidency, full-time undergraduate enrolment was 18,087, up by almost 80 per

Margaret Knittl of Atkinson's History Department was York's first woman dean, 1974–79.

cent over 1979. Increases in part-time and graduate enrolment were less startling, but total enrolment in 1984 was 33,083, an increase of almost 50 per cent in ten years.[31]

This growth was a mixed blessing at best. Harry Arthurs, who became president at the beginning of 1985, has commented: "From the mid-1970s to the mid-1980s, the provincial government adopted a series of adjustments to its operating grants formula which were intended to, and did, treat York and other new universities less generously than the established institutions." Growth had to be financed with discounted grants. By 1985, "York was receiving $0.79 for each dollar received by the average Ontario institution ... Similar disparities were built into capital grants."[32] Buildings were becoming overcrowded, class sizes increased, teaching and research facilities deteriorated, part-time faculty did a growing share of the teaching, the workload of secretaries and technicians became more burdensome, and institutional morale suffered.

YUSA members walked off the job on 10 October 1984, with job posting, layoffs and recall, technical change, health and safety, and salaries the issues. The university signalled its intention "to continue to operate, although it will obviously be necessary to reduce many services."[33] Once again some faculty members and students demonstrated support for YUSA's action, while others continued to meet classes and attend them. When the strike ended after a week, YUSA members had gained some key concessions, particularly in the area of training to cope with technical change.[34]

Even as the clerical and technical staff were returning to work, the CUEW went out on strike, with salaries and job security for part-time faculty the main issues. The growth of student numbers in the early 1980s had not led to a commensurate increase in the full-time faculty. With university finances as strained as they were, only the growing use of part-time teachers allowed York more or less to make ends meet. They were often fully qualified, having doctorates and publications, and they were well aware that they were being paid a lot less per course than full-time faculty. Furthermore, they were employed for eight months only, forcing them to look for summer work, usually in Atkinson College. Their goal remained to land a tenure-track position somewhere, but in the short run they looked for better salaries and benefits as well as an increased measure of security, that is, a beefed-up seniority system to govern access to all courses they were qualified to teach.

Not until 31 October did York and the CUEW reach an agreement that referred the issue of salaries to a team of three arbitrators.[35] "What I remember most is the fragile support among union members," Geoffrey Ewen, then a teaching assistant in history, said: "Many voted to strike to give the union a strong negotiating mandate but did not really want to strike. It was not clear to me that we would have been able to stay out for much longer."[36] From the student point of view, the strikers stayed out more than long enough. A plaintive editorial in *Excalibur* captured the dilemma facing students. In principle they tended to agree with the aims of the strikers, but they were aware that strikes interfered with their education. "Caught between sympathy for the union and their wish to continue their studies, students are placed in a very unpleasant situation."[37]

YUFA was next to strike. The union had come close to doing so in 1982 and 1984, and in the fall of 1985 it went all the way. Seeking a 9.5 per cent increase in salaries and an immediate end to mandatory retirement, a narrow majority of those professors and librarians who cast a ballot rejected the administration's offer, setting the stage for York's first faculty strike. It began on 8 October, even though the issue of compulsory retirement had been neutralized, the university agreeing to suspend the practice for two years while alternatives were explored. YUFA chair Hollis Rinehart told a *Globe and Mail* reporter that faculty members at the University of Toronto earned "between 8 and 10 per cent more than their York counterparts,"[38] yet the two groups faced the same housing and transportation costs.

A fascinating aspect of the strike was the attitude adopted by *Excalibur*. "The story this year is not of a greedy union nor of an exploitive management," editor Elliott Shiff stated: "Rather it is another sad side effect of the financial neglect York has suffered since the late 1970s. Simply put, there is not enough money coming into this institution to satisfy everybody ... We are not saying that York's faculty does not deserve more money, just that, for now, the institution can't afford it. And more importantly, the students can't afford a strike."[39] After the back-to-back work stoppages in 1984, many students had clearly had enough of strikes. When the YUFA strike began, Council of York Students Federation president Reya Ali said the Student Council was not taking sides, but it was meeting to "vote on whether to ask the president to implement less disruptive procedures for resolving contract disputes." If the strike were to go on for two weeks, he said, "drastic measures" would be considered, among them "asking students to withdraw from courses, requesting rebates of tuition fees, and taking court action."[40]

LEFT Picket line on the Keele campus during the 1985 YUFA strike.

RIGHT The 1985–86 CYSF executive. Left to right, front row: Vicky Fusca, Reya Ali (president), Janet Bobechko; second row: Sandra Antoniani, Robert Castle, Elise Hallewick; back row: Tim Rider, Jim Gresham.

A significant minority of YUFA members continued to teach, dividing the union as well as departments. Rinehart later said that he was "philosophical" about this: "We realized that some members would not want to think of themselves as belonging to an industrial-type union; in fact, we lost some members." However, "we were proud that so many members rallied to the cause in such an orderly and even enthusiastic way."[41] The Glendon sociologist Janice Newson, a member of the YUFA negotiating team, remembered it as "a leadership strike, supported grudgingly by the membership."[42] Penny Van Esterik, who had joined the Faculty of Arts Anthropology Department in 1984, found herself under pressure from two sides. "Half the department was on the picket line and said I would face problems with my application for tenure unless I joined them, and half were crossing the picket line and said I would face problems unless I crossed it too."[43] Two days into the strike, the university's negotiating team offered another quarter of a percentage point, and YUFA settled quickly. Rinehart conceded it was "not a great victory" but said that "professors traded wage increases for greater participation in deciding how the money should be spent."[44] He was "more relieved than disappointed," he later wrote: "We realized early on that ... this was more a demonstration than a strike. The administration's offer gave us a chance to end the strike without cost and even with a slight gain. I considered the strike a success."[45]

One unhappy aspect of labour relations in the later 1970s and early 1980s was that, in the absence of budgetary openness, it was simply too tempting for union leaders to assert that there was more money available than the administration would admit. Under George Bell, who became Ian Macdonald's executive vice-president in 1976, books were closed that had been open for several years. This had a serious downside. When Harry Arthurs told reporters in October 1985 that "although YUFA's wage demands are legitimate, the University doesn't have enough funds to 'pay our faculty what they should have,'"[46] faculty members took him at his word where their wage demands were concerned while taking his budgetary claims with a generous sprinkling of salt. "We needed something like the Senate Committee on the Budget; that might have helped," Sheldon Levy, a senior member of the administration, said. There was a distressing lack of civility, he remembered, as union representatives seemed to assume that administration negotiators were "cooking the books" and "lying about the numbers."[47] Newson, who served on nine YUFA negotiating committees between 1975 and 1990, agreed that the closed budgets of the Macdonald-Bell years exacerbated the differences between YUFA and the administration, and reinforced an "us versus them" mindset that made negotiations more difficult.[48]

In 1987 YUSA went on strike again, this time staying out for more than two weeks. A decade of relative labour peace followed. John Spencer, who was chief negotiator for the CUEW in the second half of the 1980s, credited much of this to Bill Farr and the people he hired, such as the lawyer Paula O'Reilly. "They saw it as sensible to try to reach agreement, to play softball rather than hardball ... On both sides you had people who were committed to reaching a deal."[49] For the CUEW, he recalled, the key issues were quality of work, that is, class size and seniority rights, areas where the administration had flexibility. Money was less

important: "We never imagined we could hope to get more money than YUFA." Seniority, however, "was always on the table one way or another." An important shift took place when applicants no longer had to demonstrate competence and those who were hiring them had to demonstrate incompetence. Spencer, who landed a full-time position in 1992 as a result of a provision in the CUEW contract enabling the conversion of long-serving members who could be fitted into departments, knew that some department chairs disliked the seniority clause. They wanted to hire the people they believed to be most qualified. But what would the absence of the clause have meant? he asked: "You got the job if the person hiring liked you. If a chair changed, you might be out of a job. Personal biases should not determine the choice."[50]

The construction program of the university was suspended as a result of the crisis of 1972, but in 1974 construction of a different kind was taking place. The

British sculptor Anthony Caro (he was knighted in 1987) was erecting a group of monumental works, the *Flats* series, on the Keele campus.

The story began when Edward Fry became chair of Visual Arts in 1971. Remembered by Ken Carpenter as "the best-published scholar we have ever had in visual arts," Fry had been an associate curator at the Guggenheim Museum, New York, and was well connected in the field of modern art. He was unhappy at York and did not stay long, resigning abruptly in the course of a meeting of the department in early 1974.[51] He left some unfinished business, for he had invited Caro, who had begun to work with steel beams, to come to Toronto and put up some of his work at York. Fry's sudden departure left Caro in a bind. As the Toronto collector and art dealer David Mirvish remembered the episode, in the spring of 1974 he got a phone call from Caro, whom he had met ten years earlier and whom he represented in Canada. The sculptor explained his problem, and asked: "What do I do now? Can you help me?" Mirvish phoned his acquaintance Joey Tanenbaum at York Steel to see if *he* could help. Caro needed a 100-ton crane, a crane operator, some men on the deck, and any steel that Tanenbaum's yard was not using. How much would it cost? Mirvish asked. "Joey said: 'I'll charge you a dollar a pound for the steel, and I'll throw in all the rest.'" For his part, Mirvish put up Caro and two of his assistants on the project, sculptors James Wolfe and Willard Boepple, at the Windsor Arms Hotel.[52]

After a while Tanenbaum needed the full use of his yard, and the pieces of metal needed a home where they could be completed. Mirvish or Boepple phoned Carpenter to find out whether York had space available.[53] Carpenter and then Mirvish took up the matter with Joe Green, who had succeeded Jules Heller as dean of fine arts. The phone calls came on a Friday afternoon in June, Green said, and he was unable to contact anyone in the President's Office or in the Department of Physical Plant who could direct him to a piece of land where the steel could be stored. Together with his executive officer, Tim Harris, he went looking for a suitable spot. "We found an overgrown plot of land east of a parking lot," he recalled: "It looked like a mess, so I phoned David and told him I had located some unused land and was making an executive decision to make it available to Tony."[54]

Flatbed trucks carrying lengths of steel began arriving at seven that evening. "At 9:30 I got a phone call from Bob Lundell: 'Green, what the fuck have you done to our weed reclamation project?'" The science dean was understandably annoyed that tons of steel had been dumped on a site that some of the botanists were using for an experiment. Green laughed heartily as he recalled the incident: "It cost me a dinner at Napoléon."[55]

After several weeks of work by Caro and his assistants, who had come to include André Fauteux and Howard Simkins, all thirty-seven pieces of the *Flats* series, consisting of rusted or varnished steel, each weighing between 2,000 and 3,300 kilos, were on display. In 1976, when the Tenth International Sculpture Symposium took place at York, Caro received an honorary doctorate from the university. Soon after that, the works began to disperse. Seven went to Mirvish in payment of his expenses; several were sold to collectors and museums.[56] Most went to an exhibition in Boston in 1980 and thence to Caro, back in England.[57]

Criss Cross Flats, by Anthony Caro.

He gave one piece to York in recognition of the contribution the university and Fine Arts had made to the project. *Criss Cross Flats* is on view northeast of the Curtis Lecture Halls. It is one of a number of sculptures on the Keele campus, among them works by Jocelyne Alloucherie (*Noire solaire, basse*), Alexander Calder (*Model of Man*), Enzo Cucchi (*Fontana d'Italia*), Mark DiSuvero (*Sticky Wicket*), Hugh LeRoy, a faculty member (*Rainbow Piece*), and George Rickey (*Four Squares in a Square*).[58]

Also in 1974, Fine Arts responded to a controversy that had boiled up downtown. In 1972 Toronto gallery owner Avrom Isaacs had displayed work by the controversial Montreal artist Mark Prent and had been charged with exhibiting a disgusting object. The charge was dismissed, but two years later another exhibition of Prent's work at the Isaacs Gallery brought renewed trouble with the law. "Joe then did something wonderful," Carpenter said: "He phoned Isaacs and told him York wanted the show."[59] In fact, Green made Prent's sculptures of human body parts, which were displayed in the lobby of the Fine Arts Building, the focus of a conference on censorship in the arts. A central participant was Edward Kienholz, a major U.S. installation artist whose work had frequently been attacked for its critical view of modern life. By exhibiting Prent's work in the context of a conference, Green turned it into an educational experience and at the same time took another step in drawing international attention to Fine Arts and to York.

In spite of budgetary pressures that became stronger as the decade went on, the 1970s were a good time for Fine Arts, with ample scope for experimentation. In 1969, the first year that students registered, people were more or less feeling their way, but soon the curriculum expanded. Taking the Theatre Department as

an example, by 1971–72 "there were six performance area courses, eight production area courses, and sixteen drama studies area courses listed. Among these drama studies courses was the first Canadian theatre course listed at York, 'Theatre Arts in Canada,' taught by Mavor Moore."[60]

Describing the first decade as "the chaotic early years," Don Rubin remembered stubborn individuals, stormy meetings, and an almost ungovernable department. There were no fewer than seven chairs and acting chairs of theatre in ten years: Joe Green, Robert Benedetti, Mavor Moore, Malcolm Black, William Lord, Ross Stuart, and finally Rubin himself: "I was the first to survive a three-year term."[61] By the time his term ended in 1982, things had settled down somewhat, and his successor also served three years.

At the outset, the program used the Burton Auditorium as well as a studio theatre in Atkinson College, but eventually it used fully thirteen spaces around the Keele campus. "The 1970s were the glory years of the Faculty of Fine Arts," Rubin said. "We kept growing and doing important things. You could go to Joe with some crazy idea, and he'd say: 'That sounds interesting. Let's try it.' And we did try. We were young then, and we had lots of energy."[62]

Among the accomplishments were the *York Theatre Journal*, whose first issue appeared in the winter of 1971 and which the students continued to publish after the department launched the *Canadian Theatre Journal* in 1974. In 1971–72 the department produced an ambitious *Lysistrata*, directed by Benedetti. In 1973–74 there were no fewer than ten productions, with Robert Carsen, today one of the program's most distinguished alumni, appearing in two of them. By 1974–75, there were twenty-two productions, nine of them directed by students. The directors included faculty members Malcolm Black, Jill Courtney, Neil Freeman, Joe Green, Jeff Henry, Ron Singer, and Norman Welsh. Among the twenty-two was the first Canadian play produced, Cam Hubert's *Windigo*; others would follow. Another initiative was the New Play Festival, founded by Alan Richardson in

1978–79, which continued to function throughout the 1980s. "In the 1970s we were creating something big," Rubin said somewhat wistfully: "By the 1980s we had created it, it was solidifying."[63]

Elizabeth Bradley, who spent four years in the department (1972–76), remembered "that marvellous sense of being young and in love with an art form, and getting immersed in it for four years." From the outset, she was more interested in producing and theatre management than in performance, and she found the department willing to accommodate her – "I was able to pick up some management courses in Atkinson College" – and to allow her to customize her program. The curriculum was innovative in requiring students to get courses in non-Western theatre. She spoke of Anatol Schlosser, who taught some of these courses, with affection. She also found Benedetti to be "inspirational" and greatly enjoyed talking with Moore and Welsh. In the Film Department she liked Doug Davidson and Peter Harcourt, "who taught me more about writing than anybody else." Among her fellow students she remembered Carsen, Barbara Budd, Rosemary Dunsmore, Sara Botsford, Sky Gilbert, and Jeanne Beker, all of whom "made good careers for themselves." She did not like the campus – "it was Siberia!" – or the time it took her to get downtown the year she lived in Stong College. But the faculty brought exciting performers and companies to the Burton Auditorium, such as Oscar Peterson (later chancellor of York) and Joseph Chaikin and his Open Theater ensemble. "We needed that: we were marooned out there!" She valued her years at York: "The BFA has taken me far. To say Fine Arts met my expectations is an understatement."[64]

Like theatre, visual arts went through turbulence in the early years. Joyce Zemans, who was chair of Liberal Arts Studies at the Ontario College of Art, was asked in 1974 whether she was interested in applying for the position of chair of visual arts. She turned it down, but the following year she got a phone call informing her the position had not been filled, and was she interested this time? Not really, she remembered, but she nevertheless decided to go for the interview. After "the bleakest drive I have ever had and wading through the mud to get to the Fine Arts Building," she said, she met the art historians and the studio

LEFT Cynthia Stanhope (left), Marni Walsh, and Peter Gooch in *Three Sisters*, 1983.

RIGHT Joyce Zemans joined the Visual Arts Department in 1975 and was later dean of fine arts.

LEFT   Dance students in the Raymond Moriyama-designed Joan and Martin Goldfarb Centre for Fine Arts.

RIGHT   News anchor Sandie Rinaldo studied in Fine Arts from 1969 to 1973.

people, and "got sucked in." She felt the energy in the place, and was attracted by York's philosophy and "its interdisciplinary approach to teaching."[65]

The department had gone through six chairs in six years, but Zemans managed to complete two three-year terms. The art historians and studio teachers did not always find coexistence easy, she remembered, but they learned to cooperate. Together they were "a remarkable assortment of people," among them Zdenka Volavka and Ted Heinrich in art history, Ron Bloore, Ken Lochhead, Doug Morton, and Tim Whiten in painting, Michael Greenwood, who was also curator of the art gallery, in photography, Vera Frenkel in video art, and Ken Carpenter in criticism. In 1985 Zemans became dean of Fine Arts, leaving in 1988 to become director of the Canada Council for the Arts. The great advantage of the faculty, she said, was its multidisciplinary approach, keeping the barriers between disciplines comfortably low.

That was part of the attraction of Fine Arts to Mary Jane Warner, a native of Toronto who returned to Canada from the United States in 1980 in order to teach dance at York. There were other dance programs in the country by that time, she recalled, "but the York program was the most interesting." She spoke affectionately of Grant Strate and Selma Odom, the founding director of the graduate program "and really instrumental in developing a good strong curriculum." The money had dried up by the early 1980s, and "some of the people who had arrived early were a bit disillusioned," but alumni were building successful careers, and "there was a real pride in what we were doing." Students were developing important skills and have continued to do so: "They learn discipline and team work, but they can also work independently and think creatively."[66]

Sandie Rinaldo would agree. She entered Dance in 1969, choosing it because it was new and allowed her to get a broad exposure to other subjects in the arts. She really liked the program, praising "the unique interdisciplinary nature of the Faculty." Among her instructors she found three particularly memorable: Don Coles, who made the humanities course he taught really engaging, Strate, the chair of the dance program, who "showed it was possible to set high goals and reach them," and Ahuva Anbary, a teacher of modern dance. "She did me a big favour. She told me, with her hands upon my shoulders, that I would never be a dancer." Taking Anbary's advice, Rinaldo switched to journalism. Thirty-five years after graduation, she said: "My image of York is warm and fuzzy. I met my husband there. The things I didn't like have faded; the many things I did like are what I now remember."[67]

Sheree-Lee Olson entered Fine Arts in 1975 because she had heard good things about it and because she "wanted a degree" rather than a community-college diploma. She majored in visual arts, which she found to be "tremendously eye-opening." Among the teachers she remembered were a teaching assistant, Wendy Knox-Leet, who was an innovative performance artist, as well as an "enormously charismatic" filmmaker, George Manupelli. She also studied creative writing, with Clarke Blaise, Don Coles, and Frank Davey. She particularly enjoyed a course with W.O. Mitchell, "a classic showman" who taught at York in 1976. "He taught us that writing is a technique, but that you must have something to write about." Olson fondly remembered the people she met at York, the building designed by Raymond Moriyama, and the Fine Arts faculty generally: "It was a real community."[68]

Music proved easier to govern than theatre or visual arts, with Sterling Beckwith putting in two years as chair, from 1969 to 1971, and Austin Clarkson and Alan Lessem both serving three-year terms in the 1970s. Lessem, indeed, returned for another term after his first sabbatical. The first music students registered in 1969, the first music majors were enrolled in 1970, and graduate studies began in 1977. From the outset, the department included fields like jazz and also looked beyond the Western tradition in music. This was deliberate, Beckwith remembered: he was "delighted by the existence of the Faculty of Music downtown, but aware of what it was *not* doing." There was no point in simply copying what the University of Toronto was already doing, so "we got away from the Eurocentric conservatory model; we were open to the music of the world."[69] Jon Higgins, an early member of the department who was trained in the classical music of south India, managed to interest a musician from India, Trichy Sankaran, in coming to York in 1971 for a year.[70] Except for one year at San Diego State University, he stayed at York, working in his own field but also collaborating with others, among them David Rosenboom, whose major interest was electronic music.

Joining the department in 1981 was Robert Bowman, who had entered Fine Arts as a student in 1974. Graduating with his first degree in 1978, he became, as he recalled, the first person accepted into the new MA program in ethnomusicology and "the first graduate teaching assistant the Music Department ever had."[71] His interest was in pop music, and in 1979 he was asked to do a college tutorial in Vanier College. Given a choice between "The Art of Bob Dylan" and a more general survey of rock and roll, the academic adviser chose the latter. "To make sure it got approved," Bowman remembered, "we [Bowman and Vanier's academic adviser] gave it an impressive title: 'A Social and Historical Survey of Contemporary Popular Music, 1954 to the Present.' That's how York got me to offer the first university course on post-war popular music ever given in Canada."[72]

Don Ross appreciated York's inclusive approach. He registered in 1979 after also considering the universities of Toronto and Western Ontario. "York's program seemed to be most forward-thinking," he said. He was interested in new music, and his favourite courses were in composition, with Philip Werren, James Tenney, and David Mott. A course in south Indian music with Sankaran was "fascinating": "he is such a master." Courses in theory with Casey Sokol and Steven Otto were also very worthwhile. He said of himself and other musicians who graduated from York: "We are the kind of musicians we are partly because we went to York ... The York experience helped us to be part of the vanguard." He loved the faculty, his fellow students, and the inter-arts collaboration with people in dance and film.[73]

As in visual arts, the music program sought to integrate the scholarly and academic side with the practical side. "I wanted to build this comprehensive alternative to the University of Toronto," Beckwith recalled. Having a cross-appointment in Humanities, he wanted students in both Arts and Fine Arts to become aware what the other faculty was doing. This, to him, was central to the idea of interdisciplinarity. Fine Arts students did take courses in Humanities and Social Science, he said, but Heller had opposed the idea of mounting courses that students from outside Fine Arts might take to broaden *their* horizons: "He disliked the amateurism that it implied." So did others in Fine Arts. "York, with its commitment to general education, should have offered more fine arts to students in other faculties."[74] To Beckwith, it seemed like an opportunity missed.

Not all the arts activity was located in Fine Arts. A studio course in Glendon College, staffed initially by printmaker Pat Fulford and sculptor Ray Speirs, and later by the painter Peter Kolisnyk, attracted many students. The Glendon dramatic arts program undertook a series of productions over the years, some of the more memorable being *Murder in the Cathedral*, *The Country Wife*, *King Lear*, and, in 1975, the first Canadian play in the program, *Big X, Little Y*, written by Elinore Siminovitch, designed by Ted Paget, and produced and directed by Bob Wallace. For a number of years, Alain Baudot conducted an amateur orchestra

LEFT   An ensemble of Fine Arts students making music.

RIGHT   Bruce Litvack, James Barnes, Ronn Sarosiak, Barbara Hamill, and Josette Cornelius in *Big X, Little Y*, 1975.

at Glendon College.[75] On the Keele campus, Michael Herren, a classicist who joined the Arts and Atkinson humanities programs in 1967, spoke about productions of the Titwillow Society, devoted to the production of works by Gilbert and Sullivan, in which he sang tenor roles: "I had lead parts in three of the operettas." Hollis Rinehart and Bob Fothergill also took part in them. Students mostly sang the soprano parts, Herren recalled.[76] He, Rinehart, the mathematician Joan Wick-Pelletier, and Cora Dusk of the administrative staff were also members of another group, the Demitasse Opera Company, which produced such works as Mozart's *Bastien und Bastienne* and Schubert's *Der Hochzeitsbraten*.[77]

No account of the arts at York is complete that does not acknowledge the poets, playwrights, essayists, and novelists on the teaching staff. They included Donald Coles, who published half a dozen volumes of poetry in the 1970s and 1980s; the poet, critic, literary historian, and anthologist Eli Mandel; another noted poet and anthologist, Miriam Waddington; poet and critic Frank Davey; Donald Summerhayes, whose first volume of poems, *Winter Apples*, appeared in 1982; the ebullient poet Irving Layton, who left Montreal for several years to teach at York; the playwright Bob Fothergill; and the most prolific and today clearly the best-known writer among them, Michael Ondaatje. Already a Governor-General's Award winner when he came to the Glendon English Department in 1970, he continued to publish poetry, prose, and plays of high quality at an astonishing rate. To list a few of his titles – *There's a Trick with a Knife I'm Learning to Do, Coming through Slaughter, The Collected Works of Billy the Kid, Running in the Family, In the Skin of a Lion, The English Patient* – is to refer to some of the major landmarks of Canadian literature.

Not all the work was being done in English. Hédi Bouraoui of the French Department was a noted poet. Margarita Feliciano, who joined the Linguistics and Language Training Program in the Faculty of Arts in 1969, remembered that Bouraoui encouraged her poetry, written in Italian, Spanish, and French, and that Waddington, "exuberant and outspoken, not at all typically Canadian," became a good friend. Feliciano later translated some of Waddington's poems into Spanish. Mandel, she said, was "extremely kind and gentle, very patient, a good listener." In time Feliciano began writing poetry in English as well, something Layton encouraged and helped her with. She also translated Spanish poetry into English, her own and that of Claudio Duran, a Chilean philosopher who joined Atkinson College after the military coup that overthrew Salvador Allende's left-wing government in 1973.[78]

Canadian literature loomed large at York not only because of the poetry and prose published by some of its faculty members. Starting in the early 1960s, Clara Thomas had taught a large course in American and Canadian literature. It was called AmCan, she recalled, citing it as evidence that "York, from the beginning, was teaching Canadian literature in a day when few universities did."[79] By the late 1960s, Canadian authors were writing more, new publishing houses like Anansi were actively promoting them, and interest in their work was growing. This was the positive side of the Canadian nationalism that was evident at the time. "Our literary landscape changed then, immeasurably for the better," Thomas has written: "Courses sprang up in every university because students began to demand

The poet Miriam Waddington was a professor of English in the Faculty of Arts.

Poet, novelist, and playwright Michael Ondaatje joined the Glendon English Department in 1970.

John Lennox and Clara
Thomas with a copy of
*William Arthur Deacon: A
Literary Biography*, 1982.

them, and the 'poor relation' among departmental course offerings quite suddenly became the darling of students and administration alike."[80] In 1968–69 she
taught York's first graduate course in Canadian literature. It was a seminar with
just three students, one of whom, Frank Birbalsingh, soon became a colleague.
A year later the course had twenty-two students! In 1976–77 Thomas began to
teach a course on Canadian women writers, "a good many of them forgotten and
neglected, but all of them fascinating subjects for research."[81]

John Lennox, a York alumnus who had done graduate work at the universities of Sherbrooke and New Brunswick, joined the Faculty of Arts English
Department permanently in 1974 and became a close associate of Thomas.[82] In
the early 1970s they introduced a course on Canadian fiction, anglophone and
francophone, the latter in translation. It speedily attracted large enrolments
and became a staple of the department's offerings. In 1977 they received a major
grant from the Social Sciences and Humanities Research Council of Canada to
work on William Arthur Deacon, the long-time literary editor of the *Globe and
Mail* and a noted literary nationalist from the 1920s on. Together with Michèle
Lacombe, a doctoral student, Lennox and Thomas went to work on the volumi-
nous collection of Deacon papers in the Thomas Fisher Rare Book Library at
the University of Toronto. "We worked superbly well as a threesome," Thomas
recalled.[83] In 1982 *William Arthur Deacon: A Literary Biography*, by Thomas and
Lennox, appeared, followed six years later by *Dear Bill: The Correspondence of
William Arthur Deacon*, edited by Lennox and Lacombe. Lennox's commitment
to Canadian literary history made him a logical choice to be the first director of
the university's Robarts Centre for Canadian Studies, which opened in 1984.

At Glendon College, Ann Mandel began complaining about the absence of
a course in Canadian literature soon after she arrived in the English Depart-

ment in 1968. "The result was that Michael [Gregory] told me I would be teaching Canadian literature in 1969–70!"[84] The following year, she and Bob Wallace launched a humanities course that Wallace described as "ahead of its time." Called "Strategies of Canadian Culture," it approached the subject from a variety of cultural perspectives. Mandel was influenced by Northrop Frye and Marshall McLuhan but also by her husband, Eli, whose pioneering collection *Contexts of Canadian Criticism* appeared in 1971. Wallace, too, was "strongly influenced" by Eli Mandel and his boundless enthusiasm for Canadian literature; McLuhan was another strong influence. Wallace's purpose was to introduce Canadian drama and media studies into the course. "We were swept up in the cultural nationalism of the period," he recalled.[85] They offered the course for a few years, Mandel said, but dropped it because they both wanted to pursue other interests, which in her case included a contemporary world literature course taught with Michael Ondaatje.[86]

Wallace taught the drama course at Glendon and in the early 1970s began to introduce more Canadian plays into the syllabus, such as John Herbert's *Fortune and Men's Eyes*, George Ryga's *The Ecstasy of Rita Joe*, and Carol Bolt's *Buffalo Jump*. There was an "explosion of scripts" sparked by the small theatres that were opening in Toronto by the late 1960s and early 1970s, among them the Theatre Passe Muraille, the Factory Theatre Lab, and the Tarragon Theatre. Wallace was involved in the Toronto theatre scene as a playwright and director, and it seemed to him "a natural step" in 1975 to launch a course, "English-speaking Theatre in Canada." It was the first of its kind in Canada. In 1983 études dramatiques/drama studies became an option within the Department of Multidisciplinary Studies, and Wallace became the first coordinator of drama studies.[87]

Among other scholars actively involved in the field of Canadian literature were Elizabeth Hopkins, the editor of letters by Susanna Moodie and Catharine Parr Traill, and Barbara Godard, whose *Talking about Ourselves: The Literary Productions of Native Women of Canada* appeared in 1985. A different kind of collection was compiled by Anthony Hopkins. His volume *Songs from the Front and Rear: Canadian Servicemen's Songs from the Second World War*, published in 1979, was an important contribution to Canadian cultural and social history, and a lot of bawdy fun besides.

For several years in the 1970s, the university's budget was under the supervision of the Senate Committee on the Budget (SCOB). Chaired by Pinayur Rajagopal, with Bill Farr as a key member, its function was chiefly to ensure that the numbers added up. Rajagopal's quiet but sharp sense of humour enlivened meetings. On one occasion, David McQueen said that the committee should get information of some kind. Rajagopal looked at him quizzically and asked: "Why do you want to know that, David?" "Well, Raja, wouldn't it be interesting to see the numbers?" "Perhaps, but do we need them?" McQueen said that was hard to decide until the committee saw them. Rajagopal smiled: "Don't tell us what you want to know; tell us why you want to know it."[88]

Perhaps because it lacked executive power, or perhaps because budgetary openness frightened some administrators, SCOB did not last long, and complete control of the budget returned to the central administration in 1977. Although finances were a source of continuing concern, Ian Macdonald said, "my recollection is that we didn't cut budgets as a policy at first. We froze things while reducing expenditures where we could, especially by not replacing people who left."[89] However, by 1976 it was clear that such measures would not keep the budget in balance while also reducing the debt, and the following year there were cuts in the base budgets of faculties and other units. "There was a really big budget crunch in 1977–78," the dean of education, Bob Overing said, "bigger than in 1972, in fact."[90] McQueen, principal of Glendon College from 1975 to 1980, also remembered 1977–78 as "a particularly difficult year."[91]

The man whom Macdonald had put in charge of the budget, George Bell, was the target of a lot of hostility as a result of the cuts. He had been the person responsible for planning at the Department of National Defence, with the rank of brigadier-general, before becoming an assistant deputy minister in the provincial Department of Treasury, Economics, and Intergovernmental Affairs, of which Macdonald was deputy minister, in 1972. Bell had a doctorate in international relations and "a predisposition to academic life," but "he liked administration" and, Macdonald recalled, "was good at it."[92] At the time that Macdonald invited Bell to join York as executive vice-president, Farr was in charge of the budget – Bruce Parkes had resigned in 1973 – as well as employee relations and student affairs. As a consequence, he was seriously overworked, so that Bell's appointment made sense. But his background in the military and the public service led him to take a dim view of budgetary openness.

Often called "General Bell" or "the general" behind his back, designations he reportedly disliked, Bell had the reputation of being tough. Macdonald denied this: "He was really an academic in the best sense of the word," who valued his appointment as adjunct professor of political science and helped found what eventually became the Centre for International and Security Studies. Macdonald recognized that Bell was never really accepted as an academic, and that he became something of a whipping boy for York's administration. However, he was "stoic" about this and loyally served York until his retirement in 1985. Summing up, Macdonald said: "George was an old-fashioned man of principle."[93]

Some faculty members took a less benign view of Bell. The cuts of 1977 convinced a number of people that there should be a return to academic control of budget making. Bell managed to secure a surplus, but, one senior academic said, "he seemed to have no sense of how a university should be run." By 1978, the geographer William Found said, some of the deans were agitating for the appointment of an academic vice-president. York had managed to do without one since Walter Tarnopolsky's resignation at the end of 1972, but the university had grown "too large and complex to function effectively without someone who could work with the Senate, the deans, the director of libraries, and the Office of Research Administration, and who could advise the president."[94] Matters came to a head at a research conference held in the spring of 1978 at the Cedar Glen Conference Centre in Bolton, northwest of Toronto. Jane Couchman of the Glendon French Department, who was associate principal (academic) of Glendon as well as a member of Senate APPC, remembered that most senior administrators and several members of the Board of Governors were in attendance. The discussion was wide-ranging, she said, its major decision being that "York should have an academic vice-president again."[95]

As Macdonald recalled matters, he initially decided to serve as his own academic vice-president in order to get to know York's academic side fully, and because he felt that "people wanted a president who took academic concerns seriously." For the same reason, he decided to become chair of the APPC. But tenure and promotion cases took up a lot of time, especially when the Senate committee disagreed with departmental and faculty committees. In these cases, Macdonald had to rely on his own judgment while lacking key information, such as whether a candidate's ideological outlook was at odds with the majority view in his discipline. Troubled about this aspect of the process, he worked for the establishment of a tenure appeals committee. After participating in the discussion at Cedar Glen, and having come to the view that there should be an academic vice-president, he appointed Found to the position in 1979. (In 1984 Found would be acting president for six months, bridging the transition between Macdonald and Harry Arthurs.) "I very happily turned tenure and promotion over to him," Macdonald said with a smile.[96]

Another event that fostered unhappiness with the administration was the so-called Red Book (its front cover was red, the York colour). This document had its origins in Macdonald's belief, prompted in part by conversations with John Yolton, that the York community needed to examine itself closely and to make constructive changes. As a newcomer, Macdonald did not presume to say what should be done, but he did want the institution to move forward from the difficult period it had recently passed through. In September 1975 he announced the creation of a presidential Commission on Goals and Objectives, in which he intended to play an active role.[97] Yolton and the geneticist and biophysicist Robert Haynes were elected to it by the Senate, and Naomi Wagschal represented the alumni. John Bankes, who was registered in the joint MBA-LLB program and served as the student member on the Board of Governors from 1974 to 1977, was elected by the student senators. (He later spent many years on the board as an alumni representative and served on two presidential search committees.) At least one board member, Henry Jackman, doubted that the commission would serve a useful purpose. "I have reservations about whether any professional group let alone an academic one can reach hard decisions which affect the career expectations of so many of its members," he wrote to Macdonald: "The university is collectively incapable of making decisions and in the last analysis the decision will be yours."[98]

It was not as simple as that. If recent events had demonstrated anything, it was that the Senate was determined to exercise its powers. At key moments the Board of Governors had acquiesced in this. Whatever recommendations the commission came up with, it would be difficult if not impossible for Macdonald to enact them without Senate approval.

After more than a year of meetings, by the commission itself and the four task forces it had spun off, the commission's report appeared in the spring of 1977. "The Commission has studied York's system of undergraduate education carefully," it

John Bankes was the students' representative on the presidential Commission on Goals and Objectives.

asserted, "and has determined that a radical change in the current academic, collegiate, and administrative structures must be made in order to strengthen each substantially."[99] One task force, chaired by Don Rickerd, had examined the future of the college system. Research had been the subject of a task force chaired by the sociologist Anthony H. Richmond. Douglas Verney had chaired a task force on the philosophy of undergraduate education, and Joe Green one on the physical and cultural ambiance of the Keele campus. A research group on "factors influencing student enrolment, performance and experience at York University" had involved a number of scholars, among them Found, Ted Olson, the geographer J. Tait Davis, the sociologist Clifford Jansen, Christine Furedy of the Social Science Division, and the psychologist and dean of graduate studies, Graham Reed.

All these groups made useful proposals; a number of them were included in the Red Book's recommendations. But after the report appeared, attention quickly came to focus on just one of the main recommendations. The report proposed the division of the Faculty of Arts into three colleges, General Studies, Letters, and Social and Environmental Studies, each to be headed by a principal. The Atkinson College dean would also become a principal. The College of General Studies, comprising the divisions of Humanities and Social Science, would be located in the Ross Building. The College of Letters, comprising English, French, foreign languages, history, philosophy, political science, and Canadian studies, would occupy Founders, Vanier, Winters, and McLaughlin colleges. The College of Social and Environmental Studies, which would include anthropology, economics, geography, psychology, sociology, urban studies, and the Faculty of Environmental Studies, would be located in Stong and Bethune colleges.[100] These changes were supposed to be made in the summer of 1978.

The dean of arts was Sydney Eisen, who strongly opposed the carving up of his bailiwick. It was not simply a matter of resisting the reduction of the faculty or the elimination of his own position, he recalled, for he was in any case due to vacate the deanship in 1978. It was a matter of retaining for the entire faculty the interdisciplinarity and intellectual coherence exemplified by the Division of Humanities. That division "had become the core of Arts in a way that the Social Science Division had not."[101] Humanities was very largely staffed with "full-time scholars"; Social Science mostly "picked up pieces from the departments." (A recent document outlining the development of humanities at York, prepared by Hugh Parry and William Whitla, has demonstrated the soundness of Eisen's assessment at least where the Humanities Division is concerned.[102]) Small wonder that those associated with Humanities, like Whitla, saw the Red Book as a threat.[103] But so did others.

Ted Spence, who was chair of the Faculty of Arts council at the time, said that Eisen charged him and associate deans Whitla and Rod Byers with organizing the faculty's self-defence.[104] A special meeting of the Senate, called to discuss the report of the Commission on Goals and Objectives, had to be held in the Moot Court of Osgoode Hall Law School in order to ensure that all those interested had an opportunity to attend. The meeting must have been an unpleasant experience for Haynes and Yolton, and also for Macdonald, as speaker after

speaker attacked one or another of the report's recommendations. Especially the proposal to dismantle the Faculty of Arts ran into very heavy weather. Couchman, who worked with Byers, Spence, Whitla, and Robert Allan of the Faculty of Science to defeat the report, remembered that Haynes and Yolton looked "very uncomfortable."[105]

The response surprised John Bankes. He had valued his membership on the commission – "my proudest association with York was through my work on that commission," he recalled – and he thought it had done good work. "There's a lot of good stuff in the 100 pages of the report," he asserted: "A comment on the uninspired design of the Ross Building, the idea of a reflecting pool at the university entrance, the relocation of the art gallery, the need for a student centre, the launch of a university-wide visual identity program, a redefinition of the role of the colleges, the final rites for the Master Plan of 1963, subway access to the Keele Street campus, the need for a faculty club, a focus on quality (rather than the more popular term today, 'excellence'), the emphasis on research, the relocation of the President's Office to the 2nd or 3rd floor, etc."[106] Although he could understand "the passion of the attack," he said, he was disappointed that the debate avoided dealing with many of the commission's recommendations. He was also dismayed by the tone of some of the criticism, "verging on being nastily personal," directed against men he had learned to admire. He remembered Haynes as "big physically and huge intellectually, with a fine sense of humour" and Yolton as "a real scholar" who, like Haynes, "was very much focused on research." Furthermore, he thought much of the criticism was unfair. "Our report was multidimensional; it did not have a narrow focus." It did have flaws, he thought. One was the failure to ask what the proposed changes would cost, and this at a time when money was tight; another was to deal with York largely in isolation from the surrounding community. But nobody talked about these things: "Everybody wanted to talk about the Faculty of Arts."[107]

The opponents of the report were successful, something Spence came later to regret, having reached the view that the colleges really should be more closely aligned with disciplines.[108] "Maybe we overdid it by talking about distributing the Faculty of Arts around," Macdonald commented, adding: "Looking back, the report *did* get people thinking about York."[109] Couchman remembered as one positive result the inter-faculty friendships that were forged during the struggle.[110] With Eisen as the organizer, a group of faculty members, among them Couchman, Arthur Haberman, and the political scientists Harold Kaplan (Eisen's successor as dean) and Michael Stevenson, a later dean of arts and academic vice-president, continued for years to meet on a regular basis to discuss various aspects of the university.[111] And by no means all of the commission's recommendations went unheeded. For example, Rickerd's task force on the colleges had reported that "the Tutorial Programme, which once seemed an imaginative and distinctive academic contribution to be made by the colleges, has been soured by penury ... to the extent that it is now likely that several of the colleges will not voluntarily contribute tutorials after 1977–78."[112] The commission therefore recommended that "the College Tutorial cease to be offered."[113] The college tutorials ended in 1981, to be replaced by "college courses" paid for by the Faculty of Arts. These were distributed among the colleges, but, unlike the college tutorials they replaced, they were under the control of Arts.

The debate around the Red Book led Whitla to compose "The Battle of the Book, or the Rape of the York," in imitation of Alexander Pope's mock-epic "The Rape of the Lock." To those (like myself) who attended the two days of meetings, and perhaps to others as well, many of its lines make for amusing reading:

> ... All censured what was writ, none paused to praise:
> The *Book* was damned. Yet many tried to raise
> Grave ghosts of goals thought dead, bring back to life
> The whole man, and, perhaps, his wholier wife ...
> Much was referred, but even more thrown out,
> All ended more with whimper than with shout.
> The Senate rose, its mighty task was done:
> Two days had passed, two settings of York's sun. ...
> True wits had with advantage York addressed:
> What here was fought was ne'er so well suppressed.[114]

It was a serious business, though, and York suffered a loss as a result. Macdonald said he believed John Yolton moved to Rutgers University in 1978 in part as a result of his disappointment over the reception of many of the Red Book proposals.[115]

If the debate generated by the report of the Commission on Goals and Objectives was largely negative, other, more positive things were happening as well. Scholars and scientists were continuing to work; so were visual and performing artists. On occasion their work won major prizes. Ramsay Cook's *The Regenerators: Social Criticism in Late Victorian English Canada* (1985), for example, won the Governor-General's Award for non-fiction. Sometimes it had a significant public impact, such as *Three Civilizations, Two Cultures, One State: Canada's Political Traditions* (1986) by Douglas Verney, and *The Federal Condition in Canada* (1987) by Donald Smiley.[116] The hard-hitting book by Irving Abella and OISE's Harold Troper, *None Is Too Many: Canada and the Jews of Europe 1933–1948* (1982), shed needed light on an aspect of Canadian history that few remembered much about and many would just as soon have forgotten.

By the time this book appeared, a number of York people had become involved with another group of refugees. Howard Adelman has written: "The tens of thousands of Vietnamese who fled their homeland in 1979–80 were called the Boat People; they were only a proportion of the far larger number who fled from Indochina as a whole, from Laos and Cambodia as well as Vietnam. Canada took in 60,000 of these refugees during 1979 and 1980."[117] Adelman's own involvement in Operation Lifeline was related to his Jewish heritage. The awareness that hostility to Jewish immigration in the 1930s had cost many lives was a strong motivation in helping the Indochinese refugees.[118] He credited the establishment of the Centre for Refugee Studies to Abella, who obtained a grant of $50,000 from the

David Bell (left), Ian Macdonald, and Ramsay Cook at a reception in the True Davidson Reading Room, Rare Books and Special Collections, Scott Library, 1984.

Social Sciences and Humanities Research Council for the Refugee Documentation Project. "That got things moving," Adelman said.[119]

The Centre for Refugee Studies was part of an orientation towards the larger world that also informed the Kenya Project and the Centre for Research on Latin America and the Caribbean (CERLAC) among others. It was part, too, of York's growing international visibility in the 1970s. As the economist Louis Lefeber said: "York had an attraction for professors who had come to feel uncomfortable in the United States."[120] Usually they were leftists of one persuasion or another, among them the mathematician and civil rights activist Lee Lorch, the revisionist historian of U.S. foreign policy Gabriel Kolko, the political scientists Neal Wood, Ellen Meiksins Wood, and Joseph Starobin, and Lefeber himself. York also attracted several socialist scholars from Europe, such as Andreas Papandreou, a Greek-born and U.S.-educated economist, Ralph Miliband, the Belgian-born and British-educated Marxist thinker, and István Mészáros, a Hungarian-born political theorist whose Marxism temporarily impeded his immigration from Great Britain into Canada. Home-grown left-wing scholars felt York's attraction as well: the political scientists Leo Panitch and Reginald Whitaker both left Carleton University in the mid-1980s to come to York.

What became CERLAC had its origins in the interest that several mostly left-leaning young scholars had in Latin America. The event that got the centre going was the military coup in Chile in September 1973. Lefeber knew that country because he had written a report on it in 1962 under the auspices of the Alliance for Progress. After the Chilean government was overthrown, he expressed public opposition to the coup. This drew him to the attention of several young Latin Americanists, such as Margarita Feliciano, Judith Hellman, Edgar Dosman, Liisa North, and Juan Maiguashca, as well as Sydney Eisen, who wanted to establish a program in Latin American studies. "The trouble was that the youngsters did not have grey hair," Lefeber said. "I *had* grey hair and a long academic career."[121] He became the front man for an appeal to the Donner Foundation, which provided money to get the centre started. Although Lefeber himself had "no great interest" in the Caribbean region, several scholars interested in that area, among them William Found, Marilyn Silverman, and Patrick Taylor, attached themselves to the centre.

Lefeber recalled that in the early years of CERLAC the centre often had a difficult time maintaining its scholarly bona fides in Latin America, which meant keeping a distance from universities and institutes controlled by the military. At the same time, CERLAC had to satisfy York's administration and potential providers of financial support that it was not simply "a Marxist snake pit," as one of the scholars involved in it later called it. Eisen defended CERLAC's autonomy, but other administrators at York, notably George Bell, sought to have CERLAC forge links that in Lefeber's opinion would have compromised it in Latin America, where scholars tended to oppose the military dictatorships of countries such as Chile, Argentina, and Brazil. It was not easy, he said, but after a couple of "blow-ups" in the mid- to late 1970s, "they left us alone."[122]

Aside from the Centre for Refugee Studies and CERLAC, several other research centres with an international dimension have developed over the years. The York Centre for International and Security Studies, the Canadian Centre for German and European Studies, and the York Centre for Asian Research all testify to the interest of scholars at York in the larger world, as, indeed, does York International, the university's central international office that was originally the brainchild of Ian Macdonald.

When he began to look for teaching staff in 1960, Murray Ross got a telephone call from Fulton Anderson, the head of philosophy at the University of Toronto. "He had a faculty member for me," Ross wrote: "'Lionel Rubinoff – he's just finishing his doctorate and he's the most brilliant student we've had for years.' 'If he's so able, why wouldn't you keep him?' I asked. 'Murray, you know we have one of them in our department now. I can't have another.' 'Them,' of course, were Jews."[123] On an earlier occasion, Ross wrote, the dean of medicine had reported that his Faculty Council would not support a scheme giving free tuition to all first-class honour students as long as they retained first-class standing. Why not? These scholarships "would all go to those people," by which, Ross quickly realized, the dean meant Jews and women.[124]

For many decades, racism, including anti-Semitism, and misogyny were the rule in Canadian universities.[125] Into the 1950s only male Caucasians of British (or, in the case of the francophone universities, French) stock were really welcome on the teaching staff. People of African or Asian background were not. Some Jews did gain appointment over the years, but they were not many. When Sydney Eisen was a history undergraduate at the University of Toronto in the early 1950s, Frank Underhill said to him: "Go to the States and don't come back." Both men knew that Jews had an easier time getting academic positions there. Eisen was teaching at the City College of New York in 1965 when Jack Saywell urged him to come to York, assuring him that there would be no prejudice.[126]

Not only Jewish academics were affected by the prevailing prejudices. By appointing Bertrand Gerstein to the Board of Governors in 1961, York was ahead of most Canadian universities. In 1967 Bora Laskin joined Gerstein. Could a Jew become board chair? His father once told him, Irving Gerstein recalled, that a prominent board member had said: "Bert, you'd make a great chairman. Too bad you're Jewish."[127] The Toronto business community, Robert MacIntosh said, retained an anti-Semitic tone longer than the academic world.[128] Brian Dixon remembered that Barry Richman had become painfully aware of this during his brief term as dean of administrative studies in 1972.[129] Not until 1975, after James Lewtas was appointed to succeed MacIntosh but then died suddenly, did Bertrand Gerstein become chairman of the Board of Governors.

For several decades, gentile women had an easier time getting appointed than Jews of either sex, at least in some parts of the university, but appointments, promotions, salary increases, and tenure were more readily available to men. Jean

Burnet, who accepted Escott Reid's invitation in 1967 to become Glendon's chair of sociology, taught at the University of New Brunswick in the late 1940s and the University of Toronto in the 1950s and 1960s. Of these experiences she has written: "Women who aspired to academic careers were told straightforwardly that they should not set their sights too high: that, for example, many years of service and high scholarly productivity might possibly lead as far as an associate professorship. Nor should they hope for many women colleagues."[130] Women on governing boards were even fewer. During the 1960s, Signy Eaton, almost always referred to as Mrs John David Eaton, was the only woman on the York board. After her resignation in 1971, board chairman Robert MacIntosh, determined to increase the number of women on the board, secured the appointment of Doris Anderson (1971), Adrienne Clarkson (1972), and Anne Dubin (1973).[131] Virginia Rock joined the board in 1971–72 after being elected to it by the Senate. Clarkson said that attending board meetings was a little bit like attending debates in Hart House, University of Toronto, when she was an undergraduate in the late 1950s. (Women were not admitted to membership in Hart House at the time and had to sit in the gallery, looking down at the young men debating and posturing below.) "Doris and I used to giggle at times about the games the men were playing," she recalled.[132] Into the 1980s women continued to be very much in the minority on the board.

As a new university, York had no long-established appointment practices or traditions. What it did have was a need for large numbers of qualified faculty. This not only permitted but imposed a greater degree of inclusiveness than prevailed in older Canadian universities. As a consequence, race and ethnicity counted for little or nothing. Wallace Northover, "a black of Jamaican descent," as he called himself, recruited into the Department of Psychology and Division of Social Science by Mortimer Appley in 1965, said that the issue of race never came up.[133] Other early recruits into the Faculty of Arts, such as Norman Endler, Harvey Simmons, Arthur Haberman, and Esther Greenglass, said that they were not aware of any anti-Semitism at York.[134] Simmons claimed that by the end of the 1960s close to 40 per cent of the political scientists were Jewish, many of them from the United States. (In 1966 or 1967 one of my fellow graduate students at the University of Toronto snidely referred to York as "the Jewish American University of Toronto.")

York's sensitivity to Jewish concerns found expression in the decision, made in the early 1970s, not to hold classes or exams on Rosh Hashanah, Yom Kippur, and Passover. In 1971 the first days of the academic year, 20 and 21 September, coincided with the first and second days of Rosh Hashanah. Responding to a request from the Jewish Students Federation of York University, the Executive Committee of the Faculty of Arts approved a directive to departmental chairs advising them "not to expect a full attendance on the Monday and Tuesday" and asking them to "refrain from discussing critical matters concerning the course during the first lecture period." Jack Saywell added: "Of course, I know that you will respect the religious beliefs of members of your department, freely permitting the cancellation of classes by those who request it."[135] When informed of the issue, David Slater referred it to the Senate Executive Committee, but it was the

Faculty of Arts that brought it to the Senate. (At the time, each faculty had its own sessional dates.) On 16 December 1971 the Senate passed a motion permitting the Faculty of Arts to cancel classes on Rosh Hashanah (two days) and Yom Kippur, and recommending that exams not be held on the first two and last two days of Passover.[136] These provisions soon spread to the entire university. In May 1974 the Senate made it "explicitly official" that no classes would be scheduled on Rosh Hashanah and Yom Kippur, and the evenings before these days, and that no exams would be scheduled on the first two and last two days of Passover as well as the evenings before them, although the university offices would be open.[137]

York University may have been free of racism, but not of misogyny. Endler, one of the first faculty members recruited, said: "Murray was not anti-Semitic, but he *was* anti-woman."[138] Clara Thomas confirmed this, adding that Ross was not alone at York in his somewhat negative attitude to women academics: "One coped with the prejudice." Asked whether York was more enlightened about appointing women than the University of Western Ontario, where she taught before coming to York, she replied that "no clear answer" was possible.[139] The sociologist Thelma McCormack perceived a lack of respect for women faculty members in the early days.[140]

The attitudes of the 1960s were on display during the early "Tea and Talk" series, when faculty wives, including on at least one occasion Dee Appley, the wife of graduate studies dean Mortimer Appley and herself a faculty member, poured the tea![141] The political scientist Kenneth McRoberts remembered that, when he joined York in 1969, his wife received an invitation to join a faculty wives' association.[142] It is not clear when this group ceased to exist, but we do know there was never an association of faculty husbands.

Data collected by Gill Teiman, who was for many years involved in human rights and equity issues at York, indicate that of the eighty-five faculty members the university had on 30 June 1965, sixteen, or 18.8 per cent, were women: "not bad at all for the times."[143] Cyndi Zimmerman, appointed in 1967, said that being a young woman was not exactly an advantage, but that the Glendon English Department was a good place for women: she had half a dozen female colleagues.[144] Ann Wilbur MacKenzie, who came to York in 1968, said that she did not experience the Glendon Philosophy Department as "in any way chilly."[145] Joan Gibson, who joined the Division of Humanities in Atkinson College in 1970, said that "it was a very collegial department." This sentiment was shared by Ann (Rusty) Shteir, who arrived in 1972.[146] Of course, the proportion of women in humanities departments was greater than in most other fields. And in many ways, big and small, York was still a man's world. Gail Cuthbert Brandt, who entered the PHD program in history in 1969, was impressed by the quality of her professors and fellow students, but nevertheless felt "a bit alienated" when it became clear that the exclusively male faculty members of the graduate program invited only the male students to play squash.[147] Wendy Mitchinson remembered learning from another graduate student that Sydney Eisen had some extra money available for graduate students. When she went to ask for her share, he regarded her questioningly: "But you're married." "Yes," she replied, "but he's an artist." Eisen nodded understandingly and gave her the money.[148]

Susan Houston, who joined History in 1970 and got a tenure-track appointment the following year, remembered the department of the early 1970s as a men's club. It housed a few other women – Cynthia Dent (the first to be appointed), Virginia Hunter, Margo Gewurtz, Diana Lary – but, since there were no other female Canadian historians, she was the only woman on the corridor in Vanier College where the Canadian section was located. "I didn't have lunch with anyone for a year. It was Ramsay [Cook] who first asked me: 'Don't you ever have lunch?'" He invited her to the Common Room, where at first she was "not entirely comfortable." When she succeeded Paul Stevens as chair of the department in 1980, one thing was clear to her: "I was perceived not as a woman but as a Canadianist."[149]

One area where women were at a clear disadvantage was that of salaries. This resulted from a tendency in some fields to offer women less than men, but it also reflected a reality that persisted for years: women were much more reluctant than men to negotiate their starting salaries and, more generally, the terms of their employment. When Ross offered her a job, Thomas said in her memoirs, "it never occurred to me to have any requests, let alone demands, of my own, and when Ross told me my pay would be $5000, I was delighted."[150] Recruited by Eisen almost a decade later, Hunter said she did not even ask what the salary was:

"I was glad to have a job."[151] A number of interviews with faculty women suggests that this grateful attitude was typical.

Information about the salaries received by other faculty members was sketchy at first – it was thought to be slightly improper to talk about such things. But even before 1970 it was dawning on some women that they were being paid less than men of similar experience and achievements. By the late 1960s, "second-wave" feminism was gaining support, and this prompted increased interest in the overall status of women in the academy, including salaries. Sandra Pyke, who came to York in 1966, was soon meeting with others in the Toronto Women's Caucus and also became active, with fellow psychologists Esther Greenglass and Mary Stewart, in a group promoting greater recognition for women and women's issues within the Canadian Psychological Association.[152] They would draw inspiration from the 1970 Report of the Royal Commission on the Status of Women in Canada, chaired by Florence Bayard Bird.[153] (She received an honorary degree from York at the 1971 fall convocation.)

If one had to choose a date when the position of women at York began to change, the year 1971 would serve nicely. Johanna Stuckey, who had taught in the Humanities Division since 1964, returned from a sabbatical in the fall of 1971 convinced that "she needed to do something about women at York," and, after consulting with Virginia Rock, she moved the establishment of a Senate task force on the status of women.[154] Stuckey became its chair; its members included representatives of the board, faculty, library staff, administration, support staff, and students. Those who signed the task force report included Howard Adelman, Doris Anderson, Vicky Draper, Bill Farr, Esther Greenglass, Elsie Hanna of YUSA, and the librarian Eirene Landon.

During the next three years, the task force and its committees did a lot of work. David Slater was very helpful in getting things moving, Stuckey remem-

Ian Macdonald, Johanna Stuckey, and Shelagh Wilkinson in the Nellie Langford Library, 1982.

Jane Banfield Haynes was the first adviser to the president on the status of women.

bered: "He cut through a lot of barriers and insisted that information on salaries be released to the committee." Even so, a good deal of information was simply not available. "Of all the studies undertaken," the report's preamble stated, "the full-time faculty study gave the Task Force the least trouble, and yet even that study has taken a good *two* years."[155] A basic problem identified in the report was that "at all levels women at York are subtly (or not so subtly) discouraged from seeking advancement." But there were also other issues, ranging from salary differentials to inadequate daycare. "York University can – and must – start by declaring itself an 'equal opportunity employer,' and by righting any wrongs done to women at present employed at York," the report asserted. It should also actively encourage women to seek advancement. "What York must do is become an agent of change, not only by declaring itself willing to provide equal education and employment for women, but also by taking positive action to ensure that such a declaration will mean something!"[156]

When the report appeared, Ian Macdonald was well into the first year of his presidency. One of the report's recommendations which he accepted was that he open a status-of-women office; another was that he appoint a president's adviser on the status of women, and he selected Jane Banfield Haynes for a two-year term. Soon after she took office, the York Women's Centre, housed in Atkinson College, was officially opened. Banfield, who had taught in the Division of Social Science since 1968, had a PHD but also a degree in law, which she believed might have appealed to Macdonald. Taking a study of full-time faculty salaries carried out for the task force by Esther Greenglass as her starting point, Banfield devised a further study, which was carried out by a special presidential committee. Each woman on the faculty was asked to select two men in her department who were at the same point in their careers, and each department chair was asked to do the same thing for each woman in the department. The procedure was to compare the status, background, experience, academic credentials, teaching responsibilities, and research performance of the woman and the chosen "comparators." This was not always easy or even possible: "There were few women in the law school and Administrative Studies," Banfield recalled. Science presented difficulties as well. Still, the study had an unambiguous outcome: with exceptions, women were paid less. "There were not a lot of huge differentials, but some women were quite egregiously underpaid."[157] Women also found it more difficult than men to get elected to important committees like the Senate APPC or to gain administrative office.

In the fall of 1976 Banfield conveyed the committee report to Macdonald. It showed that there were 856 male and 183 female full-time faculty members, in the tenure stream and with sessional contracts. Of the 183 women, fifteen had declined to be interviewed and nineteen more were ineligible for review because they had joined York on 1 July 1975, leaving 149 women who were reviewed. Of these, ninety-three, or rather more than six in ten, received a salary adjustment that averaged $1,184.[158]

The report cast a revealing light on academic staffing at York in the mid-1970s. First of all, 18.3 per cent of the full-time faculty was female (16.5 per cent of the tenured and probationary faculty), a proportion slightly smaller than it had been

a decade earlier. Secondly, in some parts of York women were conspicuous mainly by their absence. Whereas Glendon College, with its large French Department, had thirty-four women and seventy-five men teaching full time, Administrative Studies had only one woman, Alice Courtney, among its fifty-six full-time professors. In three other faculties, Environmental Studies, Osgoode Hall Law School, and Science, women made up less than 10 per cent of the full-time teaching staff. Within the three arts faculties, there were interesting variations. Computer Science, Economics, Geography, and Mathematics were almost entirely staffed with men. History, Philosophy, Political Science, and Sociology were also largely male preserves. Only Anthropology, English, French, foreign languages, and Psychology went noticeably against this trend. In Fine Arts, eight of eleven teachers in Dance were women; the other four departments were male-dominated. Had it not been for the five women in Biology, the Faculty of Science would have been overwhelmingly male: none of the twenty-six chemists and only one of twenty-eight physicists was female.[159] Thirdly, women were under-represented among full professors (4.4 per cent) and associate professors (13 per cent), and over-represented among assistant professors (24.7 per cent) and others – visiting faculty, sessional lecturers, and teachers in the so-called alternate stream, mainly sports coaches and language instructors (34.6 per cent).[160]

The low representation of women and their relatively junior rank largely reflected the realities of hiring in the period from 1965 to 1972. These were years when women were just beginning to enter graduate school in fields that, before this time, had not attracted them or had resisted their entry. Still, at a time when the number and proportion of women students were growing steadily, the result was an environment that some of them, and some of their female professors, found less than congenial.

In 1973–74 Marion Lane pointed out in a report to the Long-Range Academic Planning Committee of Osgoode Hall Law School that there were no permanent women professors in Osgoode even though 18.7 per cent of the student body and 23 per cent of the first-year students were female.[161] Lane recalled that most of her professors, among them George Adams, Brian Bucknall, Gerald LeDain, and Paul Weiler, were very good, and although she never took a course with Peter Hogg, "considered to be one of the best teachers," she recalled with pleasure working with him on the Academic Planning Committee.[162] But some students found the atmosphere excessively masculine, she said. One of her recommendations was that women be added to the faculty, providing female students with role models and "curbing the all-pervasive male domination of the law school."[163] Former Liberal cabinet minister Judy LaMarsh was a visiting professor from 1973 to 1975, and Marcia Neave, on sabbatical from Monash University in Australia, was a visiting professor in 1974–75. The first tenure-track appointments were those of Louise Arbour and Mary Jane Mossman in 1976–77; Sharon Williams followed soon after.[164] Being a single woman in a male environment was not easy, Mossman remembered. "Louise had an easier time because she had a partner, but the men didn't really know how to socialize with me."[165] Other women joined the teaching staff during the next few years, but it continued to be very largely male even as the proportion of female students grew steadily.

The issue that mainly interested Banfield and her subcommittee was the salary structure of York faculty members, but they had other concerns as well, such as the place of women in the library system and the professional and managerial ranks. Noli Swatman, who worked as a research officer for many years, recalled that the professional and managerial area was not simply "a man's club" but that she and other women felt that there was systemic discrimination, though, she added, "it was subtle and hard to prove."[166] Also of interest was YUSA, in which women greatly outnumbered men, the experiences of female students at the undergraduate and graduate levels, health services for women, and childcare services. But "the major thrust" during her two-year term was the correction of salary anomalies, she said: "The trouble was that the subcommittee didn't have time to look at everything." Furthermore, finding money for new projects was always a problem in the lean 1970s. Still, other universities were showing interest in what York was doing.[167]

Universities are not renowned for embracing change eagerly, but York *was* changing. In 1969 Virginia Rock became the master – asked for her preference, she had said she preferred "master" to "mistress" – of what soon became Stong College. She said she believed "a couple of men" had been asked first, and she was hesitant about taking the job herself, but she found it "exciting" once she got going and served until 1978. She did feel lonely at times, however. Invited soon after her appointment to attend a reception for senior administrators at the York Club, she was the only woman in the room.[168]

When Atkinson College Faculty Council elected the historian Margaret Knittl in 1974, York got its first woman dean and quite possibly the first woman dean of an arts faculty in Canada. She recalled that her election became assured when the other candidate remaining after three ballots, Howard Adelman, withdrew his name. He contradicted this: "She beat me fair and square."[169] "I was *so* green," she recalled: "I didn't realize the value of networking and how it might help. By the time I finished I had finally figured it out." It helped that "Ian Macdonald was a very open kind of president ... He was very gracious to me. I didn't feel I was being short-changed." Bill Farr and Sheldon Levy were also "very kind."[170] But, like Rock, Knittl felt a bit lonely. Until Anne Woodsworth became director of libraries in 1978, she was the only woman on the president's Executive Council. The first woman to be vice-president was Elizabeth Hopkins, appointed in 1990; the first woman president was the historian Susan Mann in 1992. (By way of contrast, Anne Scotton was elected president of the student body in 1974, the first woman to hold that position. Not until 1988 did another woman, Tammy Hasselfeldt, gain the CYSF presidency.)

Others besides Knittl have praised Macdonald's role in encouraging women faculty and promoting women's issues. Sandra Pyke served as his adviser on the status of women in the later 1970s. She noted that "York was a congenial environment" for pursuing women's concerns, including the expansion of women's studies. "If York did not actually encourage 'deviant' behaviour, it did allow it." One consequence was the early development of guidelines on sexual harassment. Some administrators were more helpful than others, but only "a new and relatively open" university like York "would have encouraged the early development of programs for women. This has contributed to York's image as being in the vanguard of promoting women's issues."[171] Rusty Shteir, who succeeded Pyke, said that "responsiveness was part of the York story. Ian Macdonald was wonderful." Bill Farr, too, "was always ready to listen to what we had to say. There was a lot of good spirit." And in the President's Office, Yvonne Aziz was "a very important figure in our early efforts. She knew exactly whom we should see."[172]

In universities generally, courses focusing on women and their concerns began to be taught in the very early 1970s. York was in the vanguard in developing this field. Lesley Lewis remembered taking a course in women's studies with Louise Rockman at Glendon College in 1970–71, then helping to design a similar course when she became a graduate student in sociology at OISE.[173] A growing number of women's studies courses became available in the 1970s, taught by scholars such as Stuckey, Greenglass, Mossman, Naomi Black, Virginia Hunter, Jane Couchman, Gail Cuthbert Brandt, and Joan Gibson. The task force on the status of women recommended that a women's studies program be established.[174] But the Senate did not respond at once. Black, a political scientist who served a term as the president's adviser on the status of women in the mid-1980s, noted in 1984 that "in all respects except formal standing ... Women's Studies grew rapidly at York in the 1970s and 1980s."[175]

By 1976, a Resource Centre for Women's Studies housed a growing collection of library and archival material that later became the core of the Nellie Rowell Langford Library. Among its supporters was the University Women's Club of

Naomi Black, co-author of *Canadian Women: A History* and the president's adviser on the status of women in the mid-1980s.

North York, which from 1984 to 2003 gave almost $3,500 to the Langford Library.[176] A key appointment was that of Shelagh Wilkinson to the Atkinson College Humanities Division in 1983. She had been at Atkinson as a mature student in the 1960s and was a tutorial leader in the Atkinson English Department in the early 1970s while doing graduate studies at the University of Toronto. After a year at New College, Oxford, using a fellowship secured for her by John Yolton – "he was a great man, a Lockean through and through"[177] – she became director of a new Centre for Women at Sheridan College and also began to develop bridging courses that women who had not completed high school education could take to prepare them for university studies. Atkinson College, where she taught a course in 1974–75, was the possible destination.[178] In 1978 she moved to Centennial College, where she started the journal *Canadian Woman Studies*. Five years later, when Dean Ron Bordessa wanted a women's studies centre in Atkinson College, he hired both Wilkinson and Meg Luxton. Ian Macdonald then arranged to make an office available to *Canadian Woman Studies*. "I'm very happy that York took it on," Wilkinson said; it is published at York University to this day. The bridging courses program for women continues as well. "York and Atkinson were open to innovation, allowing women to do new things," Wilkinson stated. She became the founding director of the Centre for Feminist Research in 1991, but above all she loved her teaching: literary theory and criticism, women's literature, and Canadian women writers.

A degree-granting program in women's studies in the Faculty of Arts got Senate approval in 1983; Atkinson's degree in women's studies gained approval two years later.[179] A landmark of a different kind was the book *Canadian Women: A History*, published in 1988. Of its six authors, five – Black, Cuthbert Brandt, Beth Light, Wendy Mitchinson, and Alison Prentice – had an association with York, as students, faculty members, or both.[180] Penny Van Esterik, who arrived in 1984 after teaching at Notre Dame University in Indiana and Cornell University, found York to be comparatively very friendly to women: "I thought I had died and gone to heaven."[181]

In part because, other than in the professional faculties, there was little recruitment between 1975 and 1985, the proportion of women faculty barely changed during the decade, inching upward by less than a percentage point. In 1984–85, 16.8 per cent of tenured and probationary faculty, and 19 per cent of all faculty, were female.[182] The limited availability of female faculty in some disciplinary areas also contributed to this state of affairs, as did traditional attitudes to women. In Administrative Studies, Brenda Gainer recalled, it was only after Deszö Horváth became dean in 1988 that the number of women faculty members began to grow significantly: "He wasn't having any of the old arguments against appointing women."[183]

As a 1985 document pointed out, although much had been accomplished, much remained to be done. "Equity for Women: The First Decade" was an update of the 1975 Senate task force report. Prepared by Stuckey, the adviser to the president on the status of women at the time, who was assisted by a committee that included Black, Pyke, Shteir, and Banfield, the report stated: "Since 1975 York University has become a model in status-of-women matters."[184] Many of the recommendations in the 1975 report had not been implemented, however, so that it seemed to the committee "appropriate to move to a system of more actively supporting changes in the status of women in York University." Using the term "employment equity" (coined by Justice Rosalie Abella in a 1984 Royal Commission report on equality of employment),[185] the committee proposed "to speak of an Equity Programme for Women at York, to encompass the range of positive measures needed to compensate for systemic barriers to equality for women in this university."[186] In response to this document, the Board of Governors committed itself to the achievement of full employment equity for women at York.[187] At the beginning of 1989, Gill Teiman, a member of the part-time faculty in English, became York's first coordinator for employment equity, a position she held for fifteen years.[188] In a variety of ways, the board, the Senate, the administration, YUFA, and YUSA were all taking steps towards making equity for women a reality.

The tendency to look for past golden ages and to celebrate them is common, even though upon close examination the ages often don't gleam quite as much as we like to think. Still, sports at York in the 1970s and 1980s do represent something of a golden age. This owed less to the facilities available, some of which were substandard, than to the ability and dedication of the teachers, coaches, and student athletes.

Foremost among them was Bryce Taylor, the chair and director of the Department of Physical Education and Athletics from 1967 to 1976, and professor in the department until his premature death in 1989. His commitment to sport at the national level can be inferred from his leadership positions in organizations such as the Canadian Gymnastic Federation, the Canadian Coaching Association, the Canadian Olympic Association, the National Advisory Council on Fitness and Amateur Sport, and the organizing committee for the 1988 Olympic Winter Games in Calgary. His commitment to sports at York was evident in the recruitment of a number of first-rate coaches, many of whom spent most or all of their working lives at York. Among them were Bob Bain (basketball), Dave Chambers (hockey), Merv Mosher (volleyball), Patricia Murray (synchronized swimming), Marina Vandermerwe (field hockey), Carol Wilson (swimming), and, in gymnastics, Natasa Bajin and Tom Zivic. Taylor himself was particularly interested in cross-country running.

Bain said Taylor's philosophy was that "coaching would be done by academically qualified people, who would divide their time between teaching and coaching."[189] That was demanding, but it made for better coaching. Until Bain arrived, the men's basketball team was coached by Vice-President Arthur Johnson, a man who loved the game but had no training as a coach, and then by a part-time coach, Bob McKinney. A dissatisfied member of the team who was acquainted with Bain helped to bring him to York in 1973. The program took a while to develop, Bain recalled, since much depended on attracting students with the necessary talent. He visited high schools in the Toronto area in order to identify promising players and to encourage them to come to York. By the late 1970s, "the glory years" of the York Yeomen had begun, with the likes of David Coulthard, John Christensen, and Tim Rider as mainstays of the squad. Coulthard, described in his citation in the York Sports Hall of Fame as "perhaps the finest male basketball player in York's 40-year history,"[190] played for the Yeomen from 1977 to 1982, years when he made the provincial second all-star team once and the first all-star team four times. "Those were the years we grew into a national contender," Bain said: "We could play with any team in the country. We never won a national championship, but we got close. We were consistently in the top ten."[191] In 1979–80 the Yeomen were Ontario champions; they became champions again in 1981–82, 1983–84, and 1984–85.

Rider came in 1981 mainly because Christensen, whom he knew, was already at York and because he knew of the "excellence" of York's basketball program. "I had a ton of fun at York," Rider recalled: "I was able to do things I wouldn't have been able to do at a U.S. school." He studied economics, taking five years for his degree, and was a don in Stong College in the fifth year. John Ridpath, who taught the introductory course, got him interested in the practical applications of economics, but "the biggest influence" on Rider was Bill Farr, whose son Matthew was the ball boy for the basketball team for two years. When Rider became

Tim Rider is looking for a rebound in a 1985 game against the Varsity Blues; John Christensen is in the background, right.

CYSF director of finance in 1985, Farr proved very helpful. "He told me how to deal with campus politics, how to create a budget ... He gave great advice on how to avoid landmines." Another strong influence was Bain. "We had a stormy relationship," Rider said. "I was very aggressive and competitive; I didn't take direction very well. But now I often quote him."[192]

Mary Lyons was an early recruit to the faculty, Taylor having asked her to come to York in 1967. Her responsibilities included teaching, administration – she took charge of women's athletics – and coaching the badminton and women's volleyball teams. There were fewer women's programs than men's, she recalled, and they got little attention even when they scored successes: "The Toronto papers were terrible that way."[193] But York came to have "quite a presence in women's sports" at the provincial and national levels, especially in volleyball, field hockey, and gymnastics.

Under the watchful eye of several highly capable coaches, the women's gymnastics team won many provincial and national championships in the 1970s and 1980s. Men's gymnastics was also a very strong program, and, although declining interest in gymnastics at other Canadian universities led to an end to national competitions and to the closing of the programs in 1993, no other sport has put more participants in the York Sports Hall of Fame, among them Susan Buchanan, who was York's first women's national champion, Lise Arsenault, Nancy McDonnell, Bob Carisse, Marc Epprecht, Thomas Kinsman (who also distinguished himself in diving), and, best known of them all, Steve MacLean. The Canadian Interuniversity Athletic Union all-round national champion in 1976, McLean won the Murray G. Ross Award, the highest honour given to a York undergraduate student for academic distinction and notable contributions to campus life, in 1977. In 1980 he coached the women's gymnastics team to a CIAU title. After completing his PHD in physics in 1983, he went to work for the Canadian Space Agency and became the second Canadian to walk in space.[194]

Merv Mosher, recruited by Lyons in 1978, took women's volleyball to new heights. He had "a wonderful time," he recalled, teaching and coaching. Along with field hockey, women's volleyball was "one of the top two women's team sports at the university": in nineteen years the team won the provincial championship thirteen times. He remembered with special pleasure the years from 1981 to 1985, when Trish Barnes, Jill Graham, Donna Kastelic, and Marla Taylor – all four are members of the Sports Hall of Fame – played for the team that won four straight Ontario championships. "Other players then came to us because York was strong."[195]

Marina Vandermerwe moved to York from the University of Toronto in 1971 to coach field hockey. She came because a very strong student of hers, Carol Anne Letheren, had joined York in 1970, but also because of "Bryce Taylor's PR." She remembered him very positively: "He was my mentor; he strongly guided me into getting higher degrees ... York gave me the opportunity to grow, academically and emotionally."[196] She took a PHD in health science from the University of Ohio and was able to teach a range of courses in the department. But coaching field and indoor hockey was her great love, and between 1971 and 1999 she coached not only York's women's field hockey teams but also Canada's Olympic squads in 1984, 1988, and 1992. It took most of a decade to turn York, which had finished last in 1971, into a championship team, but by 1980 the women's team was a powerhouse. Sparked in the later 1970s by Sheila Forshaw and in the 1980s by Sharon Creelman, Sandra Levy, and Sharon Speers, York won several Ontario titles and was competitive at the national level. Vandermerwe remembered Forshaw as "one of the greatest players in field hockey that Canada has ever produced."[197] Forshaw, who was twice York's female athlete of the year, acknowledged a debt of gratitude to Vandermerwe and Lyons, describing her decision to go to York as "the best move I ever made. I loved the honours program in physi-

LEFT Heidi Clark performs her floor routine.

RIGHT Steve MacLean was a champion gymnast, got a PHD in physics, and became an astronaut.

cal education, because it allowed me to go to university and get a degree in an area I love while playing on the national team."[198] If Canada had not boycotted the 1980 Games in Moscow, she would have played in three Olympic Games. She also played in several World Cup tournaments, winning a silver medal with the team in 1984.

Carol Wilson joined the faculty in 1970, hired by Taylor to initiate women's recreational programs as well as to teach and coach. Although her sport had been golf, she took charge of swimming, coaching the women until 1984 and both men and women from 1984 to 1988. She enjoyed her years at York: "Overall it was great!" But the absence of an Olympic-size fifty-metre pool was a disadvantage, and during the 1970s and 1980s there were just two truly outstanding swimmers. Neil Harvey was a backstroke specialist who won several national titles between 1976 and 1982. Gary MacDonald had been an Olympic silver medalist as a member of the 4 x 100 metre freestyle relay team in 1976, before he came to York. While at the university, he won eight gold medals at the national championships in 1978 and 1979. There were some "huge struggles," Wilson remembered, "a real battle for women's sports. Bryce Taylor believed in equal opportunity for men and women, but he worked in an environment where that was neither the norm nor the expectation."[199] Mosher, too, remembered that it was a struggle getting more support and more gymnasium time for the women's volleyball teams he coached.[200]

A large part of the problem was that York's facilities were seriously inadequate. Built in 1966, the Tait McKenzie building had reached capacity by the early 1970s, but the second and third phases of the athletic centre were never built for lack of money. The combined needs of athletes and recreational users were impossible to accommodate to everyone's satisfaction. Vandermerwe remembered giving Forshaw a key to the gymnasium so that she could work out at times when no one else was using it.[201] The swimming pool was only twenty-five metres, with a shallow end that was not suitable for synchronized swimming, Patricia Murray recalled.[202] She was recruited in 1972 to coach synchronized swimming and badminton, as well as teach physiology labs and the practicum courses required of every student in kinesiology. The pool proved a disadvantage in recruiting suitable students with experience, she said, but it was not the only inadequate facility. "The big problem for outdoor sports was that we didn't have a stadium." Football had to be played off campus for three decades. So did soccer, even though in 1977–78 the Yeomen won the CIAU soccer championship. On the other hand, Murray noted, athletes got a state-of-the-art indoor track after the 1976 Olympic Games, used by runners such as Molly Killingbeck, winner of a silver medal in the 1984 Olympic Games, Nancy Rooks, Desai Williams, and Mark McKoy.

Hockey was well established by the early 1970s, when players like Steven Latinovich and Murray Stroud laid the basis of their eventual entry into the York Sports Hall of Fame. Other standouts of the 1970s were Douglas Dunsmuir, Al Avery, and Tim Ampleford. But the hockey team played its home games in an arena that made almost no provision for spectators, which tended to weaken fan support. Women's hockey scored some notable successes in the 1980s. Led by forward Sue Howard, York finished second in Ontario in 1980–81 and 1981–82 before taking the championship for the first time in 1982–83.

The story of football at York was one of hope long deferred. Jamie Laws registered in Arts in 1969 and spent several years as an assistant athletic trainer, helping trainer Mert Prophet with the football, men's hockey, and men's basketball squads, later branching out into women's sports as well, taping ankles and the like. York wanted a team that would soon be competitive, he said, and in 1968 recruited Norbert (Nobby) Wirkowski to be football coach as well as men's athletic coordinator.[203] This was a real coup: Wirkowski had been quarterback as well as head coach of the Toronto Argonauts, and at the time of his move to York he was the Argos' director of player personnel. His ambition was to see York play football with "the big boys" – Toronto, Western, Queen's – and to this end he helped to negotiate the formation of the Ontario Universities Athletic Association in 1971. The new league was not kind to the Yeomen. Wirkowski's name attracted some good players to York, and Osgoode Hall Law School and Administrative Studies usually yielded several men who had played for other university teams and had some eligibility left. On the whole, "football was exciting, but no one likes to lose," Laws remembered: "We'd win only one or two games a season."[204]

LEFT   Mauro Ungaro heads the ball in a game against Trent University.

RIGHT   Former Toronto Argos' quarterback Nobby Wirkowski joined York to teach physical education and coach the football team.

LEFT   1970s football star Bill Hatanaka is today co-chair of the York to the Power of 50 campaign.

RIGHT   Physical Education chair Frank Cosentino is flanked by colleagues Tom Duck (left) and Dave Chambers.

So what brought Bill Hatanaka to York in 1973? A star athlete at Winston Churchill Collegiate in Scarborough, he wanted to become a professional football player. But rather than go to the University of Toronto, "a strong franchise in those days," he chose York. "I had Nobby Wirkowski's bubble gum card when I was a kid," Hatanaka said: "Besides, I was a contrarian."[205] He took a combined honours degree in economics and sociology, and played for the Yeomen as a slot back, wide receiver, and kick-off and punt returner. An OUAA all-star, he was chosen in the first round by the Ottawa Rough Riders at a time when, in sports enthusiast Steve Dranitsaris's words, "the Yeomen were the doormat of the league."[206] Soon afterwards, Hatanaka made Grey Cup history by returning a punt seventy-nine yards for a touchdown in Ottawa's 23–20 victory over Saskatchewan.

The football team's weak performance began to bother Frank Cosentino after he came to York in 1976 after six years at the University of Western Ontario, succeeding Bryce Taylor as chairman of physical education and athletics. Cosentino had been the all-star quarterback of the University of Western Ontario Mustangs in the late 1950s and played in the CFL for Hamilton, Edmonton, and Toronto. There was pressure to drop the football program at York, he found, because it was giving the department and York a bad name. "I didn't want to see football cancelled on my watch," he recalled, so in 1978 he began to coach the Yeomen.[207] During his three years as coach, the team's fortunes changed, with wins matching losses, and the program survived. His term as chairman having come to an end in 1981, he devoted himself full time to teaching, until his successor, Stuart Robbins, asked him in 1984 to resume coaching the football Yeomen. He agreed and kept the position for four more years.

In 1984, too, Robbins was able to persuade Dave Chambers to take on the hockey team once more. He had stepped out in 1977, but enjoyed a triumphant coaching return as the Yeomen won the 1984–85 CIAU championship. Mark Applewhaite, the all-star goalie of that and two subsequent championship-winning teams, is yet another member of the Sports Hall of Fame. It was an agreeable coincidence that the victory came in 1985, the year York celebrated its twenty-fifth anniversary.

Throughout the 1970s, newcomers to the faculty, library, and administrative staff continued to arrive, although the rate of faculty recruitment slowed down dramatically after 1972. They augmented programs that were still growing or replaced people who had left. Carole Carpenter joined the Division of Humanities in 1971, intrigued by its "breadth and potential." York's commitment to interdisciplinarity also attracted her, and she found the community at York "exciting." She taught part of a course with Eli Mandel, Ron Bloore, Michael Quealey, and Richard Teleky, and was particularly impressed with Mandel. "Eli was a gifted teacher. He had a way of being very human with a large class. He loved baseball and would often say something about baseball that made people laugh. His lectures were crystal clear ... If there is one person whose pedagogical approach in a lecture I have tried to follow, it is him." Carpenter also sang the praises of Winters College, in whose common room she had long conversations with colleagues like Norm Endler, John Warkentin, and Bob and Jane Banfield Haynes. "Those early years in the colleges were really important in promoting interdisciplinarity."[208]

Suzanne Klein joined the Division of Social Science in 1971 and taught there full time and part time for more than twenty years. "I loved teaching at York," she remembered: "I loved the freedom I had, I loved the creativity. It was exhilarating to come to teach in an interdisciplinary program, and to learn while you were teaching." The students were not necessarily great, but her colleagues were creative and interesting. "York was the most fun place at which I ever taught."[209]

Yet another 1971 recruit was Paul Lovejoy, a historian of Africa. He came to York because he wanted to be in Canada and in Toronto. He knew that Suzanne's husband, Martin Klein, also an Africanist, was at the University of Toronto, and he hoped to work closely with him. In the late 1980s he became associate vice-president for research, something he felt strongly about. Some professors seemed to think that teaching and research tended to exclude each other, he recalled. He disagreed with that. But, in spite of sometimes rancorous differences of opinion over this matter within his own department, he was positive in assessing York. "It has been a good place to be. It has changed a lot; it has got better. The students have got better." After Sidney Kanya-Forstner joined the department to teach African history, Lovejoy enjoyed working with him: "Colleagues like that have been great."[210]

Ellen Hoffmann joined the library staff in 1971. Her husband, the historian Richard Hoffmann, had been recruited by Sydney Eisen, who had asked Director of Libraries Tom O'Connell "to make a job for a faculty wife." She smiled as she remembered this: "That could still be done back then." Having disliked "the conservative and hierarchical" atmosphere of the Yale library where she worked for several years, she loved York: "There was lots of psychic space to do things."[211] Mostly this was due to her boss, Joan Carruthers: "She was wonderful to work for." Hoffmann became head of reference in 1973 but quit in 1975 to have a baby. "There was no university plan for maternity leave yet. You had to go to the unemployment office." Three years later she returned to York as assistant to the new director of libraries, Anne Woodsworth. In 1983 Hoffmann became director of

Ellen Hoffmann was director of libraries from 1983 to 2001.

libraries herself, holding that position until she retired from it in 2001 and gave way to Cynthia Archer.

The two underlying realities of the period, she recalled, were budgetary cuts and technological change, leading to the digital library. The collections budget was protected, but everything else suffered, especially staff numbers. Fortunately, computers, which were costly in the 1960s and 1970s, dropped steadily in price. By 1971, computer terminals were being used by the circulation department, and their use soon expanded. The big challenge of the 1970s was to get the catalogue into machine-readable form. That led in turn to a debate about whether the old catalogue cards should be retained (the cards lost). Unionization had an effect as well, as the technicians joined YUSA and the professional librarians found a home in YUFA. In summary, "the library changed from a conservative, traditional book-centred library to a less hierarchical, technology-based library." Hoffmann sounded nostalgic as she said: "The university I grew up in was that of Bill Farr and Sheldon Levy. They built up a culture that I think is gone. When you made a deal with them you didn't have to get it written down."[212]

Arthur Forer received a joint appointment in the Faculty of Science and Atkinson College in 1972. A biologist who had obtained his doctorate from Dartmouth University, he was teaching at Odense University in Denmark but found the university reforms there uncongenial: "Students and others in the department and university interfered with my research and teaching." He did not want to return to the United States because he opposed the war in Vietnam, and, since he knew Robert Haynes and Ronald Pearlman, both molecular biologists, he applied for a job at York. He was willing to go anywhere but the United States to escape from Denmark, he recalled: "I came here; lucky for me."[213]

Another biologist, Kenneth Davey, became chairman of York's Department of Biology in 1974. An animal physiologist who had been director of McGill's Institute of Parasitology, he said a bit facetiously that he had "barely heard of York" when he was first approached. When he looked at the university and the department, however, he found that "there were good people here ... Biology had an extraordinary record of research, unusual in a university in which science did not loom large." What he also liked was that both faculty and students at York seemed to have a "strong commitment ... to simple social justice."[214] In 1982 he succeeded Bob Lundell as dean; three years later he became academic vice-president. But he always made time for research, coming into his lab early every morning.

Rodger Schwass left the business world in 1976 to become dean of environmental studies. "I came for five years," he said: "I stayed for twenty-eight." York as a whole and FES in particular he described as "a tremendously exciting place that has pioneered in ways that few other universities have done, and none in Ontario."[215]

Also arriving in 1976 was Desző Horváth. Hungarian-born and Swedish-educated, he was made head of the Policy Department in Administrative Studies in 1978 and associate dean of the faculty in 1981. He became aware of York when he was at a conference in Toronto in the early 1970s, he said, and was struck by the ample resources available to FAS compared with Swedish business schools. Impressed by the opportunities here, he accepted an invitation from a Canadian acquaintance on the FAS faculty, Charles McMillan, to teach business strategy for a year. Horváth was on leave from Umeå University in Sweden, but Dean Wallace Crowston persuaded him to stay at York. "The faculty was really welcoming," he recalled. Upon becoming dean in 1988, he set out to make the school more globally oriented and launched a new international MBA degree.[216]

Not long after arriving, Horváth became a member of the Senate Committee on Research, in time becoming its chair. In that capacity he worked with Noli Swatman, secretary of the committee and herself a recent arrival at York. In 1976 she left a downtown legal firm to become a part-time secretary in the Osgoode Hall Law School, working for Harry Arthurs. Before long she became administrative assistant in the Office of Research Administration, working with Bill Found and Horváth: "I got to do all sorts of things!" She loved her work as a research officer. "I came to York when you could accomplish a lot because it was an emerging organization," she said: "I wouldn't have worked anywhere else ... I enjoyed the freedom to achieve. And I worked with the best!"[217]

One of those she worked with was the geographer Bryan Massam, who left a teaching position at McGill in 1977 to come to York. "I was intrigued, from a distance, by the idea of the colleges," he said. He was also ready for the challenge of working in an institution that was "less established" than McGill. Soon upon his arrival he became director of the Graduate Department and in 1980 the first dean of research. Ian Macdonald created the position as part of an effort to raise the profile of research, Massam recalled, and this trend continued: after he left the position in 1986 it was upgraded to the level of associate vice-president. The research office was a good place to work; Swatman and Horváth were "unforgettable." He sounded nostalgic as he thought back to his first few years at York. "People had a lot of time for each other" in the early days, he said: "There was lots of promise, and new ways of doing things."[218] In the bigger and more centralized institution that York later became, these possibilities seemed to narrow.

Susan Spence came close to echoing Massam's words. She joined York in 1979 as a part-time computer programmer, working in the York-Ryerson Computing Centre (YRCC) that had been founded in 1974. Huge changes in the way computers were used in the university were taking place. She remembered that Sheldon Levy understood their value at an early stage and spearheaded the move from mainframes to distributed computing. When the YRCC was dissolved in 1984, Spence had a managerial position in academic computing; in 1991 she became the director of Academic Computing Services. She experienced the transition from dealing with "a small and tolerant user group to a large and not necessarily tolerant or patient user group." Early on, she recalled, "we got to do pretty well what we wanted to. It's much more like a business now."[219]

Sheila Embleton was working on her PHD in linguistics at the University of Toronto when she took a one-year position in the Department of Languages, Literatures, and Linguistics in 1980. She had not been looking for a job, but Robert Fink had drawn her attention to the opening after getting her name from the University of Toronto's Linguistics Department. "I had somehow fallen into a

Marilyn Pilkington (third from the right), dean of Osgoode Hall Law School, with mock trial winners, 1994.

job," she recalled: "I didn't realize how tough the job market was until a year later." Her appointment was extended because she accepted the undergraduate directorship of the linguistics program, which she held until 1983, and in 1981–82 she competed successfully for a tenure-track position. The future academic vice-president never considered applying to any other university, she said, because she was happy at York. Besides, "there weren't any other jobs anyway."[220]

Jobs were scarce in the later 1970s and 1980s, especially in the humanities and social sciences. Finding employment in Osgoode Hall Law school was easier, however, because the turnover of faculty members was higher. People can and do move from the practice of law into teaching and vice versa. Marilyn Pilkington was in the litigation department at Torys when Dean Stanley Beck and future Dean Peter Hogg recruited her in 1980 to teach constitutional law. Osgoode's "international reputation for contextualizing law" attracted her, she recalled. There *was* a downside: York was very much a commuter university. "There were and are no cosy areas nearby. It's not in a university neighbourhood." She enjoyed the contact with colleagues and students, however, and in 1993 became dean and thereby the first female law dean in Ontario. "But I don't dine out on that," she said, smiling.[221] One of her successors, Patrick Monahan, was a student at Osgoode from 1977 to 1980. He registered there, he recalled, "because I wanted to explore the law in context, and there was a broader range of perspectives at Osgoode" than elsewhere. He enjoyed his student days. "The faculty were very stimulating," he said, and the one-bedroom apartment he had in a graduate residence on Assiniboine Road was reasonably priced and convenient. In 1982 he returned to Osgoode as a professor, finding it "a fantastic experience."[222] He stayed on and succeeded Peter Hogg as dean in 2003.

David M. Smith came to York in 1966 and never left (he is currently director of management information in the Office of Institutional Research and Analysis). A science student who took a degree in mathematics and computer science and then an MBA, he was also a star athlete, the national cross-country champion in 1968 and 1970, and the first president of the Men's Intercollegiate Athletic Council. He started working for the university even before he had completed his studies, he recalled, taking a junior administrative position in the Department of Physical Education. "I really liked Bryce Taylor; we became good friends." Later he became the executive officer and facilities coordinator of Physical Education while also coaching cross country and track and field for a number of years, working with the likes of Nancy Rooks and Molly Killingbeck. By the mid-1980s, he was employed in institutional research, working for Sheldon Levy and Bill Farr, who was once again in charge of the budget. He respected both men greatly and remembered Farr's office with amusement: "There were piles of stuff everywhere, but he knew exactly where everything was." Looking back he said: "I enjoyed my days as an athlete and getting involved with the athletic council. I enjoyed being a coach."[223] York evidently suited him.

Another student who ended up working at York was Dorothy Moore. She entered the Faculty of Arts as a mature student in 1973 and took the Law and Society program, which she linked to psychology. She appreciated its interdisciplinary nature, "but what was really incredible was the amount of attention you got from the faculty. They were very approachable ... It made me love being a student."[224] Three professors who stood out were Jane Banfield, who directed the program, the sociologist Desmond Ellis, and the political scientist George Szablowski. After graduating, she did graduate work at York in interdisciplinary studies and political science, then went to work for the university. She was the first coordinator of the Sexual Harassment Education and Complaint Centre before moving into the President's Office. "Harry Arthurs," she said admiringly, "was the quickest study I have ever met." Later she began to teach in the Law and Society program herself.

Fred Granek entered Environmental Studies in 1974, having earlier taken a York degree in physics. "Ralph Nicholls was really memorable," he said. Granek became a generalist ecologist – later he would work in pollution prevention – and found that "the critical, analytical skills I learned in physics worked beautifully. The connection between ecology, physics, and pollution prevention seems much clearer when you have worked through it." The absence of hard science in FES did not bother him: "I found it elsewhere. The faculty gave you the opportunity to look for yourself. They weren't going to spoon-feed you." Among his professors John Page was "wonderful." Two others, William Leiss and John Livingston, also had a "huge influence" on him: "It was exciting to watch them work together and learn from each other." On balance he remembered FES very positively. "It was eclectic, innovative, diverse ... They gave you rope: you could make macramé or you could make a noose. I don't think any other faculty would have given me the same freedom."[225]

Chris Gates went from the Faculty of Arts to Environmental Studies. He studied honours anthropology and geography, and in 1973 he was one of thirty students to go on the nine-week Kenya tour. "It opened my eyes to the importance of human ecology." Upon graduating in 1974, he marked time for a year, auditing a few courses. One by the tropical ecologist Howard Daugherty impressed him, and in 1975 he registered in FES. "The fact that it was a self-directed program was my salvation ... The faculty allowed me to sample from many disciplines without too much risk." He studied with several professors he admired, among them David Morley, Michel Chevalier, and the two men who influenced him most, Daugherty and Reginald Lang. His major paper on the Oak Ridges Moraine got him "great job offers" when he graduated. What did he like most about the Keele campus? "The wood lots were a lovely sanctuary."[226]

At the same time that Gates and Granek were in FES, Eileen Mercier (currently a member of the Board of Governors) was a part-time student in Administrative Studies. With a background in English literature, she was just finding her way into the business world and had to start the MBA program by taking two courses in statistics: "I met a lot of engineers there. I helped them with their research papers; they helped me get through statistics."[227] In 1976 there were five women in the policy course, who banded together to write a paper on the Toronto Stock Exchange under the supervision of William Dimma. "We told them that their Achilles heel was the poor information systems they had. We didn't comment on the absence of women." Dimma had a lot of credibility with the part-time students because he had been one himself, she recalled. Other notable professors were Isaiah Litvak and Donald Thompson. But the most memorable event during her time at York was the great snow storm of 3 April 1975. She was working on a project in the library of the Administrative Studies Building when someone announced that the university had closed. Seeing no hope of piloting her Volkswagen Beetle through the snowdrifts, she thought she was stuck on campus for the night. Late in the evening, however, a fellow student who had snow tires on his car asked for three passengers who could push his vehicle in case he got stuck. She volunteered. The drive was far from easy, but "an hour later we were at Finch station and I took the subway home."[228]

Public transportation dominated Ed McDonough's campus memories: "When I remember York, I remember the TTC." A student in FAS from 1981 to 1983, he lived in Scarborough and depended on buses and the subway to get him to York and back. This typically took about ninety minutes each way. "I'm not sure I fully understood the implications of the campus's location when I registered," he said wryly. He had a degree in commerce from the University of Toronto, but applied to FAS because it had a better reputation than Toronto's business school and had positioned itself as a more critical place than the business school at the University of Western Ontario. "The training was good; I think I got my money's worth."[229]

Also an FAS student in the very early 1980s, Bob Gagne (now York's chief information officer) found the program "very intense, but very rewarding." Among his professors he mentioned Horváth, David Dimick, and Bernie Wolf as being "particularly good." What he remembered most vividly, however, was the grow-

Eileen Mercier, a student in Administrative Studies in the 1970s, became vice-chair of the Board of Governors.

ing use of computers. Up to 1980 they had been used chiefly for programming in statistical and finance courses, but between 1981 and 1983 there was a huge growth in their use to write letters, memoranda, and other documents. In 1981 his class was among the first to use a computer to do their reports, he said, using a dumb terminal and dial-up modem into the faculty's minicomputer. This was "very slow" but it was clearly the wave of the future. Wires were strung throughout the building, he recalled, in order to provide secretaries with terminals that replaced their electric typewriters. Soon the long-ubiquitous punchcards were obsolete.[230]

Guy Burry was studying physical education at the University of Toronto when, after three years, he wanted to switch to the social sciences. When the Faculty of Arts and Science would give him credit for only one year, his future father-in-law, Bob Lundell, suggested he try his luck at York. With its more interdisciplinary approach, Burry recalled, York's Faculty of Arts was willing to give him credit for non-arts courses, and allowed him to enter third year. He studied sociology and economics but also took a course in Canadian business history with Tom Traves, soon to succeed Harold Kaplan as dean of arts. "Tom *was* terrific; he put business in context." Unlike some, Burry did not find the campus architecture off-putting. "My family was in concrete," he said, smiling, "so I loved the Keele campus."[231] For nostalgia's sake he secured two pieces of the Ross Building ramp when Harry Arthurs had it torn down. Graduating in 1982, he became active in the Alumni Association soon afterwards and was its president in 2008.

Allan Bonner entered York after attending *two* other universities, New Brunswick and Regina. He had started working on an MA in political science but switched to York in 1983, having gained "the impression that York had the premier political science department in the country." Ed Broadbent had taught here, James Laxer was teaching here, "so I came to have some courses with 'the flaming Marxists.'" He laughed: "I say that with great affection."[232] He ended up studying the media with Fred Fletcher – "not at all a flaming Marxist" – and a course on Marxist political economy with Robert Albritton. "*Das Kapital* was the text; I needed all my economics for that course." Bonner recently completed an LL.B at Osgoode. Like Burry, he became active in the Alumni Association.

Currently associate dean of science and engineering (student affairs), Paula Wilson had a very unusual student career. Registering in Glendon College because of its bilingual program in 1979, she studied economics because science was not taught there. She enjoyed courses with Brian Bixley and J. Ian McDonald – "he really cared about his students" – but it was one in urban history with Ian Gentles that led her to go to the Keele campus in third year for a course in urban studies. She also took a first-year course in biology, enjoyed it, and did extremely well. Arthur Forer (he described her in an interview as "one of the most brilliant students I ever had"[233]) encouraged her to think of graduate school. The universities of Toronto and Guelph wanted her to do a BSC degree first, but York, more flexible than the others, was prepared to admit her if she took a year of science courses and did well in them. She did and entered graduate school at York, taking a PHD in biology in 1989. "The department was warm, friendly, and lively," she remembered, staffed with a number of internationally known scientists, among them Forer, Robert Haynes, Kenneth Davey, Ronald Pearlman, Peter Moens, Doris Nicholls, Brent Heath, Barrie Coukell, and Elizabeth Pearce: "It was a good department to be in."[234] The same sentiment could have been expressed by many York students.

The celebrations marking the twenty-fifth anniversary of the university's opening in September 1960 began on 9 May 1985, when Harry Arthurs was installed in Burton Auditorium as the university's fourth president and vice-chancellor. Planning had begun in January, when the York 25 Committee, co-chaired by Marilyn Pilkington and Joe Green, got to work. The committee coordinator was Sylvia Zingrone, a former York employee who had returned to York after an eight-year absence. The university in 1985 felt "demoralized," she recalled: the effects of years of cutbacks were evident everywhere. But when she joined the President's Office, she found that "Harry really wanted to bring the place to life again."[235] The York 25 Committee tried to oblige. Money was so scarce that Bill Farr, who had become vice-president (finance and employee relations) in 1983, insisted she raise money from the central service departments to help pay for the installation.

At a special twenty-fifth anniversary convocation in June, honorary degrees were conferred on Jules Heller, the former dean of fine arts, Reginald Godden the pianist, who had taught in Heller's faculty for several years, and Walter Sisulu, the South African fighter against apartheid. The festivities proper began in September with a free rock concert sponsored by the CYSF and attended, in spite of a rain delay, by more than a thousand students.[236] A few days later, the Faculty of Fine Arts began a retrospective showing of films that had been released in Canada in 1960, including such classics as Billy Wilder's *The Apartment*, Alfred

Acting President William Found (left) congratulates President Harry Arthurs as 1985 begins.

Convocation 1984, Glendon campus. From left to right: Philippe Garigue, Jane Couchman (Senate chair), J. Tuzo Wilson (chancellor), Ian Macdonald, Mavis Gallant (honorary graduate), Bruce Bryden (board chair).

Hitchcock's *Psycho*, Jean-Luc Godard's *Breathless (À bout de souffle)*, Alain Resnais's *Hiroshima mon amour*, Michelangelo Antonioni's *L'Avventura*, and the funniest satire about labour-management relations ever filmed, John Boulting's *I'm All Right Jack*. The President's Silver Jubilee Symposium, held on 20 September, brought the heads of Harvard, Oxford, and the University of Paris to York to speak about "Excellence in a Democratic Society: The Challenge for Universities."[237] On 7 October, Leon Major directed *The Best of York*, performed in the Burton Auditorium by participants from all years of the theatre program, with Barbara Budd, who had completed the BFA degree in 1974, as master of ceremonies.[238] The next day Administrative Studies inaugurated the Annual Distinguished Entrepreneur Lectures, with Frank Stronach speaking about "Managing in the 1980s." On 15 October the Status of Women Office celebrated its tenth anniversary as well as York's twenty-fifth with a lecture by Rosalie Abella about "Employment Equity." A birthday party with a cake took place in Vanier College Dining Hall on 16 October.

On 19 October the Yeomen beat the McMaster Marauders 18–14 in the Homecoming Game before roughly 1,000 cheering fans at North York Civic Stadium, the highlight being Joe Pariselli's 100-yard punt return for a second-quarter touchdown. With the win, the Yeomen clinched a playoff berth. Noting that the York team had beaten the University of Toronto Varsity Blues at Varsity Stadium for the second consecutive year (after thirteen straight losses!), a Toronto *Star* reporter wrote: "The Yeomen, once the 'doormats' of the OUAA, have proved their accomplishments are not flukes. York is ranked No. 6 in Canada and head coach Frank Cosentino said his team is a legitimate contender in pursuing the provincial title."[239]

The theme of the Homecoming Dance that evening was "The Sixties." The crowd was in an excellent mood and danced the night away to music from the era, wrapping up what Mayor Mel Lastman of North York had proclaimed as "York University Week." Although in 1959 North York's government had showed considerable interest in York's plans, undertaking to donate more than a million dollars to the university in order to facilitate its establishment in North York, that interest waned after 1960. A volunteer group like the University Women's Club of North York demonstrated a greater interest in the university during the 1960s and 1970s than the township (later borough) council did.[240] Arthurs clearly thought that relations with North York could be improved. In June 1985 he pointed out to the mayor that York University had become North York's largest employer, and that half of York's faculty and staff lived in the borough and spent money there.[241] This must have caught Lastman's attention and prompted the recognition given to the university.

York 25 was an enjoyable and generally encouraging event. The Alumni Association marked the occasion by establishing the Silver Jubilee Scholarship Fund, while an alumnus of a different kind, Murray Ross, told Arthurs some weeks later: "The whole 25-year celebration provided a warmth of spirit and a boost to morale."[242] All the same, the YUFA strike began just three weeks after the party ended. It would take more than an anniversary bash to make everybody feel good about York. Like his predecessor, the new president faced daunting challenges.

Harry W. Arthurs Common, looking towards the Ross Building; York Lanes on the right.

People who last visited the Keele campus during the York 25 celebrations will barely recognize the campus today (2008). If they come through the main entrance, they will find that the Boynton Woods and Danby Woods south and north of York Boulevard are unchanged, and that the parking lot to the north is still where it was. But that is where the familiar features end. Beyond the parking lot, the Harry Sherman Crowe Co-operative housing development dates from 1993. The Lorna R. Marsden Honour Court and Welcome Centre (2000) at the top of York Boulevard is relatively inconspicuous, but its neighbours to the south stand out: the Seymour Schulich Building, constructed in 2003 in part with funds obtained from the province's SuperBuild program,[1] and the Executive Learning Centre (2004).

The prospect from the intersection of York and Ian Macdonald boulevards is strikingly different from what it was in 1985. Where the Ross Building ramp used to be, Vari Hall, constructed in 1990–91 with assistance from philanthropists George and Helen Vari, now stands. South of the Harry Arthurs Common, an attractive green space with a wading pool and fountain, three Fine Arts buildings have joined the Burton Auditorium and blocked the view of the northern exposure of Raymond Moriyama's building: the Centre for Film and Theatre (1988–89) and Accolade East and West (2005–06), both constructed with SuperBuild money and other resources, including borrowed funds. North of the Common and east of the Student Centre (1988–91) and the York Lanes retail and office building, constructed by the York University Development Corporation (1990–91), the York Research Tower and the new headquarters of the Archives of Ontario are under construction. The road around the Common is closed to all traffic except emergency vehicles and public transportation. Buses – some 1,600 of them every weekday – deliver passengers from all over the Greater Toronto Area (GTA) and pick them up to return whence they came. A TTC "Rocket," part of the express bus service that connects the campus with the Downsview subway station, arrives in front of York Lanes every few minutes of the day. The effect is

LEFT   Robert Castle and Mourad Mardikian await the construction of the Student Centre.

RIGHT   Helen and George Vari with an architect's drawing of Vari Hall, 1989.

a bit overpowering. Everyone looks forward to the day when the Spadina subway line is extended to York and beyond it to the new transportation interchange north of Steeles.[2]

The changes can have a disorienting effect on old-timers. Jacques Pauwels, who received his doctorate in history during the 1970s, visited the Keele campus in 2006 for the first time in almost twenty years. Although he had received directions on how to get to Accolade West, once on campus he had to phone an acquaintance for help. The "masking" of the Ross Building by Vari Hall had thrown him off, he reported.[3]

The changes elsewhere on campus are less immediately noticeable from the main entrance but no less dramatic, as the built-up area has been extended to the north and west. The West Office Building and Lumbers Academic Building were built in 1984; the Physical Resources Building, housing several service departments, dates from 1989. Also built in 1989, the Computer Methods Building near Keele and Steeles is not a university facility, but it houses some university functions. In 1990 Calumet College and its residence finally went up; the graduate residences between The Pond Road and Passy Crescent followed in 1991. Construction began that year on an additional science building, which ultimately came to house the Department of Chemistry.

By the time this structure was completed, Harry Arthurs had been succeeded in the presidency by the historian Susan Mann. She served until 1997, when she in turn gave way to the sociologist Lorna Marsden. It was on Mann's watch that physical education and various sports programs finally got facilities they had needed for a long time: an addition to the Field House in 1994, the 3,000-seat York Stadium in 1995, and the Ice Gardens, now the Canlan Ice Sports complex, a shared facility, in 1996. At this time, construction of the Seneca @ York Building, designed by Raymond Moriyama, began along The Pond Road between Ian Macdonald Boulevard and Seneca Lane.

In the early years of the new century there was a further burst of construction. The Computer Science and Engineering Building (2001) filled in the space between Farquharson and Steacie. The Technology Enhanced Learning Building, a facility shared with Seneca College and constructed with funds in part obtained from the SuperBuild program, was completed west of Seneca Lane in 2003. The William Small Centre, housing Security Services and the Computing Commons, with a parking garage attached, opened in 2003 east of Stong College and south of the new Chemistry Building. By that year the Student Services Centre and Parking Garage was under construction, as was the Rexall Centre, built for Tennis Canada close to Black Creek south of Shoreham Drive. The centre, which alternates with the Uniprix Stadium in Montreal in hosting the annual men's and women's Rogers Cup (the Canadian open tennis championships), consists of a 12,500-seat stadium, a 5,000-seat grandstand court, and sixteen other courts. These facilities were completed in 2004, as was The Pond Road Residence. The Tait McKenzie Physical Education Centre was expanded in 2005. In 2008 the Sherman Health Science Research Centre was under construction on the site of the old Ice Palace. On the south campus, Tribute Communities has been building a planned housing development consisting of 836 dwellings called the Village at York University.[4]

Back in 1985, the Keele campus resembled a sprawling suburb more than anything else. An excess of open spaces made walking around it a thoroughly unpleasant experience in winter: the words "windswept" and "Siberia" have come easily to the lips of people interviewed for this book. By the time the second of the Accolade buildings opened in 2006, however, the campus had been built up and looked rather like a sizable town. The comparison is apt. Given that enrolment is now approximately fifty thousand, and that the faculty and administrative and support staff number over seven thousand, the Keele campus has a weekday population larger than the central Ontario town of Belleville. And just as towns are friendlier to pedestrians than suburbs, so the campus of today is more agreeable to walk around in than the one of 1985. The most brilliant innovation in this respect is the enclosed walkway that skirts the Common from Accolade East all the way to and along York Lanes. The campus has also become more pleasant because the trees planted in the early years have reached full size, supplementing the older woods that fringe the built-up campus.

The Keele campus, then, has matured. The area north and west of it has also changed and developed. The population of the GTA continues to expand, with rapid growth north and west of Toronto. In the 1970s the campus was still very much on the outskirts, with farm land close at hand north of Steeles Avenue. Even the Glendon campus was perceived as being out in the suburbs. By 2008, however, Glendon was well within what people regard as mid-town Toronto, and the Keele campus was near the demographic centre of the Toronto conurbation. A large and growing proportion of the student body as well as faculty and staff live outside the boundaries of the amalgamated city. To those who live south of Lawrence Avenue or east of the Don Valley Parkway, the campus may still seem remote. (In February 2008 I attended a recital by Catherine Robbin, a distinguished singer who has become a member of the Music Department, in the Tribute Communities Recital Hall. During the intermission I chatted with two acquaintances, both long-time residents of Toronto, who admitted that this was their first-ever visit to the Keele campus. They were impressed, they said, and one

The historian Susan Mann was president and vice-chancellor from 1992 to 1997.

The Keele campus from the air, 2006.

of them added: "You know, it didn't take nearly as long to get here as I thought it would.") More and more people are realizing that the Keele campus is no longer, to use Stephen Leacock's phrase, "behind the beyond."

Not only the architectural face of York has changed. So has its human face. Reflecting the changing demographic profile of the GTA, the campus population has become steadily more diverse. Over the years, York, especially the Keele campus, has always attracted a significant number of students who were the first in their families to attend university. Many were immigrants or the children of immigrants. Into the 1980s their origins tended to be in southern Europe, but more recently they have come from all over the world. An estimate based on census data suggested that by the fall of 2006 members of visible minorities constituted more than a third of York's student body, with those of Chinese and South Asian ancestry easily the two largest groups.[5] The teaching faculty and the administrative and support staff have changed less rapidly, but they, too, have changed. A prominent alumnus from the mid-1970s, Bill Hatanaka, said: "I love the diversity that now exists at York. This is how things are supposed to be."[6]

YFS president Hamid Osman represents the present and future of York. Born in Afghanistan, he came to Canada at age five and grew up in Scarborough. He registered at York in January 2004, began to study political science, and got involved in politics in his second year. The issues that galvanized him were rising tuition fees and the war in Iraq, both of which he opposes. A member of Stong College, he was elected a YFS councillor in 2006, became acting vice-president (external) later that year, ran successfully for the presidency in 2007, and was handily re-elected in 2008. He spoke with passion about the barriers to higher education faced by poorer students, about the benefits of living in residence, and about the plight of commuter students. In his first year he lived in Stong College residence, where he had a roommate from New Liskeard in northern Ontario. "Our backgrounds were completely different," he recalled, "but we got along together, and I think we both learned a lot."[7]

One of his key concerns has been to get commuter students more involved in campus life, a cause, he noted, that also engages President Mamdouh Shoukri and Vice-President (Students) Robert Tiffin. Many commuter students leave the campus when their courses end; Osman thinks most of them are on their way to the part-time jobs they take to help pay for their education. As a result, residence students have a better university experience. This strikes him as unfair.

Higher education should be a right, Osman believes, and he is unhappy that it is in the process of becoming "more of a privilege." He has no real complaints about his own studies. The large classes he attended in his first couple of years were intimidating, but his tutorials and upper-year courses have been smaller and more rewarding. "The faculty are excellent," he said, "they really take the time to help you." How does he see the future of York? "I see us growing. I see us becoming more diverse. I see York becoming one of the top universities."[8]

The growing heterogeneity of the student body does present challenges, as students from very different backgrounds are brought into close contact, sometimes for the first time. These challenges are not new, of course. The issue of "race" has been contentious over the years, with scholars like the anthropologist Frances Henry working hard to identify it and to propose ameliorative measures. In the past there have been confrontations between groups with conflicting views of sensitive issues such as the struggle in the Middle East. Hateful graffiti and other evidence of ill feeling on the Keele campus in the fall of 2007 prompted Shoukri, the vice-presidents, and the deans to issue a statement of York values in February 2008. "York University is a community renowned for its diversity and commitment to free inquiry and expression," they wrote: "Yet some of the events that have happened here on the campus in recent months run the risk of alienating community members from each other." Calling for tolerance of those who look different or hold different opinions and beliefs, and for "a reciprocity of respect," the senior administrators urged that "debates on controversial subjects ... be conducted civilly without invective or hostility ... It is imperative not to let our own opinion – however sincerely held – be the tool with which we attempt to oppress, alienate or silence others."[9]

The occasion chosen for issuing this statement was the university's fifth annual Multicultural Week. Organized by "York is U," the student-alumni program, it lasted for four days in early February, with more than sixty student groups and clubs participating. An opening ceremony was followed by a multicultural parade and a food fair; other activities included a global fashion show and cross-cultural workshops. "We have a significant number of international students at York," said Farhan Ali, student director of the event. "Multicultural week really

Jazz legend Oscar Peterson was chancellor from 1991 to 1994.

Accolade East seen from the Harry W. Arthurs Common. The Executive Learning Centre is in the background.

provides a platform for us all to learn more about ourselves while developing a greater sense of community."[10] On the final two days of the event, the entire first floor of Accolade East was sectioned into "continents" where the clubs had an opportunity to depict their cultures. In addition there were performances in the Sandra Faire and Ivan Fecan Theatre, including music, dance, and other forms of art by the clubs and outside groups such as Toronto's Russian Folklore Theatre and the step-dance group Black Ice. It was a thoroughly enjoyable event.

The appearance of York and its people has changed. Other important internal changes are having the effect of turning York into a comprehensive full-faculty university. The ambition to become such an institution found expression near the end of Harry Arthurs's presidency in a Green Paper with the title "2020 Vision: The Future of York University." Endorsed by the Senate in January 1992 and by the Board of Governors in March of that year, the report sought to outline York's development over the next three decades. Its main recommendation was that "York should strive to become a 'comprehensive' university. We should not necessarily replicate the disciplines, structures and styles of other institutions; indeed we have the chance to develop our own distinctive idiom. But we ought to offer our faculty and students, and the community, a much wider range of intellectual perspectives, teaching programs, research activities, and external relationships than we do at present."[11]

Greater comprehensiveness could be achieved in three ways: by growing in areas where York was already active but less so than it might be, by "recombining existing program elements to form the nucleus of new programs," and by "adding totally new programs and their student populations where the availability of new resources permitted." The Green Paper expressed caution with respect to unrestrained growth in the well-established and largest programs, because it might interfere with the improvement of quality, prevent small programs from attaining an appropriate share of York's population, and even cause the total size of the university to escalate out of control. The report anticipated that, over time, the balance of disciplines within the university would change somewhat, and enrolment on the two campuses would increase by roughly 10 per cent. "Finally," the paper stated, "both growth and diversification should always be purposeful. They should occur only to the extent that they can be reconciled with a commitment to quality, in order to achieve specific academic objectives, and when supported by adequate resources."[12]

The continued underfunding of Ontario universities slowed implementation of the Green Paper's recommendations. Although Susan Mann and the two academic vice-presidents she worked with, Stephen Fienberg (until 1993) and Michael Stevenson, operated within the guidelines of the Green Paper, it was not until the presidency of Lorna Marsden that major changes took place. One signal of the new dispensation was raising the research portfolio from an associate vice-presidency to a vice-presidency in 2000, with former education dean Stan Shapson the first incumbent of the upgraded position. More momentous was the establishment of the Faculty of Health in 2006. The new unit, based in the former Administrative Studies Building, which it shares with Environmental Studies, has incorporated several units from Arts, Atkinson, and Science and Engineering – kinesiology and health science, health policy and management, psychology, and nursing, as well as the LaMarsh Centre on Violence and Conflict Resolution, and the Milton and Ethel Harris Research Initiative on Child Development. The faculty is also a primary partner with the Centre for Vision Research (CVR), and the York Institute for Health Research.

What the Faculty of Health currently is, however, pales alongside what it is hoping to become. The dean of the new faculty, Harvey Skinner, said: "If we get this faculty right, focusing on health, we will be well positioned to make the case for a medical school and be leaders in integrating prevention with health care." The key, in his view, is the burgeoning population of York region and its growing need for patient-centred care and collaborative health-care teams. Hospitals in the area are interested, he said: "Within three to five years we have to look seriously at a new type of medical school."[13] Skinner's prediction is that his faculty "will be seen as the model and catalyst for what York University will be in the next fifty years." The university is trying to become more research-intensive, and a medical school would complement that objective.

Certainly the new president agrees. "The GTA needs another medical school," Mamdouh Shoukri said recently, "and the university has the intellectual capacity to support one."[14] This reinforced the message he delivered during his installation address. He does not see a new faculty of medicine doing what the University of Toronto medical school is already doing, namely, high-end research and specialization. The need is for primary care, family practice, and preventive care, thereby filling a gap that other institutions are not well positioned to fill.[15]

Shoukri's own field is engineering, and his appointment as president clearly indicated that the search committee was looking in what was a new direction for York. His six predecessors were all from the humanities and social sciences or from professional fields closely linked to them, social work and law. His selec-

Marshall A. (Mickey) Cohen has been chair of the Board of Governors since 2000.

Mamdouh Shoukri became York's seventh president and vice-chancellor in 2007.

President Mamdouh Shoukri delivers his installation address, October 2007.

tion reinforced the growing importance of engineering at York. In 1989, when the physicist Kimmo Innanen was dean, a task force report led to the renaming of the Faculty of Science, which became the Faculty of Pure and Applied Science. In the fall of 2001 it launched a specialized engineering program (computer, geomatics, and space engineering). This quickly became a full part of the faculty, and in 2004 the Faculty of Science and Engineering got its new name. Nick Cercone, who came from Dalhousie University in 2006 to become dean, expressed the view that engineering should in time become an independent faculty.[16] York had been denied faculties of medicine and engineering in the early 1970s, but at age fifty it was well on the way to having both.

Both Cercone and his predecessor, the medical biophysicist and immunologist Gillian Wu, perceived the need to enhance the research culture at the university, as prescribed in the University Academic Plan (UAP) for 2005–10.[17] "York has a robust research culture," the plan stated, but there were "challenges" to be faced. One was the "relatively high proportion of scholars at York eligible for SSHRC [Social Sciences and Humanities Research Council] grants and the relative impoverishment of SSHRC." Another was "the relatively low proportion at York eligible for NSERC [National Sciences and Engineering Research Council] and other science and health-related grants, especially for very large research projects." A third challenge, and here seems to be the crux of the matter, was "the external emphasis placed on monetary measures for research achievement."[18]

The prevailing prejudice is that costly research is necessarily better or more important research. "The assessment of research ... is often conducted by means of crude monetary indicators. If we are to assert our rightful place among top-flight research universities, we will need to enhance our performance and ranking on these indices to avail ourselves of opportunities based on indices that exist while developing instruments of measurement attuned to York's particular blend of research cultures." Recognizing that a number of other universities face the same challenges, the drafters of the plan continued: "The University should work with others, including granting agencies, in a concerted effort to devise better indices of research activity and impact."[19]

The drafters of the plan were no doubt aware that developing such indices would be no easy matter. Measuring output, such as the number of publications or the number of pages published, is possible, but what, if anything, does the measurement say about the *quality* of what is being assessed? Citation indices, though not without their critics, are widely used in the sciences,[20] but they are much less useful in the social sciences and the humanities. In part this is because there is no broad agreement as to how important citations really are. After all, if a scholar is only one of a few working in a given field, she probably will not be cited frequently in journals. Does this make her work less important? There is disagreement, too, about the inclusion or exclusion of specific journals, and how much weight should be given to books as compared with scholarly articles. Citations in books often go unnoticed. Yet in a number of fields the scholarly monograph far outranks any article, and to have one's works quoted or cited in books is greatly prized. Dean of Education (until 2008) Paul Axelrod, a historian, noted that the Thomson Indices for the Arts and Humanities and for the Social Sciences do not include books or book chapters, a policy he characterized as "ridiculous" and "infuriating."[21] Besides, of how much use is an index, devised in the United States, for scholars working in Canada on Canadian subjects? he asked. Arts dean Robert Drummond, a political scientist, made a similar point. "How do you assess work published in journals that Americans don't consider important?" he asked, adding that there was resistance in most Arts departments to "crude measurement tools."[22]

York's humanists and social scientists, whether in cooperation with colleagues in other universities or not, may be able to develop more sophisticated and appropriate assessments of research performance in their fields. That would be a welcome development. However, the course York has adopted will probably make the attempt largely irrelevant. With a president who is committed to raising the university's research profile, and with an increasing number and proportion of faculty members and researchers working in health as well as in pure sciences and engineering, York is bound to attract more research dollars in the future.

The increased emphasis on research in the University Academic Plan has implications for teaching that clearly worry some people. Commenting on the UAP's clarion call to "make the crucial decisions to transform York into a more research-intensive university," Jack Saywell has recently written: "Lower teaching loads will follow as surely as night follows day."[23] This is already evident at the research-intensive universities of the country, the so-called G13 group that York is aspiring to join. Saywell is undoubtedly right in arguing that this has implications for undergraduate education at institutions from coast to coast. The teaching load of full-time faculty is going down at York, as it is elsewhere. Department chairs in the Faculty of Arts have confirmed that, while formal teaching loads continue to be two-and-a-half courses in an academic session, many faculty members now teach two courses, with the time once devoted to the additional

half-course assigned to research.[24] The argument, the Glendon economist James Savary said, is that York needs to match the standard set by other institutions.[25]

Unless student numbers go down, an unlikely event as enrolments in Ontario continue to increase,[26] a reduction in the teaching hours of full-time faculty means a shift to increased teaching by part-time faculty, a resort to larger classes, or both. In Ontario the government is seeking, by means of "Multi-Year Accountability Agreements," to ensure that the universities comply with the government's agenda: increased access, improved quality, and greater accountability. The quality that universities are focusing on, motivated by the values of their faculty members as well as the concerns of government, is in research, especially in the form of public-private partnerships that offer the promise of practical applications. It is a matter of faith that benefits will accrue to undergraduates, but a recent study of the effects of faculty research on undergraduate teaching suggests that, at present at least, this faith may be largely misplaced.[27]

It is a matter of faith, too, that Ontario (or other provinces) can afford to support a significantly increased number of research-intensive universities. Saywell, for one, is sceptical: "As dean, I fought any suggestion that York should not get into serious science or develop graduate programs. I never imagined that today I would write that we must have the courage to speak the simple truth that mass education is not affordable without institutional differentiation in level and substance and ... of faculty and faculty salaries."[28] His words indicate that a man who for a decade was at the centre of the university's growth entertains serious misgivings about York's current plans and hopes. It is unclear whether misgivings like these will have any effect on the course of events.

In the midst of expansion, York is losing the Joseph E. Atkinson Faculty of Liberal and Professional Studies and the Faculty of Arts. Their merger will be consummated on 1 July 2009; the name of the joint entity will be the Faculty of Liberal Arts and Professional Studies.

Atkinson College was the second of York's faculties to be established, and its disappearance may startle its graduates as well as others interested in the university. How did it happen? Sociologist Rhonda Lenton, who became Atkinson's dean in 2002, explained that all universities in Ontario were hard hit in the 1990s by the declining demand for part-time education from mature students, and this adversely affected Atkinson.[29] Changes in the other faculties, especially the Faculty of Arts, also weakened the college. The most significant of these changes was a move towards part-time education during the daytime. Some students have always had part-time jobs during the academic session, but during the last three decades their number, and the number of hours they work, have increased steadily. In order to help finance their education in an era of rising tuition fees, Hamid Osman emphasized, the majority of students have to work for pay *while* they try to study.[30] Even when students dropped to two courses per term, however, the other faculties did not turn them over to Atkinson. Then other faculties gained permission to teach courses in the evening as long as Atkinson did not already teach similar courses. Under the leadership of the geographer Ron Bordessa, who was then the dean, Atkinson launched the health departments, notably nursing, and with social work already in the faculty, it recreated itself in 2000 as the Atkinson Faculty of Liberal and Professional Studies.

The creation of the Faculty of Health ushered in a new phase in Atkinson's history. Nursing and psychology were both assigned to the new faculty. With part-time and mature students having become the responsibility of all the faculties, some were asking: "Do we still need an Atkinson College?" According to Lenton, Atkinson faculty members continued to believe that "if you really want to do mature education, you have to have a faculty devoted to it."[31] Others evidently disagreed. In any event, a long-time member of the Atkinson faculty, Joan Gibson, said: "It was increasingly hard to offer programs, as people who retired were not replaced ... Atkinson was weakened."[32] After a lengthy process of consultation and discussion, York's decision-making bodies moved to dissolve the faculties of Arts and Atkinson and to create a new faculty. The transition steering committee, chaired by Academic Vice-President Sheila Embleton, described this as "more than a merger. It is a chance to fashion a brand-new faculty ... a unique occasion to re-shape the University's future in York's fiftieth year along the lines of the UAP."[33]

The official position is that Atkinson is not being swallowed by Arts: "Both faculties will officially be disestablished effective with the opening of the new, consolidated Faculty."[34] Without wishing to be quoted, a couple of senior administrators suggested that Arts, being much larger, is bound to set the tone for the merged faculty. However, the merging process is unlikely to be a simple one. The new faculty will have to accommodate several professional schools currently based in Atkinson, such as administrative studies, information technology, public policy and administration, and social work, which have no counterparts in Arts. In addition, Atkinson houses the Division of Continuing Education, which offers a number of certificates but no degrees. Furthermore, the general education requirements of the two faculties have diverged over time. Atkinson requires its students to take six units (one full-session course) in each of humanities, social science, natural science, and "Modes of Reasoning." In Arts, the Modes requirement disappeared in 1969, while the introductory courses in humanities and social science have been nine units each since 1996, when the General Education program became the Arts Foundations program.[35] John Spencer, chair of the Faculty of Arts Centre for Academic Writing and a member of a committee whose interim report on the General Education program appeared in the summer of 2007,[36] has pointed out that "it won't be easy" to reconcile the two requirements.[37] Mutual accommodation will be essential.

The Atkinson name survives in the Atkinson Centre for Mature and Part-time Students, established in August 2007 and located in Central Square. There it will certainly be useful to the York University Mature Students' Organization (YUMSO), founded in 2004 by Edward Fenner. After twenty years as a writer and editor in the corporate sector, he came to York because he found that "if you don't have the letters behind your name, you don't get the promotion."[38] Interested in meeting other students in his position, he soon discovered that the York Association of Mature Students (YAMS) had expired several years earlier. Undeterred by this dispiriting information, he started his own group. YUMSO is flourishing, he reported: it has an executive, an office in Vanier College, a satellite group on the Glendon campus, a website, and a Facebook site. By the beginning of 2008, its newsletter had more than 600 subscribers, and members were meeting socially with increasing frequency. "We've been well received at York," he noted: "We've had lots of support from deans and from the academic staff." Since there are more than 8,000 students aged twenty-five and over at York, YUMSO has a significant role to play. Fenner, who is about to leave the presidency, expects to graduate with an honours degree in professional writing fairly soon. "I will have to pass this on to someone else," he said: "Part of what I wanted to do was raise the profile of mature students, and I think I've done that."[39]

Another faculty whose name has disappeared is Administrative Studies. In this case, however, the faculty was not dissolved. After entrepreneur and philanthropist Seymour Schulich made a $15-million donation to the faculty in 1995, its name was changed to the Seymour Schulich School of Business in recognition of his generosity. The gift contributed to the school's move from the increasingly

Entrepreneur Seymour Schulich has been a major benefactor of the university.

dated Administrative Studies Building to the new headquarters built between Ian Macdonald Boulevard and James Gillies Street.

The school has steadily augmented its international reputation. Deszö Horváth recalled: "When I became dean in 1988, life in business schools was still quiet … By the 1990s schools faced new challenges, including making the curriculum more relevant to the real world." Business schools had begun to compete globally, in tandem with the growth of transnational corporations. Horváth's Swedish background – his family moved from Hungary to Sweden when he was young – proved helpful here. Sweden is a small country whose corporations do compete and rank internationally, he said. "The Canadian approach to international trade has often been that we are too small to compete globally. But the Swedish approach has been: 'We are too small *not* to compete globally.'"[40] Business schools had to take a more cosmopolitan or global approach, something Horváth saw as the major challenge of the 1990s. The school needed more money so that it could attract better students and better faculty; it also needed a new building. Increased tuition fees and more successful fund-raising, from alumni and from others, were the keys to securing lasting improvement in the school. However, Horváth said that the school "wanted the very best students from around the world, regardless of their ability to pay the fees," so a high level of student financial support was put in place.

By his third term, which ran from 1998 to 2003, Horváth saw things coming together as the school's rankings steadily rose. This, in turn, led to an increase in the number of students, including international students. Enrolment doubled from 1995 to 2004, and has continued to rise, reaching almost 3,000 by the fall of 2006.[41] Higher rankings also led to the expansion of the executive training program. By 2006, Schulich was opening corporate training centres in Beijing, Mumbai, and Seoul, as well as a corporate governance centre in Moscow. Schulich's students came from ninety-two countries, and 70 per cent of the full-time MBA students held a passport from a country other than Canada. The school's international linkages included more than seventy academic exchange partner schools, some 150 corporate placement and internship partners, 18,000 alumni living and working in more than eighty countries, and eighty alumni chapters in twenty-seven countries.[42] These numbers, too, were all going up.

Horváth pointed out that the school not only teaches students about entrepreneurship and management, but "also about sustainability, corporate responsibility, and a wide range of specific management fields, such as health, real property, and financial services." It has appointed humanists such as Wesley Cragg, the first incumbent of the George R. Gardiner Chair in Business Ethics, and Robert Cuff, who taught business history. Brenda Gainer, who holds the Royal Bank professorship in non-profit management and leadership, pointed out that a good many faculty members have degrees in the liberal arts rather than business: "We make room for the unconventional, for critical approaches that some schools would consider marginal."[43] Her own field of non-profit management has been in the curriculum since the late 1960s. She held out the Arts Management program, which she ran jointly with Joyce Zemans of Fine Arts for ten years, as an example of the school's commitment to the innovative and unconventional. Another school, if it taught the area at all, might have assigned it to a business person who was dabbling in the arts. From the point of view of Schulich, it had to be someone who was knowledgeable about the arts. "This was a really enlightened attitude."[44]

"I feel great about the faculty today," Horváth said with a broad smile: "It has been a lot of fun to be in this faculty."[45] He has grounds to keep smiling. In the early fall of 2007, the *Economist* annual survey of business schools ranked Schulich first among Canadian MBA programs for the sixth straight year and twenty-fourth overall among the world's top one hundred programs.[46] At much the same time, the *Wall Street Journal* ranked Schulich first in Canada and eleventh among schools around the world, and *Forbes* also ranked Schulich very high. The *Financial Times* recently ranked the Kellogg-Schulich Executive MBA highest in the country. Business schools live and die by these rankings, which attract top students and faculty members.[47]

Patrick Monahan also has reason to smile. Osgoode Hall Law School is about to acquire a new wing that will house classrooms, offices, and a new student centre. Two scholars have recently been appointed to new named chairs, Edward Waitzer, a former chair of the Ontario Securities Commission, to the Jarislowsky Dimma Mooney Chair in Corporate Governance (jointly with Schulich), and Cynthia Williams, a recent arrival from the University of Illinois, to the Osler Chair in Business Law. Furthermore, the Ontario Law Commission, created by the Ontario government late in 2006, is being housed at Osgoode. And, just as the business school now has the Miles S. Nadal Management Centre on Bay Street between King and Wellington, so the law school has the Osgoode Professional Development Centre near the provincial courthouse. Initiated while Marilyn Pilkington was dean, the professional-development program moved to its first downtown location at Yonge and Dundas in 2000 during Peter Hogg's deanship. Its success in reaching the profession has led Osgoode to renew the lease. Relations with the profession and many alumni are still "a bit difficult" because of York's location in Downsview, Monahan said, but they are improving. At the same time: "I think we've found our place at York over the last forty years. For the present faculty, York is home. The period of adjustment is behind us."[48]

Monahan pointed at the Osgoode 2006–10 academic plan, entitled "Making a Difference," and said: "We continue to think of ourselves as pioneers." He noted that the faculty had done a major overhaul of the first-year curriculum, introducing a compulsory course in legal ethics and requiring students to do forty hours of unpaid work serving the public. Parkdale's legal clinic continues to thrive, he said: "It is an essential part of legal education to understand the lawyer's role in broader terms, to realize that you serve not merely private interests, but that you serve a public interest." Osgoode's commitment to re-examine itself, which began with the 2000 Plan, has contributed to raising the school's stature: for the second time in three years, *Canadian Lawyer* magazine ranked Osgoode first among Canadian law schools in 2008.[49]

Another dean who is smiling is Kenneth McRoberts, the principal of Glendon College. When he succeeded the psychologist Dyane Adam in 1999, the

LEFT   Seven Osgoode Hall Law School deans smile for the camera. From left to right: Harry Arthurs, Stanley Beck, John McCamus, James MacPherson, Marilyn Pilkington, Peter Hogg, Patrick Monahan.

RIGHT   Glendon College political scientist Sylvie Arend (front row, second from the right) with students at Queen's Park, 1996.

college was subjected to a searching examination by a university task force. In the second half of the 1990s, enrolment had fallen steeply, from 2,200 in 1994 to under 1,700 in 1998, with the number of FTE students reaching a low point of 1,282 in 1999–2000, so that there was once again concern about Glendon's future.[50] By 2007–08, that concern had vanished. Enrolment was up by 44 per cent since 2001, McRoberts reported, while admission standards had risen.[51] An international BA (iBA) that recognizes courses with an international dimension and encourages study abroad had been launched. So had MA degree programs in Translation and Public and International Affairs, with the Bank of Montreal providing generous funding for the School of Public Affairs. A doctoral program in Francophone Studies is well advanced, and one in Translation is in the works.

Having attained an enrolment of 2,500 students (2,000 FTEs) in 2007–08, Glendon had gone well beyond the capacity of its physical plant. But help was on the way. In late February 2008 the Ontario government announced that Glendon would be the site of a Centre of Excellence for French-Language and Bilingual Postsecondary Education, and that $20 million would be devoted to that end.[52] More than half of this will be used to enlarge the physical facilities.

Glendon has also become the site of a Faculty of Education program in French-language education for immersion schools, something that both McRoberts and education dean Paul Axelrod mentioned. The major expansion of Axelrod's faculty in recent years, however, has been in offering so-called Additional Qualification (AQ) courses, with enrolment rising from approximately one thousand to six thousand in five years.[53] Graduate enrolment also rose, though not as dramatically. At the same time, the program has made a concerted effort to strengthen relations with its alumni and to make its work better known in the world of primary and secondary education. In 2005, for example, it held the first annual alumni teaching award dinner, the occasion being the thirtieth anniversary of the faculty's first graduating class.[54] The event attracted more than a hundred people, and planning began at once to repeat it in 2006 and subsequently. Over the past decade, the faculty has cultivated its reputation for community-based education. It manages the Westview-York University partnership which offers some thirty educational and outreach programs to students and youth in the Jane-Finch area. In 2002 the faculty opened an off-campus consecutive-education site (one of several in the Greater Toronto area) in Regent Park.[55]

The Faculty of Environmental Studies has seen major changes in the last twenty years. In 1991 it introduced both a PHD program and a bachelor's degree for students interested in self-directed learning in an interdisciplinary context. Dean Barbara Rahder said that initially the undergraduate program "limped along" a bit as faculty members sorted out their pedagogical approach.[56] Undergraduates enjoy less flexibility than students at the graduate levels: they have to take foundation courses in two of four areas – environmental politics, urban and regional environments, environment and culture, and environmental management – and then choose one of the four. Unlike the graduate students, the undergraduates, who now make up almost two-thirds of the total enrolment, receive grades.

FES will continue to change, Rahder suggested, because of who the faculty members are and what the issues are. In 2006–07 two new professors were hired

in the field of climate change, which had come to engage at least five members of the faculty. "We don't do environmental engineering yet," she said, "but we can do many things."[57] FES is always ready to forge international links. The most intriguing of these is the operation of the Las Nubes (The Clouds) property, consisting of just over 120 hectares of rainforest in Costa Rica. Donated to York by the Toronto medical specialist M.M. (Woody) Fisher in 1997, it is leased by York to the Tropical Science Centre of Costa Rica. The site has already prompted some twenty master's theses on a variety of topics. Among them are ecological and biological inventories, geographic-information surveys and mapping, ecotourism, protected-area management, community-based conservation, environmental education, the use of medicinal plants, and the development and marketing of Las Nubes coffee. Sold across Canada by Timothy's, this sustainable coffee is produced by CoopeAgri, a farmers' cooperative, who get a price exceeding that of fair-traded coffee.[58] The Timothy's World Coffee website describes it

Since 2006 Accolade East has provided the performing arts with superb facilities.

as "smooth ... with sweet, fruity, and citrus notes" and states that "a portion of sales is donated to York University's Fisher Fund for Neotropical Conservation for environmental study in the region [of] the Las Nubes cooperative."[59]

Edmonton native and stage designer Phillip Silver came to York in 1986 from a national stage-design career that included the Stratford Festival. He became chair of York's Theatre Department in 1992. He was drawn to the Faculty of Fine Arts by its "excellent reputation" and by the likes of Joe Green and Joyce Zemans, whom he described as "amazing people with a broad knowledge of the arts."[60] He professed himself to be a strong believer in the faculty's ethos, combining theoretical and practical education: "The integrated intellectual development of the artist is every bit as important as the studio side." In 1998 he succeeded film professor Seth Feldman as dean and as a consequence has witnessed some major changes. The most obvious is the construction of the two Accolade Buildings, of which he was as proud as a parent with a new child. He was hardly alone in this pride. Mary Jane Warner of the Dance Department, for example, spoke enthusiastically about the new possibilities of Accolade East: "We have space that we haven't had for years. There is a sense of renewal; we're looking to do more performances."[61]

The Fine Arts Faculty occupies these buildings as well as the Joan and Martin Goldfarb Centre for Fine Arts (the name given to Fine Arts Phase II after the

Goldfarbs donated a major collection of modern art as well as money for capital improvements in 2001), the Centre for Film and Theatre, and the Burton Auditorium. Fine Arts now consists of seven departments, the original five of Dance, Film, Music, Theatre, and Visual Arts, and two more recently established programs, Design and Fine Arts Cultural Studies. A number of graduate programs exist, offering the MA, MFA, and PHD degrees. Silver claimed that "the dean's responsibilities have been a real joy, akin to working in the theatre – producing within a budget, making things come to life." Close to ending his term as dean, he saw a bright future for Fine Arts, now shaped by a "new cohort of teachers and researchers."[62]

The historian Douglas Peers came from the University of Calgary in 2007, taking over as dean of graduate studies from the biochemist Ronald Pearlman. "As a historian I came for the History Department, which is very strong," Peers said. But he also came because of the strength of the graduate program, and because he recognized some very appealing things about York: it was "nonconformist and a little turbulent ... There is an edginess to York."[63] Upon arrival he found it "academically appealing" but administratively confusing: "I found it hard having to come to grips with a hyperactive consultative process." At York, authority is much more diffuse than at Calgary, where the central administration exercises more control: "Here the Senate actually seems to matter!" (This echoed an observation by Nick Cercone, who said that in contrast with four other universities he taught at, "the Senate here is meaningful."[64]) Peers also noted that, although graduate studies are obviously important, he, like most graduate deans, has limited power: "We don't hire; we don't have big budgets." He does have significant influence over programs, however, since the graduate directors report to him and not to the undergraduate chairs. Graduate studies will expand, he predicted, especially in the sciences, as a consequence of York's increased emphasis on research. Scientists need graduate students as junior collaborators in the laboratory, he pointed out: "You can be a successful humanist without having graduate students, but you can't be a successful scientist without them."[65]

Laboratories are central to work in the sciences, but no entity is more important to the success of the research enterprise than a good library, just as it is of key importance to student learning. Cynthia Archer, who came from the University of Windsor in 2001 to succeed Ellen Hoffmann as university librarian, said that electronic sources and the Internet have become central to the library and the way it operates. She pointed to the important *Synergies* project in which the York library is participating. Because research published in Canadian journals in the social sciences and humanities, especially in English, is largely confined to print, this research is largely invisible on the Internet. Since many students and scholars begin and unfortunately sometimes end their background research on the Internet, *Synergies* will give Canadian research a higher profile. It will also help to legitimize online publication in the social sciences and humanities.[66] It is easier for York to become involved in this, Archer said, because the university does not have its own publishing house. All the same: "Libraries are not about print *or* electronic, but both, just as they are not about research *or* teaching, but both."[67]

Asked to comment on the reports by the deans and the university librarian, Sheila Embleton praised the efforts that have been made to involve the Scott Library in raising the quality of student life. Where the academic plan was concerned, she said that getting York research to be better known was sometimes slow going: "Things never go as fast as you'd like." But there was progress, and the next plan would very likely follow the same path as the existing one. She cautioned against worrying too much about the perception of York within Toronto or Canada, however, noting that York generally looked better and more competitive when seen from an international perspective. The social sciences were an area of real strength, and Schulich, Osgoode, and Fine Arts had a fine reputation abroad. All in all, she said she was "cautiously optimistic."[68]

The colleges on the Keele campus have come under examination three times since 1985. Doubtful that they were fulfilling their potential, Harry Arthurs appointed a presidential committee in 1986, consisting of the University of Toronto geographer F. Kenneth Hare (chair), Jane Banfield Haynes, and Jack Saywell. Their report "A Sense of Place" appeared in April 1987. The seven colleges "were set up by the founders of York to provide intimate and attractive homes for the students and faculty of what was expected to become a large university," the report stated. The colleges were supposed to ward off the alienation that beset large institutions, but they had failed in this. "The flood of incoming students and faculty has largely ignored the colleges, which have remained literally and figuratively peripheral to the University's mainstream life," and "the University itself, as an administrative body, has found no adequate role for the colleges."[69] Comments from people connected with the colleges were "overwhelmingly favourable, but ... these individuals are members of a small minority at York."[70] However, students who did not live in residence were simply left out unless they joined a club or program that also involved residence students. The committee noted that "resident students are inclined to be well satisfied with the colleges, whereas the commuters were actively critical."[71]

As for the students, so for the fellows. It was easy for them to identify with a college if they had their offices there, much harder if they did not. As a result of the shortage of space on campus, the committee pointed out, several academic units were located in one or another of the colleges: music in McLaughlin and Winters colleges, graduate English and the Writing Workshop in Stong, history in Vanier. "Though the colleges responded to the critical need for space ... the price may have been to prevent Fellows from taking their offices in the colleges, and thus weaken any developing sense of collegiality."[72]

Senior administrators seemed to be hostile to the colleges, and the university as a whole was largely indifferent to them. But the committee was unwilling to abandon them and lose the enthusiasm they inspired in the minority who did make use of them: "It is a cardinal rule of university life that enthusiasm should never be wasted."[73] The report's main recommendation was that the colleges be converted into "special cultural-intellectual identity colleges," and that "membership ... should be totally voluntary for all concerned, except for entering freshmen students."[74] Vanier and Founders should be specifically devoted to entering

students, McLaughlin to public affairs, Bethune to international and multicultural affairs, and Stong to arts and letters. Winters – this recommendation was not unanimous – should be a college for women; Calumet, still without a building in 1987, should target mature students.

This recommendation did not go far. Neither the money nor the will existed to make major changes in the colleges. In 1996 they came under examination once again, though less closely than in 1986–87, by the Task Force on Faculties, Colleges, and the First-Year Experience.[75] After the 1996 report, the colleges ceased teaching all so-called college courses, the Faculty of Arts courses that had replaced the college tutorials fifteen years earlier. Another result was that the colleges, which had been transferred to the care of the vice-president (student affairs and campus relations) after the 1987 report, became the responsibility of the vice-president (academic).[76] This proved less than satisfactory, and a few years later they became the concern of the vice-president (students).

The sociologist Lorna R. Marsden was president and vice-chancellor from 1997 to 2007.

The most recent report dates from 2006, produced by a task force chaired by Vice-President Robert Tiffin. Its chief concern was to improve the student experience. "This is a key strategic issue for York and critical to our success. The university has entered into a multi-year accountability agreement with the province in which measuring various aspects of the educational experience will be a factor in future funding."[77] The task force believed that the college system would "play an important role in the overall academic, co-curricular and social experiences of our students," as measured by the National Survey of Student Engagement (NSSE), originally developed at Indiana University to provide more reliable information about the student experience than was available from *US News & World Report*. The use of the NSSE by Canadian universities, including York, has been a response to the controversial annual issue of *Maclean's* that purports to rank Canadian universities.[78]

The task force report identified the importance of the first year in attaching students to the university. If the colleges are to help in this, however, they must have more impact on non-resident students, the report stated. Given the increase in the size of the Keele campus student body during the last thirty years, the college system must be restructured so that students, especially those entering for the first time, can be better integrated into York. Among the key recommendation of the task force was that "a primary focus of colleges be on the development and delivery of co-curricular programming and the creation of a diverse cultural experience for all York students to assist them to connect with faculty and other students ... A special emphasis will be placed on new students."[79]

Another recommendation was that, effective 1 May 2007, college masters report to the dean of the faculty to which their college was academically aligned. Some alignments already existed: Bethune was linked with Science and Engineering and FES, and Winters with Fine Arts. Not coincidentally, the task force found that these two colleges had the greatest connection to their students. By 2008, the other five colleges were also affiliated with a faculty: Founders, Vanier, and McLaughlin with the amalgamated Faculty of Liberal Arts and Professional Studies, and Calumet and Stong with Health.

President Marsden's response to the task force report was swift and generally positive. She strongly endorsed most of the recommendations, though she noted that a handful had to be referred to various bodies around the university. Her only cavil was with the final recommendation, "that the implementation of the recommendations of this report be reviewed in Fall to Winter, 2009–2010."[80] "We do not have the luxury of waiting until 2009–2010 to assess the effectiveness of these recommendations and their implementation," she wrote.[81] Instead, the assessment of results was to take place in the fall of 2007.

The current master of McLaughlin College, Ian Greene, expressed pleasure at these developments, noting in an interview that those who wanted to abolish the colleges had been in a small minority, and that the report had offered the colleges a new opportunity to prove themselves and thrive.[82] Two months later he wrote: "The latest reorganization could be very successful, depending on the quality of leadership within the colleges and the faculties ... The new system is working very well in most respects, and the mood in the colleges is one of revitalization and renaissance."[83] Marsden commented: "My sense is that after the initial objections to change [the new arrangement] is working quite well."[84] Tiffin also saw grounds for optimism. In early 2008 he wrote: "Overall we have made quite a few good strides this year ... I think very positive progress has been made in the first year of the renewal of the Colleges."[85]

Is York a university where research does not play a central role? Or is it perhaps a university where contributions to research have not been as visible as they should? The Green Paper of 1992 and the most recent University Academic Plan both expressed concern that York lacked an adequately developed research culture.

As a result of such concerns, York has beefed up research support during the last decade in an effort to meet the demands of a comprehensive research university. In 2000 Stan Shapson became the first vice-president in charge of research and innovation. (Since 1986 these responsibilities had rested with an associate vice-president.) An important unit under his supervision is the Office of Research Services, among whose concerns are technology transfer and Knowledge Mobilization. York is increasingly formalizing its technology-transfer and commercialization procedures to facilitate the patenting and commercialization of innovative research. Knowledge Mobilization, a field in which York is a leader, is a service aimed at scientists and humanists who wish to see their research developed and applied in the larger world.

To scholars in the humanities and social sciences, the concerns about research may seem strange. In history, a field that has been strong ever since the appointment of Edgar McInnis in 1960, no fewer than eight scholars have been named Distinguished Research Professor – John Bosher, Jerome Ch'en, Jack Granatstein, Michael Herren, Michael Kater, Gabriel Kolko, Paul Lovejoy, and H. Vivian Nelles. Most are now retired, though they continue to be active in research and writing. Lovejoy, who still teaches in the Faculty of Arts, recently played a central role in creating the Harriet Tubman Institute for Research on the Global Migrations of African Peoples. Its research focuses on the forced and voluntary movement of African peoples around the world; its mandate is to promote a greater understanding of the history of slavery and its legacy. Noting that many Canadians do not know that slavery existed in Canada (British North America) until 1834, Lovejoy has said that the aim of the Tubman Institute is to dispel such ignorance and help society understand the present: "We have to understand that our combined past has involved the massive enslavement of African people ... That has a legacy into contemporary times, right up to today."[86]

It is a legacy that has influenced Lovejoy's research ever since he came to York from the United States almost forty years ago: "It's hard to do work in African history without confronting the fact of slavery and its results."[87] In February 2008 the centre's Slavery, Memory, Citizenship project received $2.5 million under SSHRC's Major Collaborative Research Initiative program. Led by Lovejoy, holder of a Canada Research Chair, "a team of more than fifty Canadian and international scholars are researching the global migrations of African peoples under conditions of slavery and how the resulting racism arising from the exploitation of African peoples has shaped modern societies."[88]

Another scholar of international distinction is James Carley of the English Department in Arts. "My work is entirely interdisciplinary," he said, straddling literature, history, bibliography, and translation. His long-term project has been to prepare an edition and translation of *De viris illustribus* by John Leland (c. 1503–52), a first-generation English humanist, antiquarian, and topographer who was the last man to see and describe the libraries of many English monasteries before their dissolution by King Henry VIII. The book, which will be roughly one thousand pages, will include a biography of Leland. Although "he is one of the most cited people in the *DNB* [*Dictionary of National Biography*], rather surprisingly there has never been a biography of him."[89] (Carley has also written the *DNB* entry on Leland.) The volume is scheduled to appear in 2009, as is a book Carley has prepared for the Folio Society, a companion volume for their very costly (£1,000!) facsimile edition of the *King Henry VIII Psalter*. Carley noted that the year 2009 will mark the five hundredth anniversary of Henry VIII's accession to the throne, and this has created a lot of interest.

Carley's research has been helped along by fellowships at various English colleges. In 2005–06 he held a Leverhulme visiting professorship at Oxford: "All I had to do was give public lectures on my work." Deprecating the need for large sums of money to fund basic research of the kind he does, he said with a sunny smile: "I'm a very cheap researcher. I just need to be put in a library." Beyond travel costs there has been little need to spend money, and he has avoided the costs associated with coordinating the research of a group of scholars: "I've collaborated with others, but we're not a team."[90]

One York researcher who *is* part of a team is Colin Coates, who returned to Canada from teaching Canadian studies at the University of Edinburgh to take a Tier 2 Canada Research Chair at Glendon College in 2003. (Tier 2 chairs, tenable for five years and renewable once, are for exceptional emerging researchers, acknowledged by their peers as having the potential to lead in their field. For each Tier 2 chair, the university receives $100,000 annually for five years. Tier 1 chairs, tenable for seven years and renewable, are for outstanding researchers acknowledged by their peers as world leaders in their fields. For each Tier 1 chair, the university receives $200,000 annually for seven years.[91]) He is a member of Network in Canadian History and Environment / Nouvelle initiative canadienne en histoire de l'environnement (NiCHE).[92] Headed by the University of Western Ontario historian Allan MacEachern, in 2007 NiCHE was awarded almost $2.1 million over seven years through SSHRC's Strategic Knowledge Clusters program. Coates is the team's main researcher on the history of landscape, one of half a dozen subgroups. His current interest is in the history of Canadian utopias, both historical and fictional, which emerged from an interest in the agricultural commons that were part of the landscape of New France but were suppressed in the early nineteenth century. Utopias are usually based on the notion of common property, Coates said: "How do people deal with common or shared property?" Most of the Canadian utopias have been studied before, "but I want to find a common thread that makes sense of them all. I'm still discovering strands that I want to connect."[93]

This remark is true of many researchers. For more than a quarter of a century, the psychologist Ellen Bialystok, a Fellow of the Royal Society of Canada and a Distinguished Research Professor, has been asking questions about the effects of bilingualism on the brain. Until 1962, she said, badly conducted research that was rooted in racist assumptions suggested that bilingual children had more trouble learning than unilingual children. The bilingual children tested were usually recent immigrants from Europe who had not yet mastered English. Then a 1962 study done in Montreal seemed to indicate that bilingualism conferred significant advantages, since bilingual children scored higher than unilingual children on a range of tests. This research, too, was flawed. The bilingual children were generally from a higher social stratum and enjoyed a more stimulating life: "They were the cream of the crop."[94] But the new and revolutionary findings led researchers to re-examine the subject.

Psychologist Ellen Bialystok studies the effects of bilingualism on the brain.

Bialystok herself has been looking at the relationship between bilingualism and Alzheimer's Disease. She has found that "bilingualism does not prevent Alzheimer's, but bilingual people who develop the disease cope with it better and exhibit the symptoms at a later age." The part of the brain that controls attention is last to develop and first to decay. The attentional control of unilingual people peaks at age twenty. The attentional control of bilingual people climbs a little more quickly at first, and although it begins declining at the same time, it declines less steeply. Bilingualism has the same effect on the brain as living a very stimulating, event-packed life. Bilingual people develop a better "cognitive reserve" – she compared it to a reserve gas tank in an automobile – that enables the brain to slow down the effects of dementia: "Bilingualism improves the overall health of the brain."[95] This has implications for mental health and even public policy.

The applications of their research are important to both Allan Hutchinson in Osgoode Hall Law School and Moshe Milevsky in the Schulich School of Business. Hutchinson, who came to York from England in 1982 and was named a Distinguished Research Professor and a Fellow of the Royal Society of Canada in 2005, said that a theme in all his work has been "the connection between democracy and law." Over the last decades, Osgoode Hall Law School has encouraged critical approaches to law, he noted, and "although my work is individual to me, it does build on Osgoode's critical traditions."[96] For example, his book *The Companies We Keep* (2006) outlined an attempt to devise corporate governance for a democratic society. Corporations being extremely powerful institutions, he argued, they should be turned to better economic effect by including stakeholders as well as shareholders in their governance.

Hutchinson described his next book, *The Province of Jurisprudence Democratized* (2008), as a response to a classic nineteenth-century work by John Austin, *The Province of Jurisprudence Determined* (1832). "My book is a challenge to the modern concept of jurisprudence, a call to democratic arms ... The theme of my book is that in 1832 jurisprudence took a wrong turn and allied itself to analytical philosophy." His book will attempt to show "how legal theory might be better linked to democracy." Law, Hutchinson stated, has been a barrier to democracy, which he described as "not just a process but a culture." The new book "pulls together a lot of threads that I have been working on ... I would be happy to be judged by that piece of work."[97]

Milevsky, who joined York in 1995 as an assistant professor of finance, has a more homely but equally fascinating objective. "I am using mathematics to shed light on the personal financial decisions that people make," he explained.[98] One example is the decision to take one's pension as an annuity or as a lump sum (assuming one has the choice), an issue he discussed in the *Journal of Risk and Insurance* in 1998. In his basic research he has been working with mathematicians – he has a master's degree in mathematics himself – to develop models and probabilities. These can be applied to personal financial decisions. "It works to use math," he said: "We can save people from making mistakes." The models indicate that one's attitude to risk should be determined by one's personal financial status, not by one's gut feeling. This has particular relevance to one's choice in investments. "If your employment is secure, you can invest in stocks rather than bonds," Milevsky said, adding that he would soon be addressing this issue in a book intended for a non-specialist audience. With the intriguing title *Are*

York Lions goaltender
Kevin Druce (2004–07)
stops the puck.

You a Stock or a Bond?, the book will use mathematics to discuss asset allocation based on one's human capital.

Wesley Cragg of the Schulich School of Business and the Faculty of Arts Philosophy Department is involved in social-science and humanities research in a different way. He is the principal applicant for the Canadian Business Ethics Research Network (CBERN),[99] which was founded in 2004 and succeeded in obtaining a seven-year $2.1-million grant from SSHRC's Strategic Knowledge Clusters program in 2006–07. The purpose of the grant, Cragg explained, is to facilitate research and mobilize knowledge that already exists, and to raise the profile of Canadian research on business ethics, with a view to making people aware of what is happening and where information can be found, and "to move research findings on business ethics into the public arena."[100] The objective is not to generate publications, but to foster public dialogue by means of conferences, colloquia, and the like. A founding conference took place on the Keele campus in September 2007; the second meeting took place on the campus of the University of British Columbia in late May 2008.

The challenges that this sort of project poses may be inferred from the number of researchers and entities associated with CBERN: fourteen co-applicants from eleven different universities in Canada, thirty-two collaborators, most of them academics, domiciled in half-a-dozen countries, and twenty-four partners (universities, institutes, and corporations) in Canada and abroad. "This has been a very difficult, time-consuming grant," Cragg said somewhat wearily, "beginning with the application. I couldn't have done it if I hadn't been retired from teaching." He also had help in making the application. The political scientist David Dewitt, who is associate vice-president of research, assigned Sarah Whitaker to the project to help Cragg pull everything together in accordance with SSHRC standards. Since obtaining the grant, he has become a grant administrator: "In the first year of operation, it has taken about 50 per cent of my time and that of a project manager and secretary." The principal problem is trying to make sense of the rules for spending money, he said, since Schulich, the university, and SSHRC all have rules, and there are too many people who have a hand in interpreting them. More troubling is that the grant-administration environment is one of "lack of trust." In light of the number of people involved, "team research is a problem. The larger the budget, the larger and more dispersed the team, the greater the problem. If York is going to become a top-flight research university, the rules will have to be simplified."[101] Cragg suggested that "a more effective and efficient environment of trust and mutual respect, built on shared ethical values," needs to be developed.

In the humanities, social sciences, and law, York's scholars have gained international reputations in the past and continue to do so. Yet, in the eyes of some, research at York seems diminished because the Faculty of Science and Engineering has never been nearly as large as the Faculty of Arts, and because it is not as well known. That does not mean, however, that the scientists at York have not made their mark. The opposite is true. Beginning with the Centre for Research in Experimental and Space Science (now called the Centre for Research in Earth and Space Science), founded in 1965, York has become home to several high-

powered scientific research centres, such as the Centre for Atmospheric Chemistry (CAC), the Centre for Vision Research, and the Centre for Research in Mass Spectrometry (CRMS), and to scientists of international importance.

Robert Allan, a biochemist who arrived at York in 1966, recalled the founding dean, Harold Schiff, as "an enormous force in the faculty, through his own work and through the hiring he did ... He was a spark plug for the whole faculty ... He was hiring quality."[102] Allan mentioned that Schiff himself was interested in atmospheric chemistry and that he assembled a stellar group of physical chemists and gas-phase kineticists, among them Huw Pritchard, John Goodings, Diethard Böhme, and Tucker Carrington. Ralph Nicholls, who was a founder of CRESS, attracted other good physicists: Gérard Hébert, Kimmo Innanen, Allan Carswell, and Gordon Shepherd. Carswell did pioneering work with laser radar or lidar (light detection and ranging radar), founding his own company, Optech, in 1974 to work on practical applications of this invention.

When Schiff brought in Robert Haynes from Berkeley, he gave him a mandate "to change the character of the Biology Department, "to hire people with a molecular bent." Soon biologists like James Friesen, Ruth Hill, Ronald Pearlman, and David Logan joined the department. When Bob Lundell, "a superlative administrator" in Allan's words, became dean, he followed in Schiff's path: "He allowed the departments to flourish in their own way."[103]

Shepherd had worked on rockets at the University of Saskatchewan before he came to York in 1969. He knew that Nicholls had been involved in auroral physics since the early 1950s, and that Schiff was interested in space from the chemist's point of view. The appointments Schiff made in physics and chemistry were often intended to support research in that field, Shepherd said. This attracted him, for he, like Nicholls, wanted to understand the aurora borealis (Northern Lights).

Moreover, "York had a young department," he recalled, with scientists like Roy Koehler, James Laframboise, and Robert Young.[104]

Shepherd arrived at York with a satellite experiment in hand, an instrument called the Red Line Photometer (RLP) that was to fly on the Canadian ISIS-II satellite (ISIS stands for International Satellites for Ionospheric Studies). Launched in 1971, the RLP mapped the distribution of the mysterious "red aurora" that occurs in the daytime. Around 1980 Shepherd began to work on an idea to measure winds in the earth's upper atmosphere, about a hundred kilometres above the earth. Working under the auspices of CRESS, the team he led, drawn from a number of institutions in Canada and France, got approval to build an instrument, known as WINDII (Wind Imaging Interferometer), in 1984. It was made for the Upper Atmosphere Research Satellite (UARS), which was launched in September 1991. It continued to operate until the end of 2005, gathering a lot of information about "the global wind and temperature tides in the upper atmosphere with their seasonal variations."[105] The experiment was a government-university-industry project with participation by the U.S. National Aeronautics and Space Administration (NASA) as well as Canada and France. Given the cost of $40 million, such collaboration was essential. Canadian scientists working on the project were at Trent University and the universities of Calgary, Saskatchewan, and Western Ontario, as well as York.

The latest space project in which York is involved as the Canadian science lead is Phoenix, NASA's probe of Mars. The Phoenix mission landed in May 2008 and began to study the Martian climate, the planet's geological history of water, and the potential of its soil to support life.[106] York scientists, supported by the Canadian Space Agency, have contributed to the development of a meteorological station, known as MET, which contains a lidar system that can detect dust and clouds in the Martian atmosphere. The weather station was built by MDA in

Aerospace engineer Brendan Quine with a thermal vacuum chamber (TVAC) and a shake table, both used for testing equipment that will fly in space.

Brampton, Ont., with lidar expertise provided by Carswell's company, Optech, and with scientific input from York.[107] Carswell, by now a professor emeritus, brought York into the project, with Diane Michelangeli, who died of cancer in 2007, as the initial lead investigator. James Whiteway, who holds a Canada Research Chair, has succeeded her; also involved is Peter Taylor, program director in the Department of Earth and Space Science and Engineering.

Like Carswell, Shepherd is now retired, but he has stayed on in a part-time capacity as director of CRESS. He continues to do research and in the winter of 2008 had just completed a book, *Canada's Fifty Years in Space*, with Agnes Kruchio, a York alumna.[108] It was scheduled to appear in 2008.

Another early researcher of note was the chemist Huw Pritchard, who was named a Distinguished Research Professor in 1983, one of the first group of York academics to be honoured in that way. He was teaching at the University of Manchester in 1965 when Schiff phoned to offer him a full professorship and participation in CRESS. He decided to come for a couple of years to see how it worked out. Five of his graduate students accompanied him; one of them, Anthony Wallis, ended up staying at York to teach computer science. The experiments that Pritchard had been doing at Manchester were initially set up in Farquharson, but "when Petrie opened [in 1968] we moved all the equipment over there. It was marvellous from the point of view of doing research."[109] He would stay in Petrie until 2006, although he had closed his lab a few years earlier.

Pritchard said that CRESS quickly developed a "phenomenal reputation, due in large part to Ralph Nicholls, who talked about CRESS everywhere. I had excellent students who would never have come to me except through CRESS." Research funding was a problem for exploratory projects, because funding agencies tended to prefer the known to the unknown. Pritchard's own research into combustion would have suffered had it not been for Imperial Oil (Esso), which approached him in 1985 to do research into additives to maintain the ignition quality of domestic diesel fuel above the legislated minimum standard. "I used to take great delight in doing things that people said wouldn't work." Some did, some did not, he said, adding: "If you can bring yourself to think outside the box, as they call it, you can begin to question what the current theories say, you can devise something new ... Sometimes you have to doubt." He saw his success with Canadian diesel fuel in that light, and expressed regret that, in spite of the Kyoto accord, there was little interest in Canada in research on combustion nowadays. Asked to comment on the low profile of York science, he said that in matters of higher education, general public awareness was always well behind the times. "Perhaps we need better public relations," he suggested.[110]

One of the biggest scientific reputations belongs to physical chemist Diethard Böhme. He is one of five York professors to be a Distinguished Research Professor, a Fellow of the Royal Society of Canada, *and* the holder of a Canada Research Chair. (The others are the historian Paul Lovejoy, the physicist Eric Hessels, the theatre scholar Christopher Innes, and the political economist Leo Panitch). Hired by Pritchard on Schiff's recommendation in 1970, Böhme took all his degrees at McGill, where he met Schiff and, on his advice, did his doctorate under the supervision of John Goodings. "Harold and John both went to York," he said with a grin, "so after a couple of post-docs [post-doctoral fellowships] I came here too."[111] He became a member of CRESS and got to know Nicholls. The centre had some money for research: "That was important to me as I was starting my work."

He began by measuring with a flow-tube mass spectrometer how fast the fastest chemical reactions, those between ions and molecules, occur in the gas phase, and spent two years at a U.S. government laboratory in Boulder, Colorado, measuring reactions in the earth's ionosphere. He also became interested in studying ion-molecule reactions in solutions in the gas phase, the work that made him well known. Once at York, he also measured reactions of ions in flames, a subject Goodings was interested in. He used the mass spectrometer to simulate conditions in space, in the interstellar clouds, and started working in space chemistry: "My grail was to build amino acids, the building blocks of life, in space, by means of ion-molecule reactions. We finally achieved this about four years ago."[112] During his sabbaticals he forged strong scientific ties to Europe, collaborating with the organic chemist Helmut Schwarz in Berlin and the ion physicist Paul Scheier in Innsbruck.

Böhme's enthusiasm was infectious as he spoke about Buckminsterfullerene (C_{60}), the so-called Bucky ball, which has the structure of a geodesic dome or a soccer ball, and about the attempt to fill it with a helium atom, which he, Schwarz, and others succeeded in doing in Berlin. When Böhme returned to Canada, he "studied all kinds of chemistry on the outside of the Bucky ball." His basic research with atomic ions has application to analytical mass spectrometry, he said, and for seven years he has obtained collaborative research grants with MDS SCIEX, the company that makes the spectrometers used for weighing ions. A decade ago he was instrumental in bringing the analytical chemist K.W. Michael Siu to York, and he became a group leader in the Centre for Research in Mass Spectrometry, formed in 2000 around Siu.

In 2007 Böhme received the Chemical Institute of Canada Medal, "presented annually as a mark of distinction and recognition to a person who has made an outstanding contribution to the science of chemistry or chemical engineering in Canada."[113] Earlier recipients include Nobel Prize winners Gerhard Herzberg and John C. Polanyi. A man whose work has received much national and international recognition, Böhme asked whether it is worth trying to measure research intensity in order to promote the image of the university. He was sceptical. "It is almost impossible to properly measure research output across the university. Research takes different forms in different disciplines. What is important is to promote the research of individuals. Quality will out, and visibility will follow." His Canada Research Chair was recently renewed for seven more years, and he was looking forward to more research on ions: "I'm into the chemistry of biological ions now." He still has quite a large group of students, and he enjoys working with them: "It's a great way to stay young at heart!"[114]

Ian Howard may well echo that. Born and educated in England, he was teaching at New York University when Kurt Danziger recruited him for York's Psychology Department in 1966. He became chairman in 1968, the year the department decided to specialize in fields that the University of Toronto was not working in.

The physical chemist Diethard Böhme is one of York's most distinguished scientists and researchers.

LEFT The new science building, now called the Chemistry Building, was completed in 1993.

RIGHT The computer scientist and engineer John Tsotsos with the "Playbot" he developed, a visually-guided autonomous wheel-chair for a disabled child.

One of those fields was perception, and in the years that followed York was able to build up impressive expertise in this area. Howard spoke with quiet pleasure and pride about the colleagues who had distinguished and were distinguishing themselves: Hiroshi Ono; Leonard Theodor, who died early; Martin Steinbach, who came as Howard's post-doctoral fellow in 1968, became a member of Atkinson College, and is now a Distinguished Research Professor; and David Regan, also from England, who joined the department in 1987 while at the same time becoming a professor of ophthalmology at the University of Toronto. "He was a big acquisition," Howard said: "He began to win all the prizes."[115] Howard's own work was in human visual orientation, specifically on symptoms of disorientation among astronauts caused by weightlessness. Using a "tumbling room" located under Vari Hall, a room-sized space that rotates fully on a fixed horizontal axis, it is possible to simulate weightlessness and study how test subjects' vestibular organs (organs of balance) react to it. Most people suffer from motion illness as a result, and, Howard said with a conspiratorial grin, "some astronauts find it very hard to function. But they don't want this to be known."[116] Laurence Harris took charge of this project after Howard left it, and it continued until 2007, when the grant from NASA came to an end.

In view of all the research talent available, Howard founded a vision-research group in 1988. In 1992 it became the Centre for Vision Research. Howard was its director for the first six years; more recently (2000–06), John Tsotsos of the Computer Science Department, who now holds the Canada Research Chair in computational vision, was the director. The current director is Hugh Wilson of Biology. In 1995 the centre added a promising young scientist, Doug Crawford, who has since then made a major name for himself. "What is delightful," Howard said, "is that now we can attract the best people, good graduate students, good post-doctoral fellows, good faculty." He was very glad he came to York. "There's something to be said about a place that's starting up. It gives you a chance to grow, to develop something new. York has been very good to our centre." He continues to be active: a two-volume work, *Seeing in Depth*, appeared in 2002. At age eighty, he still has post-doctoral fellows working with him. "I guess I'll quit when I feel like it," he said with the air of a man who does not think he will feel like it any time soon.[117]

The biochemist and molecular biologist Ronald Pearlman came to York in 1968, recruited by Bob Haynes. Pearlman knew Haynes by reputation, and he also knew Harold Schiff, who had been one of his teachers when he was an undergraduate at McGill. Furthermore, he knew that his McGill classmate, Clifford Leznoff, had joined York. Pearlman moved into Farquharson, where the lab that Pritchard had used was being renovated for him. Molecular biology, he explained, deals with the organization and expression of genetic information. When recombinant DNA technology became available in the 1970s, it opened up new ways of addressing problems. Pearlman and his colleague James Friesen, who arrived when he did but moved on to the University of Toronto around 1980, worked together to have York build the first certified containment lab facility in Toronto, and perhaps the first in Canada, so that they and "a stream of mostly short-term visitors" could work on problems using recombinant DNA technology. This established York's leadership in this emerging field.[118]

"The life sciences have really been exciting from the 1960s on," Pearlman said, noting that the recent genome projects had opened up a great deal of new research.[119] "This area of biochemistry and molecular biology has seen exponen-

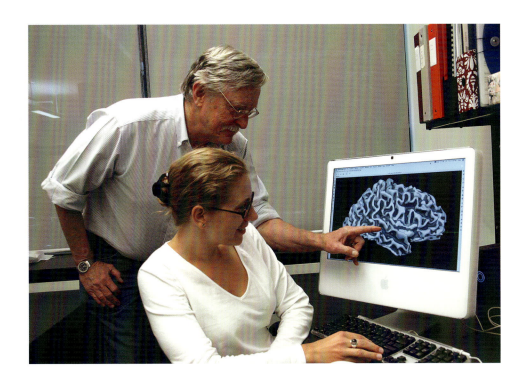

Hugh Wilson, director of the Centre for Vision Research, and post-doctoral fellow Lisa R. Betts discuss activity patterns in a scan of a human brain.

tial growth ... I have been lucky to have been part of this. I find it even more interesting and exciting now than when I began." But he noted that it has become more difficult to keep up with "the big labs and big science," such as the University of Toronto and its large hospital-based research institutes with which York competes for graduate students and post-doctoral fellows. The pursuit of funding is also "highly competitive," but York has done well. A field in which York is well respected is proteomics, the analysis of the expression, localization, functions, and interactions of the proteins encoded by the genes of an organism. Pearlman said that a key person in this context was the analytical chemist K.W. Michael Siu, much honoured and now a Distinguished Research Professor, who came to York in 1998 and works with mass spectrometers. This is "big science," in which York takes part not only in the life sciences but also through atmospheric research, which was Schiff's interest and continues to be strong, and experimental particle physics, in which Eric Hessels is an important figure as a result of his work on antihydrogen. But, while York's scientists were and are continuing to do excellent work in their fields, Pearlman regretted that "the sciences have until now loomed large neither within York nor in the general public's view of the university," which is seen as being "strong in the humanities and social sciences" but "less so in the sciences." For all that, "insiders and the granting agencies know that York has a very strong and well-deserved reputation in science."[120]

One of the star scientists identified by Pearlman, Siu said he came to York from the National Research Council because he had "always been a closet academic" and "somebody made me an offer I couldn't refuse."[121] That somebody was Robert Prince, the physicist who was dean of science from 1994 to 2001. He initiated and facilitated the process whereby Siu came to hold an NSERC Industrial Research Chair sponsored by MDS Analytical Technologies (formerly SCIEX), "one of the world's leading mass-spectrometer manufacturers and an important partner in my research."[122] Siu also serves as the director of the Centre for Research in Mass Spectrometry. He explained that spectrometers come in various sizes and shapes. The centre has more than a dozen of them; "they all do slightly different things." Each costs about half a million dollars, much less than a Stradivarius, "but just as with a Strad," he said with a smile, "you have to know how to play it."

"Playing it" involves breaking up the ion in the machine. Siu used a homely image: "You smash it against a gaseous molecule, nitrogen for example." Once it has been smacked it can be put together, giving the researcher an idea what it is. Siu described this as "putting together a jigsaw puzzle without a picture." But it is not a game. It is typically used in important applications, for example, the discovery and identification of cancer biomarkers, which can be invaluable in cancer diagnostics. Siu collaborates with other York researchers, among them Pearlman, Alan Hopkinson, John McDermott, and Samuel Benchimol, a Canada Research Chair in biomedical health research, as well as with pathologists and clinicians downtown, mainly at Mount Sinai Hospital. The cancer biomarkers of interest to Siu are proteins that are characteristic of a given cancer; if the proteins produced can be identified, diagnosing the specific cancer is possible. A longer-term objective is to apply the biomarkers to prognosis, Siu said, and beyond that into therapy. "Wanting to make a difference is what drives us forward."[123]

Vision researcher Doug Crawford with his research team, 2005. From left to right: Florin Feloui, Gerald Keith, Michael Vesia, Alina Constantin, Matthias Niemeier, Doug Crawford, Jachin Ascensio-Monteon, Gunnar Blohm, Honying Wang, Farshad Farshadmanesh, Denise Henriques, Joe DeSouza, Aarlenne Khan, Jessica Klassen, Lei Ren, Saihong Sun, Xiaogang Yan.

Doug Crawford is one of York's brightest young scientists. He won the Steacie Prize in 2004, the first York scientist to do so. The $15,000 prize is named in memory of E.W.R. Steacie, a physical chemist and former president of the National Research Council of Canada. Administered by the E.W.R. Steacie Memorial Trustees Fund, it is awarded annually to a scientist or engineer in Canada aged forty or less.

Ten years earlier, Crawford was on a beach in Hawaii – he was attending a conference – when Laurence Harris, now chair of the York Psychology Department and long-time member of the CVR, spoke to him about a position in psychology the department was having trouble filling and suggested that he apply. "By the time we finished talking I had a sunburn on one side of my face," Crawford said with a smile.[124] He was still early in a post-doctoral fellowship at the Montreal Neurological Institute, where he had been working on the neural control of eye and head movements, but while he had not given much thought to York University before, the position sounded interesting. He did apply, got the appointment, and now holds the Canada Research Chair in Visual-Motor Neuroscience. The laboratory he has built up over the last thirteen years is "engaged in three areas of vision research: eye-hand coordination, 3-D gaze control, and trans-saccadic integration (piecing together perceptions across different gaze fixations)."[125]

A thoughtful man who reads ancient and medieval history for relaxation, Crawford said that he and his research team study the brain to determine "how we use vision to guide our movements and how the brain maps out where things are in space." They collaborate with several hospitals, including the stroke centre at Sunnybrook Hospital, studying people who have suffered damage to the right parietal cortex. The parietal lobe of the cerebral cortex, at the top and back of the head, is involved in taking visual input and transforming it into motor commands in the motor cortex. The application of the research is to help people overcome damage resulting from strokes, but, Crawford said, "90 per cent of my research is basic. Computer simulations allow us to make predictions as to how the brain uses vision ... We measure performance in healthy individuals and compare that to performance in patients who have brain damage, mainly stroke patients ... We also use a number of technologies that look directly at how the brain functions in this area."[126]

York will soon get its own machine to do functional magnetic resonance imaging (fMRI), Crawford said with obvious pleasure. It will cost several million dollars and will be put in the old Ice Palace, which has been renamed the Sherman Health Science Research Centre. Research is his great love, that and training his graduate students and post-doctoral fellows, and research in his field is not cheap. He has to bring in half a million dollars annually to sustain his lab; most of it comes from the Canadian Institute for Health Research and the NSERC. His Canada Research Chair also helps, not least because it was recently upgraded from a Tier 2 to a Tier 1 chair. Infrastructure money is available from the Canada Foundation for Innovation (CFI). There is also internal support. Crawford spoke highly of those at York who have encouraged him: Ian Howard ("fascinating to talk with"), Sandra Pyke ("a powerful and inspirational chair"), and administrators like George Fallis, dean of arts from 1994 to 2001, Vice-President (Academic) Sheila Embleton, and Vice-President (Research) Stan Shapson. He said he was glad he came to York: "We've got the future here, so long as we play our cards right!"[127]

Another relative newcomer to York is the limnologist Norman Yan, but his career path was very different from Crawford's. Yan joined the Department of Biology in 2000 after twenty-five years as a provincial government research scientist. He has a continuing link to the public service, because the Ministry of the Environment pays half of his salary in a partnership deal that was renewed in 2005 and will probably be renewed again since both sides seem to be happy with it. "I agreed to do a body of work that the ministry is interested in: describing and explaining what is going on with the animal plankton in Ontario's lakes."[128] Water pollution by metals, declining calcium concentrations, invading species, and climate change are some of the issues that concern him and his students, who work in laboratories at York University and in Dorset near Algonquin Park.

Yan's fascination with and evident enthusiasm for Ontario's lakes – there are some 250,000 of them measuring one hectare or more – is rooted in his love of canoeing. The lakes are "national treasures" that are worth taking better care of than we have been doing, he stated, and his tools include "the premier sets of inland-lakes data in the world" that he has generated and still has access to. "The government can generate the data sets but does not have the number of personnel needed to interpret them. That's where I and my students come in." One of his major concerns at the moment is the threat to the lakes' biodiversity represented by non-indigenous species, and more particularly the spiny water flea. Probably native to Lake Ladoga in northwestern Russia, the tiny crustacean entered the Great Lakes in the 1980s and is now invading the inland lakes.[129] Yan described it as "the greatest threat to plankton diversity since acid rain," replacing native predators and driving plankton into colder water where they grow more slowly. Warmer water is turning the lakes into something like a desert, Yan explained, as other animals, notably plankton and the fish that feed on them, diminish in number. York researchers, in collaboration with scientists at McGill University and the universities of Alberta, Toronto, and Windsor, are generating data on the current spread of the spiny water flea and doing risk assessment.

Bridget Stutchbury is concerned about animals too, but her consuming interest is in songbirds. Holder of the Canada Research Chair in Ecology and Conservation Biology, she joined the York faculty in 1991. Her love of nature is due to spending summers at her parents' cottage in the Adirondacks, she said, and it seemed to set her up to become a field biologist or ethologist. Her turn to ornithology was "a fluke." While she was an undergraduate at Queen's University, she landed a summer job at the university's biology station, and "I discovered that birds fascinated me." Taking her doctorate at Yale with a dissertation on purple martins, she has studied birds, especially the hooded warbler, and their behaviour in many places: Ontario, Oklahoma, Arizona, and Pennsylvania, where her husband's family owns an old farm with a wood lot. A study trip to Brazil to discover what was happening to the purple martins' winter grounds was an eye-opener. With the tropical rain forest being cut down, the birds, which feed on insects, have a hard time fattening up and are late getting back to their nesting grounds in North America. Many never make it back, and the breeding success of those who do is lowered. "'Oh my gosh,' I said to myself, 'I can't believe what our birds have to put up with!'"[130]

While habitat fragmentation is a serious problem, there is an even greater menace: the heavy use of insecticides, herbicides, and fungicides in Latin American agriculture. These pesticides not only affect the birds' food supply but also poison the birds directly. Latin American farmers routinely use pesticides that are banned in North America as too toxic. Coming to realize this has completely changed Stutchbury's shopping habits. She will not buy Latin American fruit and vegetables, and she will buy only shade-grown organic coffee: "I want to encourage sustainable agriculture, and I want to help save the songbirds."[131]

A Toronto *Star* story on 1 January 2005, identifying Stutchbury as one of the top people in the GTA to watch,[132] prompted a letter from HarperCollins asking whether she had time to write a book. The result was *Silence of the Songbirds* (2007), a highly readable work that was shortlisted for the Governor General's Award for non-fiction. It makes the case that human beings must change their habits and consumption practices in order to save the songbirds. In doing so, we could also be helping to save ourselves, for the birds serve a vital purpose in keeping insect populations down and fertilizing shrubs and trees. "It was a lot more fun writing the book than writing scientific articles," Stutchbury said, smiling, "and it has reached a lot more readers." She is already at work on a second book, on the social life of birds: "People are interested in animal behaviour."[133]

Sampa Bhadra and Wendy Taylor are in a significant way the new face of science at York. Bhadra, who came to York in 1994 from a research position at the University of Toronto, and Taylor, who arrived at York in 2004, are both

Ornithologist Bridget Stutchbury studies the behaviour and migration patterns of songbirds.

Particle physicists Sampa Bhadra and Wendy Taylor are fascinated by what happened in the immediate aftermath of the Big Bang.

particle physicists, and aside from Helen Freedhoff, who is a professor emerita, they are the only two women in the Department of Physics and Astronomy. Neither considered this to be particularly relevant: "We are just researchers." Bhadra spoke highly of William Frisken, who was the only experimental particle physicist in the department when she arrived – there are now six particle physicists, three experimental and three theoretical. He was extremely encouraging towards younger colleagues, she said, but so was the department generally: "We've never been pulled down in our research by an unhealthy climate."[134] Taylor added: "I feel quite comfortable at York. We have a supportive department and university."[135]

Bhadra has been involved for years in the ZEUS experiment, a collaboration of hundreds of physicists who are running a large particle detector at the electron-proton collider HERA in the DESY laboratory in Hamburg. "Our job is to find out what are the most fundamental particles in nature," she said. She is also taking part in an experiment in Tokai, Japan, and hence travels a good deal. This experiment probes the elusive properties of the neutrino, and how it has shaped the structure and evolution of the universe. Taylor, who holds a Canada Research Chair, is involved in two experiments, one at Fermilab in Chicago and the other, the ATLAS experiment, at CERN, the European Organization for Nuclear Research in Geneva which is advertised as "the world's largest particle physics laboratory."[136] It does have the largest accelerator in the world, so that it is possible to recreate extremely high temperatures in order to get a sense of what happened just after the Big Bang, when the universe was very hot. The experiment in which Taylor, along with 2,000 other physicists (including Bhadra), is involved is designed to find the so-called Higgs boson,[137] an elementary particle postulated in 1964 by the British physicist Peter Higgs that might give other particles mass. But, said Taylor, we may not find it, which would imply that there was some other mechanism at work after the Big Bang. "We would have to rethink everything. In a way that would be even more exciting than finding the Higgs boson."[138] "In the end," said Bhadra, "we are asking what happened after the Big Bang, and what explains how it happened."[139]

Bhadra went out of her way to mention the cooperation she had received from Adrian Shubert at York International, helping to support her outreach program in South Africa. Financed by the Office of the Vice-President (Academic), it was "very successful." Shubert, who has the title associate vice-president international, explained that his office deals with a range of projects and ventures abroad. They include financial assistance to students going abroad and to international degree students – there were around 3,000 of them in 2007–08 – studying at York; the international internship program; the internationalization of the curriculum; and partnerships with universities in other countries. Shubert, who joined the Faculty of Arts History Department in 1985 and has been in charge of York International since 2002, said that these partnerships include student exchanges, faculty exchanges, and research collaboration. This is an expanding field: "When I started, York had no partnerships in India, for example, except possibly through Schulich and Osgoode. Now we have a number of good partnerships." York had put together a provincial exchange program with universities in Maharashtra and Goa in India,[140] formally announced when Ontario Premier Dalton McGuinty visited India and Pakistan in January 2007. "We have been very vocal advocates for internationalization, in the province and nationally," Shubert stated: "Across the country York is now recognized as a leader."[141]

More recently Shubert reported that his journeys have proved to him that York is known abroad for the quality of its research, citing two significant rankings of the last five years. Noting that all rankings are controversial, he added that the *Times Higher Education* (*THE*) and Shanghai Jiao Tong rankings "at least … attempt to measure actual research done and its impact, not just the proxy of grant dollars."[142] Even though the latter ranking is heavily weighted towards science, medicine, and engineering, York appeared among the top 500 universities in the world. The latest version of the *THE* ranking, which came out in November 2007, put York in forty-first place in the social sciences in the world.

Shubert expressed enthusiasm about the work done in his office. Enthusiasm, too, characterized the attitude of the researchers interviewed for this book. They are strongly committed to research, their "passion," as Böhme put it, and they believe strongly in its value to the society and world in which they live. Their work has been crowned with prizes and has gained international recognition. And this chapter has done no more than scratch the surface of all the research being done at York.

Why, then, is York's research in the sciences not better known? Gillian Wu, a medical biophysicist who left the University of Toronto in 2002 to become York's dean of science, said she had never been to the Keele campus before her interview and was shocked to discover how big York was and how big the science faculty was: "When I got here I was surprised I hadn't heard more of York. Ron Pearlman was the only one I knew."[143] She necessarily started looking for answers to the question she had asked herself. One answer offered was that York researchers did

not seek attention to the degree they might have: "They don't blow their horns enough." Another was that, although science at York had always had pockets of strength, the faculty as a whole was relatively small, especially compared with the University of Toronto. For years, too, the admission standards in science were lower than those at Toronto. The image of York as a fractious, strike-ridden institution dominated by left-wing social scientists did nothing to enhance its reputation at the University of Toronto, where dominant sections of the professoriate have resisted unionization to this day. Finally, there was the shadow cast by the University of Toronto, with its large science departments, which made it hard for York scientists to gain attention.

The existence of an older, larger, better-funded university downtown has shaped York throughout its first half-century. York owed its first campus to the University of Toronto and operated under its benevolent if somewhat inattentive protection until 1965. This emphasized from the outset which was the senior and which the junior institution. To say that the two universities are fated to remain in that relationship indefinitely would attach too much weight to the fact of primogeniture. But attitudes at York as well as at the University of Toronto have helped to maintain the rank order of the 1960s.

Having been educated at the University of Alberta and Oxford, and having taught at Laurentian University for twenty-five years before joining York in 1992, Wesley Cragg has a certain detachment from Toronto and its universities, giving him a clearer view than long-time inhabitants of the city. He theorized recently that many York faculty members seem to have had a "colonial mentality" where the University of Toronto was concerned, ready to assume that things are done better near the intersection of St George and Harbord/Hoskin than near Keele and Steeles.[144]

However, as we approach the year 2010 and the fiftieth anniversary of that September day when York's first students entered Falconer Hall on the St George campus for the first time, the image of York's subordinate status and the reality that underlay it are receding. The professors and administrators who were engaged in the 1960s have very largely left the scene. Those who joined York in the 1970s are retiring or due soon to retire, though with the end of compulsory retirement in Ontario some will undoubtedly stay on. The arrival of scores upon scores of young academics who do not remember York's early days and who do not share the old attitudes and preconceptions is changing the university and its collective self-image. The newcomers have credentials that were unnecessary before 1972, when there was a shortage of fully qualified applicants. Hardly anybody gets appointed nowadays without a completed doctorate in hand and a record of publications. As a result, younger faculty seem to have a feeling of self-confidence that was often lacking among the ABDs ("all but dissertation") of the 1960s. This should help to eliminate whatever vestiges of a colonial mentality still linger.

More important, the accomplishments of York's scholars and researchers, and perhaps particularly those in science, engineering, and health, seem bound to enhance the university's reputation. Wu said she believed that York's scientists were emerging from the University of Toronto's shadow. The humanists and social scientists had already emerged from it. York's professional schools, Osgoode, Schulich, Fine Arts, Environmental Studies, and Education, found their place in the sun years ago.

York at fifty is a far cry from the small liberal arts college that took form on the Glendon campus in the early 1960s. It is now a multiversity confronted with all the challenges that can face a large institution located in a multi-ethnic metropolis. Peace and perfection are a long way off. Still, York shows signs of settling more or less comfortably into the role of a major university.

One piece of evidence of this is York's changed labour relations climate since 2001. Two disruptive strikes, one in 1997 and the other in 2000, reinforced an earlier image, dating back to the 1970s, of an institution wracked by division and discord. After a decade of labour peace, YUFA went on strike in early 1997. The key issue was the administration's decision to remove article 14 (which had governed flexible retirement since 1987) from the collective agreement after the union refused to renegotiate it. Administration negotiators argued that the article was costing more than anyone had predicted when it was first negotiated and that the university could no longer afford it; YUFA rejected this assessment. But this was not the only source of conflict. Brian Abner, who was YUFA chair from 1989 to 1993, became associate vice-president (academic resource planning) in 1995. His portfolio included labour relations, and in his view the quarrel over article 14 "crystallized four or five years of anger" over issues such as growing class sizes and computing systems.[145] The sociologist Janice Newson, who had been active in YUFA for years, stated that the strike was rooted in "frustration with the administration and its failure to bargain sensibly." Article 14 was "the flashpoint."[146] Both Abner and Newson agreed that there was a lack of trust between the two sides, and that YUFA's negotiators simply did not believe the information supplied by the administration about the university budget or the costs of flexible retirement.

The strike lasted fifty-five days, from 20 March through a chilly April into early May. By then the union had abandoned any hope of saving article 14 and had shifted its focus to pay equity for women faculty. Acrimonious and divisive, the strike was not easily forgotten, as a YUFA Internet publication in 2007 made clear.[147] It also created major problems for students and damaged York's reputation.

This was true also of the seventy-six-day strike by Canadian Union of Public Employees (CUPE) (formerly CUEW) 3903 that began in late October 2000 and did not end until early January 2001. Several part-time faculty members said that the flashpoint was the administration's attempt to "claw back" something granted in an earlier contract, the indexation of the remuneration of teaching and research assistants to match increases in tuition fees. This issue was of huge interest to TAs and to the RAs who had recently gained the right to be represented by CUPE. It was much less important to part-time faculty members like himself, Geoffrey Ewen recalled, but the two units composed of graduate students dominated the union numerically.[148] "Quite a few Unit 2 people crossed the picket line," he said, but the graduate students held firm, and ultimately the

LEFT   Vice-chair of the Board of Governors into 2008, Tim Price is also co-chair of the York to the Power of 50 campaign.

RIGHT   Avie Bennett, seen in conversation with Lorna R. Marsden, was chancellor from 1998 to 2004.

administration negotiators gave up the fight in order to save the academic year for students.

To this day these remain the last strikes York has experienced. Lorna Marsden stated that labour peace owes a lot to Gary Brewer, who became vice-president (finance) in 2002 and took charge of labour relations, and his team.[149] An observer from the other side of York's labour relations, Brenda Hart in the YUFA office, agreed that Brewer and his assistants, Executive Director of Employee Relations Barry Miller and Assistant Vice-President (Human Resources and Employee Relations) Norman Ahmet, are committed to reaching settlements without a strike. However, in her view, the altered labour relations, so far as YUFA is concerned, have at least as much to do with the changing professoriate: "I don't think there will be a faculty strike again because the faculty have no stomach for it. New faculty members tend to be more research- and career-oriented ... We're not even close to being a militant university any more."[150]

This may be the counterpart to something that Kenneth Davey, former dean of science and academic vice-president, alluded to a few years ago. After he came to York in 1974, he said, he became impressed by "the strong commitment within the university generally to simple social justice."[151] Thirty years later, he wondered whether this was slipping, both among the faculty and within the student body. He identified the emphasis on excellence and increases in tuition fees as influences producing a less socially conscious environment. Social concerns are still in evidence, as in the Centre for Research on Work and Society and the Centre for Refugee Studies, but they are less obvious than they were in the early years of York.

If the mood of many full-time faculty members is understandably quiescent, this may be less true of some contract faculty, even though, as Ewen observed, part-time faculty at York are probably the best-paid in Canada, and "the benefits are wonderful."[152] But at $14,000 per course, some may feel undervalued. As for YUSA, it last went on strike in 1987, and nobody is predicting that it will strike again any time soon. York's labour peace has certainly been agreeable, and it has benefited the institution's image.

Another piece of evidence that York may be settling into an institutional "comfort zone" is the success of the York to the Power of 50 campaign, co-chaired by Bill Hatanaka and Tim Price. Publicly launched in October 2006, the campaign is the largest and most ambitious fund-raising campaign in York's history, with a target of $200 million. By April 2008, York University Foundation president Paul Marcus reported, more than three-quarters of this had been raised.[153] Some of the gifts are princely. Seymour Schulich has continued his habit of being generous to the business school. Avie Bennett, who was chancellor from 1998 to 2004 and is now chancellor emeritus, has funded more than thirty generous undergraduate and graduate awards and scholarships. The late Milton Harris together with his wife Ethel Harris have given $5 million in support of a research initiative headed by Stuart Shanker, Distinguished Research Professor of Psychology and Philosophy, allowing him and his colleagues to test and refine the intervention techniques they have developed to help children's brain development, including children with autism. Honey and Barry Sherman have given $5 million to create a state-of-the-art research facility and provide an expanded home for the Centre for Vision Research, Ignat Kaneff has donated $2.5 million to the Osgoode Hall Law School building campaign, and the Elia Foundation has made a donation of close to $2 million to fund graduate scholarships and increase support for the Mariano A. Elia Chair in Italian-Canadian Studies, first established in 1983. At the same time, more than 11,000 alumni, honorary graduates, and students have pledged nearly $55 million to the York to the Power of 50 campaign, either personally, through their companies, or through private foundations.[154] York is attracting philanthropic support on an unprecedented scale.

York has reached a size and scope that would have astonished Wilfred Curtis, Arthur Margison, Roby Kidd, and the others who, more than fifty years ago, were hoping to found a new university. Starting with seventy-six students and fifteen faculty members, within four decades York had become the third-largest university in Canada. York has grown, sometimes according to plan, sometimes haphazardly, sometimes in response to external forces, but almost always in the spirit of "*Tentanda Via, the way must be tried.*"

Chancellor Peter deC. Cory (2004–08) addresses the 2007 Fall Convocation.

Irving Abella
Brian Abner
Nancy Accinelli
Howard Adelman
Neil Agnew
James Alcock
Robert Allan
Mortimer Appley
Cynthia Archer
Jan Armstrong
Harry Arthurs *
W.R. (Bob) Augustine
Paul Axelrod *

Bob Bain
Jane Banfield
John Bankes
Alain Baudot *
John Beare
John Becker
Sterling Beckwith
David Bell
Walter Beringer
Sampa Bhadra *
Ellen Bialystok *
Ronald Bloore
Diethard Böhme *
Allan Bonner
Hon. Marion Boyd
Elizabeth Bradley
Gail Cuthbert Brandt
Gary Brewer
Gwyneth Buck
Guy Burry

Joanie Cameron Pritchett
Paul Cantor
James Carley
Carole Carpenter
Kenneth Carpenter
Gerald Carrothers

Nick Cercone
Rt. Hon. Adrienne Clarkson
David Clipsham
Colin Coates
Hon. David Cole
Hon. David Collenette
Ramsay Cook
David Coombs
Wesley Coons *
Frank Cosentino
Jacques Cotnam *
Jane Couchman
John Court *
Wesley Cragg
Douglas Crawford
Michael Creal

Kurt Danziger
Gordon Darroch
Kenneth Davey
William Dimma
Brian Dixon
Tony Doyle
Daniel Drache
Steve Dranitsaris *
Vicky Draper
Julianna Drexler *
Robert Drummond
Bruce Dugelby *

Sydney Eisen
Frederick Elkin
Sheila Embleton
Norman Endler *
Geoffrey Ewen

William Farr
Margarita Feliciano
Edward Fenner
Arthur Forer
Sheila Forshaw

Robert Fothergill
William Found
Martin Friedland

Robert Gagne
Brenda Gainer
Chris Gates
Ian Gentles
Irving Gerstein *
Joan Gibson
James Gillies *
Alison Girling
Barbara Godard *
Frederick Gorbet
Sandra (Noble) Goss
Naguib Gouda
Jack L. Granatstein
Fred Granek *
Joseph Green
Ian Greene *
Esther Greenglass
Michael Gregory

Arthur Haberman
Judith Hardy
Brenda Hart
Bill Hatanaka
Kent Haworth
John Heddle
Frances Henry
Michael Herren
Rives (Dalley) Hewitt
Fred Ho *
Ellen Hoffmann *
Adrienne Hood
Elizabeth Hopkins
Deszö Horváth
Susan Houston
Ian Howard
Raymond Hudson
Virginia Hunter *

Adèle Hurley
Allan Hutchinson

Christopher Innes
William D. Irvine

Hon. Henry Jackman *
Vivienne James
Gerald Jordan
Lucille (Fowle) Joseph *

Ron Kanter
James Keachie *
Thomas Klassen *
Suzanne Klein
Margaret Knittl
Ildikó Kovács

Hon. Marion Lane
Michael Lanphier
Philip Lapp *
James (Jamie) Laws *
Louis Lefeber *
John D. Leitch
John Lennox
Rhonda Lenton
Marshall Leslie
Charles Levi
Sheldon Levy
Harriet Lewis
Lesley Lewis
Catherine Limbertie
Rex Lingwood
Douglas Lochhead
Paul Lovejoy
Liz Lundell
Mary Lyons

H. Ian Macdonald
Robert MacIntosh
Ann Wilbur MacKenzie
Ann Mandel
Susan Mann
Paul Marcus *
Arthur Margison *
Lorna Marsden
Nick Martin
Bryan Massam
John McCamus
Thelma McCormack *
Edward McDonough
John McFarland
Heather (McClary) McGoey

John McNee
Barbara McNutt *
Kathryn McPherson
David McQueen
Kenneth McRoberts
Eileen Mercier *
Hon. Ruth Mesbur
Moshe Milevsky
David Mirvish
Wendy Mitchinson
Patrick Monahan
Ann Montgomery
Dorathy Moore
Merv Mosher
Mary Jane Mossman
Alex Murray
Patricia Murray
Robert Myers

John Nagel
Earle Nestmann
Janice Newson
Doris Nicholls
Ralph Nicholls *
Wallace Northover

Myriam Obadia-Hazan
Sheree-Lee Olson
Theodore Olson
John O'Neill
Hamid Osman
Robert Overing

Julie Pärna
Donna Paterson
Jacques Pauwels
Ronald Pearlman
Douglas Peers
Willard Piepenburg
Marilyn Pilkington
Tim Price
Huw Pritchard
Bill Purcell
Sandra Pyke

Barbara Rahder
Pinayur Rajagopal
Malcolm Ransom
Timothy Reid
Marie Rickard
Donald Rickerd
Tim Rider *
Sandie Rinaldo *

Hollis Rinehart
Jackie Robinson
Virginia Rock *
Marc Rosen
Don Ross
Peter Ross
Don Rubin *
Lionel Rubinoff *
Clayton Ruby
Rasma Rugelis
George Rust-D'Eye *
Hon. Douglas Rutherford *

Rick Salutin
Allan Sangster
James Savary
John T. Saywell
Rosemarie Schade
Daphne Schiff
Harold Schiff
Richard Schultz
Rodger Schwass
John Seeley
Stanley Shapson
Gordon Shepherd *
Mamdouh Shoukri
Ann (Rusty) Shteir
Adrian Shubert
Phillip Silver
Harvey Simmons
Helen Sinclair *
K.W. Michael Siu
Harvey Skinner
Enid Slack
William Small
David M. Smith
Denis Smith
Marilyn Smith
Peter L. Smith
D. McCormack Smyth *
Daniel Soberman
Edward Spence *
Susan Spence
John Spencer *
Paul Stevens
Cathie Stone
Richard Storr
Murray Stroud
Johanna Stuckey
Bridget Stutchbury *
Noli Swatman

Dale Taylor

Wendy Taylor
Gill Teiman
Walter Tholen *
Clara Thomas *
Robert Tiffin
David Trick
Albert Tucker *
Stanley Tweyman

Marina Vandermerwe *
Penny Van Esterik

Douglas Verney

Robert Wallace *
Robert Waller *
John Warkentin
Mary Jane Warner
William Whitla *
Shelagh Wilkinson *
Penny Williams *
Carol Wilson
Paula Wilson

Eric Winter
Bernard Wolf
Berton Woodward *
Gillian Wu

Norman Yan

Frederick Zemans
Joyce Zemans
Cynthia Zimmerman
Sylvia Zingrone

* also supplied documents or photos

Chancellor

Wilfred A. Curtis	1961–68
Floyd S. Chalmers	1968–73
Hon. Walter L. Gordon	1973–77
Hon. John P. Robarts	1977–82
John S. Proctor	1982–83
J. Tuzo Wilson	1983–86
Larry D. Clarke	1987–91
Oscar E. Peterson	1991–94
Arden R. Haynes	1994–98
Avie J. Bennett	1998–2004
Hon. Peter deC. Cory	2004–08
Hon. R. Roy McMurtry	2008–

President and Vice–Chancellor

Murray G. Ross	1959–70
David W. Slater	1970–73
Richard J. Storr (acting)	1973
John W. Yolton (acting)	1973–74
H. Ian Macdonald	1974–84
William C. Found (acting)	1984
Harry W. Arthurs	1985–92
Susan Mann	1992–97
Lorna R. Marsden	1997–2007
Mamdouh Shoukri	2007–

Chairman/Chair, Board of Governors

Hon. Robert H. Winters	1959–65
William Pearson (Pete) Scott	1966–71
Robert M. MacIntosh	1971–75
James L. Lewtas	1975
Bertrand Gerstein	1975–79
John S. Proctor	1979–82
R. Bruce Bryden	1982–92
William A. Dimma	1992–97
Charles H. Hantho	1997–2000
Marshall A. (Mickey) Cohen	2000–

Chairman/Chair, Senate

Murray G. Ross	1960–70
David W. Slater	1970–71

John W. Yolton	1971–72
Howard S. Robertson	1972–73
J. David Hoffman	1973–74
John D. McFarland	1974–75
John H. Warkentin	1975–76
Gwenda Echard	1976–77
C. Michael Lanphier	1977–78
Graeme H. McKechnie	1978–79
David M. Logan	1979–81
Howard Adelman	1981–82
T. Harry Leith	1982–83
Jane Couchman	1983–84
Victor V. Murray	1984–85
George E. (Gene) Denzel	1985–86
K.H. Michael Creal	1986–87
H. Michael Stevenson	1987–88
Allan D. Stauffer	1988–89
Naomi Black	1989–90
John B. Crozier	1990–91
Louise M. Ripley	1991–92
Stuart G. Robbins	1992–93
A. Saber M. (Sal) Saleuddin	1993–94
Ruth A. Grogan	1994–95
Paul F. Wilkinson	1995–96
George Tourlakis	1996–97
Helen M. Doan	1997–98
Maurice S. Elliott	1998–99
Allan C. Hutchinson	1999–2000
Robert J. Drummond	2000–01
Joan Wick-Pelletier	2001–02
Bonnie Kettel	2002–03
C. Ian Greene	2003–04
Patricia Bradshaw	2004–05
Ross A. Rudolph	2006–07
Brenda Spotton Visano	2007–08
Celia Haig-Brown (elect)	2009–

Secretary, Board of Governors

P.R. Woodfield	1959
William W. Small	1959–66
James L. Flynn	1966–69

Secretary, Senate

William W. Small	1960
Denis Smith	1961
Donald S. Rickerd	1961–68
William D. Farr	1968–69

Secretary, University

William D. Farr	1969–73
Malcolm W. Ransom	1973–98
Harriet I. Lewis	1998–

Vice-President (Academic)

Edward L. Pattullo	1964–65
James M. Gillies	1966–68
Dennis M. Healy	1968–70
Walter S. Tarnopolsky	1972
William C. Found	1979–85
Kenneth G. Davey	1986–91
Stephen Fienberg	1991–93
H. Michael Stevenson	1993–2000
Sheila Embleton	2000–

Vice-President (Administrative – various)

William W. Small	1965–83
H. Bruce Parkes	1965–73
Arthur C. Johnson	1969–73
William D. Farr	1973–94
George G. Bell	1976–85
Ian H. Lithgow	1985–97
Sheldon Levy	1988–97
Elizabeth D. Hopkins	1990–96
Deborah Hobson	1997–2002
Phyllis Clark	1997–2002
Gary J. Smith	1998–2002
Stanley Shapson	2000–
Gary Brewer	2002–
Bonnie Neuman	2002–05
Robert J. Tiffin	2005–

Dean, Faculty/Arts and Science/Arts

George Tatham	1961–62
Rollo Earl	1962–64
John T. Saywell	1964–73
Sydney Eisen	1973–78
Harold Kaplan	1978–83
Thomas D. Traves	1983–91
Ross A. Rudolph (acting)	1988
H. Michael Stevenson	1991–93
Robert J. Drummond (acting)	1993–94
George B. Fallis	1994–2001
Robert J. Drummond	2001–

Dean, Joseph E. Atkinson College/Atkinson Faculty of Liberal and Professional Studies

Douglas V. Verney (acting)	1961–62
Neil M. Morrison	1962–63
D. McCormack Smyth	1963–69
Harry S. Crowe	1969–74
Margaret M. Knittl	1974–79
Harry S. Crowe	1979–81
Ronald Bordessa	1981–87
Stephen Griew	1987–90
Thomas A. Meininger (acting)	1990–92
Harold A. (Skip) Bassford	1992–97
Livy A. Visano	1997–98
Ronald Bordessa	1999–2001
Joanne Magee (acting)	2001–02
Rhonda Lenton	2002–

Dean, Graduate Studies

Edgar W. McInnis	1963–65
Mortimer H. Appley	1965–67
John W. Yolton (acting)	1967–68
Frederick Elkin (acting)	1968–69
Michael Collie	1969–73
Richard J. Storr (acting)	1971–72
Graham F. Reed	1973–81
Barry Argyle (acting)	1975
David V.J. Bell	1981–87
Sandra Pyke	1987–92
David R. Leyton-Brown	1992–99
John W. Lennox	1999–2005
Ronald E. Pearlman (interim)	2005–07
Douglas Peers	2007–

Principal, Glendon College

Escott Reid	1965–69
Albert V. Tucker	1970–75
David L. McQueen	1975–80
Philippe Garigue	1980–87
Elizabeth D. Hopkins (acting)	1987–88
Roseann Runte	1988–94
Jean-Claude Jaubert (acting)	1994
Dyane Adam	1994–99
Kenneth H. McRoberts	1999–
Françoise Boudreau (acting)	2004

Dean, Administrative Studies/ Schulich School of Business

James M. Gillies	1965–72
Barry Richman	1972
Brian Dixon (acting)	1973–74
William A. Dimma	1974–75

Wallace B. Crowston	1975–84
Alan B. Hockin	1984–88
Deszö J. Horváth	1988–

Dean, Science/Pure and Applied Science/ Science and Engineering

Harold I. Schiff	1966–72
O. Robert Lundell	1972–82
Kenneth G. Davey	1982–86
O. Robert Lundell (acting)	1986
Kimmo A. Innanen	1986–94
Robert H. Prince	1994–2001
Gillian E. Wu	2001–06
Nicholas Cercone	2006–

Dean, Osgoode Hall Law School

Gerald E. LeDain	1968–72
Harry W. Arthurs	1972–77
Stanley M. Beck	1977–82
John D. McCamus	1982–87
John M. Evans (acting)	1987
James C. MacPherson	1988–93
Marilyn L. Pilkington	1993–98
Peter W. Hogg	1998–2003
Patrick J. Monahan	2003–

Dean, Environmental Studies

Gerald A.P. Carrothers	1968–76
Rodger D. Schwass	1976–82
Edward S. Spence	1982–92
David V.J. Bell	1992–96
Peter A. Victor	1996–2001
David Morley	2001–04
Joni Seager	2004–07
Barbara Rahder	2007–

Dean, Fine Arts

Jules Heller	1968–73
Joseph G. Green	1973–80
Lionel H. Lawrence	1980–84
Donald A. Newgren (acting)	1985
Joyce Zemans	1985–88
Alan Lessem (acting)	1988–89
Joy Cohnstaedt	1989–93
Seth Feldman	1993–98
Phillip Silver	1998–2008
Barbara Sellers–Young	2008–

Principal, Lakeshore Teachers College

William C. McClure	1971–75

Dean, Education

Robert L.R. Overing	1972–80
Joan E. Bowers (acting)	1980
Andrew E. Effrat	1980–90
Stanley Shapson	1990–98
Jill S. Bell (acting)	1998–99
Terry Piper	1999–2001
Donald Dippo (acting)	2001
Paul Axelrod	2001–08
Alice Pitt	2008–

Dean, Research

Bryan H. Massam	1980–86

Dean, Health

Harvey Skinner	2006–

Librarian/Director of Library Services/ Director of Libraries/University Librarian

Douglas G. Lochhead	1960–63
Thomas F. O'Connell	1963–76
William Newman (acting)	1976–78
Anne Woodsworth	1978–83
Ellen J. Hoffmann	1983–2001
Cynthia Archer	2001–

President, York University Development Corporation

Philip A. Lapp	1986–89
Gregory Spearn	1989–90
Bret Biggs	1991–93
Ronald Hunt	1993–2002
Norman W. (Bud) Purves	2002–

President, York University Foundation

Paul Marcus	2002–

Distinguished Research Professor
(limit of twenty at any time)

Norbert Bartel	2005
Ellen Bialystok	2002
Diethard K. Böhme	1994
Deborah P. Britzman	2005
James P. Carley	1999
Stephen R. Gill	2005
Eric A. Hessels	2006
Allan C. Hutchinson	2006
Christopher D. Innes	1996
Paul E. Lovejoy	1996
John C. McConnell	2004
C. Kent McNeil	2007
Gareth Morgan	1991
Leo Panitch	1998
Debra Pepler	2007

Stuart G. Shanker	2004	James M. Gillies
K.W. Michael Siu	2007	Joseph G. Green
Brian J. Slattery	2008	Arthur Haberman
Martin J. Steinbach	1999	Peter W. Hogg
John K. Tsotsos	2008	Bryan H. Massam

Distinguished Research Professor Emeritus

John F. Bosher

Jean-Gabriel Castel

Jerome Ch'en

Lorraine Code

Kenneth G. Davey

Jack L. Granatstein

Philip H. Gulliver

Michael Herren

Ian P. Howard

Ian C. Jarvie

Michael H. Kater

Gabriel Kolko

A. Barry P. Lever

Clifford C. Leznoff

H. Vivian Nelles

John O'Neill

Hiroshi Ono

Huw O. Pritchard

David M. Regan

Gordon G. Shepherd

Reginald Whitaker

David L. McQueen

Willard W. Piepenburg

Robert H. Prince

Sandra Pyke

Stuart G. Robbins

A. Saber M. (Sal) Saleuddin

John T. Saywell

Ronald L. Sheese

Johanna H. Stuckey

Albert V. Tucker

Shelagh Wilkinson

Joyce Zemans

University Professor

(limit of twenty at any time)

Eshrat Arjomandi	2006
George B. Fallis	2008
Seth Feldman	2001
John H. Lennox	2008
Varpu Lindström	2006
John D. McCamus	2005
Mary Jane Mossman	2007
Ronald D. Owston	2007
Ronald E. Pearlman	2004
Ross A. Rudolph	2007
Leslie C. Sanders	2003
George Tourlakis	2007

University Professor Emeritus

Harry W. Arthurs

Hédi A. Bouraoui

Gerald A.P. Carrothers

Sydney Eisen

Maurice S. Elliott

Frederick J. Fletcher

William C. Found

Canada Research Chair	**Tier**
Samuel Benchimol	1
Nantel Bergeron	2
Diethard K. Böhme	1
Colin M. Coates	2
Rosemary J. Coombe	1
J. Douglas Crawford	1
Caitlin Fisher	2
Gordon L. Flett	1
Joshua Fogel	1
Eric A. Hessels	1
David A. Hood	1
Christopher D. Innes	1
Joel Katz	1
Sergey N. Krylov	2
Paul E. Lovejoy	1
Janine Marchessault	2
Stephen N. Mason	1
Sylvie Morin	2
Catriona Mortimer-Sandilands	2
Leo Panitch	1
Bridget J.M. Stutchbury	2
Wendy Taylor	2
John Tsotsos	1
Leah Vosko	2
K. Andrew White	2
James A. Whiteway	2
Jianhong Wu	1
Peer Zumbansen	2

Fellow of the Royal Society of Canada

Irving M. Abella	1993
Joseph Agassi	1993
Harry W. Arthurs	1982
Alain Baudot	1993

Ellen Bialystok	2003	Brian J. Slattery	1995
Ronald Bloore	2007	Clara Thomas	1983
Diethard K. Böhme	1994	John H. Warkentin	1982
John F. Bosher	1976	Sharon A. Williams	1993
Hédi Bouraoui	1997	Ellen Meiksins Wood	1996
James P. Carley	2002		
Allan I. Carswell	1984		
Jean-Gabriel Castel	1979		

President/Chairperson, York University Student Council/Student Representative Council/ York Student Federation/York Federation of Students

Jerome Ch'en	1981	Douglas Rutherford	1960–62
Lorraine Code	2005	Gary Caldwell	1962–63
Michael Collie	1987	Anthony D. Martin	1963–64
G. Ramsay Cook	1969	Victor Hori	1964–65
Robert W. Cox	1992	Alan Young (Glendon)	1965–66
Kurt Danziger	1989	Malcolm Jackson (Keele)	1965–66
Kenneth G. Davey	1977	Gary J. Smith	1966
Arthur Forer	1984	Keith Kennedy	1966–67
Vera Frenkel	2006	Kenneth Johnson	1967–68
James R. Gibson	1989	John Adams	1968–69
Stephen R. Gill	2003	Paul Koster	1969–70
Jack L. Granatstein	1982	Paul Axelrod	1970–71
Philip H. Gulliver	1982	Michael Fletcher	1971–72
I. Brent Heath	1996	John Theobald	1972–73
Frances Henry	1989	Michael Mouritsen	1973–74
Michael Herren	1999	Anne Scotton	1974–75
Eric A. Hessels	2005	Dale Ritch	1975–76
Peter W. Hogg	1988	Barry Edson	1976–77
Michiel Horn	2002	Paul Hayden	1977–78
Allan C. Hutchinson	2004	David Chodikoff	1978–79
Christopher D. Innes	1992	Keith Smockum	1979–80
Ian C. Jarvie	1987	Malcolm Montgomery	1980–81
Evelyn Kallen	1989	Greg Gaudet	1981–82
Michael H. Kater	1988	Maurizio Bevilacqua	1982–83
Stanislav J. Kirschbaum	2002	Chris Summerhayes	1983–85
Gabriel Kolko	1986	Reya Ali	1985–86
Philip A. Lapp	1982	Gerard Blink	1986–87
Lee Lorch	1968	Drew McCreadie	1987–88
Paul E. Lovejoy	1989	Tammy Hasselfeldt	1988–89
Neal Madras	2002	Peter Donato	1989–90
Susan Mann	1985	Jian Ghomeshi	1990–91
Bryan H. Massam	1995	Michelle Hughes	1991–92
John D. McCamus	2006	Nikki Gershbain	1992–93
John C. McConnell	2001	Jeff Zoeller	1993–94
H. Vivian Nelles	1985	André Bastian	1994–96
Michael Ondaatje	2005	Wayne Poirier	1996–97
John O'Neill	1985	Jayson Chizick (interim)	1997
Fernand Ouellet	1967	Dawn Palin	1997–99
Leo Panitch	1994	Horace Dockery	1999–2000
Huw O. Pritchard	1979	Hasrat Gafoor	2000–01
David M. Regan	1989	J. Wallace (interim)	2001
Anthony H. Richmond	1980	Desmond Cherrington	2001–02
R.L. Liora Salter	1992	Angie Joshi	2002–03
John S. Saul	2004	Michael Novak (interim)	2003
Gordon G. Shepherd	1981		

Paul Cooper	2003–04
Omari Mason	2004–06
Corrie Sakaluk	2006–07
Hamid Osman	2007–09

Chairman/Chairperson/Chair, York University Faculty Association

Hugh N. Maclean	1961–62
C. David Fowle	1962–63
Dennis C. Russell	1963–64
Alex L. Murray	1964–65
T. Harry Leith	1965–66
Albert J. Robinson	1966–67
Lewis Hertzman	1967–68
Frederick F. Schindeler	1968–69
Wesley H. Coons	1969–70
George E. Eaton	1970–71
Magnus Gunther	1971–72
Michiel Horn	1972–73
Dennis C. Russell	1973–74
Harvey Simmons	1974–75
Jack L. Granatstein	1975–77
David J. Clipsham and	1977
Virginia J. Hunter (joint)	
William E. Echard	1977–78
Michael D.G. Copeland	1978–79
Allan D. Stauffer	1979–80
Howard I. Buchbinder	1980–82
Janice A. Newson	1982–84
Robert J. Drummond	1984–85
Hollis Rinehart	1985–87
Michael D.G. Copeland	1987–89
Brian D. Abner	1989–93
Paul Laurendeau	1993–94
Patricia McDermott	1994–96
David J. Clipsham	1996–99
Penni Stewart	1999–2001
Susan Dimock	2001–03
Arthur Hilliker	2003–

President/Chair, York University Alumni Association

R. Bruce Bryden	1964–66
Peter Wallis	1966–68
Colin Campbell	1968–69
James Avery	1969–70
Douglas Neal	1970–72
Gregory Cooper	1972–73
John Stiff	1973–74
Israel Y. Aharoni	1974–75
E. Naomi Wagschal	1975–76
Alan Sheffman	1976–77
Drago Samsa	1977–79

Garth D. Wood	1979–81
David B. Johnson	1981–85
Michael Shook	1985–87
Joan Wood	1987–91
Don Berkowitz	1991–94
Andrew Sherwin	1994–96
Dale Lastman	1996–2005
Guy Burry	2005–

President, York University Staff Association

YUSA was founded as a voluntary association in 1970 and became a certified union late in 1975. The names and dates of the pre-1976 presidents cannot be fully verified.

Gabrielle Paddle	1976–77
Laura Avens	1977–80
Karen Herrell	1980–83
Roderick Bennett	1983–85
Shirley Ittas	1985–86
Celia Harte	1986–91
Jane Grant	1991–93
James Streb	1993–98
Albert Scragg	1998–99
James Streb	1999–2001
Joanie Cameron Pritchett	2001–

Convener/Director/President, Confidential, Professional and Managerial Employees Association

The Professional and Managerial Employees Association was founded in 1978. Confidential employees joined in 1999, and the name of the association was changed accordingly. At first it was led by three conveners; in 1986 they became directors. Since a change in the constitution in 2004 CPMEA has had a president.

Issie Goldman	1978–79
Rolly Stroeter	1978–79
Michele Young	1978–79
Magda Davey	1979–81
Michael London	1979–80
Ron Lowe	1979–80
Fred Marsden	1980–81
Mal Reader	1980–82
Bob Binnie	1981–82
Ann Montgomery	1981–82
Lynn Cornett	1982–83
Bob Howard	1982–83
Noli Swatman	1982–84
Barbara Abercrombie	1983–84
Sheila Cann	1983–85

Fred Marsden	1984–85
Julius Suraski	1984–85
Noli Swatman	1985–86
Catherine McPhun-Beatty	1985–86
Colin Deschamps	1985–86
Bob Howard	1985–87
Ann Montgomery	1986–87
Barbara Tryfos	1986–87
Jacques Aubin-Roy	1987–88
Magda Davey	1987–89
Barbara Moffat	1987–88
Shirley MacDonald	1988–89
Joanne (Sibley) Carlberg	1988–90
Donald Wallace	1989–90
Jane Crescenzi	1989–90
Pat Zuest	1989–92
Jayne Greene-Black	1990–91
Clark Hortsing-Perna	1990–91
Gilles Fortin	1991–92
Dianne Bates	1991–93
Kieron Brunelle	1991–96
Robert Flood	1992
Pat Zuest	1993–94
Bob Goldman	1994–96
Jayne Greene-Black	1994–96
Gilles Fortin	1996–2001
Dale Hall	1996–2000
Clark Hortsing-Perna	1996–97
Marc Wilchesky	1997–99
Steve Dranitsaris	1999–2002
Debbie Ham	2000–01
Debbie Hansen	2001–03
Sean Squires	2001–04
Siobhan McEwan	2002–03
Margaret Miceli	2002–03
Lillian A. Nasello	2003–04
Rose Orlando	2003–04

President

Lillian A. Nasello	2004–05
Sharon McLeod	2005–06
Lillian A. Nasello	2006–

Chair, Canadian Union of Educational Workers/ Canadian Union of Public Employees 3903

Records are incomplete before 1982.

Charles Doyon	1982–85
Ross Arthur	1985
Gary Hackenbeck	1985
Larry Lyons	1985–88
Margaret Watson	1988–90
Larry Lyons	1990–91
Helen Fielding	1991
Douglas Allen	1991
Joseph Kispal-Kovacs	1991–92
Margaret Watson	1992–93
Scott Forsyth	1993–94
Richard Wellen	1994–97
Michel Roy	1997–98
Miriam Yaacov	1998
Fred Ho	1998–2000
Joseph Kispal-Kovacs	2000–01
Joseph Tohill	2001
Fernando Soto	2002
Amy Lavender Harris	2002
Jesse Payne	2002–03
Manzur Malik	2003–04
Ryan Toews	2004–05
Brian Fuller	2005
Rajiv Rawat	2005–06
Kristin Hole	2006–07
Darius Dadgari	2007–08
Juliane Edler	2008–09

York University is home to twenty-six Organized Research Units that are organized under a faculty if they relate solely to disciplines or departments associated with that faculty, or under the Office of the Vice-President (Research and Innovation) if they bring together researchers from across the university. Research centres and institutes provide collaborative support to researchers and are an important part of the research culture at York.

Centre	Director
Canadian Centre for German and European Studies	Klaus Rupprecht
Centre for Atmospheric Chemistry	Geoffrey W. Harris
Centre for Feminist Research	Linda Peake
Centre for Jewish Studies	Sara Horowitz
Centre for Practical Ethics	Susan Dimock
Centre for Public Policy and Public Law	Bruce B. Ryder
Centre for Refugee Studies	Susan L. McGrath
Centre for Research in Earth and Space Science	Gordon G. Shepherd
Centre for Research on Language Contact	Raymond Mougeon
Centre for Research on Latin America and the Caribbean	Eduardo Canel
Centre for Research in Mass Spectrometry	K.W. Michael Siu
Centre for Research on Work and Society	Norene J. Pupo
The City Institute at York University	Roger Keil
The Harriet Tubman Institute for Research on the Global Migration of African Peoples	Paul E. Lovejoy
Institute for Research and Innovation in Sustainability	Dawn Bazely
Institute for Research on Learning Technologies	Ronald D. Owston
Institute for Social Research	Michael D. Ornstein
The Jack and Mae Nathanson Centre on Transnational Human Rights, Crime and Security	Craig Scott
LaMarsh Centre for Research on Violence and Conflict Resolution	Jennifer Connolly
Muscle Health Research Centre	David Hood
Robarts Centre for Canadian Studies	Seth Feldman
York Centre for Asian Research	Susan Henders
York Centre for Education and Community	Carl James
York Centre for International and Security Studies	Robert Latham
York Centre for Vision Research	Hugh R. Wilson
York Institute for Health Research	Marcia H. Rioux

Most of the early Keele campus was built by the UPACE (University Planners, Architects, and Consulting Engineers) joint venture, which was approved in principle by the Board of Governors on 11 June 1962 and gained authorization to proceed with plans on 20 February 1963. UPACE consisted of John B. Parkin and Associates, Gordon S. Adamson and Associates, and Shore and Moffat Partners. The assignment of buildings, up to the Ross Building, to these companies is based on a confidential 1966 UPACE document. It is supported by handwritten comments on a document in the William Greer Fonds (F0185), Clara Thomas Archives, York University, which also assigns some buildings after the Ross Building.

Dates given are dates of occupation of building by York, in some cases spread over several years.

Glendon Campus

York Hall (1961, 1962, 1964) – Marani, Morris and Allan

Central Utilities Building (1962) – Marani, Morris and Allan

Leslie Frost Library (1963) – Allward and Gouinlock

E.R. Wood Residence (1963) – Mathers and Haldenby

John S. Proctor Field House (1964) – Allward and Gouinlock

Marion Hilliard Residence (1966) – Mathers and Haldenby

Keele Campus

Founders College and Residence (1965) – UPACE (Adamson for College, Parkin for Residence)

Steacie Science Library (1965) – UPACE (Adamson)

Burton Auditorium [Fine Arts Phase I] (1965) – UPACE (Adamson)

Farquharson Natural Science Building (1965) – UPACE (Shore and Moffat)

Central Utilities Building (1965, 1968) – H.G. Acres

Vanier College (1966) – UPACE (Parkin)

Behavioural Science Building (1966) – UPACE (Adamson)

Stedman Lecture Hall (1966) – UPACE/Gordon S. Adamson and Associates

Tait McKenzie Centre, Phase I (1966) – UPACE/Shore and Moffat Partners

Atkinson College Phase I (1966) – Allward and Gouinlock

Physical Plant Workshops (1966) – UPACE (Shore and Moffat)

Vanier College Residence (1967) – UPACE (Adamson)

Winters College and Residence (1967) – UPACE (Parkin)

East Office Building (1968) [Temporary Office Building] – Internorth Construction

Artificial Ice Arena (1968) – converted into the Sherman Health Science Research Centre (2009), NXL Architects

Petrie Science Building (1968–69) – UPACE (Shore and Moffat)

McLaughlin College and Residence (1968–69) – UPACE (Shore and Moffat for College/Parkin for Residence)

Ross Humanities and Social Sciences Building (1968–70) – UPACE (Adamson)

Central Square (1969) – UPACE (Parkin)

Osgoode Hall Law School (1969) – Marani, Rounthwaite and Dick

Graduate Student Residence #1 (1969) – Ontario Student Housing Corporation (OSHC)/Julian J. Trasiewicz

Curtis Lecture Halls (1970) – UPACE (Parkin)

Graduate Student Residence #2 (1970) – OSHC/ Julian J. Trasiewicz

Graduate Student Residence #3 (1970) – OSHC/ Julian J. Trasiewicz

Kinsmen Building (1970) – Clifford and Lawrie

* pre-existing structures not included

Stong College (1970–71) – UPACE (firm unknown)

W.P. Scott Central Library (1970–71) – UPACE
(Shore and Moffat Partners)

Stong Residence (1971) – OSHC/Julian J. Trasiewicz/
A.J. Chapkin and Associates

Atkinson College Phase II (1971) – Allward and
Gouinlock

Administrative Studies Building (1972) – Marani,
Rounthwaite and Dick

Bethune College (1972) – UPACE (firm unknown)

Bethune Residence (1972) – Julian J. Trasiewicz

Graduate Student Residence #4 (1972–73) – OSHC/
Julian J. Trasiewicz

Fine Arts Phase II (now Joan and Martin Goldfarb
Centre for Fine Arts) (1973) – Raymond
Moriyama

Atkinson Residence (1973) – Cadillac Development
Corporation

Scott Religious Centre (1974) – Page and Steele

Tennis Centre (1976–78) [this and the Track and
Field Complex were not built by York, but York
got use of them because they were built on land
leased to the agencies that built them]

Track and Field Complex (1978) – Moffat, Moffat
and Kinoshita, Architects [shared facility]

West Office Building (1984?) – Allen and Sheriff
Architects

Lumbers Academic Building (1984) – Kelton and
Lacka Architects

Fine Arts Phase III, Centre for Film and Theatre
(1988–89) – Kuwabara, Payne, McKenna and
Blumberg and Barton Myers

Calumet College Building (1990) – Martin
Liefhebber, Architect and Carrothers Shaw

Vari Hall (1990–91) – Moriyama and Teshima

Student Centre (1988–91) – A.J. Diamond, Donald
Schmitt and Company

Physical Resources (1989) – Ian W. Nicoll Architect

Computer Methods Building (1989?) – Richard D.
Young of Robbie/Young and Wright Architects
[not a York facility, but York uses space]

York Lanes Mall (1990–91) – Beinhaker/Irwin
Associates

Passy Gardens Graduate Residences (1991) –
Beinhaker/Irwin Associates

Chemistry/Computer Science Building (now the
Chemistry Building) (1991–93) – Robbie/Young
and Wright Architects with Daicon Contractors

York Student Field House (1994) – Alfred Szeto,
Szeto Architects

Canlan Ice Sports-York (1995–96) – Anthony
Jackson, Jackson Ryder Architects [shared
facility]

Seneca@York (1996–99) – Raymond Moriyama [not
a York facility]

York Stadium (1995) – Cansult Group

Lorna R. Marsden Honour Court and Welcome
Centre (2000) – Stephen Teeple and Associates

Computer Science and Engineering Building (2001)
– Van Nostrand and Di Castri Architects/Busby
and Associates

Technology Enhanced Learning Building (2003)
– Moriyama and Teshima [shared facility]

Seymour Schulich Building and Executive Learning
Centre (2003–04) – Hariri Pontarini Architects
with Robbie/Young and Wright

William Small Centre (2003) – Robbie/Young and
Wright/Rich and Associates

Student Services Centre and Parking Garage
(2003–04) – Hariri Pontarini Architects with
Robbie/Young and Wright

Rexall Centre (2004) – Robbie/Young and Wright
[not a York facility]

The Pond Road Residence (2004) –
architectsAlliance

Tait McKenzie Expansion (2005) – Bregman and
Hamann Architects

Accolade East and West (2005–06) – Zeidler
Partnership/Bregman and Hamann Architects

Ontario Archives and York Research Tower (2009)
– Bregman and Hamann Architects [shared
facility]

Notes

Preface

1 Peter Seixas, "What Is Historical Consciousness?" in Ruth W. Sandwell, ed., *To the Past: History Education, Public Memory, and Citizenship in Canada* (Toronto: University of Toronto Press 2006), 21.

Chapter 1

1 Only the University of Toronto and the Université de Montréal had more students in 2006–07.
2 http://www.yorkinfo.yorku.ca/factbook.asp ?Year=2006%20-%202007, 1, 267–8, 281.
3 Interview with James Keachie, Toronto, 18 Sept. 2003.
4 Blair Neatby and Don McEown, *Creating Carleton: The Shaping of a University* (Montreal and Kingston: McGill-Queen's University Press 2002), 3–5.
5 James Lemon, *Toronto since 1918: An Illustrated History* (Toronto: Lorimer 1985), 113.
6 Ibid., 194.
7 Keachie interview.
8 Paul Litt, *The Muses, the Masses, and the Massey Commission* (Toronto: University of Toronto Press 1992), 166.
9 E.F. Sheffield, "Canadian University and College Enrolment Projected to 1965," *National Conference of Canadian Universities, Proceedings 1955*, cited in Sheffield, "The Post-War Surge in Post-Secondary Education," in J. Donald Wilson, Robert M. Stamp, and Louis-Philippe Audet, eds., *Canadian Education: A History* (Scarborough, Ont.: Prentice-Hall 1970), 420.
10 Paul Axelrod, *Scholars and Dollars: Politics, Economics, and the Universities of Ontario, 1945–1980* (Toronto: University of Toronto Press 1982), 23.
11 Ibid., 63.
12 Keachie interview.
13 York University Libraries, Clara Thomas Archives and Special Collections (CTASC), F0074, 1987–021 (001), Organizing Committee, Minutes, 25 Nov. 1957.
14 Ibid.
15 Ibid.

16 John Court, "A White Rose by Any Other Name: Revealed at Last, the Wellspring of the Name, York University," *York University Gazette Online*, vol. 25, no. 27, 7 April 1999, http://www.yorku.ca/ycom/gazette/past/archive/040799/issue.htm.
17 Interview with Arthur D. Margison, Cobourg, Ont., 6 Oct. 2003.
18 Claude Bissell, "The University and the City," Empire Club of Canada, *Addresses 1957–58* (Toronto: Empire Club 1958), 323.
19 "Toronto Needs York U.C.," Toronto *Telegram*, 8 Aug. 1958.
20 "York University Must Go Ahead," Toronto *Star*, 23 May 1959.
21 Archives of Ontario (hereafter AO), RG 3–23, Office of the Premier (Frost), box 204, file 292-G, Board of Governors, University of Toronto, Eric Phillips to Nathan Phillips, 28 Aug. 1958; Eric Phillips to Leslie Frost, 28 Aug. 1958.
22 University of Toronto Archives (hereafter UTA), A88–0029/03, Office of the Vice-President, Business Affairs, Chairman's Correspondence, Claude Bissell to Eric Phillips, 7 Nov. 1958.
23 CTASC, F0074, 1987–021(001), Organizing Committee, Minutes, 8 Dec. 1958.
24 John Court, "Getting Our Act Together: A Look at the Genesis of York's Charter Legislation between 1955 and 1959," *York University Gazette Online*, vol. 29, no. 25, 24 March 1999, www.yorku.ca/ycom/gazette/past/archive/032499/current.htm.
25 AO, RG 2–217/4, Department of Education, University Subject Files, Committee on University Affairs, 1959–1960, Minutes, 23 Dec. 1958.
26 AO, RG 3–32–3, box 11, Office of the Premier, Outgoing Correspondence. Leslie M. Frost to W. Beverley Lewis [MPP York-Humber], 6 Feb. 1959.
27 *Ontario Statutes*, 5th Session, 25th Legislature, c. 145, An Act to Incorporate York University, 572.
28 Margison interview.
29 Ibid.
30 Library and Archives Canada (hereafter LAC), MG 31, J 39, A.D. Margison Papers, vol. 8, file 13, Facilities Planning Committee, Minutes, 6 Nov. 1958.

31 Ibid., James D. Service to A.D. Margison, 12 Aug. 1959.

32 Margison Papers, vol. 8, file 8, Minutes, provisional board of governors, 20 Aug. 1959.

33 Ibid., vol. 8, file 13, N.C. Goodhead to Leslie Frost, 29 Oct. 1959.

34 Ibid., Frost to Goodhead, 5 Nov. 1959.

35 Ibid., Margison to Paul T. Hellyer, 5 Nov. 1959.

36 Margison interview.

37 "We regarded the present site of York as undesirable," Margison added. Ibid., vol. 8, file 18, A.D. Margison to Margaret Wente, 10 Jan. 2001. I am grateful to Mr Margison for providing me with a copy of this letter.

38 AO, RG 3–26, Office of the Premier (John Robarts), box 435, York University 1961–1965.

39 Margison Papers, vol. 8, file 9, "York University Can't Afford Henry Site," Toronto Star, 10 Nov. 1959.

40 Ibid., Bascom St John, "High Cost of Site York U's Problem," Globe and Mail, 12 Nov. 1959.

41 Ibid., "Opening Date Stands for York University," Globe and Mail, 10 Nov. 1959.

42 Claude Bissell, Halfway up Parnassus: A Personal Account of the University of Toronto 1932–1971 (Toronto: University of Toronto Press 1974), 68; see also Axelrod, Scholars and Dollars, 67–8.

43 Margison Papers, vol. 8, file 17, Minutes, meeting of the Organizing Committee, 2 July 1959.

44 UTA, A71–0011/37 (12), Office of the President, "York University," Murray Ross to Claude Bissell, 16 July 1959.

45 Margison Papers, vol. 8, file 17, Minutes, meeting of the Organizing Committee, 2 July 1959.

46 Ibid., vol. 8, file 7, Minutes, meeting of the provisional board of governors, 17 Sept. 1959.

47 Keachie interview.

48 UTA, A71–0011/37 (12), Office of the President, "York University," Murray Ross to Claude Bissell, 16 July 1959; Claude Bissell to Wilfred Curtis, 30 Sept. 1959.

49 "Appoint Winters York University Board Chairman," Globe and Mail, 27 Nov. 1959.

50 AO, RG 3–32–3, box 12, Office of the Premier, Outgoing Correspondence, Leslie Frost to John Bassett, 3 Dec. 1959.

51 James D. Service, letter to the editor, Globe and Mail, 8 Dec. 1959.

52 CTASC, F124, 2003–0029/001, York University Provisional Board, Minutes, 11 Dec. 1959.

53 Interview with John D. Leitch, Toronto, 12 Dec. 2005.

54 Margison Papers, vol. 8, file 7, press release, 19 Dec. 1959.

55 "New President, 3-Point Plan for York U," Telegram, 4 Dec. 1959.

56 Margison interview.

Chapter 2

1 John P.M. Court, "Out of the Wood Work: The Wood Family's Benefactions to Victoria University," Papers of the Canadian Methodist Historical Society, vol. 11, 1997, 43–5.

2 Murray G. Ross, The Way Must Be Tried: Memoirs of a University Man (Toronto: Stoddart 1992), 66.

3 AO, RG 2–217/4, Department of University Affairs, University Subject Files, "Committee on University Affairs 1959–60."

4 Interview with Denis Smith, Port Hope, Ont., 9 June 2003.

5 Interview with Vicky Draper, Thornhill, Ont., 4 July 2003.

6 Ross, The Way Must Be Tried, 22.

7 John Warkentin, The Art of Geography: The Life and Teaching of George Tatham (Toronto: University of Toronto, Department of Geography / University of Toronto Association of Geography Alumni 2002), 52.

8 Interview with Douglas Rutherford, Ottawa, 2 Nov. 2006.

9 Interview with Lionel Rubinoff, Peterborough, Ont., 14 Sept. 2006.

10 Interview with Norman Endler, Toronto, 16 Oct. 2002.

11 CTASC, 2000–044/001, Board of Governors, Minutes, 11 April 1960; Rubinoff interview.

12 William Christian, George Grant: A Biography (Toronto: University of Toronto Press 1993), 198–204.

13 Interview with John McFarland, Toronto, 30 Jan. 2007.

14 Interview with Penny Williams, Toronto, 8 March 2007.

15 CTASC, President's Office, press release, 16 May 1960.

16 Communication from John Court, 16 Oct. 2006; Toronto Star, 22 July 1960.

17 CTASC, 2000–044/001, Board of Governors, Minutes, 26 July 1960, appendix F.

18 George Rust-D'Eye, "A Brief History of York University during the Lost Years," Pro Tem, "Lost Years Issue, Reunion '88," 14 May 1988.

19 Rutherford interview.

20 Interview with Clayton Ruby, Toronto, 17 Nov. 2006.

21 Communication from Rick Salutin, 7 Dec. 2006.

22 Interview with Dale Taylor, Toronto, 15 Aug. 2006.

23 Interview with Heather (McClary) McGoey, Toronto, 22 Jan. 2007.

24 Rust-D'Eye, "A Brief History of York University during the Lost Years."

25 Interview with Fred Gorbet, Toronto, 31 May 2007.

26 Interview with David Bell, Toronto, 25 Oct. 2002.

27 William Wordsworth, *The Prelude, Book xi.*

28 McClary interview.

29 Clara Thomas, *Chapters in a Lucky Life* (Ottawa: Borealis Press 1999), 153.

30 Communication from John Court, 3 Nov. 2006.

31 Rubinoff interview. See also Murray G. Ross et al., *These Five Years ... 1960–65: The President's Report* (Toronto: York University [1965]), 68.

32 Interview with Douglas Lochhead, Sackville, N.B., 26 Sept. 2005.

33 McFarland interview.

34 Interview with Clara Thomas, Toronto, 26 Sept. 2002.

35 Ross, *The Way Must Be Tried*, 47.

36 Endler interview.

37 Rubinoff interview.

38 Communication from John Court, 12 Feb. 2004.

39 John Court, "Glory Days," *Profiles*, September 1997. Available at: http://www.yorku.ca/ycom/profiles/past/sept97/current/features/article1.htm.

40 Interview with John Court, Toronto, 30 Nov. 2006; communications from John Court, 30 Nov. 2006, and 1 Feb. 2007, quoting from his forthcoming book on the University of Toronto and botanical gardens.

41 UTA, A71–0011–43(03), President's Office (Smith/Bissell), "Glendon" file, J.W.B. Sisam to Claude Bissell, 31 March 1960.

42 Communication from John Court, 25 Oct. 2006.

43 AO, RG 3–32–3, box 13, Office of the Premier, Outgoing Correspondence, Leslie Frost to Robert Winters, 7 June 1960.

44 CTASC, 2000–044/001, Board of Governors, Minutes, 20 June 1960.

45 Toronto *Telegram*, 26 Jan. 1961; *Globe and Mail*, 28 Jan. 1961.

46 Ross, *The Way Must Be Tried*, 44.

47 *Globe and Mail*, 25 and 27 Feb. 1961.

48 CTASC, 2000–044/001, Board of Governors, Minutes, 10 April 1961.

49 Endler interview.

50 *Globe and Mail*, 20 Oct. 1961.

51 Ruby interview.

52 Taylor interview.

53 Bell interview.

54 Rutherford interview.

55 Communication from Douglas Rutherford, 3 Nov. 2006.

56 Conversation with Donald Rickerd, Toronto, 3 April 2002.

57 Interview with George Rust-D'Eye, Toronto, 13 Aug. 2007.

58 Interview with John Lennox, Toronto, 13 Dec. 2002.

59 Taylor interview.

60 Ross, *The Way Must Be Tried*, 95–8.

61 CTASC, 2000–0044/007(10), Senate, Minutes, 9 Nov. 1961.

62 Rust-D'Eye interview.

63 Ibid.

64 Rubinoff interview.

65 Ibid.; CTASC, 2000–44/001, Board of Governors, Minutes, 8 Nov. 1963.

66 George Tatham, "Student Activities at Glendon Campus," in Ross et al., *These Five Years*, 69.

67 Interview with Vivienne James, Toronto, 30 Nov. 2006.

68 Tatham, "Student Activities at Glendon Campus," 70.

69 Rubinoff interview.

70 McClary interview.

71 J.H. Langille, "The Role of Athletics," in Ross et al., *These Five Years*, 74.

72 Interview with Douglas Verney, Washington, D.C., 20 March 2007.

73 James interview.

74 Interview with Malcolm Ransom, Toronto, 5 June 2007.

75 I attended several sessions of the convention, to which a few of my friends were delegates.

76 Langille, "The Role of Athletics," 76.

77 *Globe and Mail*, 30 May 1963.

78 McClary interview.

79 Interview with Clara Thomas, Toronto, 24 Jan. 2007.

80 Interview with Alex Murray, Toronto, 13 May 2003.

81 Interview with Harold Schiff, Toronto, 3 Feb. 2003.

82 Lucille (Fowle) Joseph, "Remembrances of the Early Years at York University," unpublished manuscript [2005]. I am grateful to Ms Joseph for making a copy of this document available to me. Interview with Lucille Joseph, Toronto, 7 March 2005.

83 Rust-D'Eye, "A Brief History of York University during the Lost Years"; Rust-D'Eye interview.

84 *York University Gazette*, 20 Nov. 1963.

85 Williams interview.

86 Rutherford interview.

87 Martin Friedland, *The University of Toronto: A History* (Toronto: University of Toronto Press 2002), 510–11.

88 CTASC, 2000–044/001, Board of Governors, Minutes, 16 May 1960; interview with William Small, Toronto, 18 Nov. 2002.

89 CTASC, 2000–044/001, Board of Governors, Minutes, 15 Sept. 1960.

90 Interview with D. McCormack Smyth, Hamilton, Ont., 14 July 2006.

91 City of Toronto Archives, Fonds 220, Series 11, file 682, Metro Chairman's File on York University, 1960–65, Frederick C. Gardiner to Executive Committee of Metro Council, 21 July 1961.

92 CTASC, 2000–044/001, Board of Governors, Minutes, 15 Oct. 1962.

93 *Globe and Mail*, 14 Oct. 1960.

94 Murray G. Ross, *The New University* (Toronto: University of Toronto Press 1961), 10–11.

95 Ibid., 79.

96 Ibid., ix.

97 Interview with John Seeley, Toronto, 21 May 2003.

98 AO, RG 2–217/6, Department of Education, University Subject Files, "York University," Robert Winters to John P. Robarts, 27 Feb. 1962.

99 AO, RG 3-26, Office of the Premier, box 435, File "York University 1961–1966," Winters to Robarts, 23 Nov. 1962.

100 CTASC, 2000–044/001, Board of Governors, Minutes, 15 Oct. 1962.

101 Committee of Presidents of the Universities of Ontario, *Post-Secondary Education in Ontario, 1962–1970*, May 1962 (revised January 1963), 8.

102 CTASC, 2000–0044/007(10), Senate, Minutes, 15 Nov. 1962.

103 Ibid., meeting, 18 Oct. 1962.

104 Ibid., meeting, 15 Nov. 1962.

105 Verney interview.

106 McClary interview.

107 CTASC, John Seeley Fonds, 1975–012/008 (063), John Seeley to Murray Ross, 22 Oct. 1962, is a key letter.

108 Endler interview.

109 Smith interview.

110 Barbara Moon, "The Perils and Pleasures of a Brand-New University," *Maclean's*, 7 April 1962, 54.

111 Verney interview.

112 "Administrative Muddle Charged, 10 Staffers Quit York University," *Globe and Mail*, 29 June 1963.

113 Ibid.

114 "York University Aide Denies Revolt," *Globe and Mail*, 1 July 1963.

115 Smyth interview.

116 Seeley interview.

117 "Board to Meet Today on Staff Complaints about York University," *Globe and Mail*, 3 July 1963; Smith interview.

118 CTASC, Norman Endler Fonds, 2003–040/032 (13), Hugh Maclean to Endler, 2 July 1963.

119 Lochhead interview.

120 "Board to Meet Today on Staff Complaints about York University," *Globe and Mail*, 3 July 1963.

121 Ruby interview.

122 Rutherford interview.

123 McClary interview.

124 Ross, *The Way Must Be Tried*, 31–2.

125 "York Staff Complaints Rejected by Governors," *Globe and Mail*, 4 July 1963; "Governors Back Ross in York University Row," Toronto *Daily Star*, 4 July 1963.

126 Interview with John D. Leitch, Toronto, 12 Dec. 2005.

127 Verney interview.

128 Clara Thomas interview, 24 Jan. 2007.

129 CTASC, Norman Endler Fonds, 2003–040/032 (13), York University Faculty Association, meeting of 5 July 1963, resolution.

130 Ibid., John Brückmann to Endler, 5 July 1963.

131 Interview with Johanna Stuckey, Toronto, 23 Nov. 2006.

132 Conversation with Walter Beringer, Nelson, B.C., 6 Aug. 2003.

133 Williams interview.

134 Interview with John McNee, New York, 19 March 2007.

135 Hugh Parry and William Whitla, "Humanities at York: The Early Years," unpublished ms., n.d. I am grateful to Professor Whitla for giving me a copy of this document.

136 Interview with William Whitla, Toronto, 9 Feb. 2006.

137 Interview with John T. Saywell, Toronto, 14 Nov. 2002.

138 Ross, *The New University*, 30.

139 Ibid., 39.

140 George Tatham, "The Curriculum – Part I – Planning," in Ross et al., *These Five Years*, 33.

141 CTASC, Lionel Rubinoff Fonds, 2003–035/001 (08), John R. Seeley to the Second-Stage Committee, 6 Dec. 1960, emphasis in the original; Seeley interview.

142 Ibid., Hugh Maclean, reply to Seeley's statement.

143 Ibid., "The Curriculum."

144 Ibid., 2003–035/001 (10), Denis Smith, "Summary of Discussions of the Interim Report of the Curriculum Committee at Meetings of the Faculty Council … May 10, 1961."

145 Rubinoff interview; Tatham, "The Curriculum – Part I – Planning," 35.

146 CTASC, Lionel Rubinoff Fonds, 2003–035/001 (10), Report of the Curriculum Committee, 12 Dec. 1961.

147 Ibid., 2003–035/001 (05), Lionel Rubinoff, Confidential Memorandum I and Confidential Memorandum II, 5 March 1962.

148 Ibid., David Fowle, Hugh Maclean, and Douglas Verney, Report of Co-chairmen of Curriculum Committee Subcommittees, "The New Curriculum," 9 March 1962.

149 Moon, "The Perils and Pleasures of a Brand-New University," 54.

150 CTASC, 2000–004/007 (6), Senate, Minutes, 6 April 1962, appendix D, "Description of the New Curriculum for York University Calendar, 1962–63."

151 CTASC, President's Office, 1970–0012/001, H.N. Maclean, "York's Second Year: From Romance to Realism," 17 April 1962, 8.

152 Ibid., 10.

153 Rubinoff interview.

154 Clara Thomas interview, 24 Jan. 2007.

155 McFarland interview.

156 CTASC, 2000–044/007 (11), R.O. Earl, Report of the Committee on Undergraduate Studies, 11 Dec. 1962.

157 Seeley interview; Ruby interview.

158 Ross, The New University, 13–14.

159 J.R. Kidd, 18 to 80, Continuing Education in Metropolitan Toronto (Toronto: Board of Education 1961), 142. Emphasis in original.

160 CTASC, President's Papers, press release, 8 March 1961.

161 D. McCormack Smyth, "The Joseph E. Atkinson College of York University, the First Four Years 1961–1965," 15 April 1965, 7. I am grateful to Professor Smyth for giving me a copy of this report.

162 Smyth interview.

163 Ibid.

164 Smyth, "The Joseph E. Atkinson College," 20.

165 Wesley Coons Private Papers, Atkinson College, press release, 25 May 1965. I am grateful to Professor Coons for making these papers available to me.

166 Smyth, "The Joseph E. Atkinson College," 29, and appendix D, "Population Distribution in Metropolitan Toronto." See also Kidd, 18 to 80, 14.

167 Smyth, "The Joseph E. Atkinson College," 28.

168 Paul Axelrod, Scholars and Dollars: Politics, Economics, and the Universities of Ontario 1945–1980 (Toronto: University of Toronto Press 1982), 68.

169 Ross et al., These Five Years, appendix E, "Benefactions to York University for the Years ending June 30, 1961 to 1965."

170 York University Gazette, 15 Sept. 1963, 28 Oct. 1963; President's Report 1965–66, 4.

171 Interview with Wesley Coons, Caledon, Ont., 25 Sept. 2007; CTASC, Norman Endler Fonds, 2003–040/032 (06), "A Brief History of the York University Department of Psychology," September 1998.

172 York University Gazette, 31 July 1968.

173 Ralph W. Nicholls, "The Department of Physics and Astronomy, York University (1965–)," Physics in Canada, vol. 54, no. 1 (1998): 32–4.

174 Interview with Ralph Nicholls, Toronto, 3 Dec. 2002.

175 Ibid.

176 Schiff interview; Communication from Doris Nicholls, 2 Oct. 2007.

177 York University Gazette, 31 Oct. 1965.

178 Ross, The Way Must Be Tried, 47.

179 George Whalley, ed., A Place of Liberty: Essays on the Government of Canadian Universities (Toronto and Vancouver: Clarke Irwin 1964).

180 Ross, "The President's Report," in Ross et al., These Five Years, 17–18.

181 Ontario Statutes, 3rd Session, 27th Legislature, York University Act, 1965, c. 149.

182 Ross, The Way Must Be Tried, 48.

183 Ibid., 68.

184 Interview with Willard Piepenburg, Toronto, 29 Dec. 2006.

185 Ross, The Way Must Be Tried, 68.

186 Williams, "The Lost Years"; Rust-D'Eye, "A Brief History of York University during the Lost Years."

Chapter 3

1 Patricia W. Hart, Pioneering in North York: A History of the Borough (Toronto: General Publishing 1968), 214–17, 225–6.

2 Communication from Harriet Lewis, 27 Feb. 2007.

3 Paul Axelrod, Scholars and Dollars: Politics, Economics, and the Universities of Ontario 1945–1980 (Toronto: University of Toronto Press 1982), 68.

4 Murray G. Ross, The Way Must Be Tried: Memoirs of a University Man (Toronto: Stoddart 1992), 51.

5 Axelrod, Scholars and Dollars, 69.

6 Ibid., 73.

7 Ibid., 74.

8 Ibid., 75.

9 Ibid., 75.

10 Murray Ross, Those Ten Years 1960–70: The President's Report on the First Decade of York University (Toronto, 1970), 35.

11 Murray Ross, "The President's Report," in Ross et al., These Five Years ... 1960–65 (Toronto: York

University 1965), 11; *York University Gazette*, 1 Nov. 1962.

12 Eric Dowd, "Fancy-Free Designers Evolve 'Grand, Exciting, Pioneering' York U Campus," *Globe and Mail*, 5 Dec. 1963.

13 *York University Gazette*, 1 Nov. 1962.

14 Interview with Donald Rickerd, Toronto, 15 Feb. 2007.

15 Communication from Steve Dranitsaris, 1 March 2007.

16 Interview with Steve Dranitsaris, Toronto, 20 April 2004.

17 Interview with Nancy Accinelli, Toronto, 15 May 2007.

18 Interview with John Becker, Toronto, 24 Jan. 2003.

19 *York University Gazette*, 29 Feb. 1964.

20 Ibid.

21 Ibid., 31 Oct. 1965.

22 Interview with Brian Dixon, Kingston, Ont., 29 Nov. 2007.

23 Interview with Frances Henry, Toronto, 11 July 2007.

24 Interview with John Warkentin, Toronto, 1 Nov. 2004.

25 Ross, *The Way Must Be Tried*, 86.

26 Ibid.

27 Lester J. Pronger, "A Proposal for the Small Campus of York University," 26 Dec. 1962 (revised 18 Dec. 1963). I am grateful to Professor Cotnam for giving me a copy of this document.

28 Ibid.

29 CTASC, Senate, Minutes, 19 Dec. 1963.

30 Interviews with Clara Thomas, Toronto, 24 Jan. 2007, John McFarland, Toronto, 30 Jan. 2007, and Donald Rickerd, Toronto, 15 Feb. 2007.

31 Interview with Jacques Cotnam, Quebec City, 25 June 2004.

32 Communication from John T. Saywell, 4 Dec. 2007.

33 LAC, Escott Reid Fonds, MG 31, E46, vol. 39, Murray Ross to Escott Reid, 30 July 1964.

34 Ibid., Tim Reid to Escott Reid [August 1964]. See also Escott Reid, *Radical Mandarin: Memoirs* (Toronto: University of Toronto Press 1989), 341–2.

35 Interview with Timothy Reid, Toronto, 30 March 2003.

36 LAC, Reid Fonds, vol. 38, Reid to Murray Ross, 20 Nov. 1964.

37 Kenneth McRoberts, *Quebec, Social Change and Political Crisis*, 3rd ed. (Toronto: Oxford University Press 1993), 128–72.

38 LAC, Reid Fonds, vol. 38, memorandum, Reid to the president, 15 April 1965.

39 Ibid., vol. 39, Jacques Cotnam to Escott Reid, 12 May 1965.

40 Cotnam interview.

41 LAC, Reid Fonds, vol. 39, Norman MacKenzie to Reid [August 1964].

42 Ibid., Frank Underhill to Reid, 5 Feb. 1965.

43 LAC, Frank H. Underhill Fonds, MG 30, D204, vol. 13, Reid to Underhill, 10 Feb. 1965.

44 McFarland interview.

45 Interview with Bob Augustine, Toronto, 30 May 2007.

46 Escott Reid, "Glendon College," 16 Sept. 1965. A copy with critical annotations by Edgar McInnis is currently in my possession but will be donated to the Glendon College Archives.

47 Gary J. Smith, "Glendon To Be Hotbed of Politics," *Globe and Mail*, 1 Jan. 1966.

48 Interview with Lionel Rubinoff, Peterborough, Ont., 14 Sept. 2006.

49 Interview with David Clipsham, Toronto, 10 May 2004.

50 Interview with Michael Gregory, New York, 22 March 2007.

51 Bob Waller, "Pro Tem Notes," October 1996, 8–9. I am grateful to Mr Waller for supplying me with a copy of this document.

52 *Report of the Presidential Committee on Glendon College, June 1969* ([Toronto]: York University 1969), 11.

53 Interview with Albert Tucker, Toronto, 5 Nov. 2002.

54 The *coopérants* were able to satisfy the military-service requirement by teaching French language, literature, or cultural affairs abroad.

55 Alain Baudot, "In Praise of Glendon Students," address at Founders College on the occasion of the 40th anniversary of York University, 26 March 1999.

56 Interview with Alain Baudot, Toronto, 15 July 2003.

57 Interview with Lesley Lewis, Toronto, 27 Sept. 2007.

58 Ibid.

59 Interview with David Cole, Toronto, 8 May 2007.

60 Communication from David Cole, 5 Nov. 2007.

61 Graham Fraser, "René Lévesque: The Anglais Cheer as He Calls for Canada's Break-Up," *Maclean's*, May 1969, 47–9.

62 Interview with Rives (Dalley) Hewitt, Toronto, 22 Nov. 2007.

63 Interview with Ruth Mesbur, Toronto, 18 Oct. 2007.

64 Cole interview.

65 Lesley Lewis interview.

66 Conversation with Ron Kanter, Toronto, 26 Dec. 2007.

67 Communication from Jan Armstrong, 13 Aug. 2007.

68 Interview with Jan Armstrong, Toronto, 25 Nov. 2002.

69 Interview with Julie Drexler, Toronto, 12 Dec. 2002.

70 Dalley interview.

71 Interview with John McNee, New York, 19 March 2007.

72 Interview with Adrienne Hood, Toronto, 14 Nov. 2007.

73 Interview with Helen Sinclair, Toronto, 1 June 2004.

74 Interview with Paul Cantor, Toronto, 25 May 2004.

75 Interview with Bob Drummond, Toronto, 12 March 2007.

76 Interview with Marion Boyd, Toronto, 13 Nov. 2006.

77 Gregory interview.

78 Interview with Richard Schultz, Montreal, 10 Dec. 2007.

79 Interview with David Collenette, Toronto, 1 Feb. 2006.

80 Interview with Malcolm Ransom, Toronto, 5 June 2007.

81 Interview with Clara Thomas, Toronto, 26 Sept. 2002.

82 Gregory interview.

83 Interview with Harriet Lewis, Toronto, 7 Dec. 2006.

84 Interview with Kurt Danziger, Toronto, 8 Dec. 2006.

85 Interview with Neil Agnew, Toronto, 7 March 2007.

86 Interview with Sandra Pyke, Toronto, 24 April 2007.

87 Interview with Johanna Stuckey, Toronto, 26 Nov. 2006.

88 Interview with Sandra Noble Goss and Jackie Robinson, Toronto, 17 Jan. 2007.

89 Interview with Esther Greenglass, Toronto, 11 Nov. 2002.

90 Robinson interview.

91 Interview with Ronald Bloore, Toronto, 20 Feb. 2007.

92 Robinson interview.

93 Goss interview.

94 Interview with Cathie Stone, Toronto, 6 Feb. 2007.

95 Interview with Rex Lingwood, Waterloo, Ont., 30 March 2007.

96 Goss interview.

97 Interview with John Nagel, Toronto, 18 Jan. 2008.

98 Harriet Lewis interview; interview with Marie Rickard, Toronto, 8 Feb. 2007.

99 Interview with Wendy Mitchinson, Waterloo, Ont., 30 March 2007; Lingwood interview.

100 Interview with Paul Axelrod, Toronto, 11 Dec. 2006.

101 Mitchinson interview.

102 Communication from Paul Axelrod, 3 Dec. 2007.

103 *Excalibur*, 30 Jan. 1969, cited in Marcel Martel, *Not This Time: Canadians, Public Policy, and the Marijuana Question 1961–1975* (Toronto: University of Toronto Press 2006), 40–1.

104 Ibid., 48–9.

105 Interview with Rasma Rugelis, Toronto, 22 May 2007.

106 Wesley Coons Private Papers, "York University Announces Appointments for 1965–66," 24 May 1965.

107 Interview with Raymond Hudson, Toronto, 18 Aug. 2005.

108 Ross, *The Way Must Be Tried*, 91–2.

109 Interview with Vicky Draper, Thornhill, Ont., 4 July 2003.

110 Interview with Bruce Dugelby, Toronto, 29 July 2004.

111 Bruce Dugelby, "Remembrances," n.d. [2004], 2–3. I am grateful to Mr Dugelby for making this document available to me.

112 *York University Gazette*, 30 Aug. 1966.

113 James Gillies and Colin Dickinson, "From the Faculty of Administrative Studies to the Schulich School of Business: The Origin and Evolution of Professional Education for Managers at York University," in Barbara Austin, ed., *Capitalizing Knowledge: Essays on the History of Business Education in Canada* (Toronto: University of Toronto Press 2000), 168.

114 Ross, *The Way Must Be Tried*, 111.

115 Interview with James Gillies, Toronto, 20 Jan. 2004.

116 Gillies and Dickinson, "From the Faculty of Administrative Studies to the Schulich School of Business," 170.

117 Ibid., 171.

118 *York University Gazette*, 31 Dec. 1965, 28 Feb. 1966.

119 Gillies interview, 20 Jan. 2004.

120 Interview with James Gillies, Toronto, 26 April 2007.

121 Interview with William Dimma, Toronto, 22 Sept. 2005.

122 Dixon interview.

123 James Gillies, "The Creation and Building of the Faculty of Administrative Studies at York University, 1966–1972: A Very Personal Memoir of a Very

Exciting Experience," unpublished ms., summer 2006, 108. I am grateful to Professor Gillies for lending me a copy of this document.

124 Gillies interview, 26 April 2007.

125 Ibid.

126 Ross, *The Way Must Be Tried*, 112.

127 Ileana Esfakis et al., eds., "1969–1989: A History of Theatre at York," *York Theatre Journal*, 31, Special Edition, 1989, 2–4.

128 Gregory interview.

129 *York University Gazette*, 31 Oct. 1966.

130 Bloore interview.

131 *York University Gazette*, 28 Feb. 1967.

132 Ibid., 30 April 1967.

133 Interview with Joe Green, Toronto, 24 March 2003.

134 Interview with Don Rubin, Toronto, 5 Dec. 2007.

135 Interview with Marc Rosen, Toronto, 19 Nov. 2007.

136 Green interview, 24 March 2003.

137 Interview with Joyce Zemans, Toronto, 6 Oct. 2005.

138 Interview with Joe Green, Toronto, 14 June 2007.

139 Lingwood interview.

140 Esfakis et al., eds., "1969–1989: A History of Theatre at York," 13.

141 Interview with Sterling Beckwith, in Sterling Beckwith, ed., *Music at York: The Founding Generation* (Toronto: York University, Faculty of Fine Arts, Department of Music 2003), 24.

142 Green interview, 14 June 2007.

143 Rosen interview.

144 *York University Gazette*, 28 Feb. 1967.

145 Ibid., 30 April 1967.

146 Interview with Alex Murray, Toronto, 15 May 2003.

147 Interview with Harold Schiff, Toronto, 4 Feb. 2003.

148 Communication from John T. Saywell, 11 Dec. 2007.

149 Murray interview.

150 Ross, *Those Ten Years*, 28.

151 Interview with Gerald Carrothers, Toronto, 13 June 2007.

152 Murray interview.

153 Interview with Sylvia Zingrone, Toronto, 6 Jan. 2006.

154 Gerald A.P. Carrothers with Stephen Kline, John Livingston, et al., *FESKIT: Essays into Environmental Studies, Being Interpretations and Amplifications of the FES Curriculum Model* (York University, Faculty of Environmental Studies, 1987 [1968]), 1.

155 Carrothers interview.

156 Schiff interview.

157 Carrothers interview.

158 Interview with Adèle Hurley, Toronto, 25 Jan. 2007.

159 C. Ian Kyer and Jerome E. Bickenbach, *The Fiercest Debate: Cecil A. Wright, the Benchers, and Legal Education in Ontario 1923–1957* (Toronto: Osgoode Society for Canadian Legal History / University of Toronto Press 1987), 210–21.

160 H.W. Arthurs, "The Affiliation of Osgoode Hall Law School with York University," *University of Toronto Law Journal*, vol. 17, no. 1 (1967): 198.

161 Interview with Harry Arthurs, Toronto, 28 Oct. 2002.

162 Philip Girard, *Bora Laskin: Bringing Law to Life* (Toronto: Osgoode Society for Canadian Legal History / University of Toronto Press 2005), 328.

163 CTASC, Board of Governors, Minutes, 11 Dec. 1972.

164 Interview with Frederick Zemans, Toronto, 3 March 2005.

165 Interview with John McCamus, Toronto, 25 Oct. 2005.

166 Interview with Marion Lane, Toronto, 23 Jan. 2007.

167 Mesbur interview.

168 Interview with Marilyn Pilkington, Toronto, 4 April 2007.

169 *York University Gazette*, January 1968.

170 Ibid., 31 March 1965.

171 Interview with Michael Lanphier, Toronto, 3 May 2005.

172 *York Communiqué*, May 1970.

173 CTASC, 1997–007/12 (08), "The Gerstein Report: A Review of the Role and Development of Atkinson College of York University," 30 Sept. 1967, 16–17.

174 *York University Gazette*, July 1969.

175 Ibid., February 1970.

176 Gillies interview, 26 April 2007.

177 Dixon interview.

178 LAC, Frank Underhill Fonds, vol. 13, John T. Saywell to Underhill, 2 Feb. 1968.

179 Interview with Frederick Elkin, Toronto, 7 Feb. 2005.

180 Interview with John O'Neill, Toronto, 18 June 2003.

181 Interview with Gordon Darroch, Toronto, 2 Oct. 2007.

182 Interview with Virginia Rock, Toronto, 25 Oct. 2004.

183 Interview with Kurt Danziger, Toronto, 8 Dec. 2006.

184 Interview with Arthur Haberman, Toronto, 3 March 2007.

185 Communication from Ramsay Cook, 8 May 2007.

186 Communication from Ramsay Cook, 30 July 2007.

187 Interview with Kenneth Carpenter, Toronto, 11 Sept. 2007.

188 Interview with Harvey Simmons, Toronto, 19 Oct. 2004.

189 Interview with Elizabeth Hopkins, Toronto, 6 March 2003.

190 Interview with Robert Fothergill, Toronto, 27 Feb. 2007.

191 Interview with Christopher Innes, Toronto, 6 March 2007.

192 Interview with Bernard Wolf, Toronto, 17 May 2004; communication from Wolf, 30 July 2007.

193 Green interview, 14 June 2007.

194 Robin Mathews and James Steele, eds., *The Struggle for Canadian Universities: A Dossier* (Toronto: New Press 1969), 1–11.

195 Interview with Joe Green, Toronto, 29 Feb. 2008.

196 *Excalibur*, 23 Jan. 1969.

197 Ibid., 8 Jan. 1970.

198 Interview with Paul Axelrod, Toronto, 29 Nov. 2002.

199 *Excalibur*, 3 Dec. 1970, 11 Nov. 1971.

200 Robin Mathews and James Steele, "The Universities: Takeover of the Mind," in Ian Lumsden, ed., *Close the 49th Parallel etc.: The Americanization of Canada* (Toronto: University of Toronto Press 1970), 169–78.

201 Interview with Thelma McCormack, Toronto, 6 April 2004.

202 Haberman interview.

203 Green interview, 14 June 2007.

204 CTASC, F0326, Michiel Horn Fonds, 1981–013/001 (06), John Boyle to YUFA executive, 7 March 1973; Jack Chambers to John Yolton, 7 March 1973 (copy).

205 Lanphier interview.

206 Wolf interview.

207 Communication from Paul Axelrod, 3 Dec. 2007.

208 Michiel Horn, *Becoming Canadian: Memoirs of an Invisible Immigrant* (Toronto: University of Toronto Press 1997), 278–9.

209 I have drawn much of the information in the following paragraphs from "25 Years of Achievement: York University Champions," compiled by Steve Dranitsaris. I am grateful to him for sending me a copy.

210 http://www.yorku.ca/sprtyork/sport_hall_of_fame/members/1980.htm

211 Ibid.

212 Interview with Bill Purcell, Toronto, 5 Feb. 2008.

213 Interview with Murray Stroud, Pickering, Ont., 13 Feb. 2008.

214 Ibid.

215 Purcell interview.

216 Interview with Steve Dranitsaris, Toronto, 3 April 2007.

217 Interview with Frank Cosentino, Toronto, 2 Nov. 2005.

218 Interview with Michael Herren, Toronto, 12 April 2007.

219 Interview with Nick Martin, Winnipeg, 30 May 2004.

220 Cyril Levitt, *Children of Privilege: Student Revolt in the Sixties* (Toronto: University of Toronto Press 1984), 13–36.

221 Peter L. Smith, *A Multitude of the Wise: UVic Remembered* (Victoria: Alumni Association of the University of Victoria 1993), 149; communication from Paul Williamson (president, University of Victoria Alma Mater Society, 1965–66), 25 Jan. 2007.

222 Schultz interview.

223 *York University Gazette*, 30 April 1967.

224 *Excalibur*, 1 and 8 Dec. 1967.

225 Ibid., 21 Nov. 1968.

226 Ibid., 12 Dec. 1968.

227 Interview with Bob Waller, Toronto, 30 Jan. 2004.

228 *Telegram*, 10 Feb. 1969; Toronto *Star*, 10 Feb. 1969; "Red Tape or Discrimination?" Toronto *Star*, 11 Feb. 1969.

229 Interview with Earle Nestmann, Toronto, 4 Dec. 2007.

230 Ibid.

231 McFarland interview.

232 *Excalibur*, 7, 14, and 21 Nov. 1968.

233 Innes interview.

234 Jim Park, "Letter to Students and Faculty Members of Glendon College," in Tim and Julyan Reid, eds., *Student Power and the Canadian Campus* (Toronto: Peter Martin Associates 1969), 78–80.

235 Student Council of Glendon College, "A University Is for People: A Manifesto," ibid., 83–6.

236 Axelrod interview, 29 Nov. 2002.

237 Drexler interview.

238 Cole interview.

239 Lesley Lewis interview.

240 Dalley interview.

241 LAC, Reid Fonds, vol. 39, several letters and memos; CTASC, 2000–044/002 (27), Board of Governors, Minutes, 10 March 1969; *York University Gazette*, July 1969.

242 Jerry Farber, *The Student as Nigger: Essays and Stories* (New York: Contact Books 1969); Pierre Vallières, *Nègres blancs d'Amérique: autobiographie précoce d'un 'terroriste' québécois* (Montréal: Éditions Parti Pris 1968).

243 Mesbur interview.

244 Interview with Albert Tucker, Toronto, 17 Aug. 2007.

245 Interview with Irving Abella, Toronto, 21 Feb. 2007.

246 *Excalibur*, 18 Sept. 1969.

247 Ibid., 20 Nov. 1969.

248 Interview with Harold Schiff, Toronto, 4 Feb. 2003.

249 Girard, *Bora Laskin: Bringing Law to Life*, 332–3.

250 Presidential Committee on Rights and Responsibilities of Members of York University, *Freedom and Responsibility in the University* (Toronto: York University 1970), 49.

251 Ibid., 38.

252 Wesley Coons Private Papers, Minutes of YUFA Executive Committee meeting, Monday [n.d.].

253 Axelrod interview, 29 Nov. 2002.

254 Communication from Paul Axelrod, 13 Sept. 2007.

255 CTASC, York Student Federation Fonds, 1974–019/031 (633), Paul Axelrod, "Towards Democracy in the University: A Response to the Report of the Presidential Committee on Rights and Responsibilities," 20 Oct. 1970, 69–71; *Excalibur*, 22 Oct. 1970.

256 Axelrod communication, 13 Sept. 2007.

257 James Duff and Robert O. Berdahl, *University Government in Canada* (Toronto: University of Toronto Press 1966), 67.

258 *York University Gazette*, July 1969.

259 George Whalley, ed., *A Place of Liberty: Essays on the Government of Canadian Universities* (Toronto and Vancouver: Clarke Irwin 1964).

260 *York University Gazette*, July 1969.

261 Douglas Verney, "The Government and Politics of a Developing University: A Canadian Experience," *Review of Politics*, vol. 31, no. 3 (1969): 293.

262 Ibid., 310, 311.

263 Levitt, *Children of Privilege*, 9, 53.

264 William G. Davis, "The Government of Ontario and the Universities of the Province," in William Cooper Mansfield et al., *Governments and the University* (Toronto: Macmillan of Canada 1966), 36–46.

265 *York Communiqué*, June 1969.

266 Carpenter interview.

267 Glendon College Forum, York University, *Quebec: Year Eight* (Toronto, 1968).

268 "Example to the Young," *Globe and Mail*, 29 Oct. 1968.

269 Dalley interview.

270 CTASC, 2000–003/24, Board of Governors, Minutes, 9 Dec. 1968.

271 Ross H. Munro, "Seek End to Family Unit," *Globe and Mail*, 25 Oct. 1969; "Women 'Sexual Objects, Slaves,'" *Telegram*, 25 Oct. 1969.

272 Munro, "Radicals Proclaim 'Year of Barricade,'" *Globe and Mail*, 24 Oct. 1969.

273 Munro, "200 Radicals March on Offices of Globe," *Globe and Mail*, 27 Oct. 1969.

274 *York University Gazette*, Aug. 1970.

275 Ibid., February 1970.

276 Dranitsaris interview, 3 April 2007.

277 *York Communiqué*, May 1970.

278 CTASC, Office of the President, 1975–023/005, file 61, York 10 – General, "York 10 Week May 26–May 31 Program."

279 Lionel Rubinoff, ed., *Tradition and Revolution* (Toronto: Macmillan of Canada 1971).

280 Interview with Barbara McNutt, Toronto, 8 Nov. 2005.

281 *York Communiqué*, May 1970; *York University Gazette*, August 1970.

Chapter 4

1 CTASC, President's Office, 1998–030/001 (51), Minutes of the meeting held 19 Feb. 1969, Executive Suite, Toronto-Dominion Centre.

2 CTASC, 1998–030–001 (51), Bora Laskin, A Statement from the Committee of Search for a New President, n.d.

3 Philip Girard, *Bora Laskin: Bringing Law to Life* (Toronto: University of Toronto Press / Osgoode Society for Canadian Legal History 2005), 333.

4 Michiel Horn, *Academic Freedom in Canada: A History* (Toronto: University of Toronto Press 1999), 253–60.

5 F.R. Scott, "The Law of the University Constitution," in George Whalley, ed., *A Place of Liberty: Essays on the Government of Canadian Universities* (Toronto and Vancouver: Clarke Irwin 1964), 33–4.

6 Interview with Harold Schiff, Toronto, 4 Feb. 2003.

7 *Excalibur*, 9 Oct. 1969.

8 Schiff interview.

9 Interview with Albert Tucker, Toronto, 5 Nov. 2002.

10 Communication from Albert Tucker, 28 Aug. 2007.

11 Interview with Michael Creal, Toronto, 17 June 2003.

12 Interview with Wesley Coons, Caledon, Ont., 25 Sept. 2007.

13 CTASC, F0169, David Coombs Fonds, 1998–035/001, Coombs handwritten notes; interview with David Coombs, Barry's Bay, Ont., 16 Dec. 2007.

14 Conversation with John T. Saywell, Toronto, 27 Jan. 2008.

15 David Coombs notes.

16 Interview with Robert MacIntosh, Toronto, 4 Oct. 2007.

17 Interview with John D. Leitch, Toronto, 12 Oct. 2007.

18 Murray Ross, *The Way Must Be Tried: Memoirs of a University Man* (Toronto: Stoddart 1992), 148.

19 Horn, *Academic Freedom in Canada*, 220–45.

20 Interview with D. McCormack Smyth, Hamilton, Ont., 14 July 2006.

21 Interview with Pinayur Rajagopal, Toronto, 4 Aug. 2004.

22 Schiff interview.

23 Coons interview.

24 Interview with Albert Tucker, Toronto, 21 Sept. 2007.

25 CTASC, President's Office, 1998–030/001 (02), untitled and undated document listing thirty-one nominees.

26 Interview with James Gillies, Toronto, 20 Jan. 2004.

27 Interview with John T. Saywell, Toronto, 14 Nov. 2002.

28 Communication from John T. Saywell, 11 Sept. 2007.

29 Creal interview.

30 Interview with Brian Dixon, Kingston, Ont., 29 Nov. 2007.

31 Communication from Ralph Nicholls, 28 Aug. 2007.

32 Ross, *The Way Must Be Tried*, 149, 150.

33 Interview with Bob Waller, Toronto, 30 Jan. 2004.

34 *Excalibur*, 11 Dec. 1969.

35 Waller interview.

36 CTASC, F0169, David Coombs Fonds, 1998–035/001 (05), transcript of interview, David Coombs with Harold Schiff [1970].

37 Loren Lind, "Three Proposed as President of York U," *Globe and Mail*, 9 Dec. 1969; *Excalibur*, 9 Dec. 1969.

38 CTASC, Coombs Fonds, Schiff transcript.

39 Ross, *The Way Must Be Tried*, 152.

40 Coombs interview.

41 Ross H. Munro, "York Dean Leaves Race for Presidency," *Globe and Mail*, 6 Jan. 1970; Munro, "York Loses Third Candidate for Presidency," *Globe and Mail*, 9 Jan. 1970.

42 CTASC, Board of Governors, 1998–030/001 (01), John T. Saywell to W.D. Farr, 5 Jan. 1970; also A.D. Allen to Bora Laskin, 8 Jan. 1970.

43 Girard, *Bora Laskin*, 334.

44 Ross H. Munro, "York University's Growing Predicament in Finding a President," *Globe and Mail*, 21 Jan. 1970.

45 Munro, "York Senate Endorses New Hunt for Head," *Globe and Mail*, 23 Jan. 1970.

46 *Excalibur*, 26 March 1970.

47 CTASC, Board of Governors, 1998–030/001 (01), Bora Laskin, Report of the Committee of Search for a New President of York University, 27 March 1970.

48 Ibid.

49 Schiff interview.

50 CTASC, Coombs Fonds, "The Presidential Search Committee," handwritten report, 4.

51 Tucker interview, 21 Sept. 2007.

52 Coons interview.

53 Bora Laskin, Report of the Committee of Search for a New President of York University.

54 MacIntosh interview.

55 CTASC, Board of Governors, Minutes, 1 May 1970, appendix B.

56 CTASC, Senate, 2000–044/008 (32), appendix A, Senate Executive Committee to chairman, Board of Governors, 15 April 1970.

57 CTASC, Senate, Minutes, 23 April 1970.

58 *Globe and Mail*, 23 April 1970.

59 Ross, *The Way Must Be Tried*, 158.

60 Schiff interview.

61 CTASC, Senate, Minutes, 23 April 1970.

62 Harry Arthurs, "The View from the Ninth Floor: 1985–1992: A Memoir" [2002], 9. I am grateful to Professor Arthurs for making this document available to me.

63 Wesley Coons Private Papers, Minutes of the special meeting of the YUFA Executive Committee, 30 April 1970; memorandum to President M.G. Ross and Board of Governors, 30 April 1970.

64 Toronto *Star*, 1 May 1970.

65 Gillies interview.

66 CTASC, Board of Governors, Minutes, 1 May 1970, appendix A, press release.

67 MacIntosh interview; *Globe and Mail*, 2 May 1970.

68 CTASC, Board of Governors, Minutes, 5 June 1970.

69 MacIntosh interview.

70 Communication from James Gillies, 22 Jan. 2004.

71 Interview with Howard Adelman, Toronto, 24 March 2003.

72 York University, "Fact Book, 1997–98."

73 AO, RG 3–26, Office of the Premier, box 435, file "York University 1961–1966," Robert Winters to John P. Robarts, 23 Nov. 1962.

74 Murray G. Ross, *Those Ten Years 1960–70: The President's Report on the First Ten Years of York University* (Toronto: York University 1970), 22.

75 Murray G. Ross, *The New University* (Toronto: University of Toronto Press 1961), 79.

76 Interview with Henry Jackman, Toronto, 11 Dec. 2007.

77 "How York Faces Love, Life and the Real World," *Toronto Life*, 4 (October 1970): 37.

78 Ibid., 88.

79 Philip A. Lapp et al., *Ring of Iron: A Study of Engineering Education in Ontario* (Toronto: Committee of Presidents of the Universities of Ontario 1970), 81, 82.

80 Ibid., 82.

81 Interview with Philip Lapp, Toronto, 21 Feb. 2005.

82 CTASC, Board of Governors, Minutes, 11 March 1968.

83 Communication from Doris Nicholls, 2 Oct. 2007.

84 CTASC, Office of the President, 1975–022/18, file 108, York University Committee to Study Education for Health Sciences, Report No. 1, July 1971, 3.

85 Communication from Doris Nicholls, 2 Oct. 2007.

86 CTASC, Office of the President, 1975–022/18, file 109, York University Committee to Study Education for Health Sciences, Report No. 2, January 1972, 3–4.

87 CTASC, Board of Governors, Minutes, 10 Jan. 1972.

88 CTASC, Senate, Minutes, 24 Sept. 1965.

89 CTASC, Senate, 2000–044/016 (23), Report of the Interim University Committee on the Planning and Implementation of a Faculty of Education at York University, 27 May 1971, 1.

90 CTASC, Board of Governors, Minutes, 14 June 1971; Senate, Minutes, 24 June 1971.

91 Interview with Peter Ross, Toronto, 14 June 2006.

92 Interview with Robert Overing, Ivry-sur-le-Lac, Que., 30 Nov. 2007.

93 Ross interview.

94 Interview with Arthur Haberman, Toronto, 3 March 2007.

95 Ibid.

96 Ross interview; Overing interview.

97 Interview with Liz Lundell, Toronto, 13 Nov. 2007.

98 Interview with Donna Paterson, Toronto, 21 Nov. 2007.

99 Frederick H. Zemans, "The Dream Is Still Alive: Twenty-five Years of Parkdale Community Legal Services and the Osgoode Hall Law School Intensive Program in Poverty Law," *Osgoode Hall Law Journal*, vol. 35, no. 3 (1997): 503.

100 Interview with Frederick Zemans, Toronto, 3 March 2005.

101 Communication from Mary Jane Mossman, 20 Feb. 2008.

102 Zemans interview.

103 Interview with Marion Lane, Toronto, 23 Jan. 2007. The title of her report was "Raise High the Roof Beams, Carpenter."

104 Lane interview.

105 York University, *Report of the Presidential Committee on Glendon College, June 1969* ([Toronto]: York University 1969), 11.

106 Glendon College, Faculty Council Office, FC 70–71–47, Minutes, 1 Feb. 1971.

107 Interview with Alan Sangster, Toronto, 21 June 2006.

108 Interview with William D. Irvine, Toronto, 2 Nov. 2007.

109 Interview with James Alcock, Toronto, 22 Sept. 2003.

110 Glendon College, Faculty Council Office, FC 74–75–32, Minutes, 23 Jan. 1975.

111 Dixon interview.

112 Conversation with Ian Gentles, Toronto, 4 Jan. 2008.

113 Glendon College, Faculty Council Office, FC 85–86–18, Minutes, 22 Nov. 1985.

114 FC 87–88–29, Minutes, 4 March 1988.

115 Interview with Irving Abella, Toronto, 21 Feb. 2007.

116 Interview with Alain Baudot, Toronto, 15 July 2003.

117 Interview with Elizabeth Hopkins, Toronto, 6 March 2003.

118 Interview with Stanley Tweyman, Toronto, 7 July 2006.

119 Interview with Gail Cuthbert Brandt, Toronto, 4 May 2007.

120 Interview with Adèle Hurley, Toronto, 25 Jan. 2007.

121 Interview with David Trick, Toronto, 21 Nov. 2007.

122 Interview with Catherine Limbertie, Toronto, 17 Jan. 2008.

123 Interview with Julie Pärna, Toronto, 28 Nov. 2006.

124 Interview with Gwyneth Buck, Toronto, 6 Dec. 2007.

125 Council of Ontario Universities, "Ontario Universities Statistical Compendium 1970–71 to 1979–80," Part B, Table B4–1.

126 Communication from Ellen Hoffmann, 8 Nov. 2007.

127 Coons Papers, York University Faculty Association, Minutes, special meeting, 28 March 1970.

128 CTASC, Board of Governors, Minutes, 11 Sept. 1972.

129 Paul Axelrod, *Scholars and Dollars: Politics, Economics, and the Universities of Ontario 1945–1980* (Toronto: University of Toronto Press 1982), 147.

130 Ibid., 165.

131 Ibid., 166.

132 Marilyn Smith, "What Do You Call a University with No People," *Excalibur*, 14 Sept. 1972.

133 CTASC, Board of Governors, Minutes, 10 Oct. 1972, appendix B, David W. Slater to members of the Board of Governors, 5 Oct. 1972.

134 Communication from Ellen Hoffmann, 8 Nov. 2007.

135 CTASC, University Secretariat, 2000–044/15 (12), Report of the Senate Committee on Tenure and Promotions, 12 Nov. 1968; Senate Committee on Tenure and Promotions, Report to Senate, May 1970.

136 Coons Papers, Senate Committee on Academic Dismissal, Minutes, 13 July 1972.

137 Interview with John Heddle, Toronto, 23 Dec. 2007.

138 Communication from Wesley Coons, 19 Nov. 2007.

139 Donald C. Savage, ed., "Guidelines concerning Reductions in Academic Appointments for Budgetary Reasons," *C.A.U.T. Handbook* (Ottawa: Canadian Association of University Teachers 1971), 49.

140 CTASC, F0326, Michiel Horn Fonds, 1981–013/003 (010), Michiel Horn to J.A.M. Heddle, 29 Sept. 1972.

141 Interview with Marilyn Smith, Toronto, 24 Oct. 2003.

142 CTASC, Board of Governors, Minutes, 10 Oct. 1972.

143 Coons Papers, SCAD file, Academic Policy and Planning Committee, Report for Information on Staff Implications of Our Financial Position, 19 Oct. 1972. Emphasis in the original.

144 CTASC, Senate, Minutes of special meeting, 19 Oct. 1972.

145 Rajagopal interview.

146 Interview with Theodore Olson, Toronto, 6 Feb. 2008.

147 CTASC, Senate, Minutes of special meeting, 19 Oct. 1972.

148 Coons Papers, SCAD file, Senate Committee on Academic Dismissal, Report to Senate, 19 Oct. 1972, Schedule II, Rules for Reductions in Teaching Staff for Reasons of Budget Necessity.

149 On tenure, see Michiel Horn, "Tenure and the Canadian Professoriate," *Journal of Canadian Studies*, vol. 34, no. 3 (autumn 1999): 261–81.

150 Conversation with Albert Tucker, Toronto, 18 Dec. 2007.

151 CTASC, Board of Governors, Minutes of special meeting, 24 Oct. 1972, appendix A, David W. Slater, A Further Report on Enrolments and Budgets, 23 Oct. 1972.

152 CTASC, Board of Governors, Minutes of special meeting, 24 Oct. 1972.

153 MacIntosh interview.

154 Interview with Adrienne Clarkson, Toronto, 19 Feb. 2008.

155 Ibid.

156 CTASC, Board of Governors, Minutes of special meeting, 24 Oct. 1972, appendix B, Statement of the Board of Governors, York University, 24 Oct. 1972.

157 Adelman interview.

158 Interview with Harry Arthurs, Toronto, 28 Oct. 2002.

159 Interview with Ann Montgomery, Ogden, Que., 30 Dec. 2007.

160 Interview with David McQueen, Toronto, 22 May 2003.

161 Communication from Albert Tucker, 26 Feb. 2008.

162 Interview with Marion Boyd, Toronto, 13 Nov. 2006.

163 Communication received 28 Feb. 2008.

164 CTASC, Senate, Minutes of special meeting, 25 Oct. 1972.

165 Ibid.

166 Ibid.

167 Ibid.

168 "Three-way Power Struggle Lurks Behind Budget," *Excalibur*, 1 Nov. 1972.

169 Overing interview.

170 Interview with Albert Tucker, Toronto, 23 Nov. 2007.

171 Boyd interview.

172 Communication from John T. Saywell, 4 Dec. 2007.

173 This alluded to the fact that, at Queen's as at other universities, the administrative responsibilities and budgetary powers of the deans of graduate faculties are limited.

174 Interview with Wallace Northover, Toronto, 8 Feb. 2008.

175 Adelman interview.

176 Jackman interview.

177 Saywell interview.

178 MacIntosh interview.

179 CTASC, Senate, Minutes of special meeting, 8 Nov. 1972.

180 The legal advice that the university received was confirmed in a legal opinion secured by YUFA. CTASC, Horn Fonds, 1981–013/003 (010), Vincent Kelly to Michiel Horn, 15 Nov. 1972.

181 CTASC, Senate, Minutes of special meeting, 8 Nov. 1972.

182 CTASC, Board of Governors, executive and finance committees, Minutes of joint meeting, 10 Nov. 1972.

183 Clarkson interview.

184 CTASC, Senate, Minutes of special meeting, 22 Nov. 1972.

185 Olson interview.

186 CTASC, 1975–022/059 (02), President's Office, Joint Committee on Alternatives, Report on Enrolments

and Income, Projections 1973–74 and 1974–75, 4 Dec. 1972, 3.
187 Ibid., 7.
188 Ibid., 12.
189 Ibid., 12.
190 CTASC, Senate, Minutes, 23 Nov. 1972.
191 Olson interview.
192 Rajagopal interview.
193 Interview with Ann Wilbur MacKenzie, Toronto, 6 July 2005.
194 Arthurs interview.
195 Interview with William Small, Toronto, 18 Nov. 2002.
196 "Tarnopolsky Feels He Is Ineffective in Job," *Excalibur*, 7 Dec. 1972.
197 Jim Daw, "Administration Fiasco Revolves around Slater," *Excalibur*, 11 Jan. 1973.
198 McQueen interview; communication from Albert Tucker, 26 Feb. 2008.
199 Arthurs interview.
200 MacKenzie interview.
201 Interview with Gerald Carrothers, Toronto, 13 June 2007; Overing and Tucker interviews.
202 MacIntosh interview.
203 CTASC, Board of Governors, Minutes, 11 Dec. 1972.
204 CTASC, Horn Fonds, 1981–013/001 (04), handwritten notes, JCOA meeting, 11 Dec. 1972. The minutes of the meeting, including the motion establishing the Coordinating Committee, are missing from the JCOA file in the President's Office Fonds.
205 CTASC, 1975–022/059 (02), President's Office, Joint Committee on Alternatives, Minutes, meeting no. 16, 12 Dec. 1972.
206 Ibid.
207 CTASC, Senate, Minutes, 13 Dec. 1972.
208 "Slater Demands Loyalty Oath; Crowe Refuses, College Agrees," *Excalibur*, 14 Dec. 1972.
209 "Dean Walks Out on York President over Loyalty Pledge," Toronto *Star*, 15 Dec. 1972.
210 CTASC, Board of Governors, 2000–044/005 (16), R.M. MacIntosh, Statement of the Board of Governors – York University by the Chairman of the Board, 22 Jan. 1973.
211 Dixon interview.
212 MacIntosh interview.
213 Donna Dilschneider, "York Dean Quits, Criticizes President," Toronto *Star*, 20 Dec. 1972.
214 John King, "Leadership Crisis Pits York Deans against President," *Globe and Mail*, 22 Dec. 1972.
215 MacIntosh interview; R.M. MacIntosh, Statement of the Board of Governors, 22 Jan. 1973.
216 MacIntosh interview.

217 CTASC, Board of Governors, 2000–044/005 (16), David W. Slater to R.M. MacIntosh, 22 Jan. 1973.
218 CTASC, Board of Governors, Minutes, 22 Jan. 1973.
219 MacIntosh interview.
220 Michael Keating, "U.S. Philosophy Professor Named 3rd York U President in 3 Days," *Globe and Mail*, 25 Jan. 1973.
221 Interview with Richard Storr, Toronto, 11 Dec. 2003.
222 CTASC, Board of Governors, Minutes, 24 Jan. 1973.
223 CTASC, Board of Governors, Minutes, 22 Jan. 1973.
224 Boyd interview.
225 Dixon interview.
226 MacIntosh interview.
227 Jackman interview.
228 "Relic of the Colonial Campus," Toronto *Star*, 25 Jan. 1973.
229 N. John Adams, "Board of Governors at York U Told Slater to Quit as President or He Would be Fired," *Globe and Mail*, 1 Feb. 1973. Those said to have been present were Robert MacIntosh, Bill Small, Bruce Parkes, Howard Robertson, Ted Olson, John Yolton, Harry Arthurs, Gerald Carrothers, Harry Crowe, Bob Overing, Barry Richman, Jack Saywell, and Albert Tucker.
230 MacIntosh interview.
231 Interview with Sheldon Levy, Toronto, 20 Feb. 2003.
232 Interview with Rosemarie Schade, Montreal, 1 Dec. 2007.
233 Communication from Marion Lane, 23 Jan. 2008.
234 Interview with Sandie Rinaldo, Toronto, 15 Jan. 2008.
235 Interview with Jamie Laws, Toronto, 29 Jan. 2008.
236 Interview with Barbara Godard, Toronto, 30 Oct. 2007.
237 Interview with Cynthia Zimmerman, Toronto, 24 Jan. 2008.
238 Interview with Daniel Drache, Toronto, 2 Nov. 2004.
239 Interview with Gerald Jordan, Toronto, 6 Nov. 2007.
240 Irvine interview.
241 Interview with Marc Rosen, Toronto, 18 Nov. 2007.
242 Dixon interview.
243 Jackman interview.
244 CTASC, Senate, 1999–072/004 (5), Mavor Moore, Communication to Senate of York University of the Search Committee for a New President, 26 Sept. 1973.
245 "Two Vie for Post of York U Head," *Globe and Mail*, 26 Oct. 1973.
246 Jackman interview.

247 "Macdonald Named York University President," *Globe and Mail*, 13 Nov. 1973.

248 "York University's Prize," *Globe and Mail*, 14 Nov. 1973.

249 "Ian Macdonald, Superclerk at the Centre," *Globe and Mail*, 17 Nov. 1973.

250 Hartley Steward, "The Invisible Whiz Who'll Be York's New President," Toronto *Star*, 24 Nov. 1973.

251 Interview with H. Ian Macdonald, Toronto, 8 Oct. 2002.

252 Interview with H. Ian Macdonald, Toronto, 8 March 2006.

253 Axelrod, *Scholars and Dollars*, 179.

Chapter 5

1 All data are from the York University *Fact Book 2006–07*.

2 Paul Axelrod, *Scholars and Dollars: Politics, Economics, and the Universities of Ontario, 1945–1980* (Toronto: University of Toronto Press 1982), 179.

3 Martin L. Friedland, *The University of Toronto: A History* (Toronto: University of Toronto Press 2002), 560–3, 567–9, 581.

4 Albert J. Robinson, "Would Collective Bargaining Increase Academic Salaries?" *CAUT Bulletin*, 16, no. 4 (1968): 74.

5 Committee of Presidents of the Universities of Ontario, Subcommittee on Research and Planning, *Towards 2000: The Future of Post-Secondary Education in Ontario* (Toronto: CPUO 1971), 25.

6 At the meeting, held on 23 May 1973, were Eaton, Jackman, Robert MacIntosh, John Yolton, and I.

7 Interview with Harvey Simmons, Toronto, 19 Oct. 2004.

8 "York Professors Ask for Union in 120–10 Vote," Toronto *Star*, 18 April 1975.

9 Interview with J.L. Granatstein, Toronto, 11 Jan. 2008.

10 Ibid.

11 Ibid.

12 Virginia Hunter, "The State of the Union," *York University Faculty Association Newsletter*, 10 Jan. 1977; interview with Virginia Hunter, Toronto, 28 Feb. 2005; interview with D. McCormack Smyth, Hamilton, Ont., 14 July 2006.

13 Interview with Virginia Hunter, Toronto, 14 Feb. 2008.

14 H.N.R. Jackman Private Papers, W.D. Farr, "Principles to Govern the Development of Management Objectives for Collective Bargaining with YUFA," 4 May 1976. I am grateful to Hon. Henry Jackman for making this and several other documents available to me.

15 J.L. Granatstein to Joan Wick-Pelletier, 3 Jan. 1977, reproduced in *York University Faculty Association Newsletter*, 10 Jan. 1977.

16 Granatstein interview.

17 Hunter interview, 28 Feb. 2005.

18 Paul Kellogg, "No More Profs this Year," *Excalibur*, 15 Sept. 1977; Agnes Kruchio, "Budget Axe Hits Part-Time Profs," *Excalibur*, 26 Jan. 1978.

19 Interview with H. Ian Macdonald, Toronto, 9 Jan. 2008.

20 Mark Monfette, "Staff Strike Could Be a Long Haul," *Excalibur*, 21 Sept. 1978.

21 Interview with Myriam Obadia-Hazan, Toronto, 11 Feb. 2008.

22 Ibid.

23 Interview with Margaret Knittl, Toronto, 27 Dec. 2007.

24 Dale Brazao, "York U Students Protest Strike," Toronto *Star*, 22 Sept. 1978.

25 Henry Mietkiewicz, "York Workers End Their Strike, Accept Pay Offer of 6.2 Per Cent," Toronto *Star*, 4 Oct. 1978.

26 Knittl interview.

27 Interview with Ildikó Kovács, Toronto, 20 May 2003.

28 Michael Monastyrskyj, "CUEW Goes on Strike," *Excalibur*, 29 Oct. 1981.

29 Berel Wetstein, "Some Cross the Line," *Excalibur*, 29 Oct. 1981.

30 "York U Classes to Resume as Strike Settled," Toronto *Star*, 3 Nov. 1981.

31 All data are from the York University *Fact Book 1997–98*, 5.

32 Harry Arthurs, "The View from the Ninth Floor: 1985–1992: A Memoir" [2002], 3.

33 Carol Brunt, "YUSA Hits the Pickets," *Excalibur*, 11 Oct. 1984.

34 Carol Brunt, "Strike's Over," *Excalibur*, 18 Oct. 1984.

35 Paul Taylor, "York University Teaching Aides to Return to Job," *Globe and Mail*, 1 Nov. 1984.

36 Communication from Geoffrey Ewen, 3 Feb. 2008.

37 "Caught in Crossfire," *Excalibur*, 18 Oct. 1984.

38 Margaret Polanyi, "York Professors Walk Out in Dispute over Salaries," *Globe and Mail*, 8 Oct. 1985.

39 "Financial Neglect Sad Source of York's Labor Woes," *Excalibur*, 26 Sept. 1985.

40 Margaret Polanyi, "Quality of Education at Risk in Wage Dispute, York President Asserts," *Globe and Mail*, 9 Oct. 1985.

41 Communication from Hollis Rinehart, 8 Feb. 2008.

42 Interview with Janice Newson, Toronto, 18 March 2003.

43 Interview with Penny Van Esterik, Toronto, 7 Feb. 2008.

44 Margaret Polanyi and Erika Rosenfeld, "York Professors Go Back to School," *Globe and Mail*, 11 Oct. 1985.

45 Rinehart communication, 8 Feb. 2008.

46 Laura Lush, "$1-Million at Issue as YUFA Hits the Picket Lines," *Excalibur*, 11 Oct. 1985.

47 Interview with Sheldon Levy, Toronto, 20 Feb. 2003. The Senate Committee on the Budget operated from 1973 to 1977.

48 Newson interview.

49 Interview with John Spencer, Toronto, 18 March 2008.

50 Ibid.

51 Interview with Ken Carpenter, Toronto, 11 Sept. 2007; interview with Joe Green, Toronto, 9 Jan. 2008.

52 Interview with David Mirvish, Toronto, 2 Dec. 2007.

53 Carpenter interview.

54 Green interview.

55 Ibid. From 1970 to 1984, Napoléon was one of Toronto's best and priciest restaurants.

56 Mirvish interview.

57 *Anthony Caro: The York Sculptures* (Boston: Museum of Fine Arts 1980).

58 http://www.yorku.ca/agyu/info/tours.html.

59 Carpenter interview.

60 Cyndi Piccolo, "The Program in Theatre: A View From the Undergraduate Calendars," in Ileana Esfakis et al., eds., *A History of Theatre at York: 1969–1989, York Theatre Journal*, 31, Special Edition, 1989, 6.

61 Interview with Don Rubin, Toronto, 5 Dec. 2007.

62 Ibid.

63 Ibid.

64 Interview with Elizabeth Bradley, Pittsburgh, 14 March 2008.

65 Interview with Joyce Zemans, Toronto, 6 Oct. 2005.

66 Interview with Mary Jane Warner, Toronto, 25 Jan. 2008.

67 Interview with Sandie Rinaldo, Toronto, 15 Jan. 2008.

68 Interview with Sheree-Lee Olson, Toronto, 16 Oct. 2007.

69 Interview with Sterling Beckwith, Toronto, 28 Feb. 2008.

70 Interview with Trichy Sankaran, in Sterling Beckwith, ed., *Music at York: The Founding Generation, 1970–2000* (Toronto: Faculty of Music, York University [2003]), 138.

71 Interview with Robert Bowman, in Beckwith, ed., *Music at York*, 38.

72 Ibid., 39.

73 Interview with Don Ross, Cannington, Ont., 9 March 2008.

74 Beckwith interview.

75 Interview with Alain Baudot, Toronto, 15 July 2003.

76 Interview with Michael Herren, Toronto, 12 April 2007.

77 Communication from Hollis Rinehart, 8 Feb. 2008.

78 Interview with Margarita Feliciano, Toronto, 19 April 2007.

79 Communication from Clara Thomas, 2 Feb. 2008.

80 Clara Thomas, *Chapters in a Lucky Life* (Ottawa: Borealis Press 1999), 161–2.

81 Ibid., 179.

82 Interview with John Lennox, Toronto, 13 Dec. 2002.

83 Thomas, *Chapters in a Lucky Life*, 189.

84 Interview with Ann Mandel, Toronto, 4 March 2008. Gregory was Glendon's chair of English.

85 Interview with Bob Wallace, Toronto, 31 Jan. 2008.

86 Mandel interview.

87 Wallace interview.

88 Interview with Pinayur Rajagopal, Toronto, 4 Aug. 2004; personal recollection (I was a member of SCOB at the time).

89 Macdonald interview, 9 Jan. 2008.

90 Interview with Robert Overing, Ivry-sur-le-Lac, Que., 30 Nov. 2007.

91 Interview with David McQueen, Toronto, 20 May 2003.

92 Macdonald interview, 9 Jan. 2008.

93 Interview with H. Ian Macdonald, Toronto, 8 March 2006.

94 Interview with William Found, Toronto, 24 Oct. 2002.

95 Interview with Jane Couchman, Toronto, 24 Jan. 2006.

96 Macdonald interview, 9 Jan. 2008.

97 Macdonald interview, 8 March 2006.

98 H.N.R. Jackman Private Papers, Henry Jackman to Ian Macdonald, 25 Feb. 1976.

99 York University, President's Commission on Goals and Objectives, Report, April 1977, 29.

100 Ibid., 33–5.

101 Interview with Sydney Eisen, Toronto, 16 Sept. 2003.

102 Hugh Parry and William Whitla, "Humanities at York: The Early Years," n.d. [2004].

103 Interview with William Whitla, Toronto, 9 Feb. 2006.

104 Interview with Ted Spence, Toronto, 18 March 2004.

105 Couchman interview.

106 Communication from John Bankes, 19 Feb. 2008.

107 Interview with John Bankes, Toronto, 15 Feb. 2008.

108 Spence interview.

109 Macdonald interview, 8 March 2006.

110 Couchman interview.

111 In 2003 its members were Jane Couchman, Sydney Eisen, Arthur Haberman, Dawn Bazely, Michael Creal, Douglas Freake, Ruth Grogan, Al Stauffer, and Mark Webber. Communication from Al Stauffer, 21 Oct. 2003.

112 Quoted in: President's Commission on Goals and Objectives, "Report," 28.

113 Ibid., 35.

114 William Whitla, "The Battle of the Book, or the Rape of the York," 1977. I am grateful to Professor Spence for making a copy of this poem available to me.

115 Macdonald interview, 8 March 2006.

116 I am grateful to Professor Klassen for proposing these titles.

117 Howard Adelman, *Canada and the Indochinese Refugees* (Regina: L.A. Weigl Educational Associates, 1982), 1.

118 Ibid., 127.

119 Interview with Howard Adelman, Toronto, 24 April 2003.

120 Interview with Louis Lefeber, Toronto, 29 Dec. 2007.

121 Ibid.

122 Ibid.

123 Murray Ross, *The Way Must Be Tried: Memoirs of a University Man* (Toronto: Stoddart 1992), 180.

124 Ibid.

125 Michiel Horn, *Academic Freedom in Canada: A History* (Toronto: University of Toronto Press 1999), 165–6, 210–16, 259–61.

126 Interview with Sydney Eisen, Toronto, 16 Sept. 2003.

127 Interview with Irving Gerstein, Toronto, 12 Jan. 2008.

128 Interview with Robert MacIntosh, Toronto, 4 Oct. 2007.

129 Interview with Brian Dixon, Kingston, Ont., 29 Nov. 2007.

130 Jean Burnet, "Minorities I Have Belonged To," *Canadian Ethnic Studies*, vol. 13, no. 1 (1981): 30.

131 MacIntosh interview.

132 Interview with Adrienne Clarkson, Toronto, 19 Feb. 2008.

133 Interview with Wallace Northover, Toronto, 8 Feb. 2008.

134 Interviews with Norman Endler, Toronto, 16 Oct. 2002; Harvey Simmons, Toronto, 19 Oct. 2004; Arthur Haberman, Toronto, 1 March 2007; Esther Greenglass, Toronto, 11 Nov. 2002.

135 CTASC, President's Office, 1977–013/051 (1401), John T. Saywell to Departmental Chairmen, 3 Sept. 1971.

136 CTASC, Senate, Minutes, 16 Dec. 1971.

137 Ibid., 23 May 1974.

138 Endler interview.

139 Interview with Clara Thomas, Toronto, 26 Sept. 2002.

140 Interview with Thelma McCormack, Toronto, 6 April 2004.

141 Gill Teiman, *Idealism and Accommodation: A History of Human Rights and Employment Equity at York University, 1959–2005* (Toronto: York University Bookstore 2007), 27.

142 Interview with Kenneth McRoberts, Toronto, 22 Feb. 2008.

143 Teiman, *Idealism and Accommodation*, 22.

144 Interview with Cynthia Zimmerman, Toronto, 24 Jan. 2008.

145 Interview with Ann Wilbur MacKenzie, Toronto, 6 July 2005.

146 Interviews with Joan Gibson, Toronto, 30 Jan. 2008; Ann (Rusty) Shteir, Toronto, 7 Jan. 2008.

147 Interview with Gail Cuthbert Brandt, Toronto, 4 May 2007.

148 Interview with Wendy Mitchinson, Waterloo, Ont., 30 March 2007.

149 Interview with Susan Houston, Toronto, 23 May 2006.

150 Thomas, *Chapters in a Lucky Life*, 139–40.

151 Hunter interview, 14 Feb. 2008.

152 Interview with Sandra Pyke, Toronto, 24 April 2007.

153 Canada, Royal Commission on the Status of Women in Canada, *Report* (Ottawa: Information Canada 1970).

154 Interview with Johanna Stuckey, Toronto, 23 Nov. 2006.

155 York University, Senate, Task Force on the Status of Women at York University, Report, 27 Feb. 1975, 2. Emphasis in the original.

156 Ibid., 4.

157 Interview with Jane Banfield, Vancouver, 25 Jan. 2008.

158 York University, Presidential Committee to Review the Salaries of Full-Time Faculty Women, Report to President H. Ian Macdonald, 15 Nov. 1976, 24.

159 Ibid., 18–22.

160 Ibid., 23.

161 Marion Lane Irvine, "Women at Osgoode: Problems and Perceptions of the Growing Minority," 15 Jan. 1974, 1–2. A copy of this report is located in the Osgoode Hall Law School Library.

162 Interview with Marion Lane, Toronto, 23 Jan. 2007.

163 Lane Irvine, "Women at Osgoode," 4.

164 Communication from Mary Jane Mossman, 20 Feb. 2008.

165 Interview with Mary Jane Mossman, Toronto, 19 Feb. 2008.

166 Interview with Noli Swatman, Toronto, 5 Oct. 2005.

167 Banfield interview.

168 Interview with Virginia Rock, Toronto, 25 Oct. 2004.

169 Conversation with Howard Adelman, Toronto, 24 Feb. 2008.

170 Interview with Margaret Knittl, Toronto, 27 Dec. 2007.

171 Pyke interview.

172 Shteir interview.

173 Interview with Lesley Lewis, Toronto, 27 Sept. 2007.

174 Task Force on the Status of Women at York University, Report, 18.

175 Naomi Black, "Women's Studies at York University," *Women's Education des femmes*, vol. 4, no. 2 (1984): 18–19.

176 Interview with Barbara McNutt, Toronto, 8 Nov. 2005; "Historical Connections between University Women's Club of North York and York University," undated document provided by Ms McNutt, to whom I am grateful.

177 Interview with Shelagh Wilkinson, Toronto, 29 Feb. 2008.

178 Shelagh Wilkinson, "Quite a Journey: A History of the Bridging Program," in Ruby Newman and Andrea O'Reilly, eds., *You Can Get There from Here: 25 Years of Bridging Courses for Women at York University* (Toronto: School of Women's Studies, York University 2006), 30–8.

179 Teiman, *Idealism and Accommodation*, 102–3.

180 The sixth author was Paula Bourne, who taught at OISE.

181 Van Esterik interview.

182 York University Status of Women Committee, "Equity for Women: The First Decade," Report to the President of York University, July 1985, 38.

183 Interview with Brenda Gainer, Toronto, 17 April 2007.

184 "Equity for Women: The First Decade," 1.

185 Canada, Commission of Inquiry on Equality in Employment, *Report* (Ottawa: Supply and Services Canada 1984).

186 "Equity for Women: The First Decade," 3.

187 Teiman, *Idealism and Accommodation*, 97.

188 Ibid., 97–100; interview with Gill Teiman, Toronto, 16 June 2005.

189 Interview with Bob Bain, Toronto, 8 Jan. 2008.

190 http://www.yorku.ca/sprtyork/sport_hall_of_fame/members/2001.htm.

191 Bain interview.

192 Interview with Tim Rider, 13 Dec. 2007.

193 Interview with Mary Lyons, Mississauga, Ont., 8 Feb. 2008.

194 http://www.space.gc.ca/asc/eng/astronauts.biomaclean.asp.

195 Interview with Merv Mosher, Toronto, 13 Feb. 2008.

196 Interview with Marina Vandermerwe, Toronto, 7 Feb. 2008.

197 Ibid.

198 Interview with Sheila Forshaw, Toronto, 20 Feb. 2008.

199 Interview with Carol Wilson, Toronto, 26 Feb. 2008.

200 Mosher interview.

201 Vandermerwe interview.

202 Interview with Patricia Murray, Toronto, 6 Feb. 2008.

203 Interview with Jamie Laws, Toronto, 29 Jan. 2008.

204 Ibid.

205 Interview with Bill Hatanaka, Toronto, 20 Nov. 2007.

206 Interview with Steve Dranitsaris, Toronto, 3 April 2007.

207 Interview with Frank Cosentino, Toronto, 2 Nov. 2005.

208 Interview with Carole Carpenter, Toronto, 1 Dec. 2006.

209 Conversation with Suzanne Klein, Toronto, 2 Feb. 2007.

210 Interview with Paul Lovejoy, Toronto, 11 Nov. 2005.

211 Interview with Ellen Hoffmann, Toronto, 29 Oct. 2006.

212 Ibid.

213 Interview with Arthur Forer, Toronto, 16 Nov. 2007.

214 Interview with Kenneth Davey, Toronto, 8 Dec. 2004.

215 Interview with Rodger Schwass, Toronto, 8 Nov. 2004.

216 Interview with Deszö Horváth, Toronto, 22 Feb. 2006.

217 Swatman interview.

218 Interview with Bryan Massam, Toronto, 30 Nov. 2004.

219 Interview with Susan Spence, Toronto, 27 March 2007.

220 Interview with Sheila Embleton, Toronto, 1 March 2006.

221 Interview with Marilyn Pilkington, Toronto, 4 April 2007.

222 Interview with Patrick Monahan, Toronto, 31 July 2007.

223 Interview with David M. Smith, Toronto, 6 March 2008.

224 Interview with Dorathy Moore, Toronto, 15 Jan. 2008.

225 Interview with Fred Granek, Toronto, 22 Jan. 2008.

226 Interview with Chris Gates, Toronto, 11 Jan. 2008.

227 Interview with Eileen Mercier, Toronto, 14 Dec. 2007.

228 Ibid.

229 Interview with Ed McDonough, Toronto, 29 Dec. 2007.

230 Interview with Bob Gagne, Toronto, 9 Jan. 2007.

231 Interview with Guy Burry, Toronto, 12 Dec. 2007.

232 Interview with Allan Bonner, Toronto, 27 Nov. 2007.

233 Forer interview.

234 Interview with Paula Wilson, Toronto, 23 Oct. 2007.

235 Interview with Sylvia Zingrone, Toronto, 6 Jan. 2006.

236 *Excalibur*, 19 Sept. 1985.

237 Most of the information provided here is from CTASC, Office of the President, 1996–018/004 (07a).

238 Esfakis et al., eds., *A History of Theatre at York: 1969–1989*, passim.

239 Mary Ormsby, "York Gets Playoff Berth by Beating McMaster," Toronto *Star*, 20 Oct. 1985.

240 McNutt interview; "Historical Connections between University Women's Club of North York and York University."

241 CTASC, Office of the President, 1996–024/005 (03), Harry Arthurs to Mel Lastman, 25 June 1985.

242 CTASC, Office of the President, 1996–024/005 (03), Murray Ross to Harry Arthurs, 21 Nov. 1985.

Chapter 6

1 The SuperBuild program, founded in 1999, encourages partnerships between the public and private sectors. http://www.fin.gov.on.ca/english/budget/ontariobudgets/1999/innovbkg.html.

2 http://www.yorku.ca/alumni/alumnimatters/dec-07/am_dec-07_subwayConstruction.php.

3 Conversation with Jacques Pauwels, Toronto, 28 May 2006.

4 http://villageatyork.ca/village.

5 Thomas Klassen, "A Review of York University Administrative Policy of Cancelling Classes in the Fall Term – A Report for the York University Senate Committee on Curriculum and Academic Standards," 15 Dec. 2007, 5.

6 Interview with Bill Hatanaka, Toronto, 20 Nov. 2007.

7 Interview with Hamid Osman, Toronto, 15 April 2008.

8 Ibid.

9 Mamdouh Shoukri et al., "A Joint Statement on Community Values from the University Leadership" [February 2008].

10 http://www.yorku.ca/mediar/archive/Release.asp?Release=1197.

11 "2020 Vision: The Future of York University," 1992. http://www.yorku.ca/secretariat/documents/2020Vision.htm.

12 Ibid.

13 Interview with Harvey Skinner, Toronto, 12 Feb. 2007.

14 Interview with Mamdouh Shoukri, Toronto, 31 Oct. 2007.

15 Elizabeth Church, "York Steps up Med School Push," *Globe and Mail*, 15 April 2008.

16 Interview with Nick Cercone, Toronto, 10 Dec. 2007.

17 Interview with Gillian Wu, Toronto, 2 Feb. 2006; Cercone interview.

18 Senate, York University, "University Academic Plan: Academic Priorities 2005–2010," 23 June 2005, 6.

19 Ibid., 7.

20 For a criticism of the system, its domination by commercial publishers, and the costs it imposes on university libraries, see Jean-Claude Guédon, *In Oldenburg's Long Shadow: Librarians, Research Scientists, Publishers, and the Control of Scientific Publishing* (Washington, D.C.: Association of Research Librarians 2001). Guédon taught natural science at Glendon College in the early 1970s. I am grateful to Julie Drexler for drawing this publication to my attention.

21 Interview with Paul Axelrod, Toronto, 11 Dec. 2006.

22 Interview with Bob Drummond, Toronto, 12 March 2007.

23 John T. Saywell, *Someone to Teach Them: York and the Great University Explosion, 1960– 1973* (Toronto: University of Toronto Press 2008), 284.

24 Conversations with John Beare and Robert Myers, Toronto, 8 April 2008.

25 Conversation with James Savary, Toronto, 8 April 2008.

26 Saywell, *Someone to Teach Them*, 285.

27 Michael J. Prince, Richard M. Felder, and Rebecca Brent, "Does Faculty Research Improve Undergraduate Teaching? An Analysis of Existing and Potential Synergies," *Journal of Engineering Education*, 96, no. 4 (2007): esp. 290–1. http://www4.ncsu.edu/unity/lockers/users/f/felder/public/Papers/Teaching-Research(JEE).pdf.

28 Saywell, *Someone to Teach Them*, 286.

29 Interview with Rhonda Lenton, Toronto, 16 Oct. 2006.

30 Osman interview.

31 Lenton interview.

32 Interview with Joan Gibson, Toronto, 30 Jan. 2008.

33 York University, Transition Steering Committee, "Creating a New Faculty Comprising the Humanities, Social Sciences, and Related Professional Programs," 1 Nov. 2007, 3.

34 Ibid.

35 John Spencer, "History of General Education at York," 5. I am grateful to Professor Spencer for making a copy of this report available to me.

36 General Education Review Team, Faculty of Arts, "Interim Report," July 2007. http://www.arts.yorku.ca/faculty_and_staff/council_agendas/2007/071011/pdf/5b%20-%20GERT%20Interim%20Report%20FINAL.pdf.

37 Interview with John Spencer, Toronto, 18 March 2008.

38 Interview with Edward Fenner, Toronto, 15 Jan. 2008.

39 Ibid.

40 Interview with Deszö Horváth, Toronto, 22 Feb. 2006.

41 Enrolment data from the *York University Factbook, 2006/2007*, 5–6. http://www.yorkinfo.yorku.ca/factbook.asp?Year=2006%20-%202007.

42 http://www.schulich.yorku.ca/ssb-extra/ssb.nsf/docs/Transnational.

43 Interview with Brenda Gainer, Toronto, 17 April 2007.

44 Ibid.

45 Horváth interview.

46 http://www.which-mba.com/.

47 http://www.schulich.yorku.ca/ssb-extra/ssb.nsf?open#.

48 Interview with Patrick Monahan, Toronto, 31 July 2007.

49 Ibid.

50 Enrolment data from the *York University Factbook, 2006/2007*, 5–6, 107.

51 Interview with Kenneth McRoberts, Toronto, 22 Feb. 2008.

52 Elizabeth Church, "York, U of T Get Millions to Renovate," *Globe and Mail*, 28 Feb. 2008.

53 Axelrod interview.

54 York University, "Planning, Budget, and Accountability Report, 2005–2006," 62. http://www.yorku.ca/presidnt/news/PBA/2005-2006%20PBA.pdf.

55 Communication from Paul Axelrod, 12 April 2008. "Consecutive education" refers to the practice of having course work followed by practicums (in contrast to concurrent education, a model that York had pioneered, where the two proceed simultaneously).

56 Interview with Barbara Rahder, Toronto, 30 July 2007.

57 Ibid.

58 York International Internship Program: Las Nubes Centre for Neotropical Conservation and Research, Costa Rica. http://international.yorku.ca/internships/placements/2005/lasnubes.htm.

59 https://www.timothys.ca/shopOnlineSingleProduct.aspx.

60 Interview with Phillip Silver, Toronto, 25 April 2006.

61 Interview with Mary Jane Warner, 25 Jan. 2008.

62 Silver interview.

63 Interview with Douglas Peers, Toronto, 19 Dec. 2007.

64 Cercone interview.

65 Peers interview.

66 http://www.synergiescanada.org/index_en.html.

67 Interview with Cynthia Archer, Toronto, 18 Dec. 2006.

68 Interview with Sheila Embleton, Toronto, 20 April 2008.

69 F. Kenneth Hare, Jane Banfield Haynes, and John Saywell, "A Sense of Place: A View of the Future of the Non-Faculty Colleges at York University," April 1987, 2.

70 Ibid., 12.

71 Ibid., 15.

72 Ibid., 11.

73 Ibid., 5.

74 Ibid., 18, 19.

75 "Task Force on Faculties, Colleges, and the First-Year Experience," *Faculty of Arts Newsletter*, April 1996.

76 York University, Task Force on the Colleges, "Strengthening York's Neighbourhoods," November 2006, 3, 4. http://www.yorku.ca/vpstdnts/pdfs/ TFOC_report.pdf.

77 Ibid., 4.

78 Harriet Eisenkraft, "Students Get Their Say," *University Affairs*, March 2006. http://www.universityaffairs.ca/issues/2006/ march/_print/students_say.html.

79 "Strengthening York's Neighbourhoods," Executive Summary, 3. http://www.yorku.ca/vpstdnts/pdfs/ TFOC_execsummary.pdf.

80 Ibid., 5.

81 Lorna R. Marsden to Robert Tiffin, 28 Nov. 2006. http://www.yorku.ca/vpstdnts/pdfs/ TFOC_presidentsresponse.pdf.

82 Interview with Ian Greene, Toronto, 25 Jan. 2008.

83 Communication from Ian Greene, 27 March 2008.

84 Communication from Lorna Marsden, 25 March 2008.

85 Communication from Robert Tiffin, 28 March 2008.

86 Paul Lovejoy, quoted in Olena Wawryshyn, "The Slavery Files," *YORKU*, Special Research Edition 2007, 30.

87 Interview with Paul Lovejoy, Toronto, 11 Nov. 2005.

88 "Global Slavery Research Project Receives $2.5 Million in Funding," *YFile*, 19 March 2008. http://www.yorku.ca/yfile/archive/issues.asp.

89 Interview with James Carley, Toronto, 28 March 2008.

90 Ibid.

91 http://www.chairs.gc.ca/web/program/index_e.asp.

92 http://niche.uwo.ca/.

93 Interview with Colin Coates, Toronto, 24 March 2008.

94 Interview with Ellen Bialystok, Toronto, 19 March 2008.

95 Ibid.

96 Interview with Allan Hutchinson, Toronto, 25 March 2008.

97 Ibid.

98 Interview with Moshe Milevsky, Toronto, 10 March 2008.

99 http://www.businessethicscanada.ca/home/index. html.

100 Interview with Wesley Cragg, Toronto, 7 April 2008.

101 Ibid.

102 Interview with Robert Allan, Orangeville, Ont., 3 March 2008.

103 Ibid.

104 Interview with Gordon Shepherd, Toronto, 6 March 2008.

105 Canada Space Agency, "Revolutionizing Our Understanding of the Earth's Upper Atmosphere" ([Ottawa]: n.d.), 4.

106 Sarah Barmak, "Canadians Feel Loss of Scientist," Toronto *Star*, 27 May 2008.

107 "York Scientists Look for Water on Mars," *Ylife*, 31 Oct. 2005. http://www.yorku.ca/ylife/2005/10-31/ phoenix-103105.htm.

108 Shepherd interview.

109 Interview with Huw Pritchard, Toronto, 20 April 2007.

110 Ibid.

111 Interview with Diethard Böhme, Toronto, 4 April 2008.

112 Ibid.

113 "York Professor Wins Canada's Highest Honour for Chemisty," *YFile*, 16 Nov. 2006. http://www.yorku.ca/yfile/archive/ index.asp?Article=7408.

114 Ibid.

115 Interview with Ian Howard, Toronto, 26 March 2008.

116 Ibid.

117 Ibid.

118 Interview with Ronald Pearlman, Toronto, 15 Dec. 2005.

119 http://www.ncbi.nlm.nih.gov/sites/ entrez?db=genomeprj.

120 Pearlman interview.

121 Interview with K.W. Michael Siu, Toronto, 17 March 2008.

122 David Fuller, "Critical Mass," *YORKU*, Special Research Edition 2007, 22.

123 Siu interview.

124 Interview with Douglas Crawford, Toronto, 20 March 2008.

125 Michael Todd, "The Mind's Eye," *YORKU*, Special Research Edition 2007, 41.

126 Crawford interview.

127 Ibid.

128 Interview with Norman Yan, Toronto, 25 March 2008.

129 http://www.invadingspecies.com/Invaders. cfm?A=Page&PID=2.

130 Interview with Bridget Stutchbury, Toronto, 26 March 2008.

131 Ibid.

132 "Bridget Stutchbury," Toronto *Star*, 1 Jan. 2005.

133 Stutchbury interview.

134 Interview with Sampa Bhadra, Toronto, 31 March 2008.

135 Interview with Wendy Taylor, Toronto, 31 March 2008.

136 http://public.web.cern.ch/Public/Welcome.html. The initials CERN are derived from the original name, Conseil Européen pour la Recherche Nucléaire.

137 http://www.exploratorium.edu/origins/cern/ideas/higgs.html.

138 Taylor interview.

139 Bhadra interview.

140 http://www.omgprogram.org/.

141 Interview with Adrian Shubert, Toronto, 11 Oct. 2007.

142 "York International's Shubert Finds Global Rankings Boost York Overseas," *YFile*, 9 April 2008; http://www.yorku.ca/yfile/archive/index.asp?Article=10271.

143 Gillian Wu interview.

144 Cragg interview.

145 Interview with Brian Abner, Toronto, 28 Oct. 2005.

146 Interview with Janice Newson, Toronto, 13 March 2003.

147 http://www.yufa.org/pubs/ActiveVoiceReactivated1.pdf.

148 Interview with Geoffrey Ewen, Toronto, 10 Nov. 2005.

149 Interview with Lorna Marsden, Toronto, 12 Sept. 2007.

150 Conversation with Brenda Hart, Toronto, 10 April 2008.

151 Interview with Kenneth Davey, Toronto, 8 Dec. 2004.

152 Ewen interview.

153 Conversation with Paul Marcus, 10 April 2008.

154 "York University Foundation Report to Donors," 2007. http://www.yorku.ca/foundatn/ROD07.pdf; "York to the Power of 50 Campaign Update," winter 2008. Communication from Cathy Yanosik, 16 June 2008.

Select bibliography

Arthurs, H.W. "The Affiliation of Osgoode Hall Law School with York University." *University of Toronto Law Journal*, 17, no. 1 (1967).

Axelrod, Paul. "Businessmen and the Building of Canadian Universities: A Case Study." *Canadian Historical Review*, 63, no. 2 (1982).

– *Scholars and Dollars: Politics, Economics, and the Universities of Ontario 1945–1980*. Toronto: University of Toronto Press 1982.

Beckwith, Sterling, ed. *Music at York: The Founding Generation, 1970–2000*. Toronto: Department of Music, Faculty of Fine Arts, York University [2003].

Bissell, Claude. *Halfway up Parnassus: A Personal Account of the University of Toronto 1932–1971*. Toronto: University of Toronto Press 1974.

Black, Naomi. "Women's Studies at York University – The Process to a Degree Program." *Women's Education des femmes*, 4, no. 2 (1984).

Butcher, Don, and Jessie-May Rowntree, eds. *York University 1960–1985: A Retrospective*. North York, Ont.: York University, Department of Communications 1985.

Court, John P.M. "Getting Our Act Together: A Look at the Genesis of York's Charter Legislation between 1955 and 1959." *York University Gazette*, 29, no. 25 (24 March 1999).

— "Glory Days." *Profiles*, September 1997. http://www.yorku.ca/ycom/profiles/past/sept97/current/features/article1.htm.

— "Out of the Wood Work: The Wood Family's Benefactions to Victoria University." *Papers of the Canadian Methodist Historical Society*, 11 (1997).

Esfakis, Ileana, et al., eds. "A History of Theatre at York, 1969–1989." *York Theatre Journal*, 31, Special Edition, 1989.

Friedland, Martin L. *The University of Toronto: A History*. Toronto: University of Toronto Press 2002.

Gillies, James, and Colin Dickinson. "From the Faculty of Administrative Studies to the Schulich School of Business: The Origin and Evolution of Professional Education for Managers at York University." In Barbara Austin, ed., *Capitalizing Knowledge: Essays on the History of Business Education in Canada*. Toronto: University of Toronto Press 2000.

Hillman, Serrell, and Robert Collins. "How York Faces, Love, Life, and the Real World." *Toronto Life*, 4 (October 1970).

Horn, Michiel. *Becoming Canadian: Memoirs of an Invisible Immigrant*. Toronto: University of Toronto Press 1997.

Mann, Edward. *A Mann for All Seasons: A Memoir*. Toronto: Lugus Publications 1996.

Monahan, Edward J. *Collective Autonomy: A History of the Council of Ontario Universities, 1962–2000*. Waterloo, Ont.: Wilfrid Laurier University Press 2004.

Moon, Barbara. "The Perils and Pleasures of a Brand-New University." *Maclean's*, 75 (7 April 1962).

Newman, Ruby, and Andrea O'Reilly, eds. *You Can Get There from Here: 25 Years of Bridging Courses for Women at York University*. Toronto: School of Women's Studies, York University 2006.

Nicholls, Ralph W. "The Department of Physics and Astronomy, York University (1965–)." *Physics in Canada*, 54, no. 1 (1998).

O'Connell, Thomas F. "The Creation of a Canadian Research Library." *Canadian Library Journal*, 26, no. 2 (1969).

Reid, Escott. *Radical Mandarin: Memoirs*. Toronto: University of Toronto Press 1989.

Ross, Murray G. *The New University*. Toronto: University of Toronto Press 1961.

— et al. *These Five Years ... 1960–65: The President's Report*. [Toronto]: York University [1965].

— et al. *Those Ten Years 1960–70: The President's Report on the First Ten Years of York University*. Toronto: York University 1970.

— *The Way Must Be Tried: Memoirs of a University Man*. Toronto: Stoddart 1992.

Saywell, John T. *Someone to Teach Them: York and the Great University Explosion, 1960–1973*. Toronto: University of Toronto Press 2008.

Smyth, D. McCormack. "The Founding of York University." *York University Gazette*, 11, nos. 34–36 (1981).

Teiman, Gill. *Idealism and Accommodation: A History of Human Rights and Employment Equity at York University, 1959–2005*. Toronto: York University 2007.

Thomas, Clara. *Chapters in a Lucky Life*. Ottawa: Borealis Press 1999.

Verney, Douglas V. "The Government and Politics of a Developing University: A Canadian Experience." *Review of Politics*, 31, no. 3 (1969).

Warkentin, John. *The Art of Geography: The Life and Teaching of George Tatham*. Toronto: Department of Geography, University of Toronto 2002.

Warner, Mary Jane. "York University, Toronto, Canada." *World Ballet and Dance 1991–92: An International Yearbook*. Bent Schønberg, ed. London: Dance Books 1991.

York Stories Collective, eds. *York Stories: Women in Higher Education*. Toronto: TSAR Publications 2000.

Zemans, Frederick H. "The Dream Is Still Alive: Twenty-five Years of Parkdale Community Legal Services and the Osgoode Hall Law School Intensive Program in Poverty Law." *Osgoode Hall Law Journal*, 35, no. 3 (1997).

Illustration credits

Index of names